STEPAN KVARDAKOV

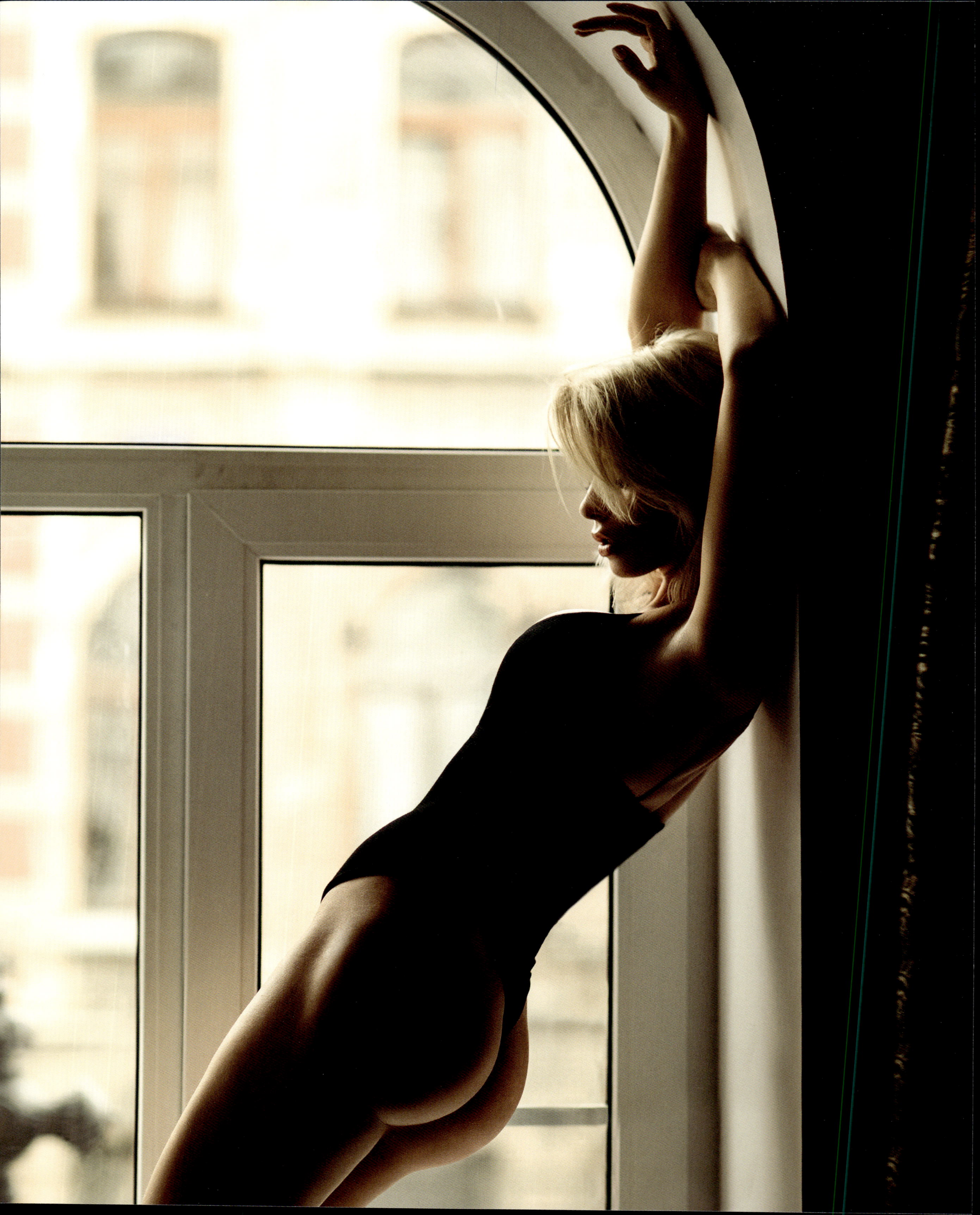

STEPAN KVARDAKOV

GIRLS, GIRLS, GIRLS!
OF ST. PETERSBURG

A PHOTO DATING ALBUM

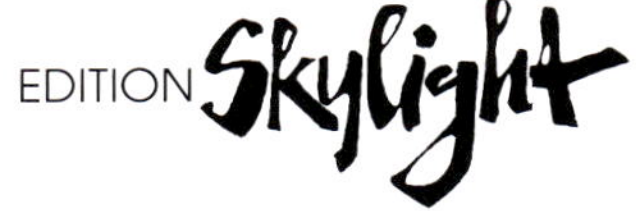

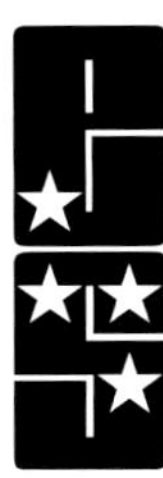

First Edition 2018

EDITION SKYLIGHT
Willikonerstr. 10
CH-8618 Oetwil am See / Zürich
Switzerland

info@edition-skylight.com
www.edition-skylight.com

ISBN 978-3-03766-669-2

Bibliographic information published by Die Deutsche Bibliothek
Die Deutsche Bibliothek lists this publication in the Deutsche Nationalbibliografie; detailed bibliographic data are available in the Internet at http://dnb.ddb.de.

PHOTOGRAPHY AGENT:
Emmanuel D. Fouquet
Artists Partners Inc
artistspartnersinc@gmail.com

English translation by: Eugene Edwards

Printed in Slovenia

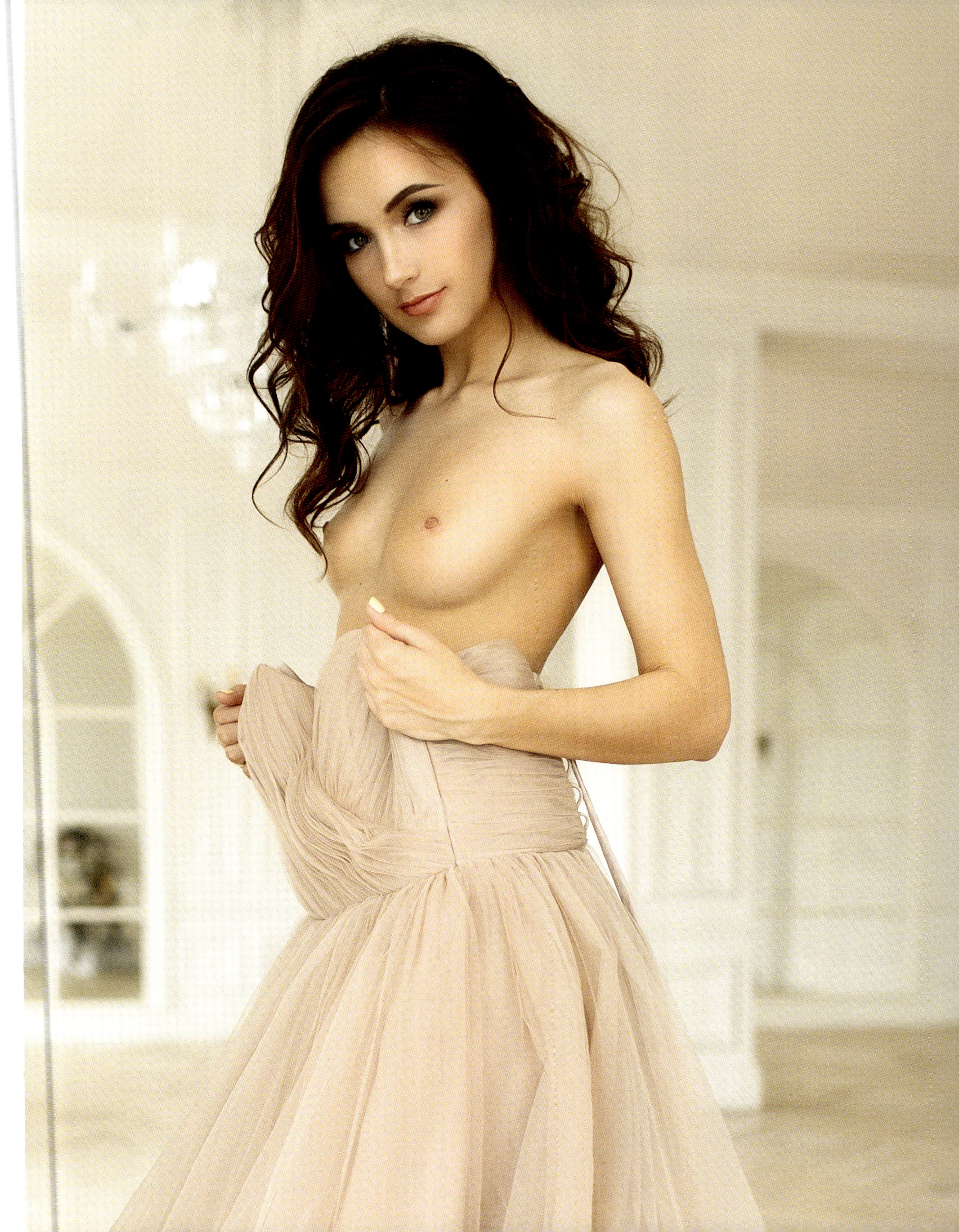

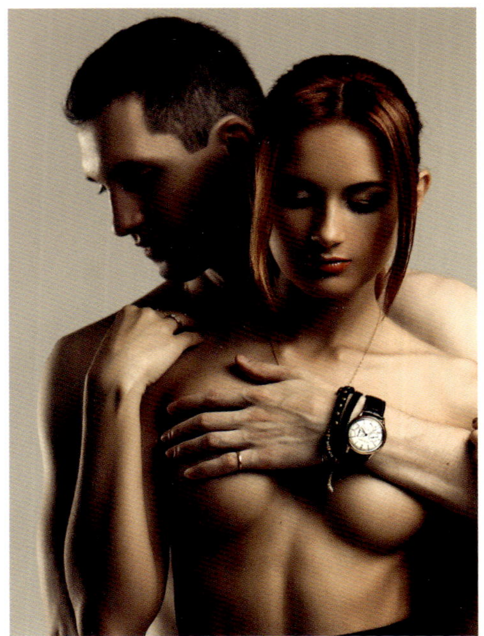

Interview

What were your first steps in the business?
It's hard to say. When I started, photography was a hobby not a career, so I didn't bother too much about money. At some point, people decided that they liked my photos so much they were willing to pay for them. The better my photos became, the more my work attracted attention from different quarters.

What was your education in photography?
I didn't have a professional photo education, but I did attend two master classes by highly skilled, professional photographers. I started to take pictures in 2014, and spent a lot of time working on my style.

Who were some of the photographers who influenced the way you photograph naked women?
When I started, I studied many talented photographers who do amazing work. They all helped me to become what I am now, because I always compared my stuff with theirs. Dan Hecho was the first. In his master class he showed me how to work with nude girls.

What is your favourite equipment?
I use a Canon 5dm3 and two lenses: the 85mm 1.2, and the 35mm 1.4. I prefer to use only fixed lenses because they produce better results, even in minimal light conditions.

Do you use flash, or do you prefer natural light?
I like natural light. The models always look perfect, and I can concentrate on communicating with them to ensure I get the photo I want. But I sometimes work in the studio with artificial lighting; these are probably test sessions, done with a model without props or interiors.

Interview

Welches waren Ihre ersten beruflichen Schritte?
Das lässt sich schwer sagen. Anfangs war die Fotografie nur ein Hobby von mir und ich kümmerte mich nicht darum, wie ich damit Geld verdienen könnte. Nach einer gewissen Zeit mochten die Menschen meine Fotos aber so sehr, dass sie bereit waren, für sie zu bezahlen. Je besser meine Aufnahmen wurden, desto mehr Aufmerksamkeit erhielt meine Arbeit.

Welche Berufsausbildung in Sachen Fotografie haben Sie durchlaufen?
Ich habe keine offizielle fotografische Ausbildung absolviert, aber an Lehrgängen von professionellen Fotografen teilgenommen. Mit dem Fotografieren begann ich 2014, und seitdem arbeite ich an meinem eigenen Stil.

Welche anderen Fotografen haben Sie in Ihrer erotischen Fotografie beeinflusst?
Zu Beginn sah ich mir viele eindrucksvolle Bilder erfolgreicher Fotografen an. Sie halfen mir auf meinem Weg, weil ich meine Arbeiten immer mit ihren verglichen habe. Dan Hecho zählt zu den ersten Fotografen, die mich inspirierten. In seinem Workshop lernte ich den richtigen Umgang mit nackten Mädchen.

Welche fotografische Ausrüstung bevorzugen Sie?
Ich verwende eine Canon 5D Mark III und zwei Objektive: das 85 mm 1,2 und das 35 mm 1,4. Am liebsten arbeite ich mit Festbrennweiten, weil sie auch bei schwachen Lichtverhältnissen optimale Ergebnisse ermöglichen.

Arbeiten Sie mit Blitzlicht oder ziehen Sie natürliches Licht vor?
Ich mag natürliches Licht. Darin sehen die Models immer perfekt aus, und so kann ich mich auf die Kommunikation mit ihnen konzentrieren, um genau das Foto zu bekommen, das mir vorschwebt. Im Studio arbeite ich manchmal mit künstlichem Licht. Dann handelt es sich meist um Probeaufnahmen mit einem Model ohne Requisiten oder Ausstattung.

Wie schaffen Sie es, dass sich die Models vor der Kamera entblößen und manchmal richtig provokant posieren?
Mittlerweile legen die Models bei mir ungehemmt ihre Kleider ab. Letzten Endes sind sie Models und deshalb auch hier. Dennoch sorge ich immer für eine freundliche Atmosphäre, und sie vertrauen mir. Provokante Posen mag ich in der Tat. Sie sorgen immer für Aufmerksamkeit. Aber sie funktionieren nicht bei jedem Model. Wenn das richtige Gefühl oder die passende Emotion fehlen, ist das Posieren ausdruckslos und somit vergeudete Zeit.

Was sagen Sie zu den Models während des Shootings? Sprechen Sie viel und empfehlen bestimmte Posen, oder lassen Sie ihnen freie Bahn?
Bei einem Fotoshooting versuche ich immer, eine Beziehung zum Model aufzubauen. Wenn totales

Интервью

Какими были Ваши первые профессиональные шаги?
Трудно сказать. Вначале фотографирование было просто моим хобби и меня не интересовало, могу ли я зарабатывать этим деньги. Но через некоторое время людям настолько стали нравиться мои фотографии, что они были готовы платить за них деньги. Чем лучше становились мои фотографии, тем больше внимания уделялось моим работам.

Какое профессиональное образование у Вас в области фотографирования?
Я не заканчивал официального обучения по фотографии, но посещал учебные курсы, предлагаемые профессиональными фотографами. Фотографировать я начал в 2014 году и с тех пор работаю над своим собственным стилем.

Какие другие фотографы повлияли на Ваше эротическое фотографирование?
Вначале я рассматривал большое количество впечатляющих фотографий успешных фотографов. Они помогли мне на моем пути, так как я всегда сравнивал свои работы с ними. Дэн Хечо - один из первых фотографов, которые вдохновили меня. На его практических семинарах я научился правильному подходу к обнаженным девушкам.

Какое фотографическое оборудование Вы предпочитаете?
Я использую Canon 5D Mark III и два объектива: 85 мм 1.2 и 35 мм 1.4. Я предпочитаю работать с фиксированными фокусными расстояниями потому что они и в условиях плохой освещенности позволяют достигать оптимальных результатов.

Вы работаете со вспышкой или предпочитаете естественный свет?
Мне нравится естественный свет. Модели в нём всегда выглядят идеально, поэтому я могу концентрироваться на общении с ними, чтобы получить именно то изображение, которое я мысленно себе представляю. В студии я иногда работаю с искусственным светом. Но обычно это пробные съёмки с моделью без реквизита или оборудования.

Как Вам удается достигать того, что модели обнажаются перед камерой и иногда принимают действительно откровенные позы?
На данный момент у меня модели уже непринуждённо раздеваются. Ведь в конце концов, это модели, и потому находятся здесь. Тем не менее, я всегда создаю дружескую атмосферу и они мне доверяют. Мне действительно очень нравятся провокационные позы. Они всегда привлекают внимание. Но такие позы срабатывают не с каждой моделью. Если нет правильного восприятия или соответствующих эмоций, позирование становится невыразительным и, следовательно, пустой тратой времени.

How do you get them to strip off in front of the camera and pose, sometimes really provocatively?
Now it's easy for me to get them to take their clothes off, after all, they are models and that's why they are here, but of course I always keep a friendly atmosphere, and they do trust me. It's true, I like provocative poses, as they always attract attention. But not all girls can do them, and posing without the right feeling or emotion is empty, and a waste of time.

What do you say to your models while you're working? Do you talk a lot and suggest poses, or do you let them do their own thing?
I always try to keep a good rapport with models on a photo session. It's hard for both of us if we spend all the time in silence. I chat about this and that, and gently correct them; tell a few jokes and stories. Sometimes I only say "yes, okay, well done!" which may be enough. Models need to feel that everything is under control; then they can relax. With regard to posing, it always depends on the model. I usually make suggestions and pose a bit myself to demonstrate. I've rarely seen a model who I can say "do what you want, I'll just press the button!"

How is it that practically nobody has ever seen your fantastic work before? What are you and your agent planning to do next?
I don't know, it's hard to say, but I have a lot of followers on social media and am popular on well-known photographic sites. My aim is to reveal the beauty of the female form to the world.

Why and how did you come to make this book?
My agent told me that the time was ripe for people to see my work on paper, which, after all, is the classic, traditional medium.

What projects are you doing next?
I don't know; let's see what the future brings.

Why did you choose to work in this particular style?
Because I like beautiful girls, especially if they're nude! Some years ago I tried my hand at taking pictures of weddings and family groups, but I didn't find it interesting enough, and the results always looked routine and mundane. Cats and flowers can't speak, so I don't find them interesting, either. So that's why I prefer to work with the girls I do.

What do you think of the erotic sector of the market in your country?
Unfortunately, in the current situation, it's completely hopeless if you want to earn money with it. On the other hand, I think that Russia has the world's most beautiful models.

Why did you choose to work exclusively in the studio, or indoors?
I like to control the situation and don't want to worry about the weather. In Saint Petersburg it's impossible to plan photo sessions outdoors, and of course, it's much less hassle to shoot indoors.

Schweigen herrscht, ist es schwierig für uns beide. Ich rede über dieses und jenes und korrigiere die Posen behutsam. Manchmal erzähle ich einen Witz oder eine Anekdote, und manchmal reicht ein: „Ja, okay, gut gemacht!" Models brauchen das Gefühl, dass alles unter Kontrolle ist. Dann erst entspannen sie sich. Die Posen hängen vom jeweiligen Model ab. Normalerweise mache ich Vorschläge und deute die Posen an. Es gibt kaum ein Model, zu dem ich sagen könnte: „Mach', was Du willst, ich drücke nur auf den Auslöser."

Wie kommt es, dass Ihre fantastische Arbeit bisher fast unbekannt geblieben ist? Was planen Sie zusammen mit Ihrem Agenten als Nächstes?
Ich weiß es nicht, und der Grund ist nur schwer benennen. Ich habe unzählige Follower in den sozialen Medien und bin auf bekannten Fotoseiten durchaus präsent. Mein Ziel ist es, der ganzen Welt die Schönheit der weiblichen Formen zu zeigen.

Warum und wie kam es zu diesem Buch?
Mein Agent riet mir zu diesem Buch. Die Zeit sei reif dafür, dass die Menschen meine Aufnahmen auf Papier sehen, meinte er. Schließlich ist es das klassische, traditionelle Medium.

Was für Projekte stehen bei Ihnen außerdem an?
Das weiß ich noch nicht. Ich lasse mich überraschen, was die Zukunft bringt.

Warum haben Sie gerade diesen speziellen Stil gewählt?
Weil ich hübsche Mädchen fantastisch finde, vor allem, wenn sie nackt sind! Vor einigen Jahren versuchte ich es mit Hochzeits- und Familienfotos. Aber mein Interesse war nicht groß genug, sodass die Aufnahmen immer routinemäßig und fast langweilig wirkten. Auch Katzen und Blumen finde ich nicht sonderlich interessant, schließlich reden sie nicht mit mir. Deshalb bevorzuge ich eindeutig das Arbeiten mit meinen Mädchen.

Was denken Sie über den momentanen Markt in Ihrem Land in Sachen Erotik?
Leider sieht in Russland die Situation für Fotografen, die mit ihren Bildern Geld verdienen wollen, hoffnungslos aus. Andererseits gibt es, meiner Meinung nach, in diesem Land die schönsten Models der Welt.

Warum entschieden Sie sich, ausschließlich im Studio oder in geschlossenen Räumen zu arbeiten?
Ich habe gerne die Kontrolle über eine Situation und möchte nicht vom Wetter abhängig sein. In St. Petersburg kann man unmöglich Fotoshootings im Freien planen. Und nicht zuletzt spare ich mir dadurch manchen Aufruhr und Ärger.

Stepan Kvardakov

Что Вы говорите моделям во время съемки? Вы много объясняете и рекомендуете определенные позы или Вы оставляете им свободу действий?
На фотосессии я всегда стараюсь установить связь с моделью. Когда преобладает абсолютное безмолствие, трудно нам обоим. Я говорю о том и об этом, и при этом осторожно поправляю позы. Я могу рассказать анекдот или смешную историю, а иногда хватает и короткого „Да, хорошо, отлично сделано!". Модели должны чувствовать, что все под контролем. Только в том случае они расслабляются. Выбранные позы зависят от модели. Обычно я что-то предлагаю и обрисовываю позу. Сложно найти модель, которой можно было бы сказать: „Делай, что хочешь, я буду просто нажимать на кнопку".

Как так получилось, что Ваши отличные работы до сих пор остались почти неизвестными? Как Вы планируете в дальнейшем действовать с Вашим агентом?
Я не знаю, причину назвать трудно. У меня бесчисленное количество подписчиков в социальных сетях, и на известных фотосайтах я вполне известен. Моя цель - показать всему миру красоту женских форм.

Почему и как появилась эта книга?
Мой агент посоветовал мне создать эту книгу. Он сказал, что настало время, чтобы люди увидели мои фотографии на бумаге. В конце концов, это классический, традиционный носитель.

Какие следующие проекты Вы задумали?
Этого я еще не знаю. Пусть будущее меня удивит.

Почему вы выбрали для себя именно этот особенный стиль?
Потому что мне нравятся красивые девушки, особенно обнаженные! Несколько лет назад я пробовал заниматься свадебной и семейной фотографией. Но так как мой интерес к этому был невелик, фотографии казались повседневными и почти что скучными. Также я не очень интересуюсь кошками и цветами, ведь они со мной не разговаривают. Поэтому я однозначно предпочитаю работать со своими девушками.

Что Вы думаете о рынке в Вашей стране в вопросах эротики в настоящее время?
К сожалению, ситуация в России для фотографов, которые своими снимками стремятся зарабатывать деньги, безнадежна. С другой стороны, я считаю, в этой стране самые красивые модели в мире.

Почему Вы решили работать исключительно в студии или в закрытых помещениях?
Мне нравится иметь ситуацию под контролем и я не хочу зависеть от погоды. В Санкт-Петербурге невозможно планировать фотосессии на открытом воздухе. И наконец: это избавляет меня от излишнего беспокойства и возмущения.

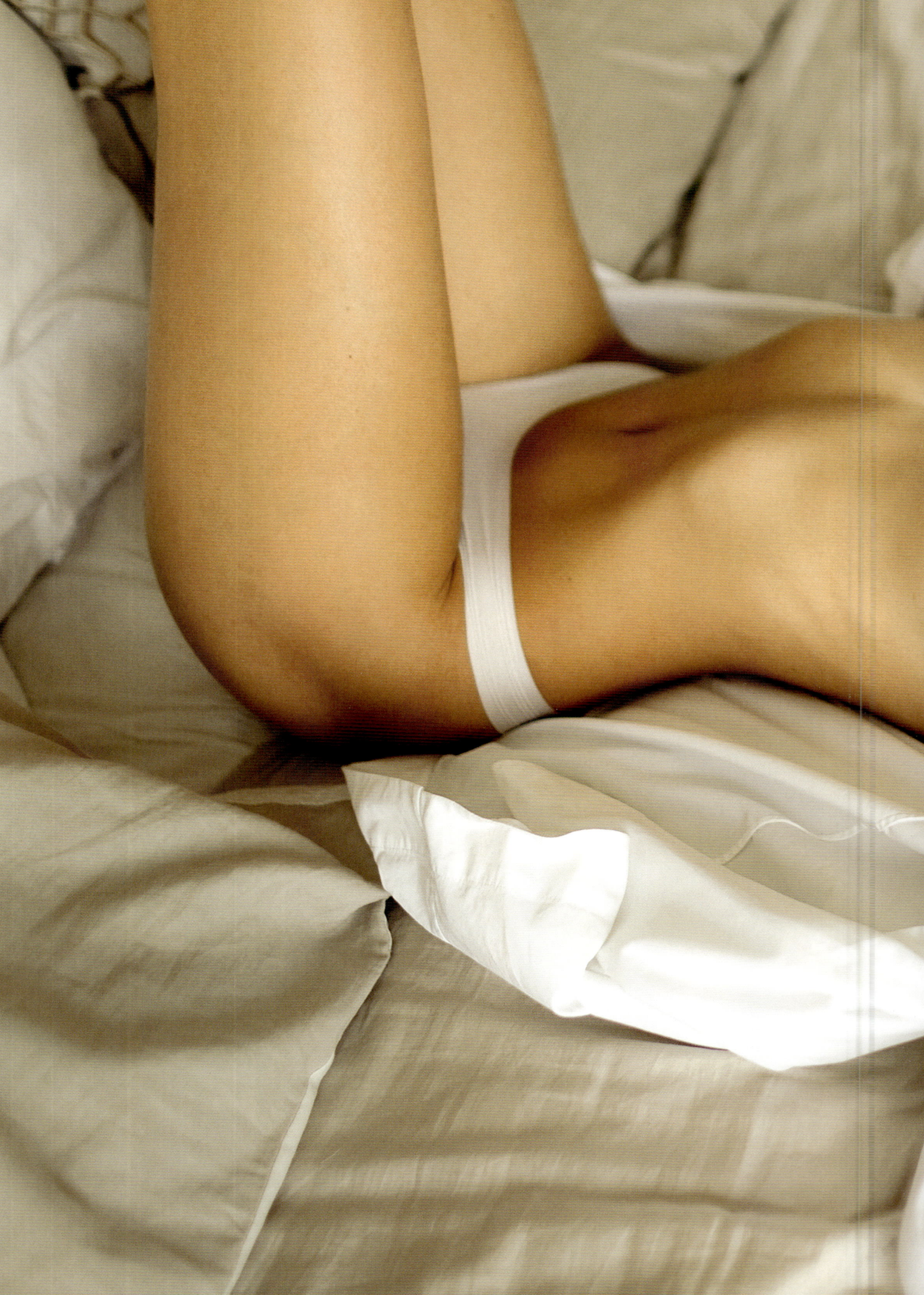

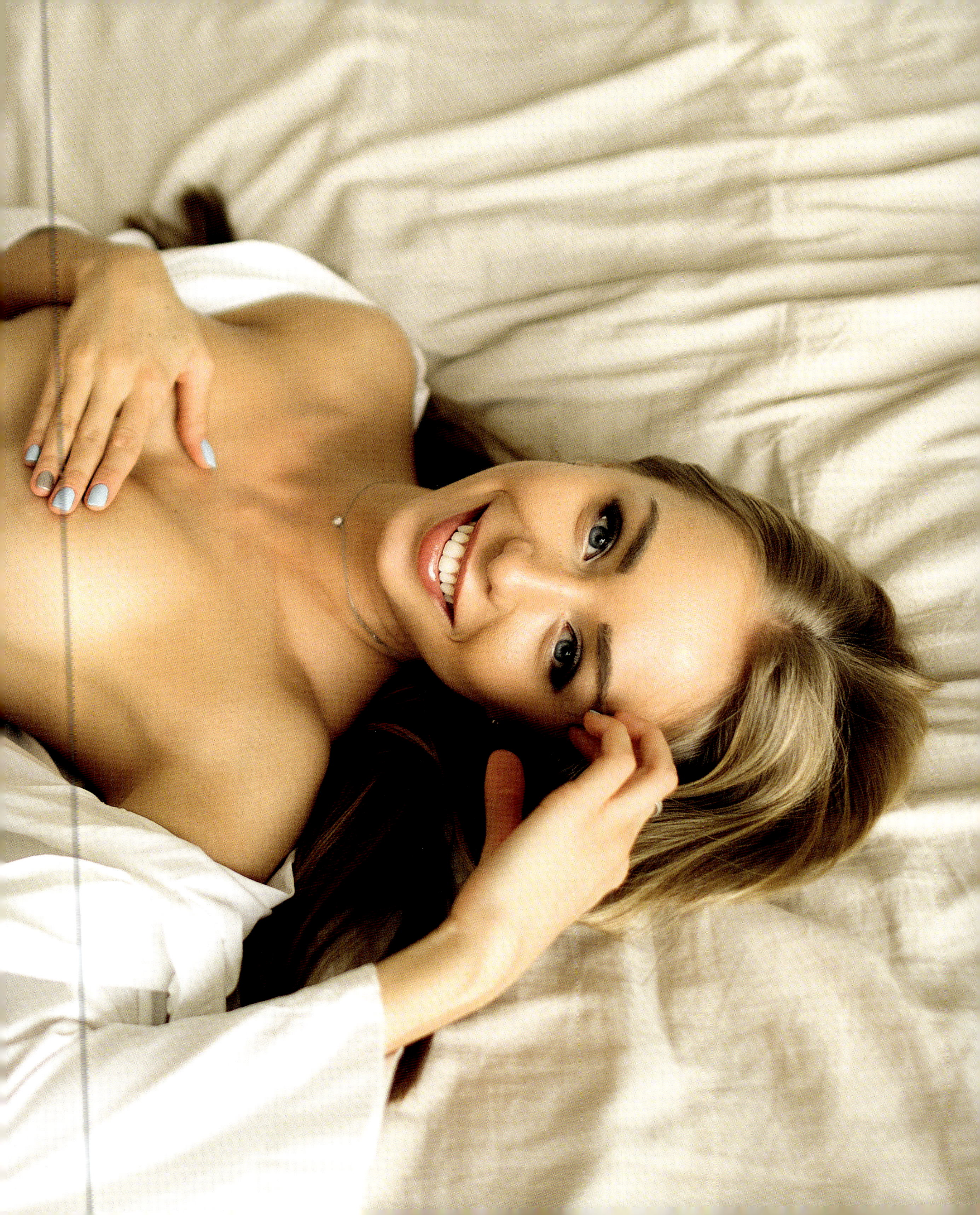

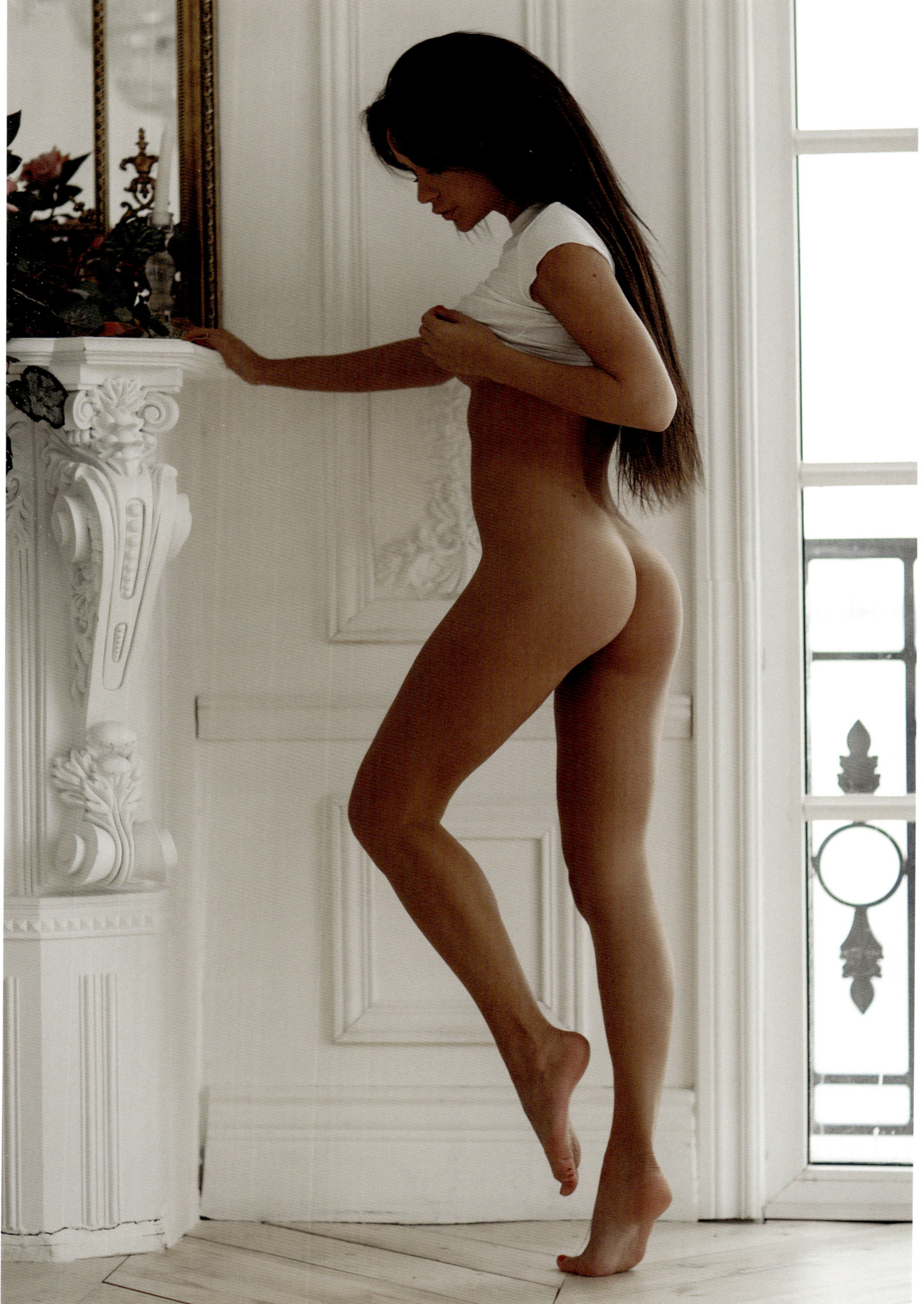

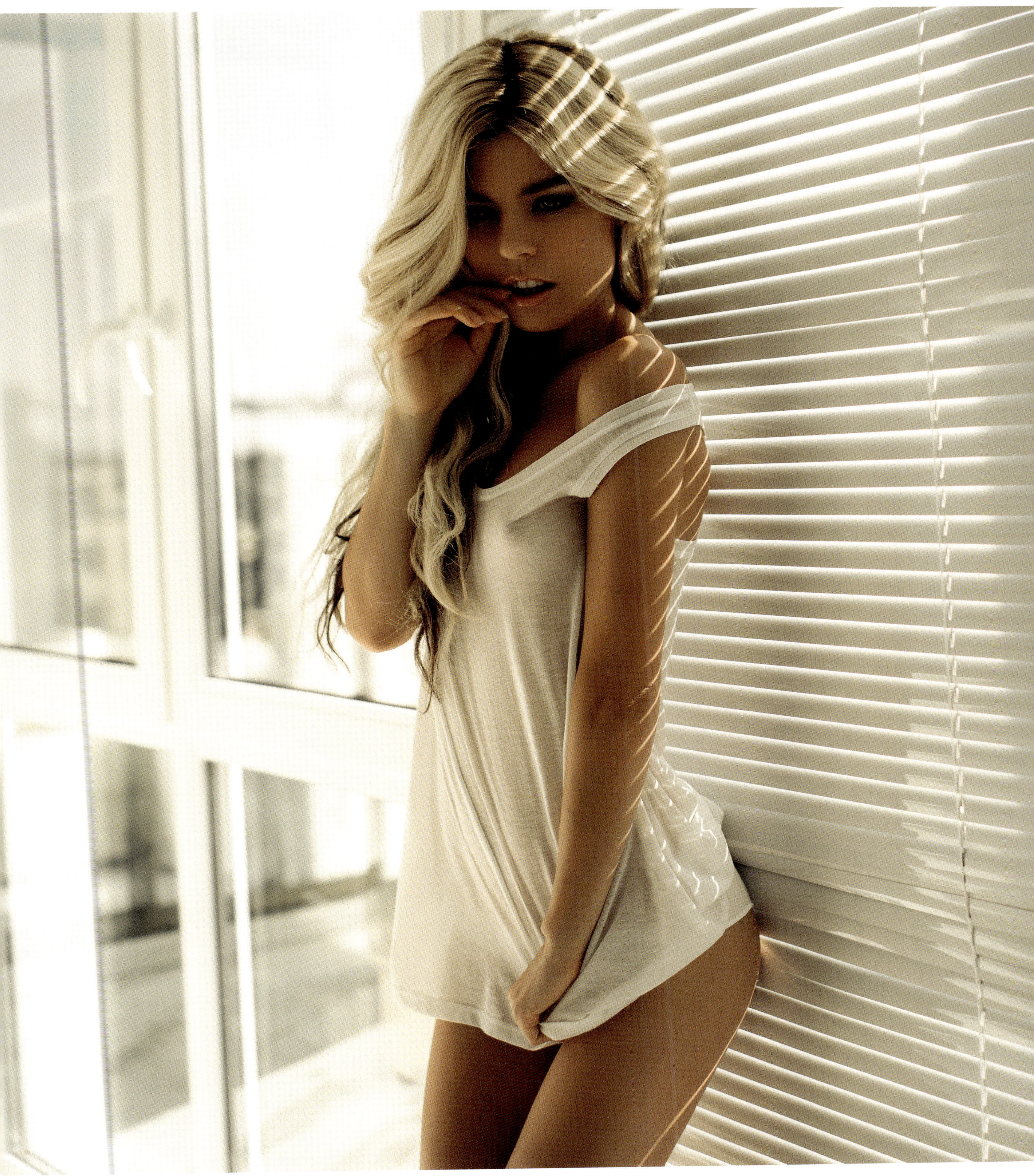

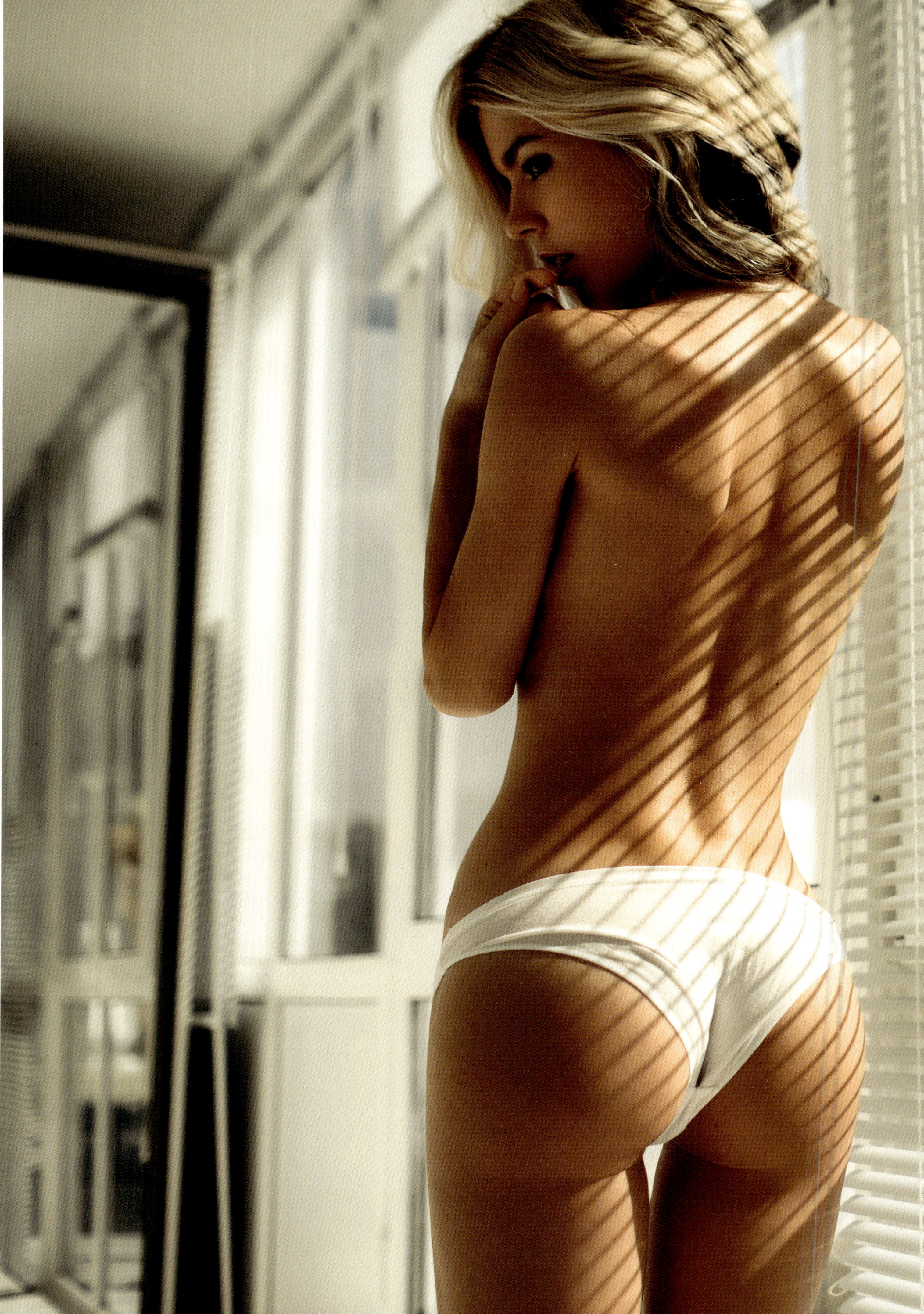

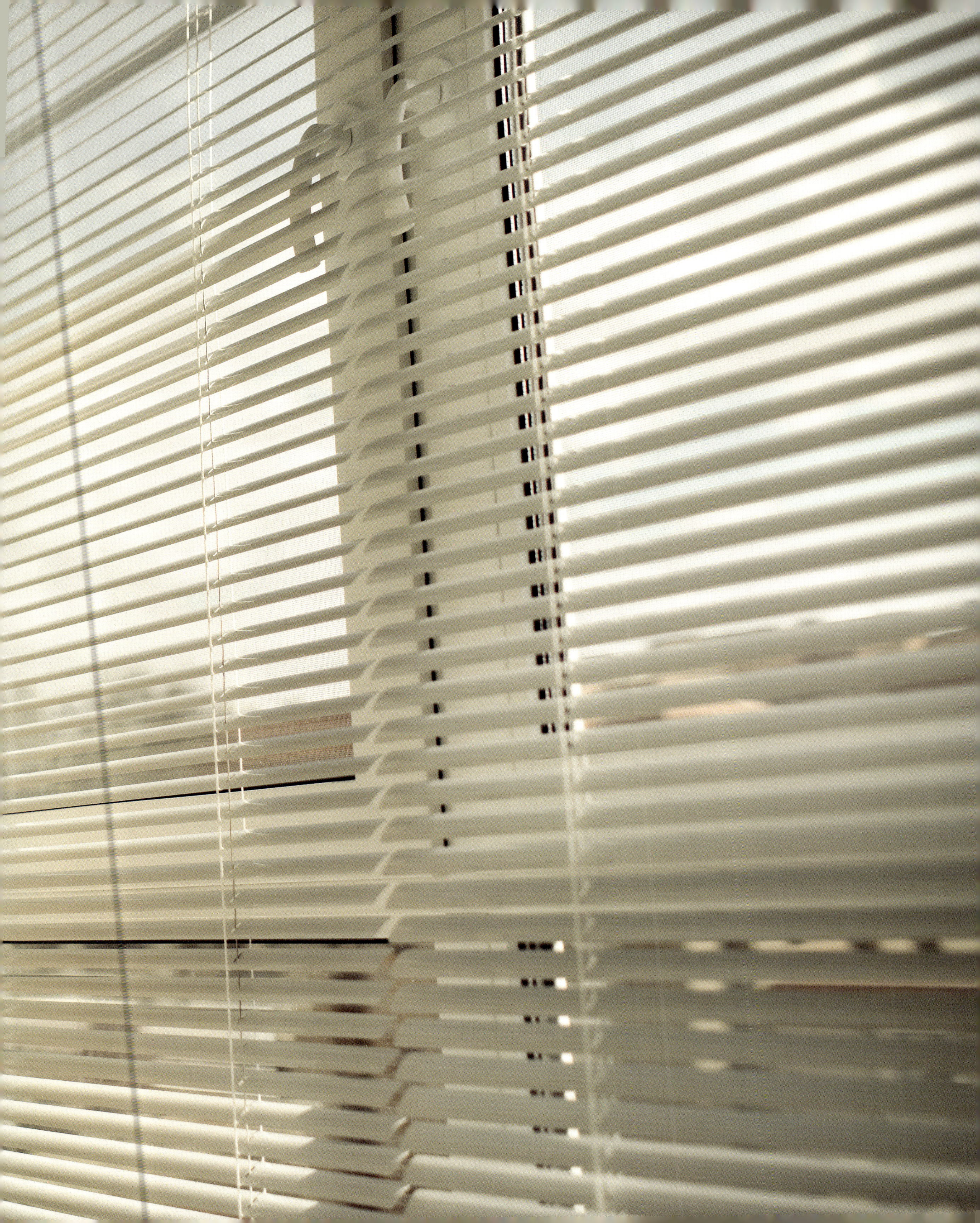

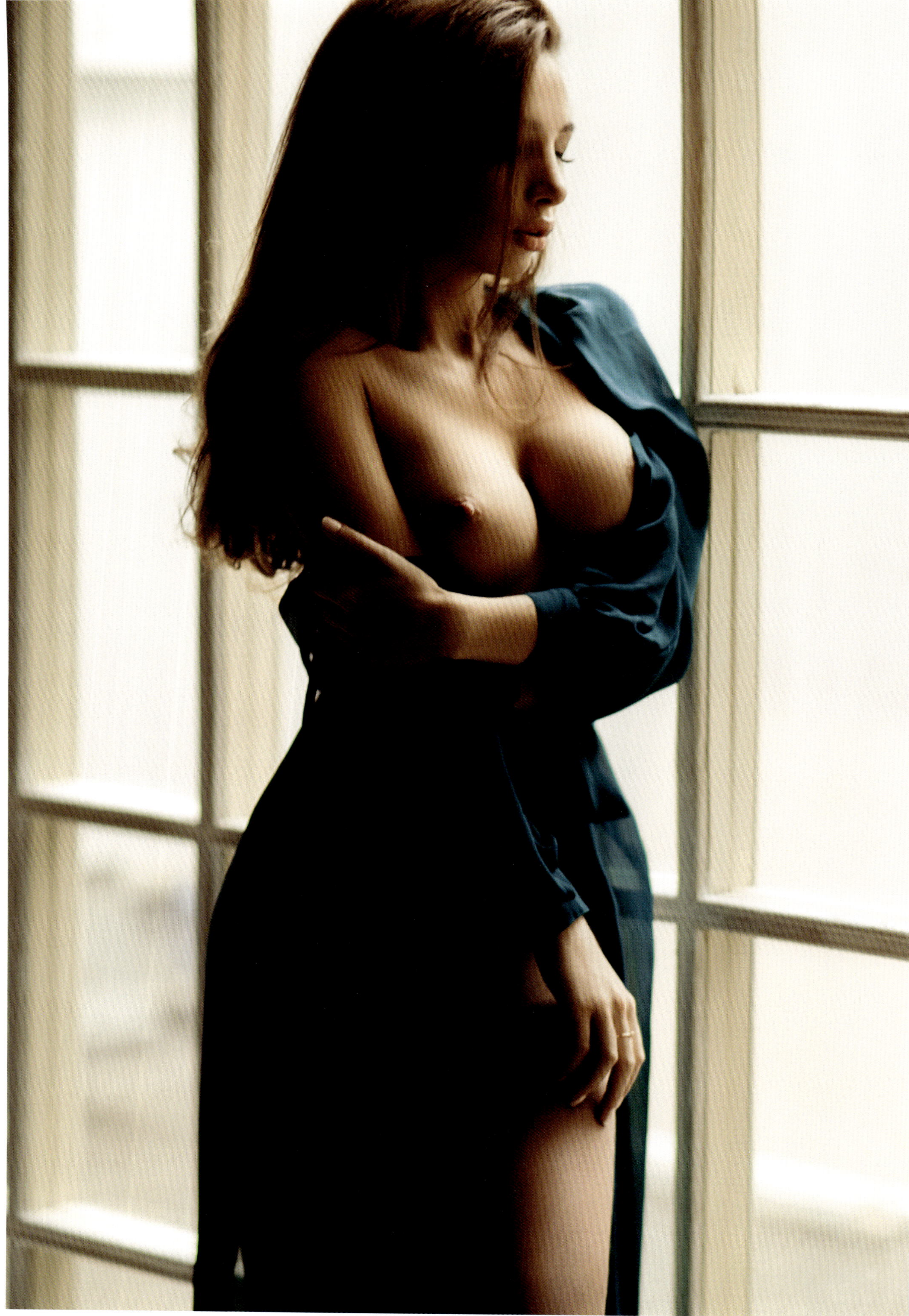

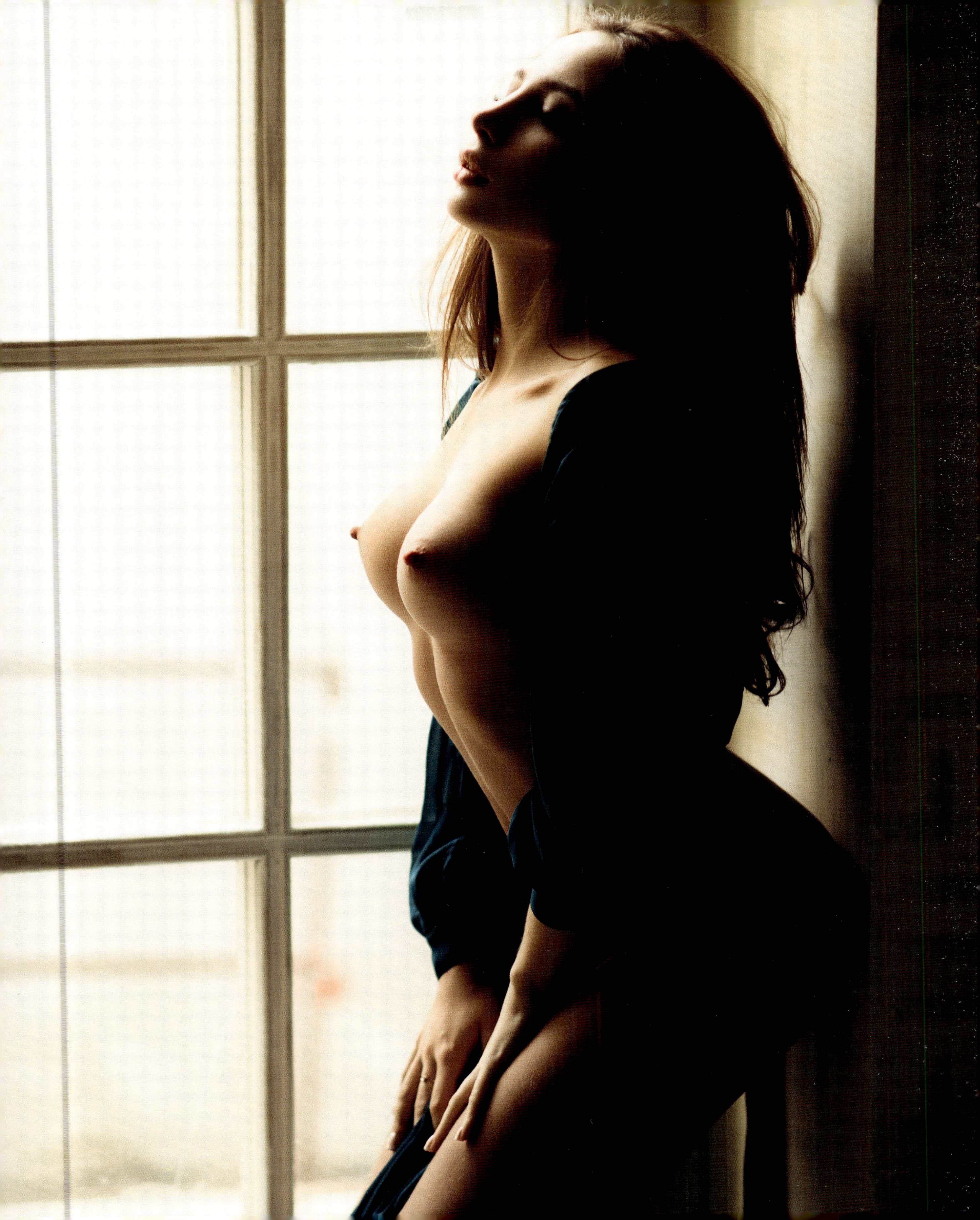

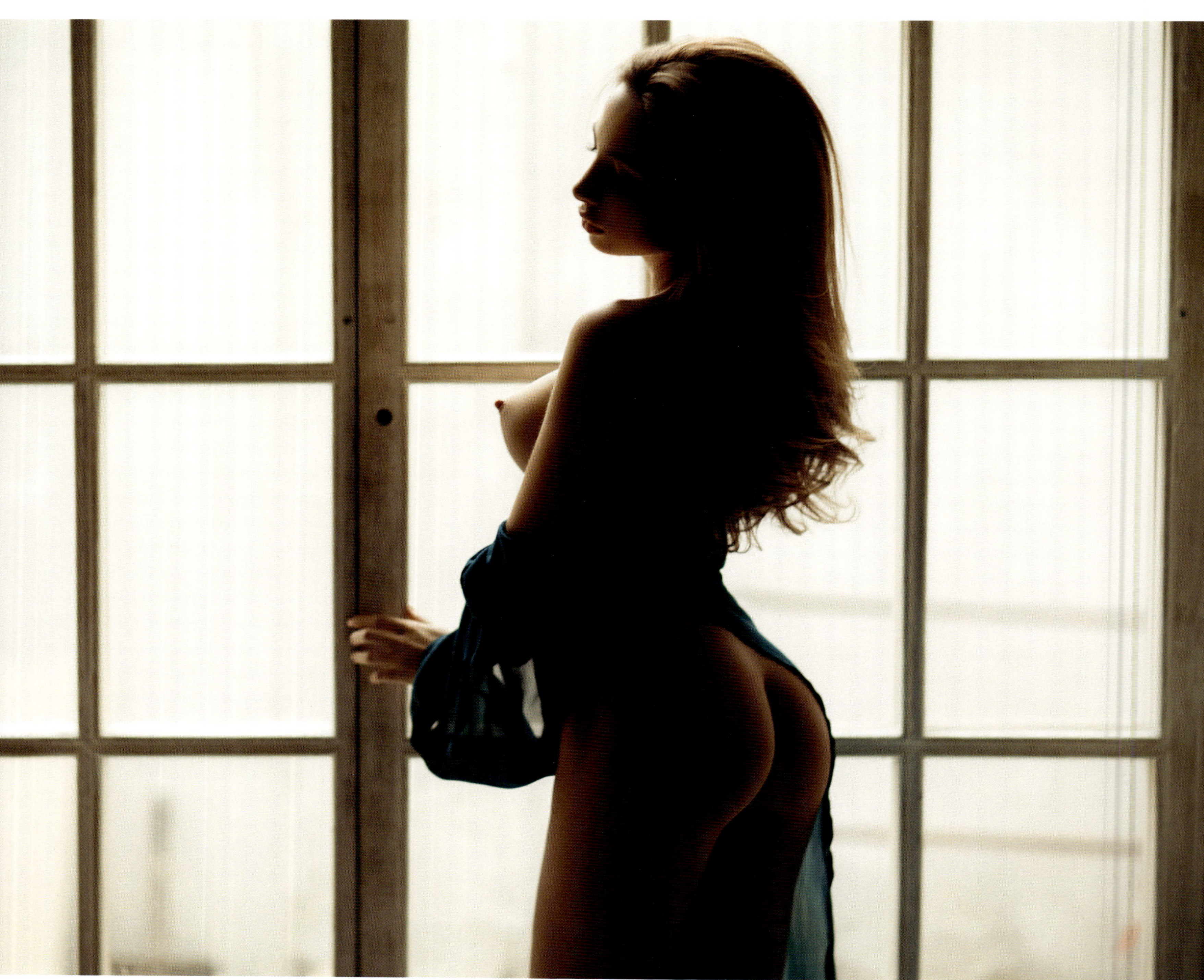

▲ АННА М. | ANNA M.

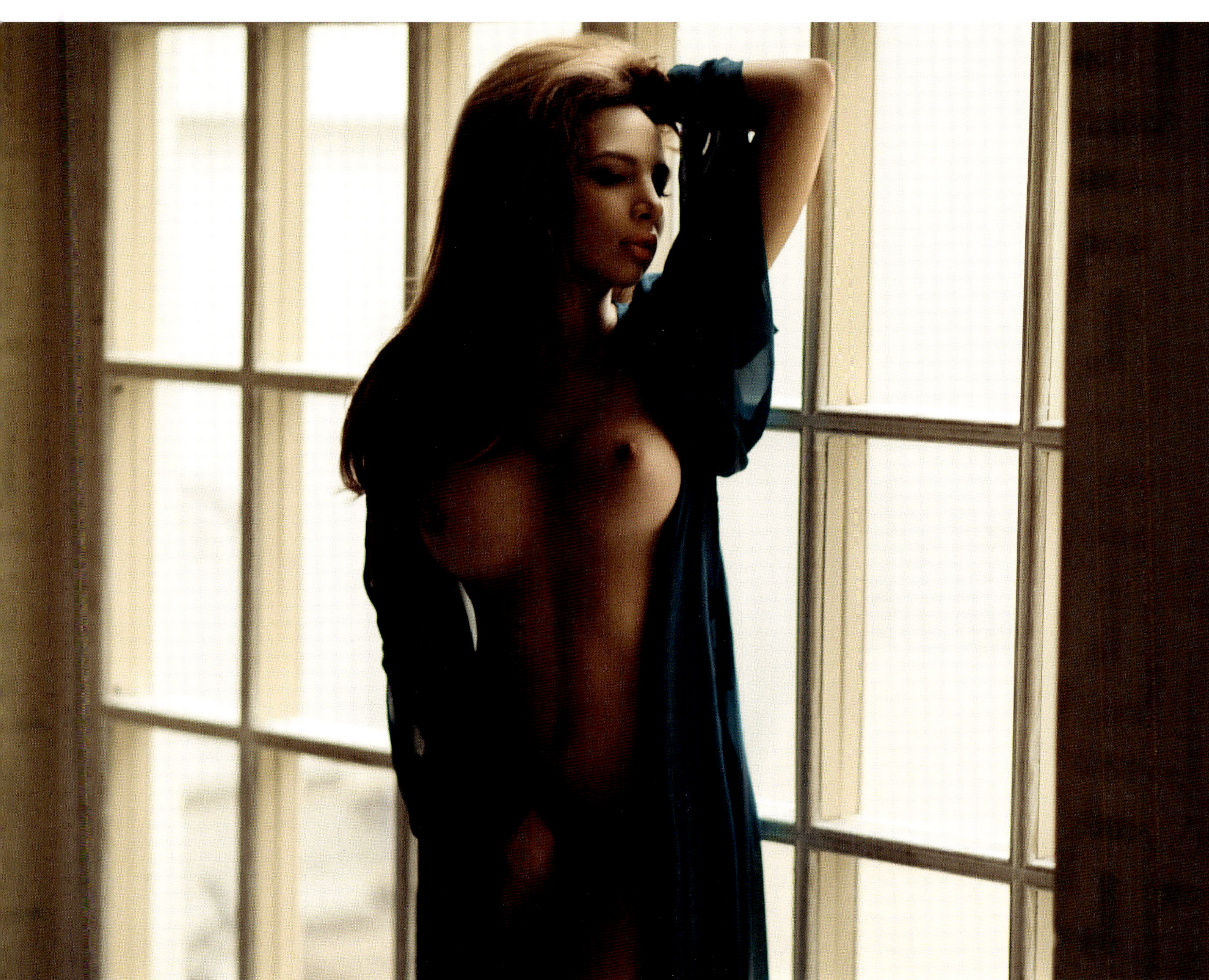

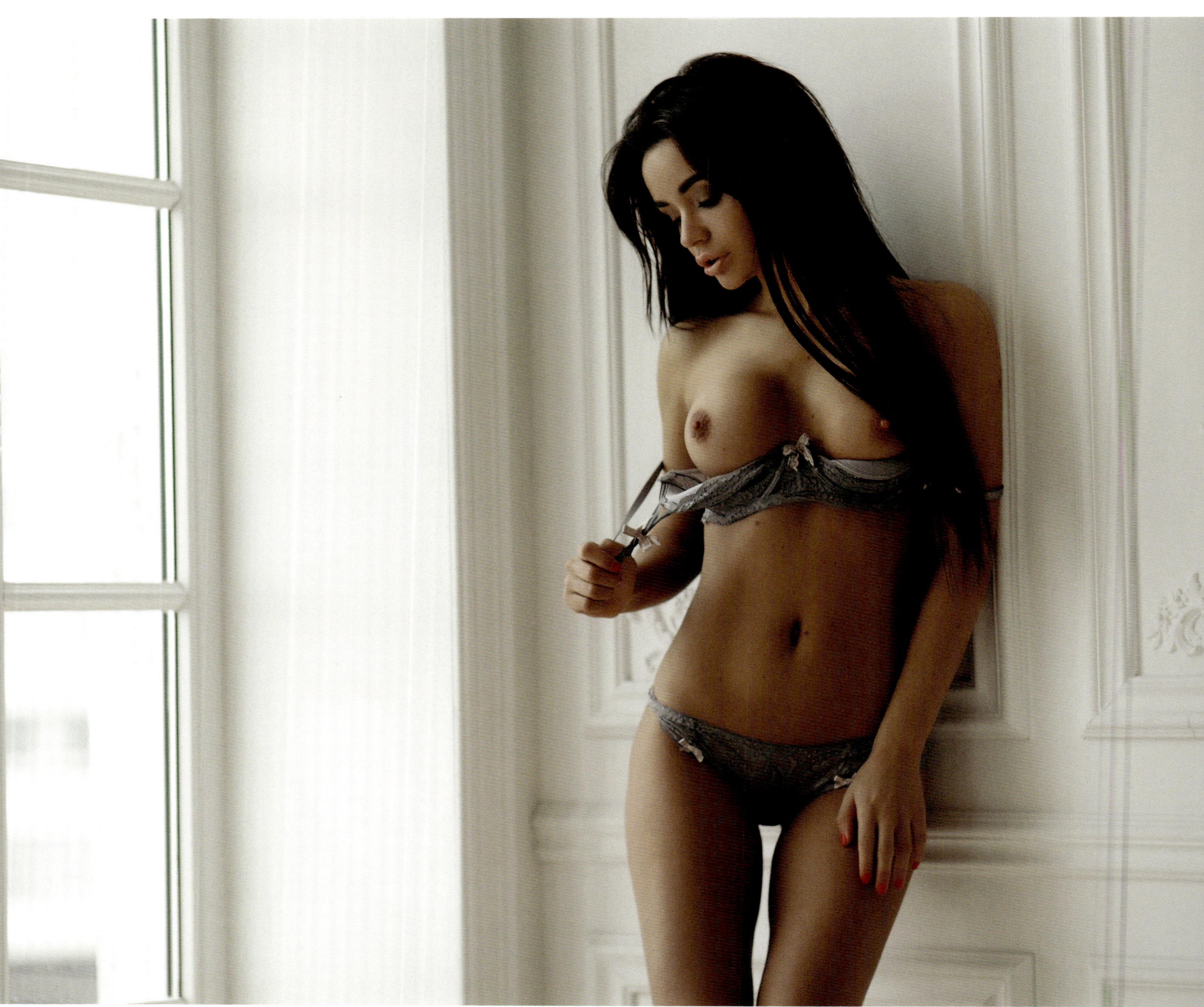

ЕКАТЕРИНА З. | EKATERINA Z. ▲

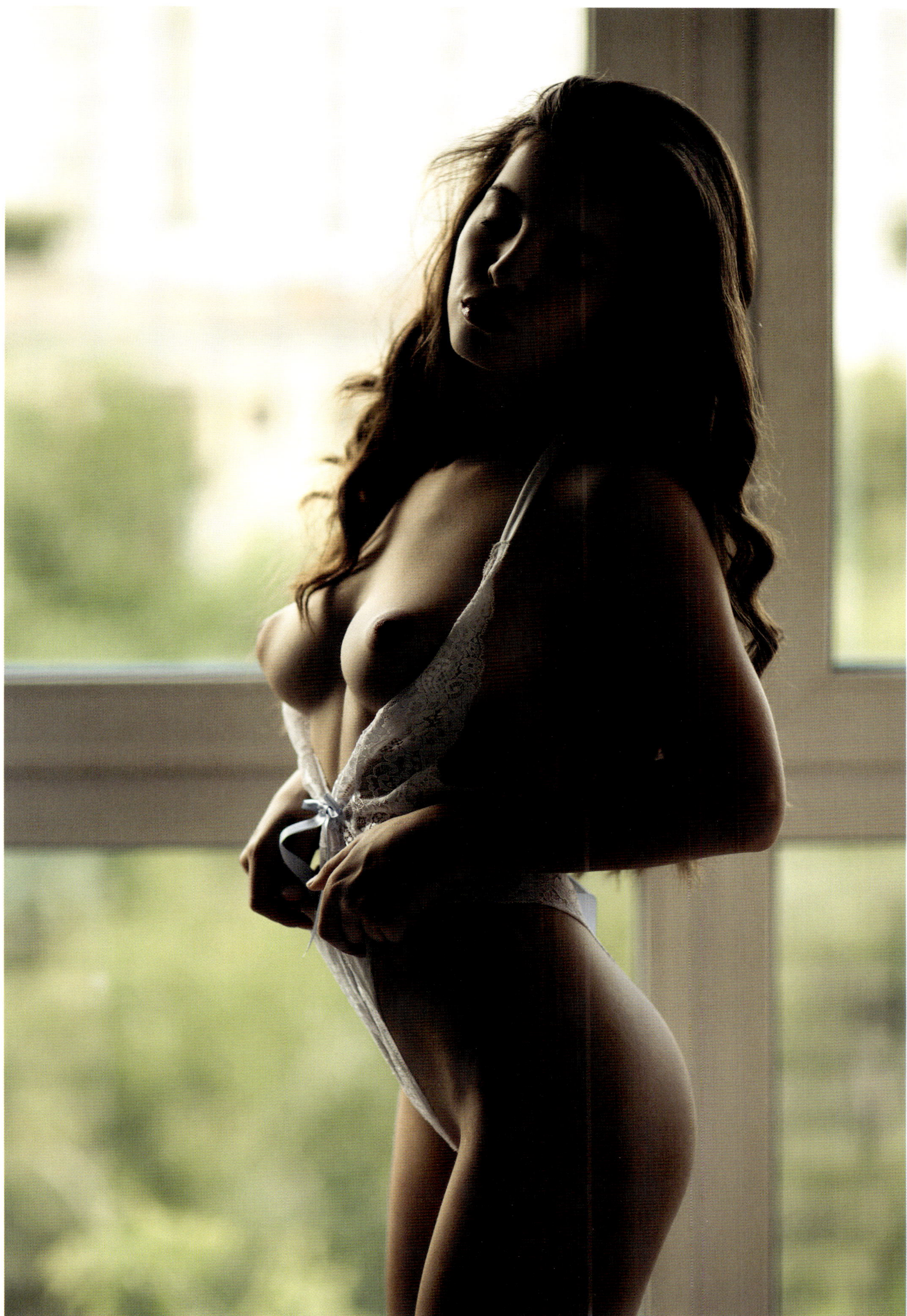

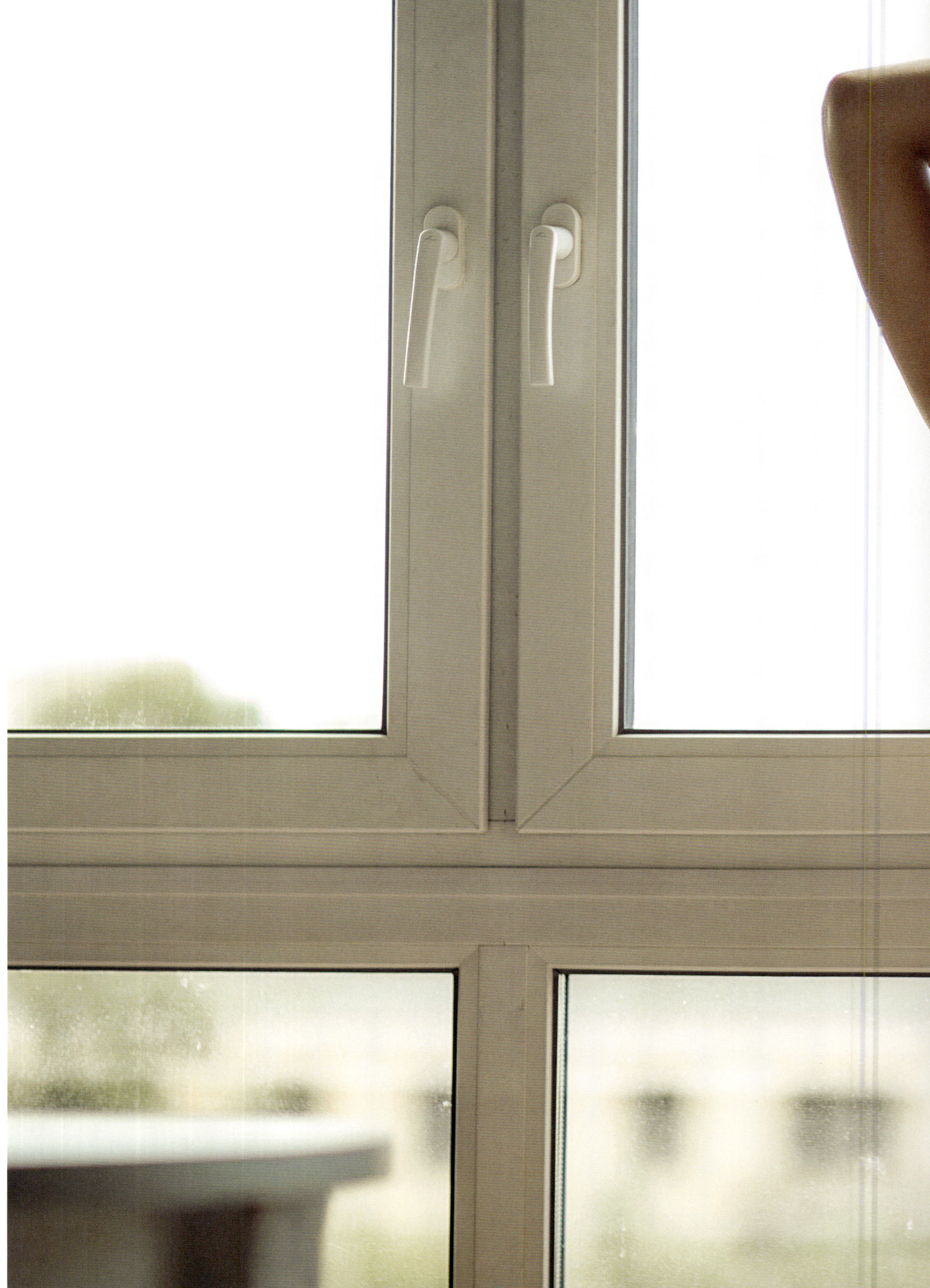

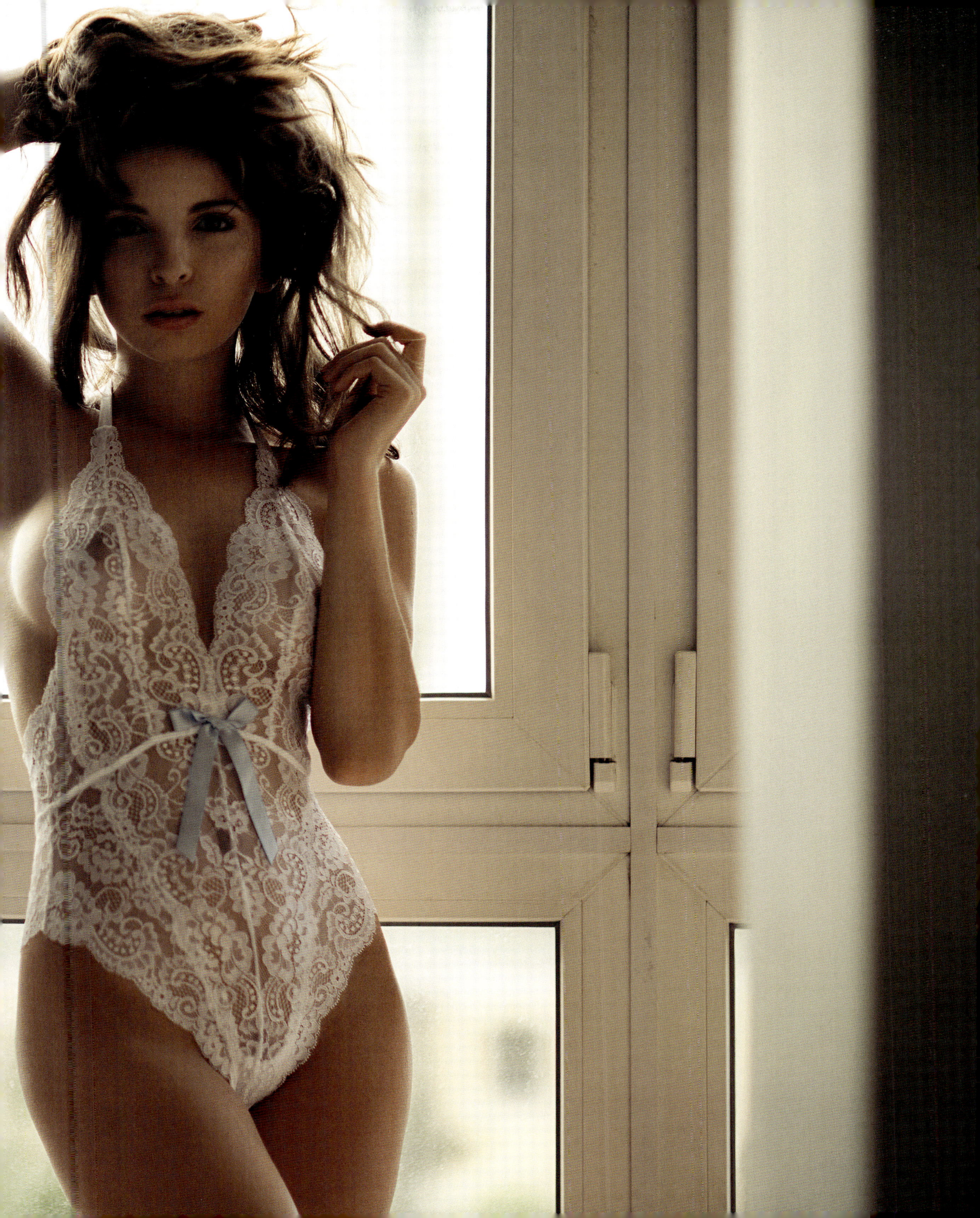

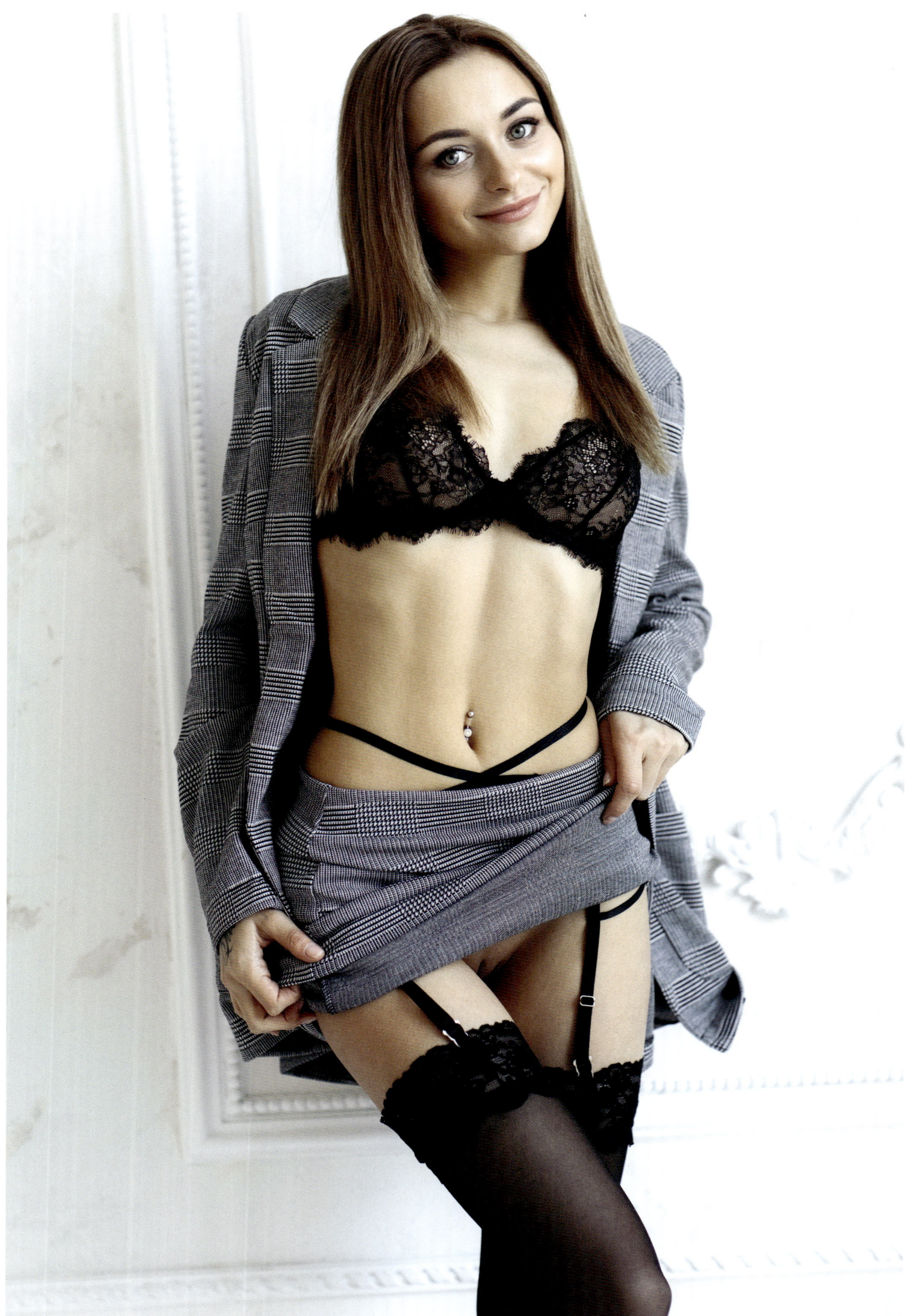

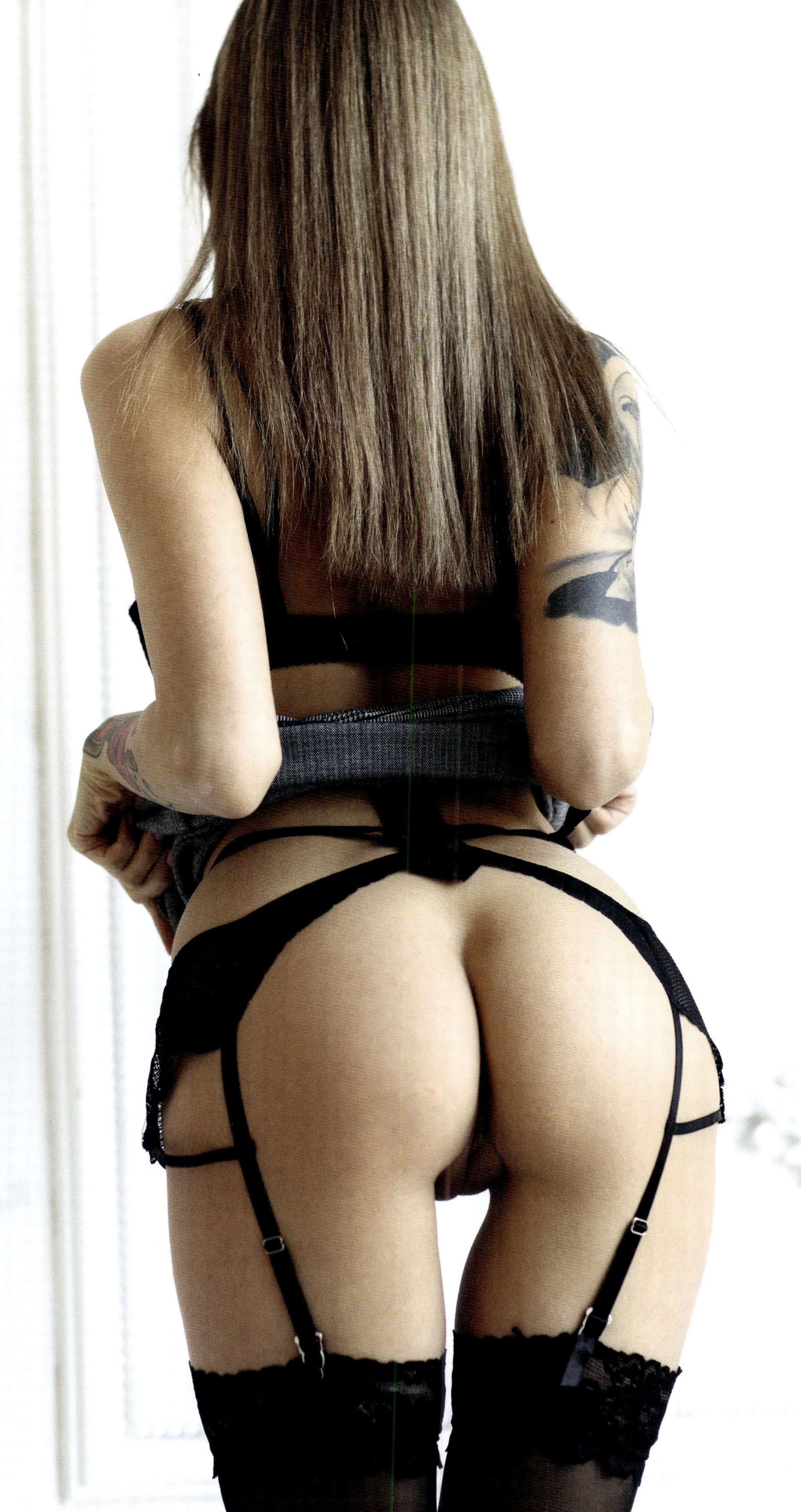

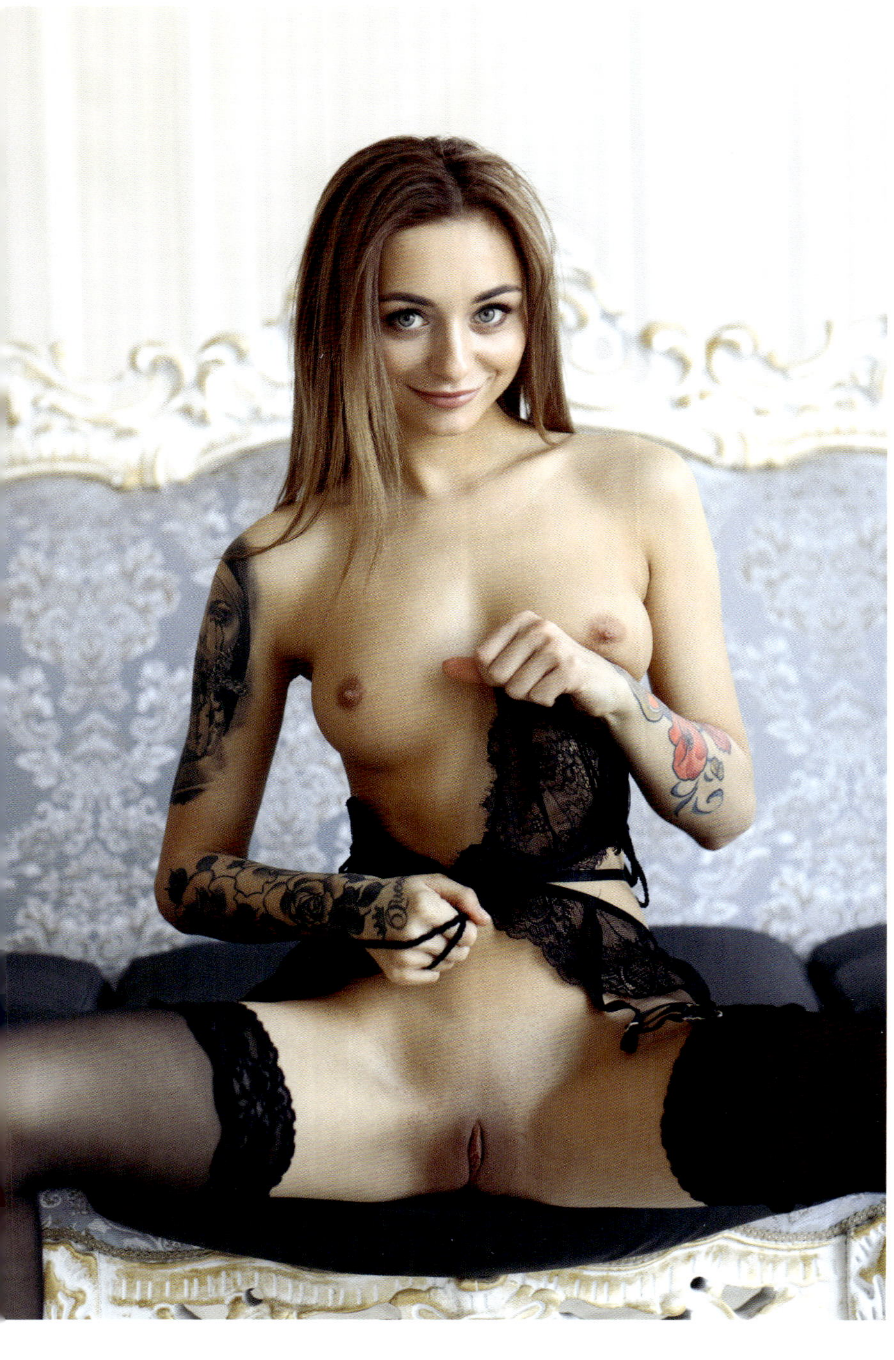

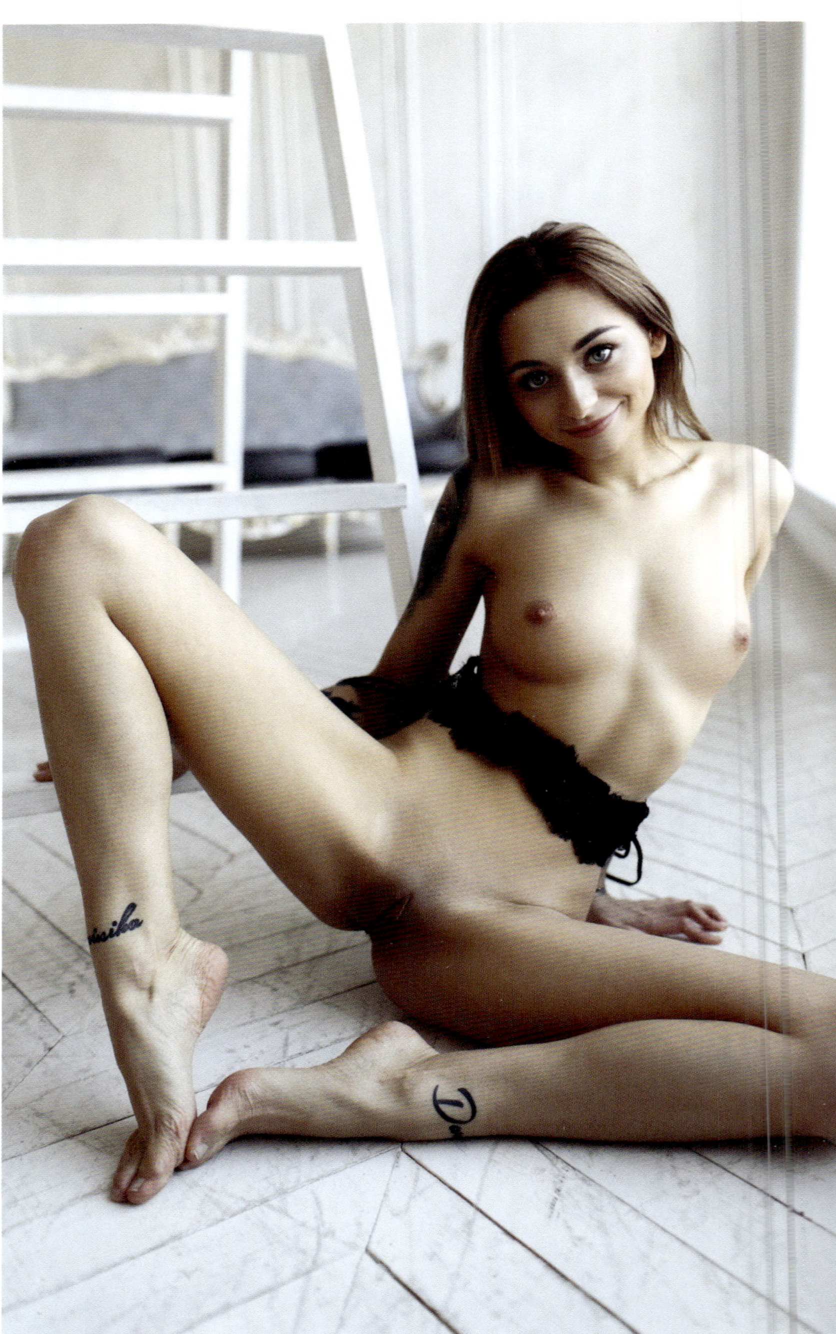

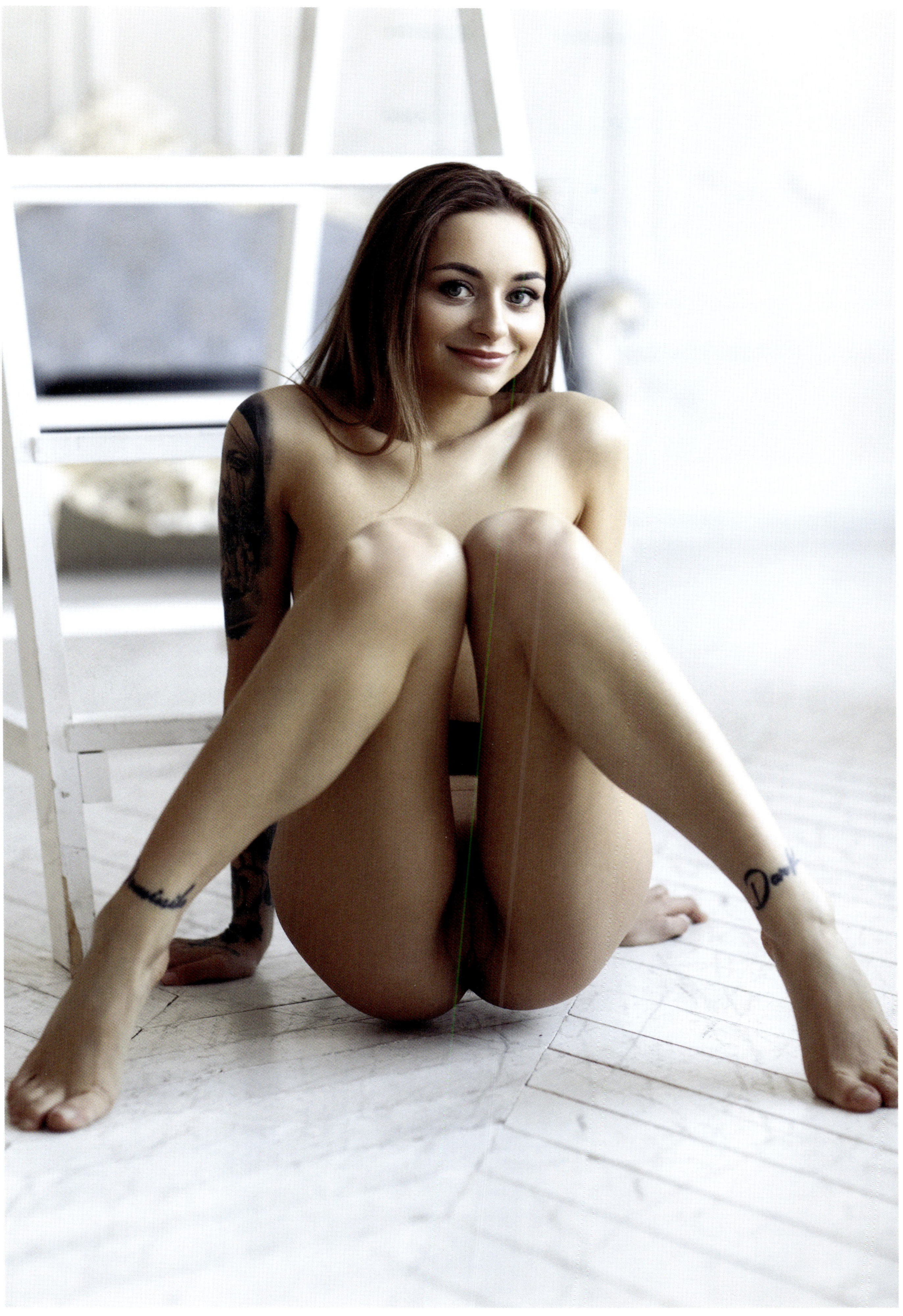

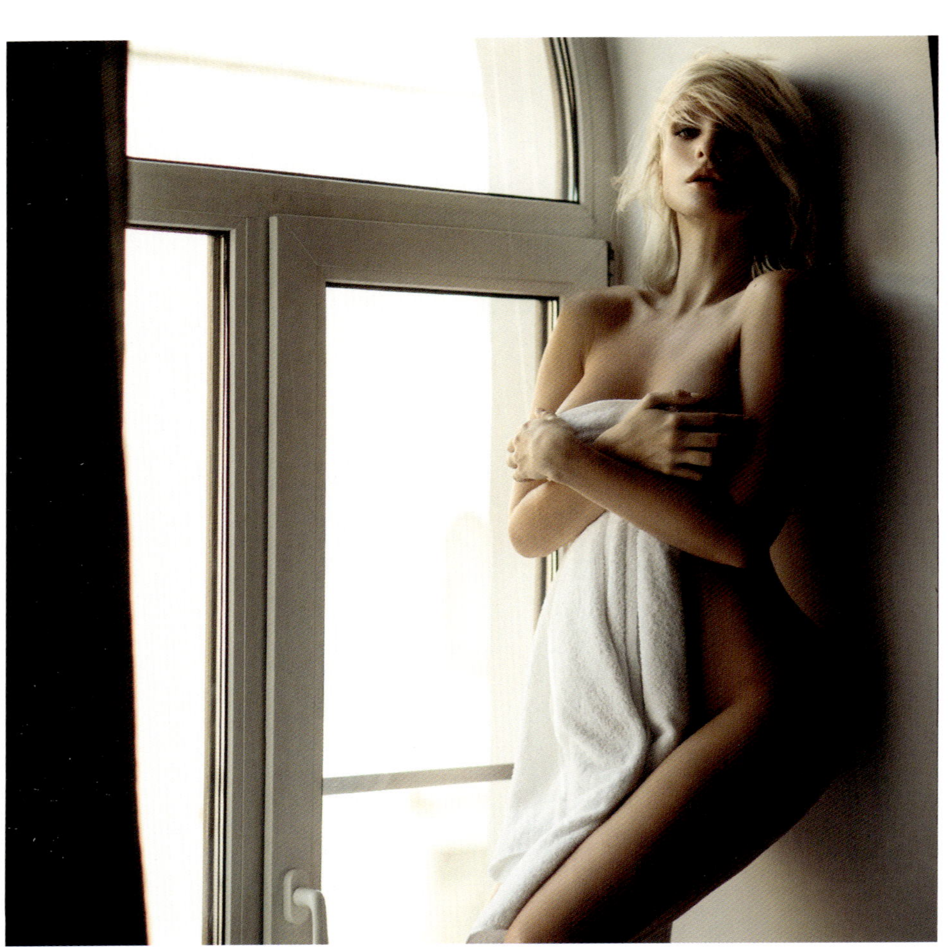

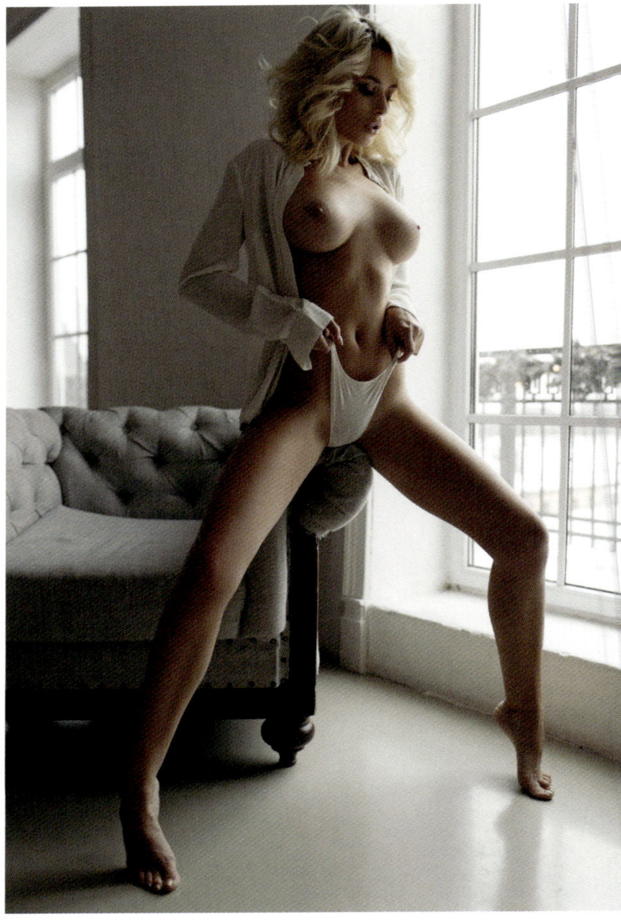

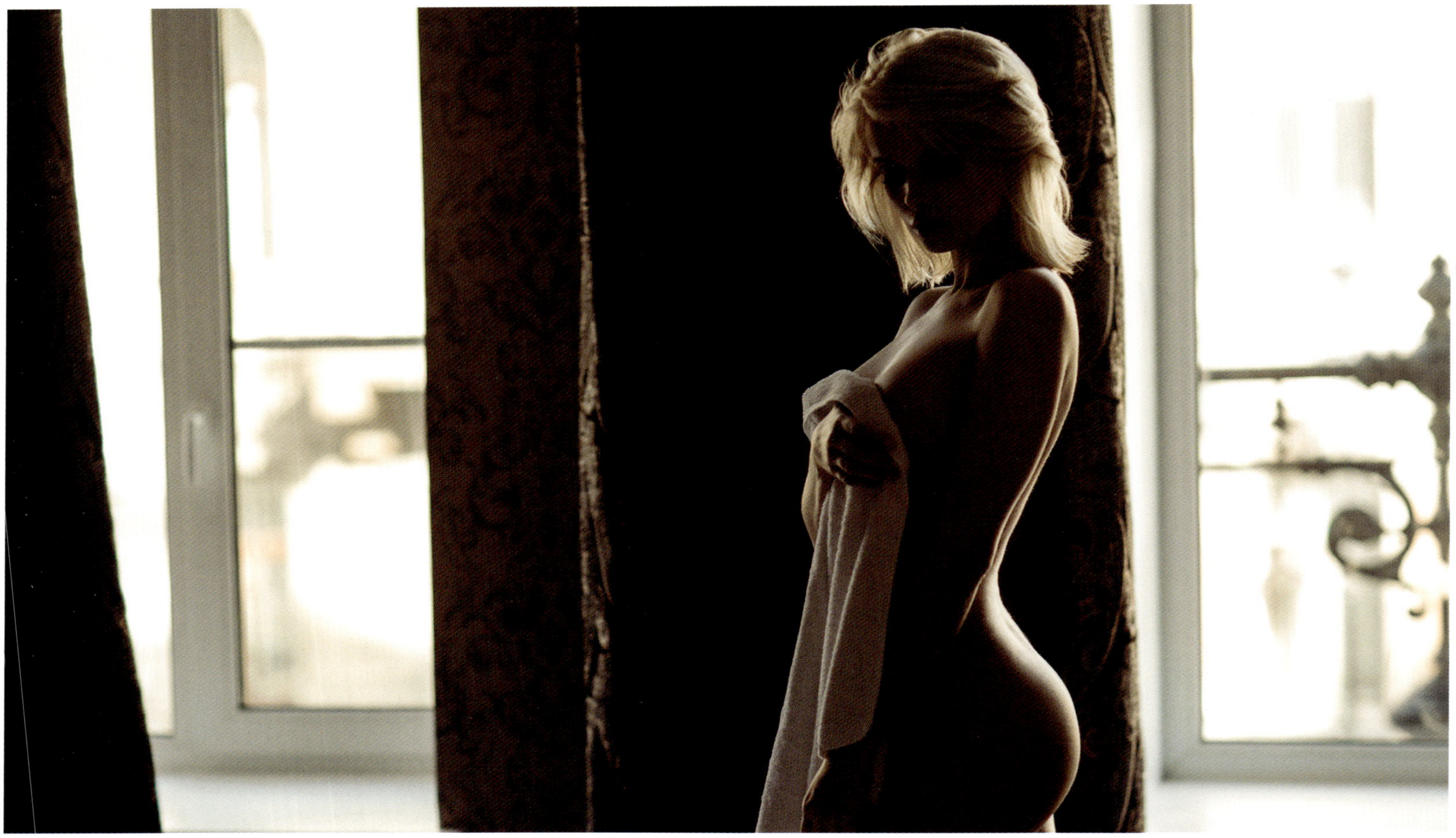

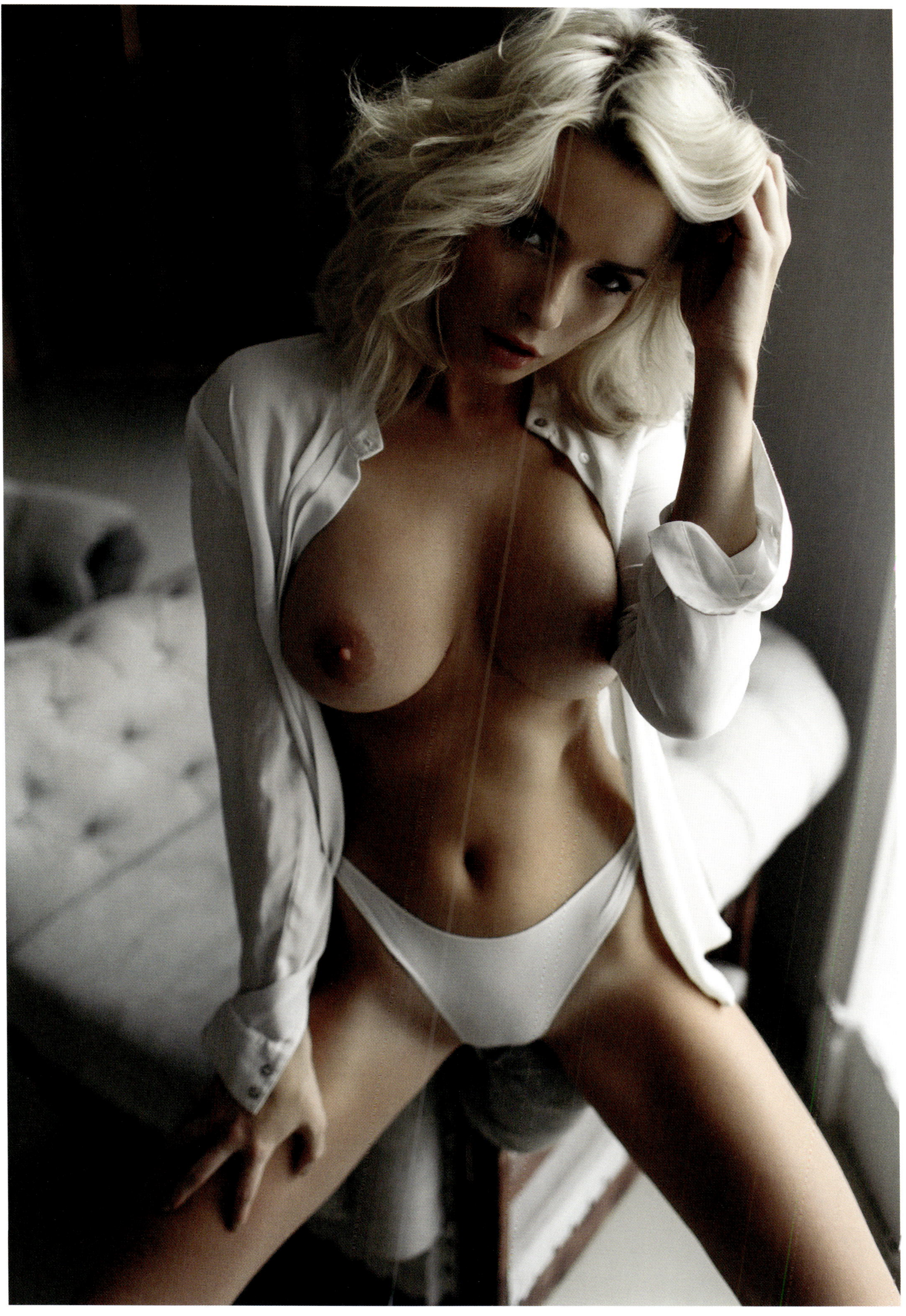

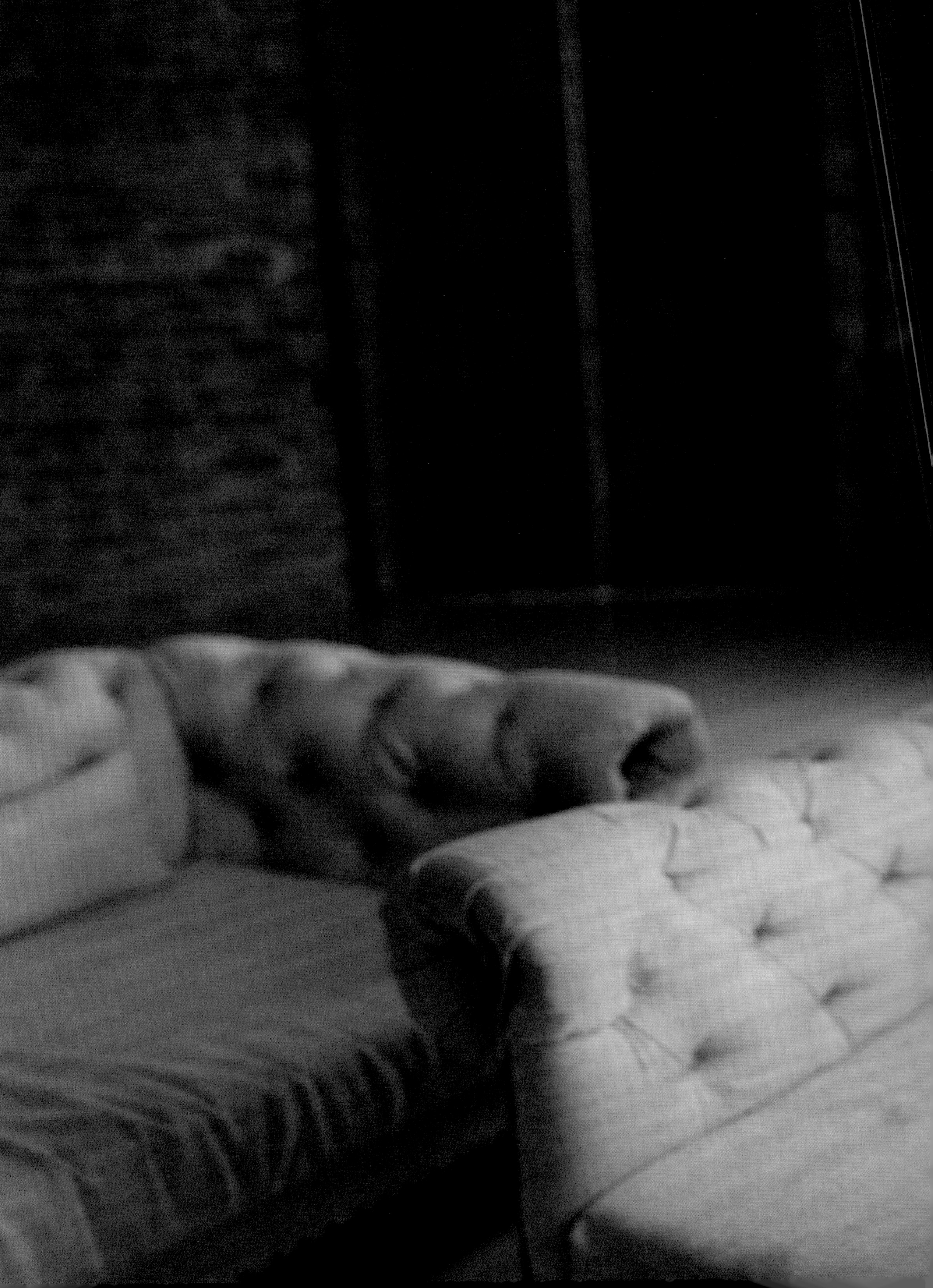

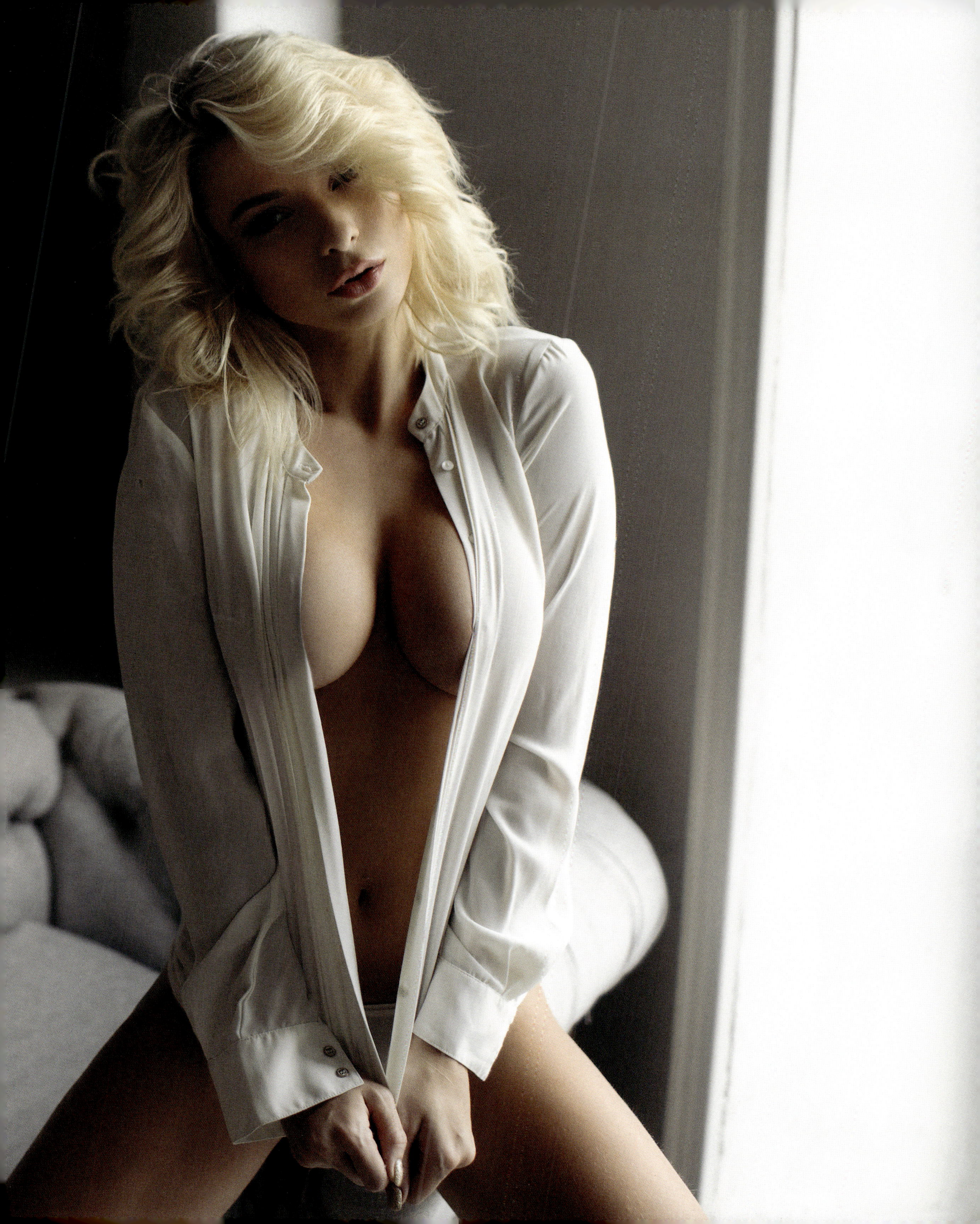

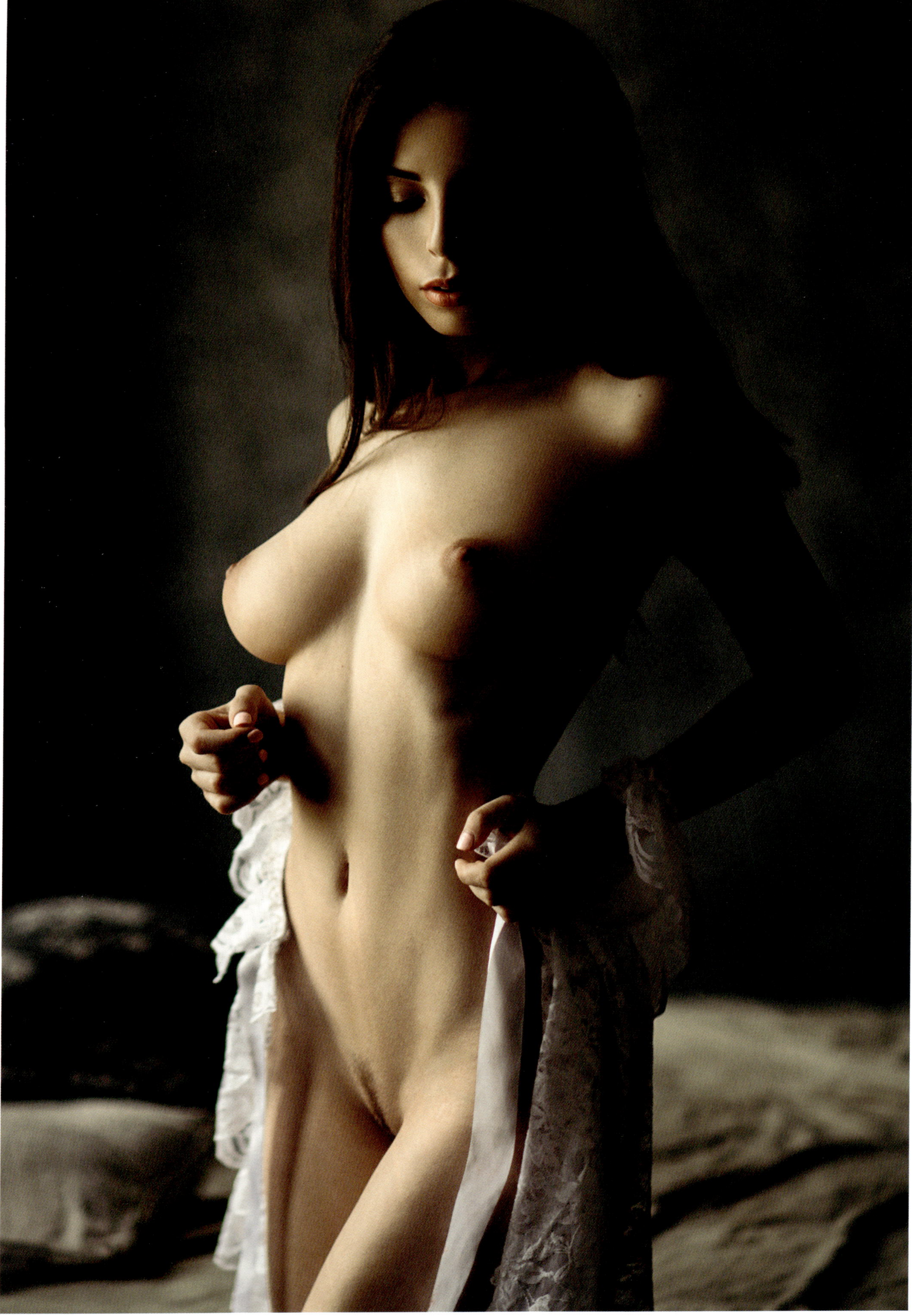

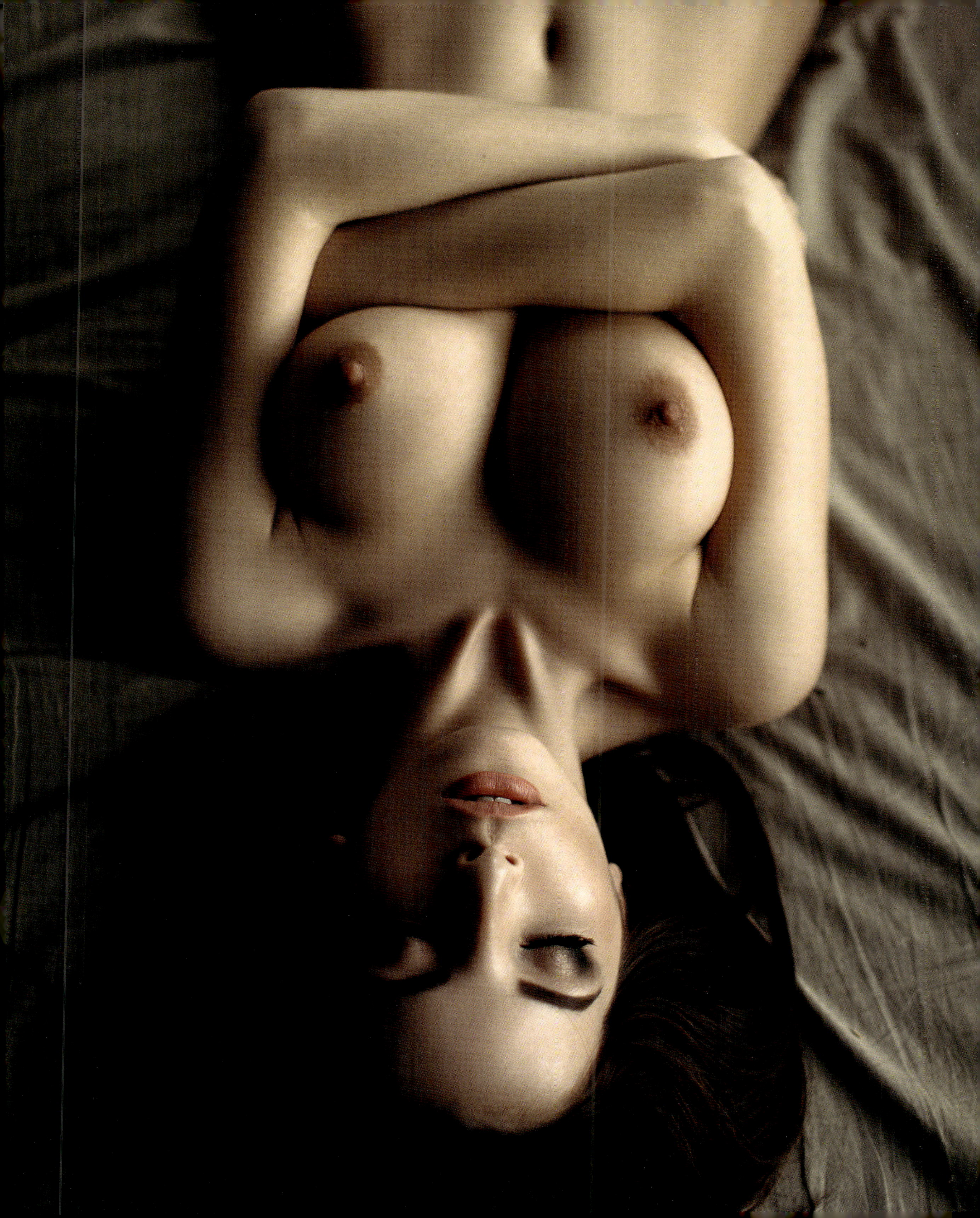

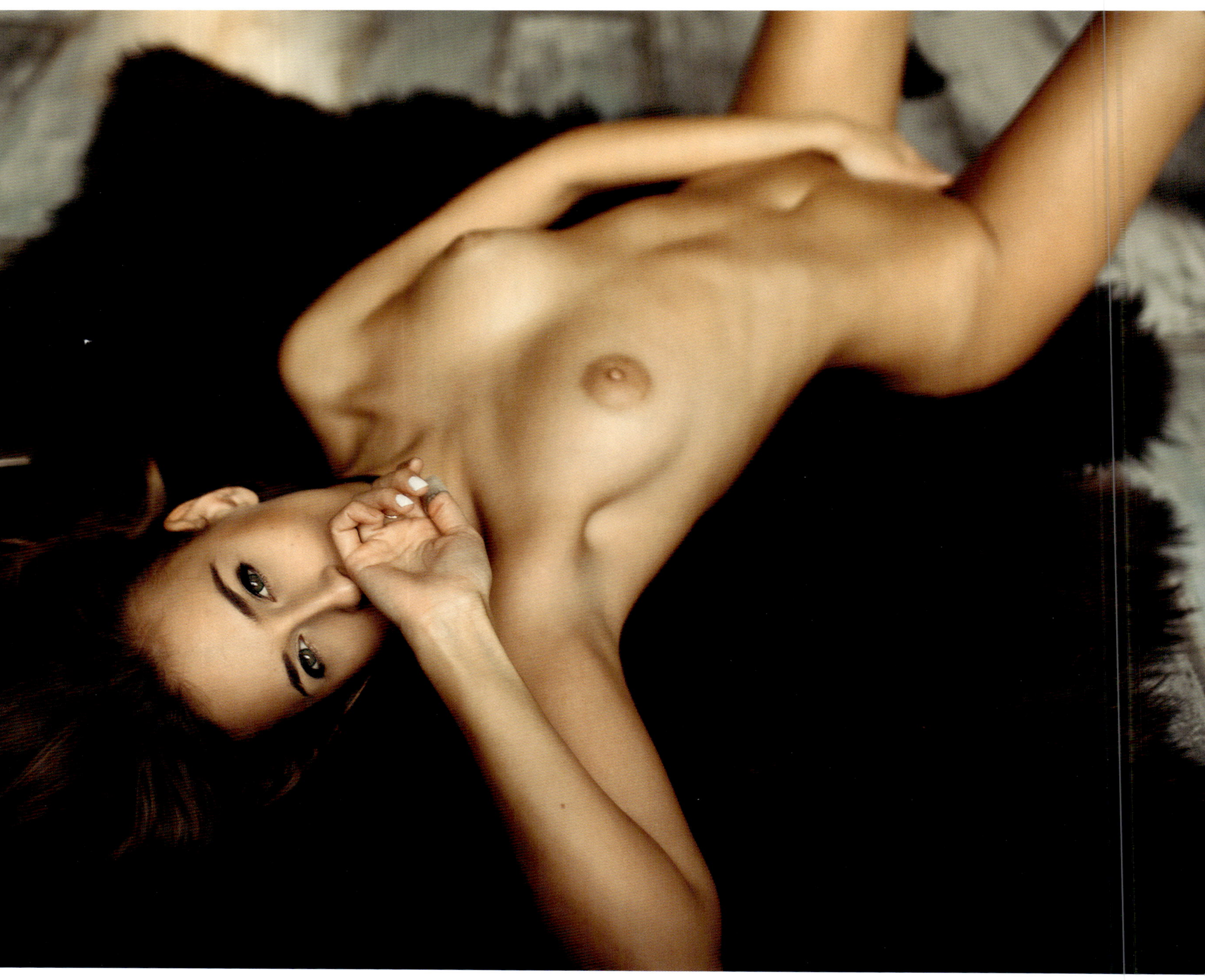

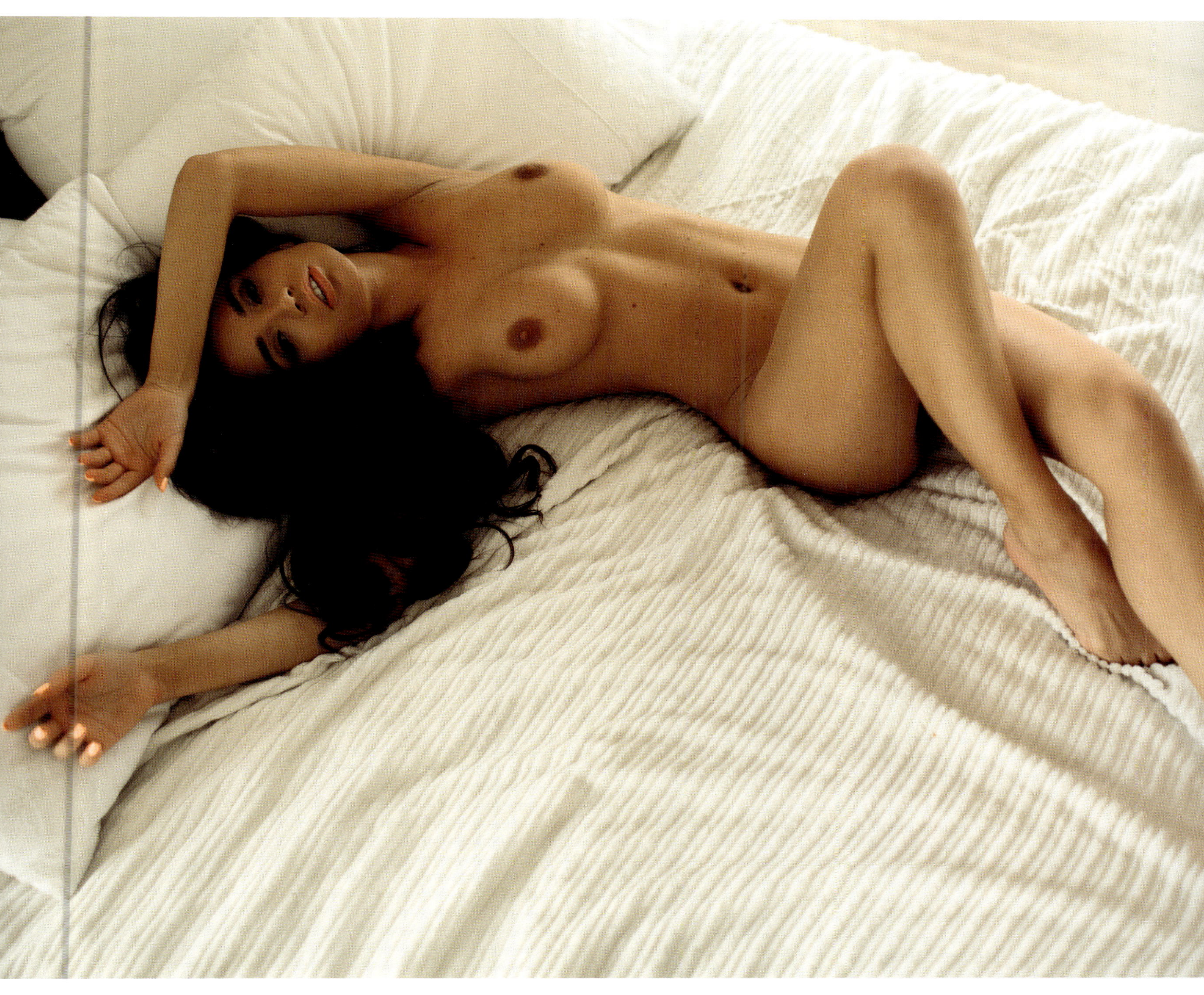

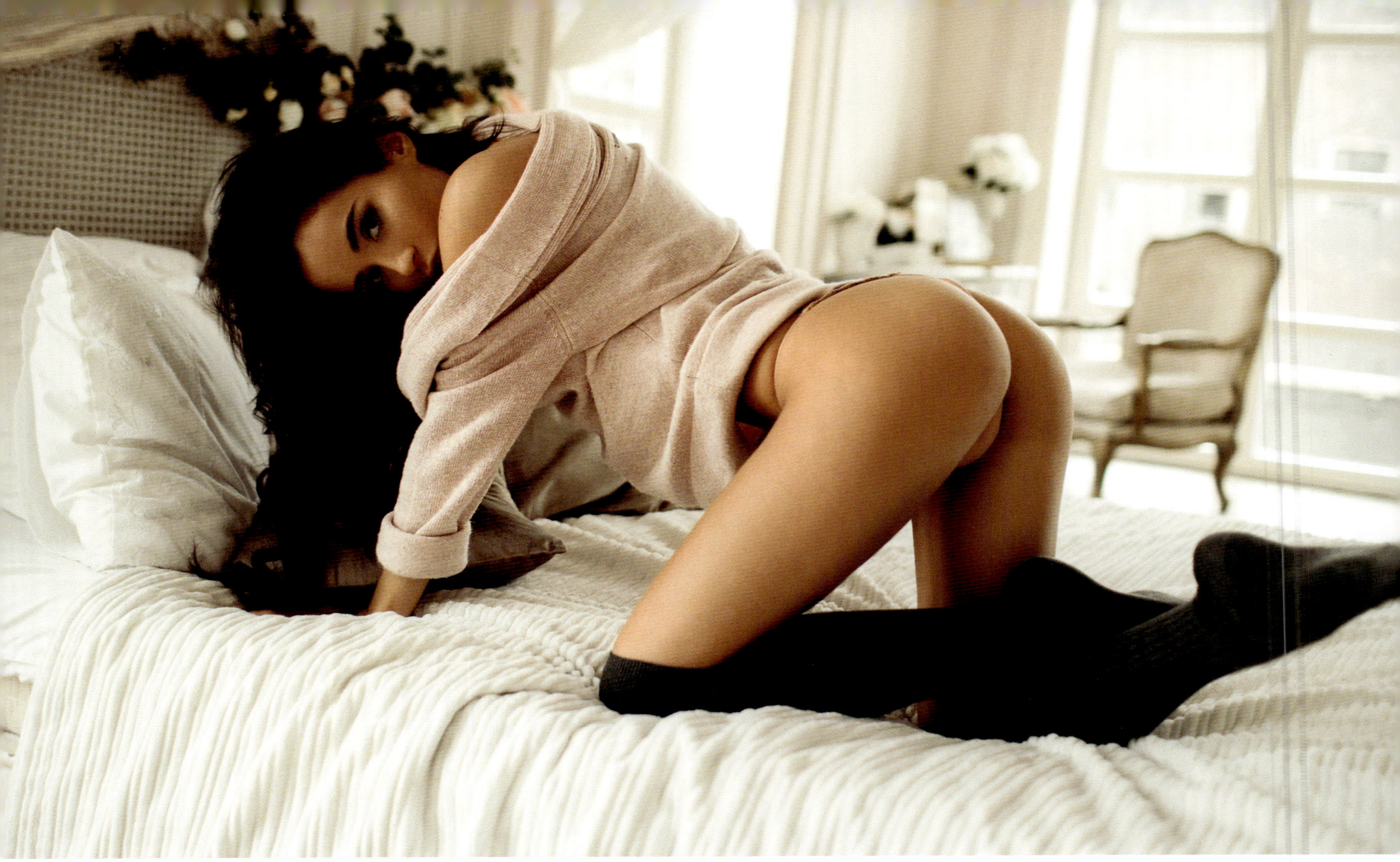

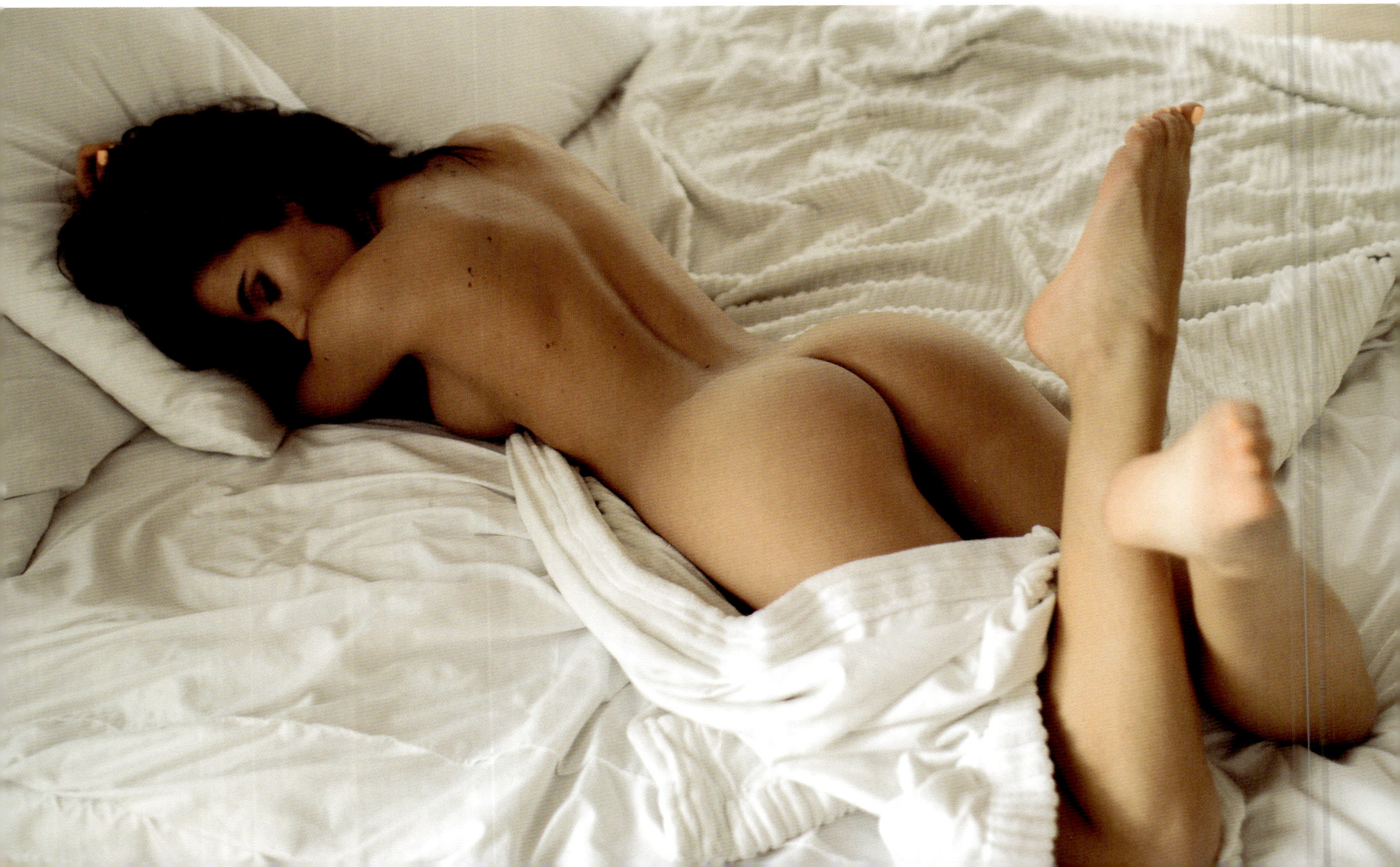

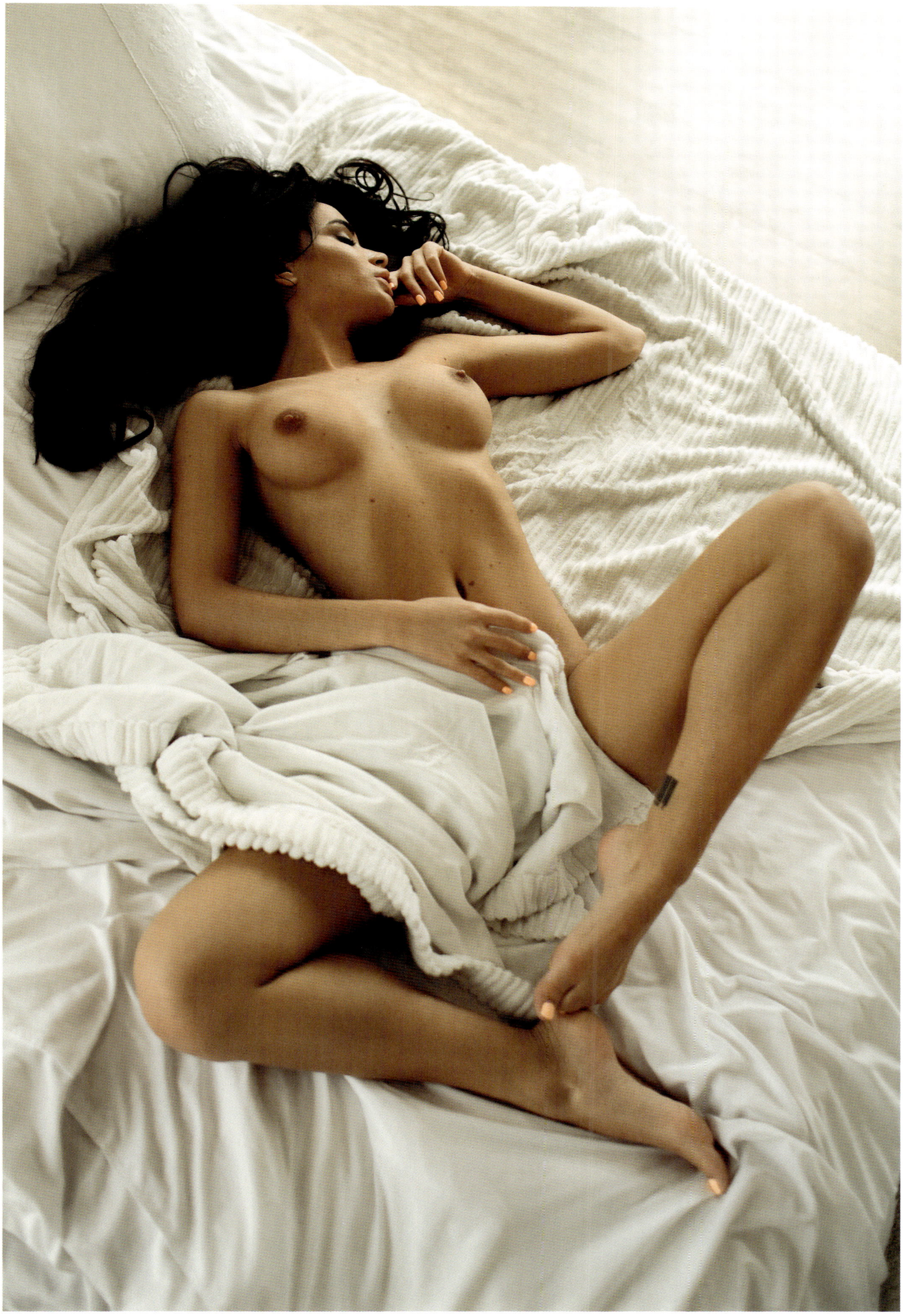

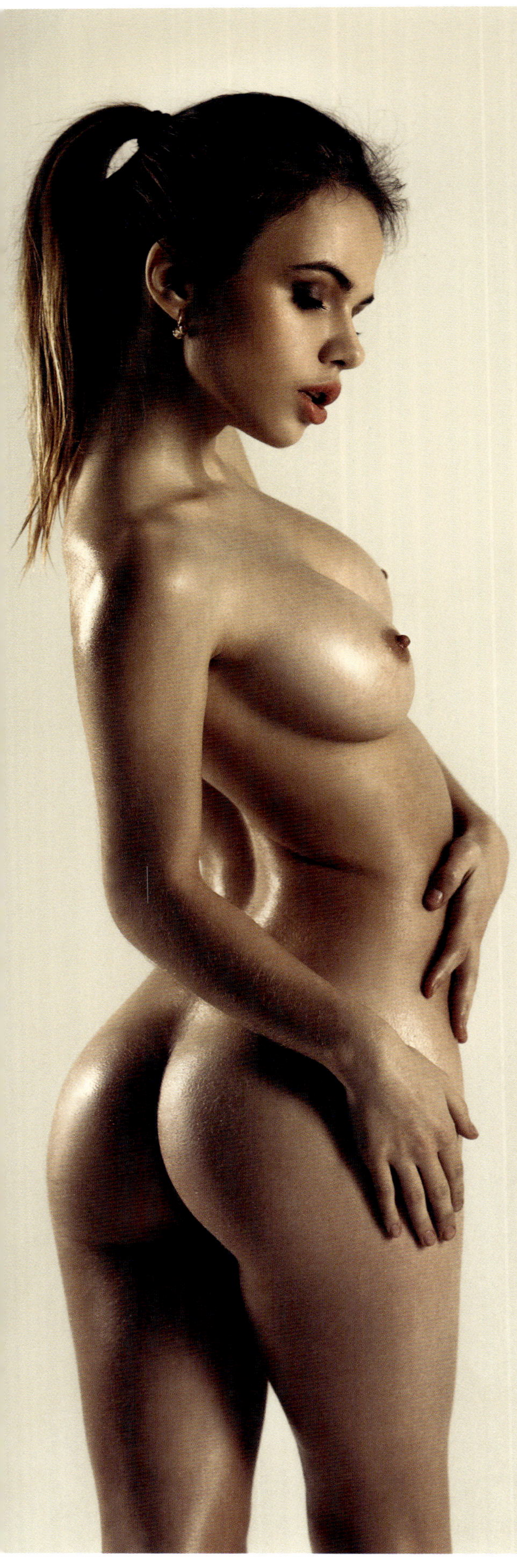

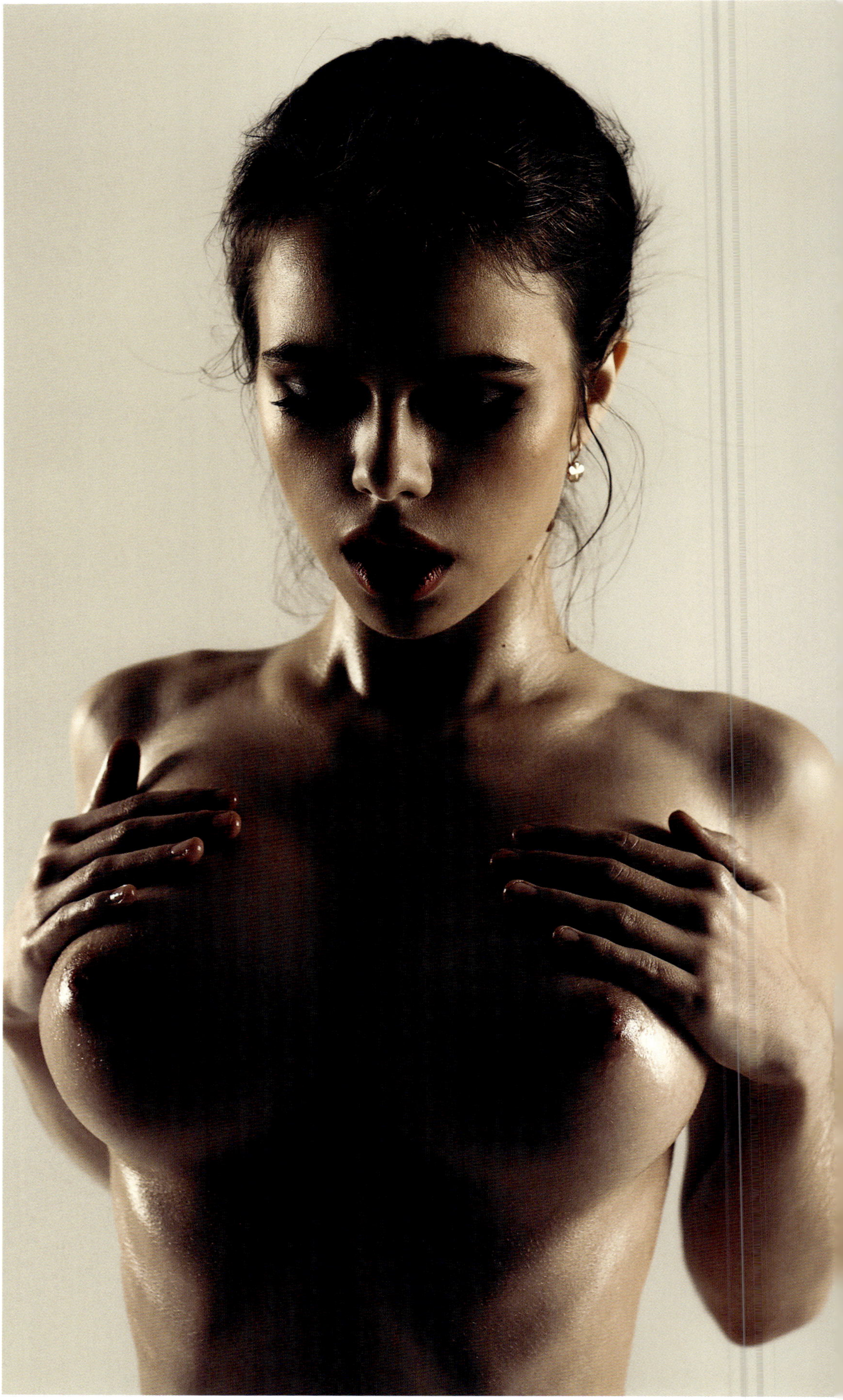

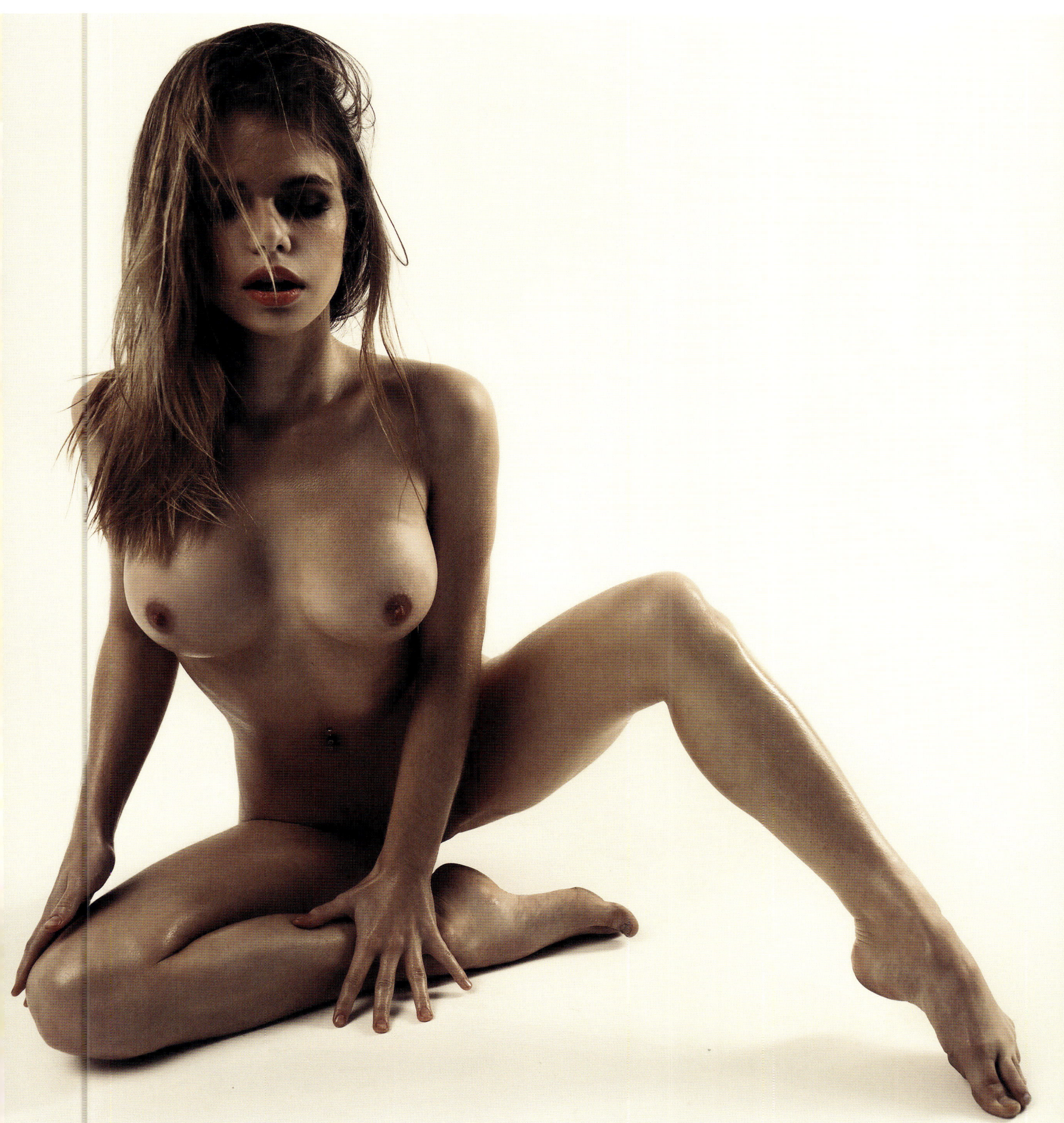

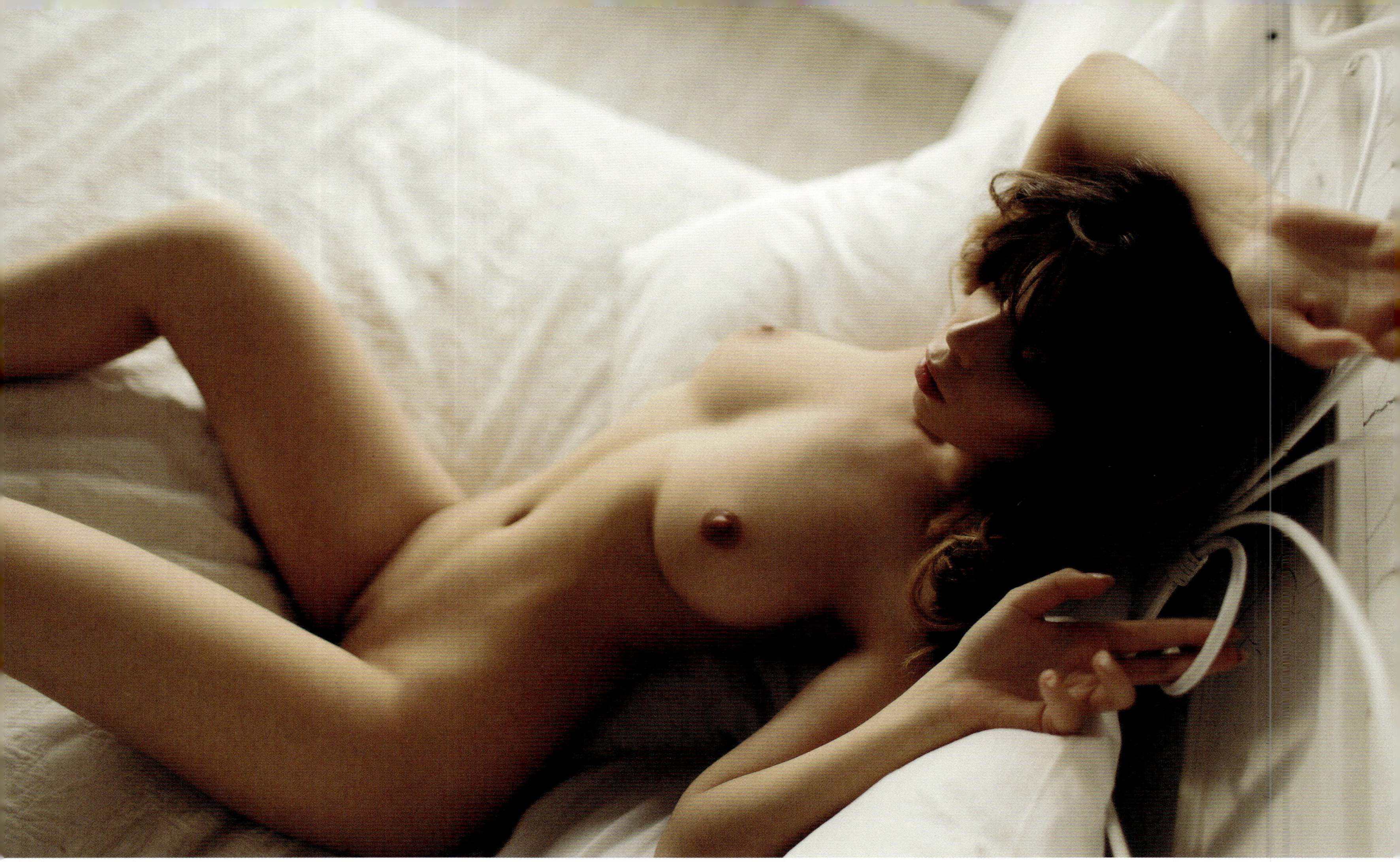

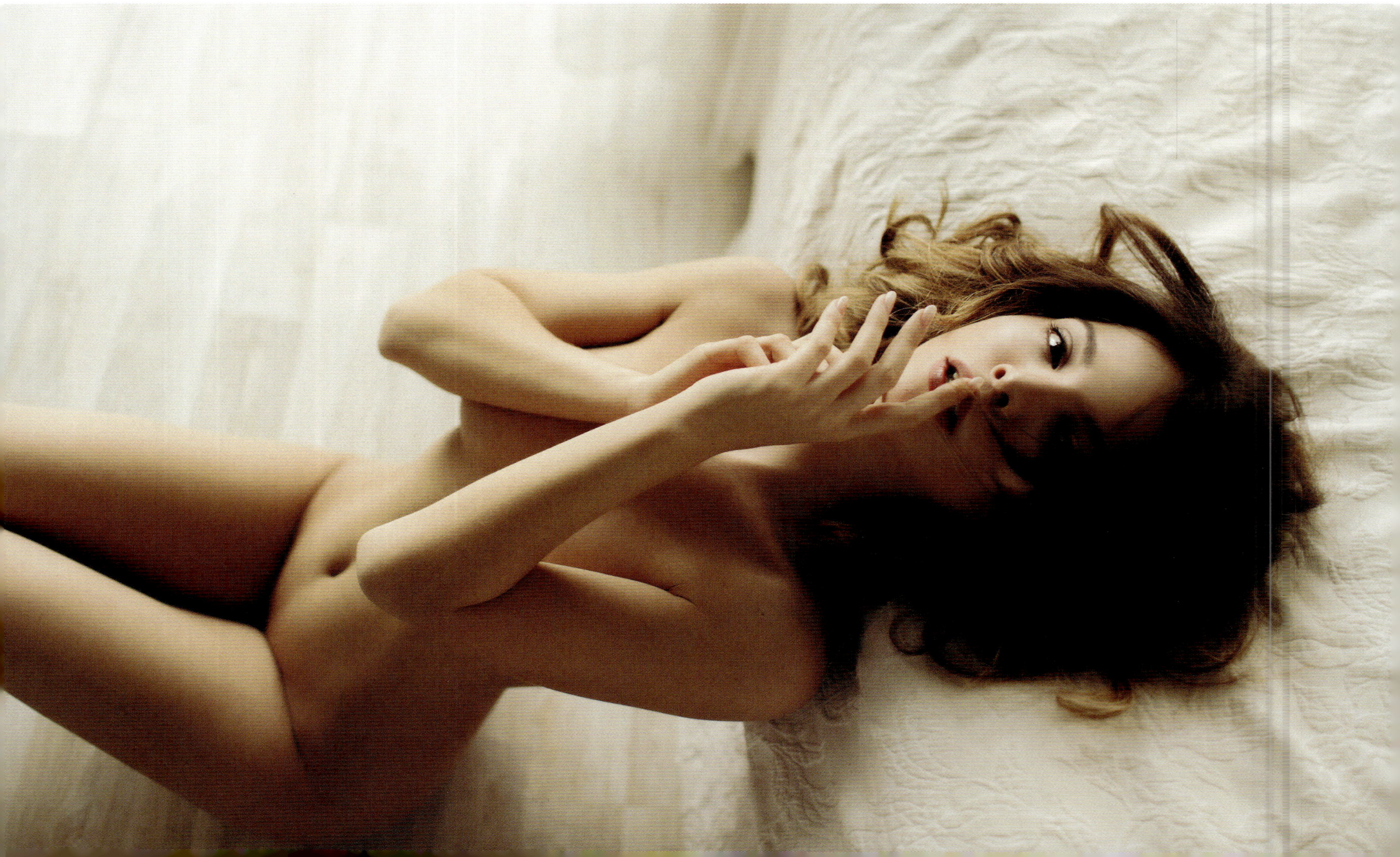

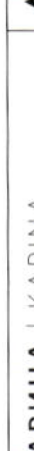

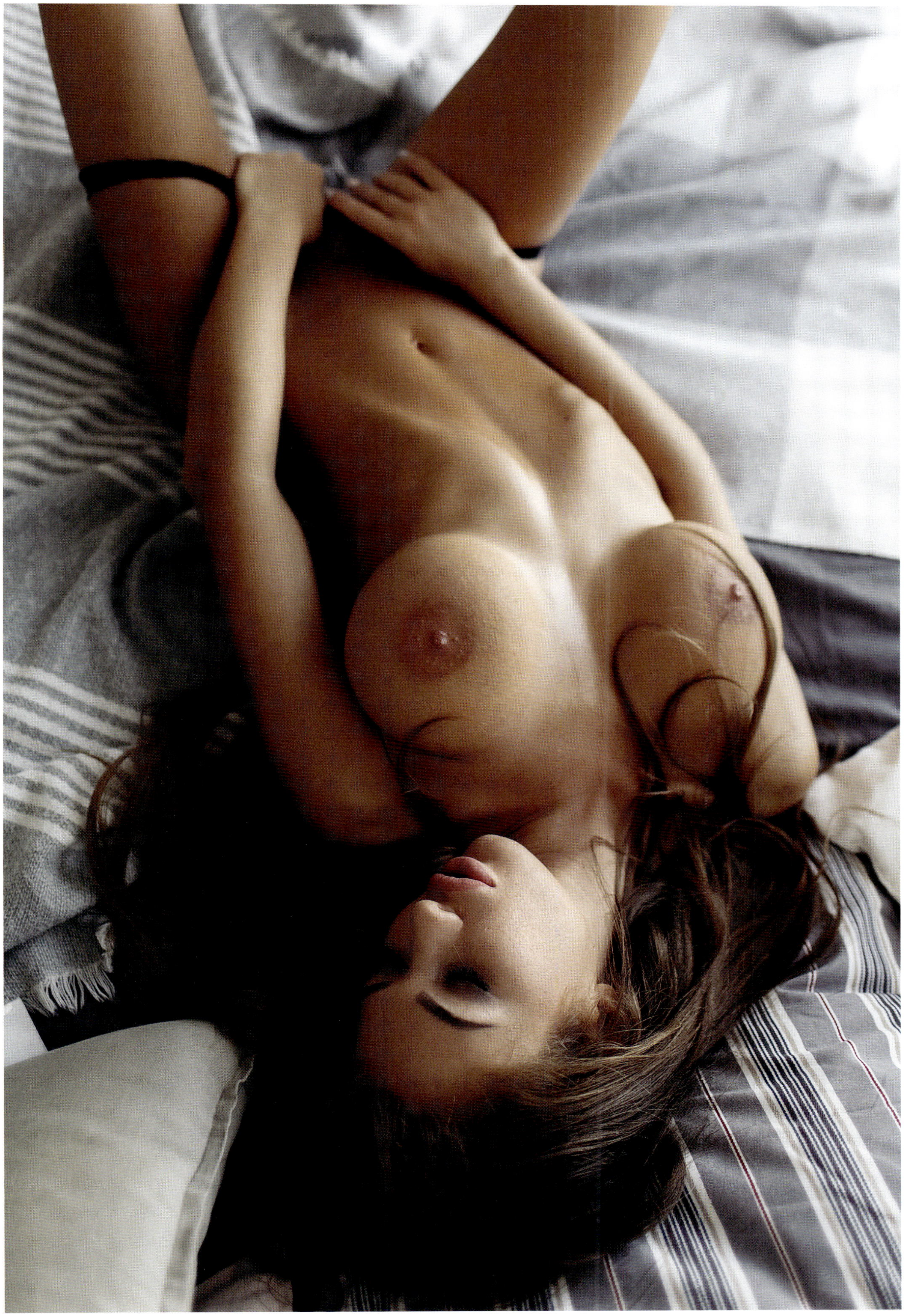

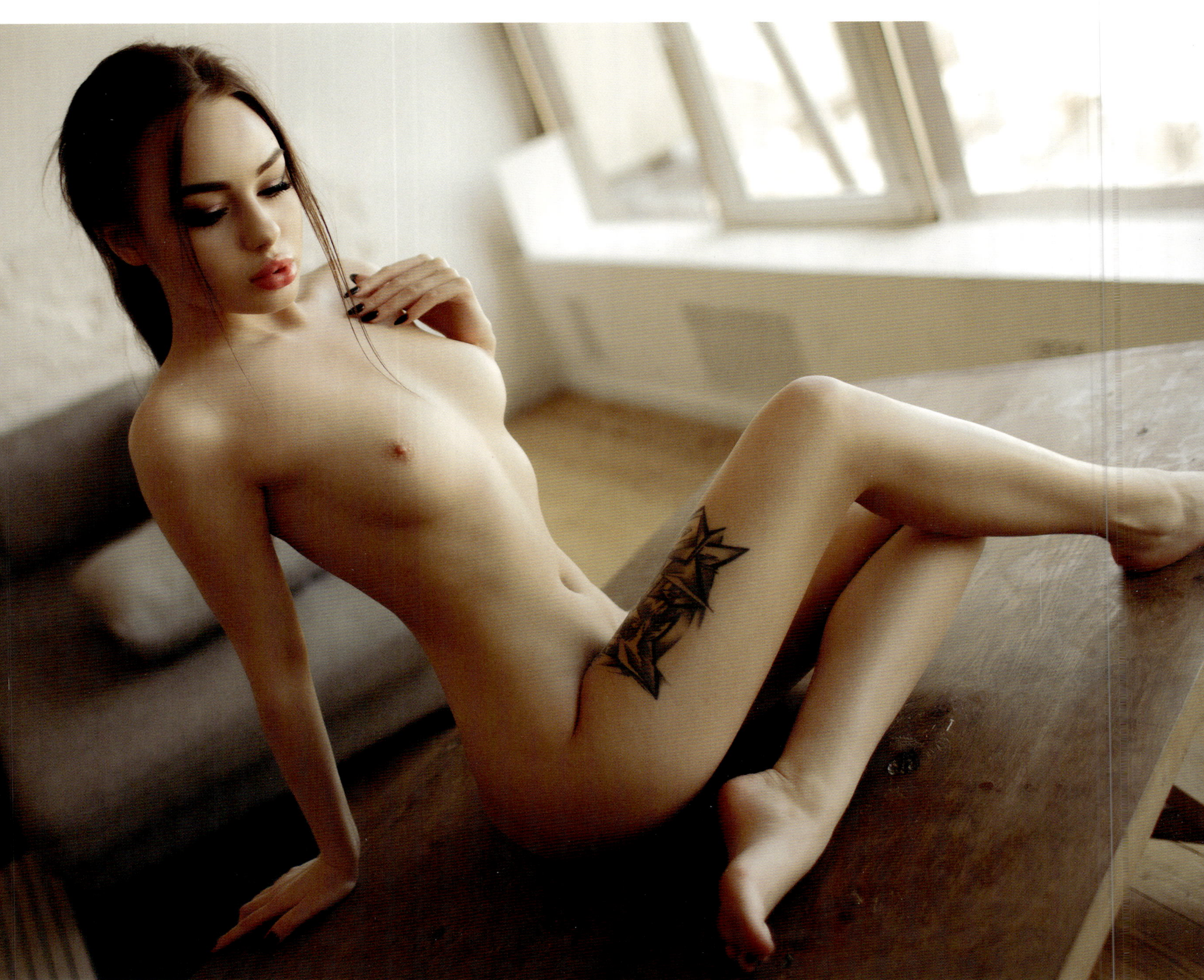

▲ АЛИСА | LISA

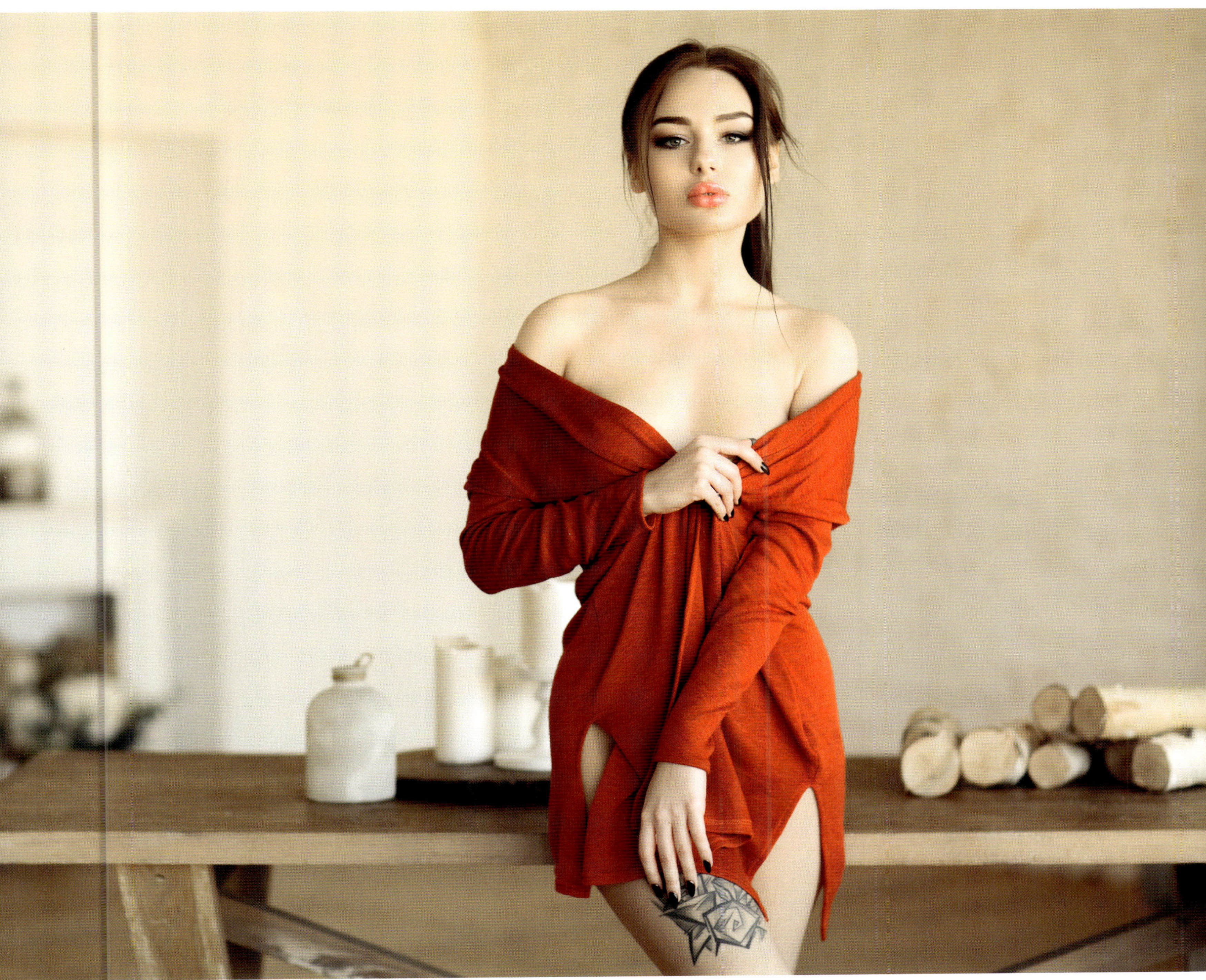

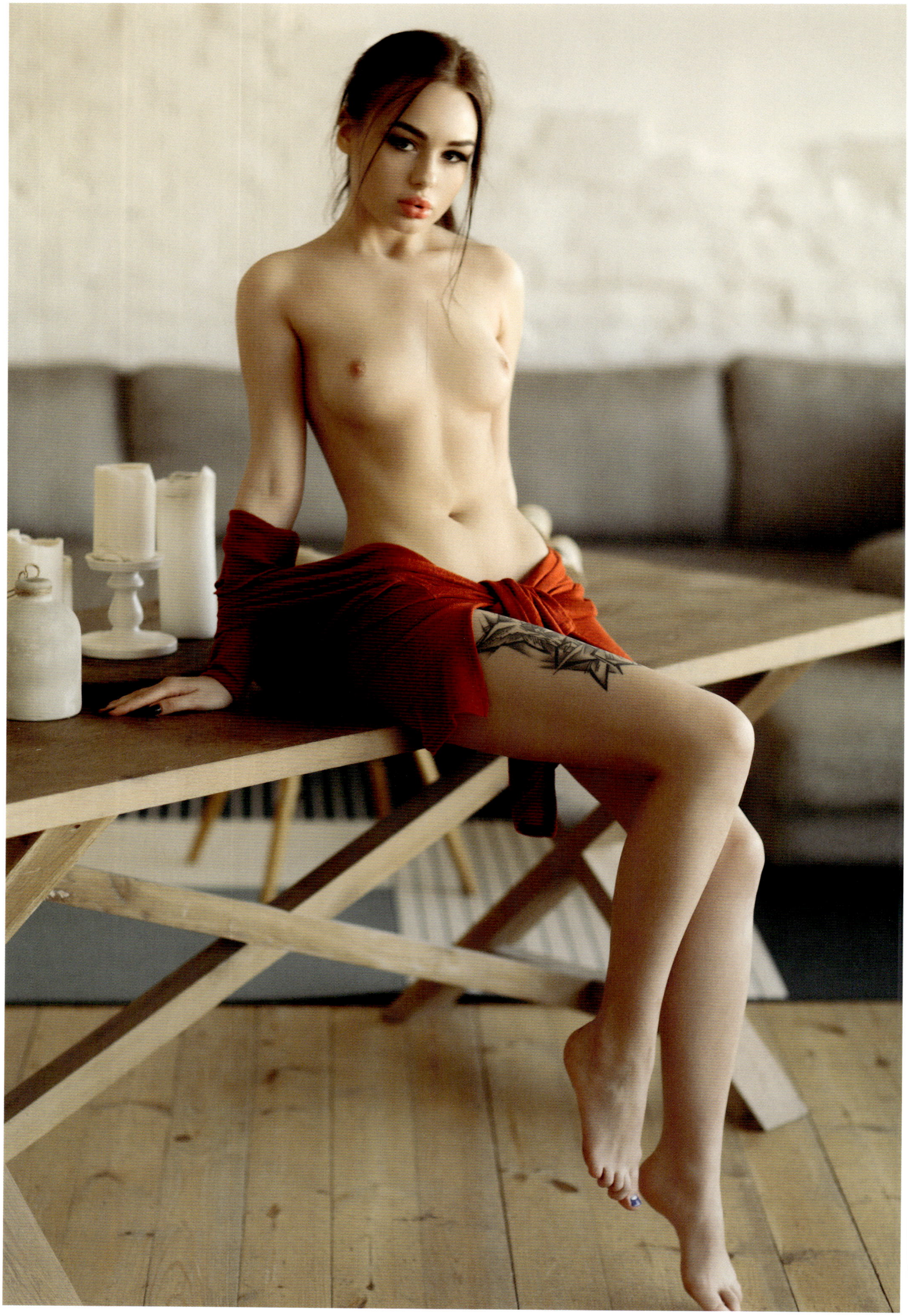

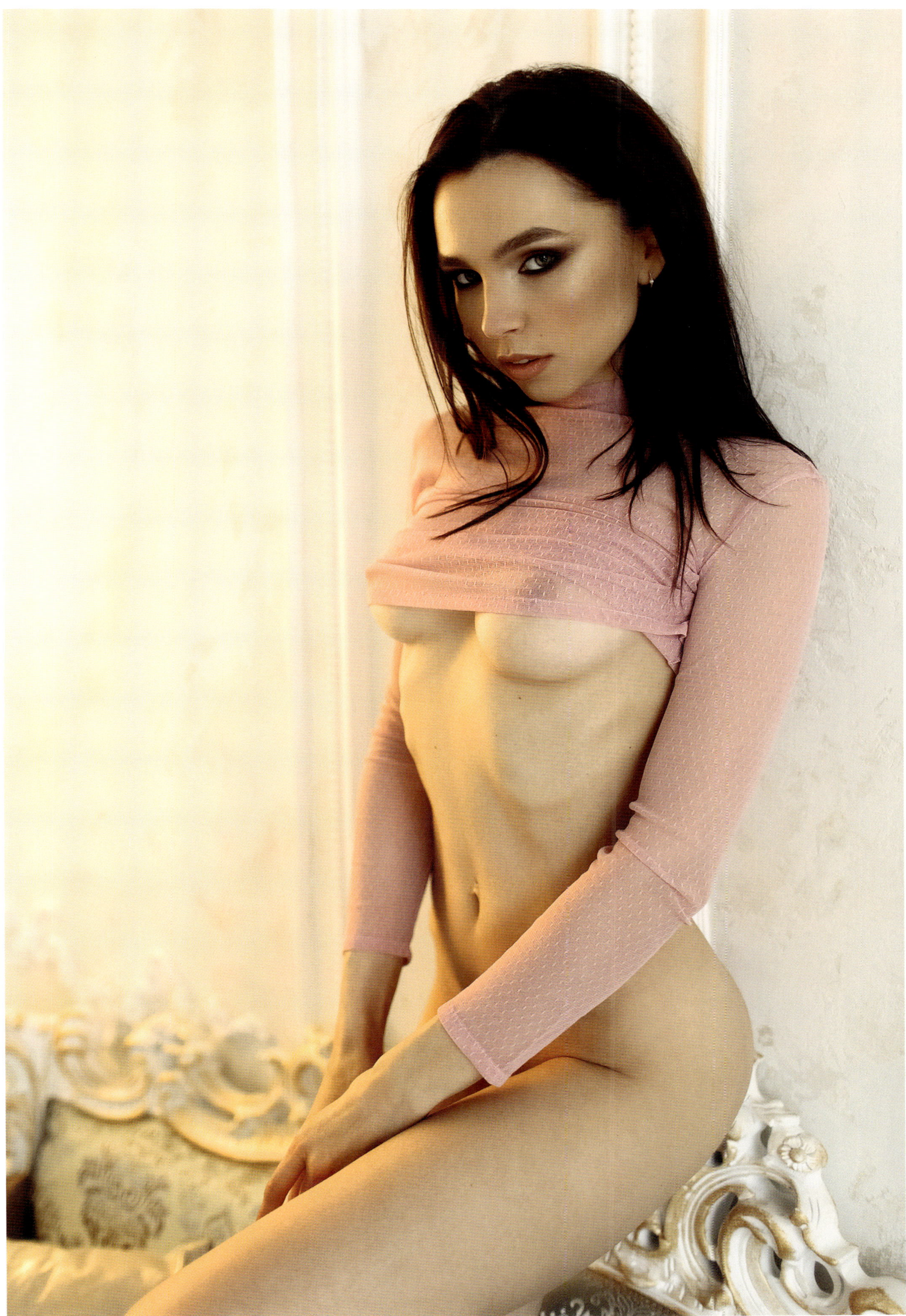

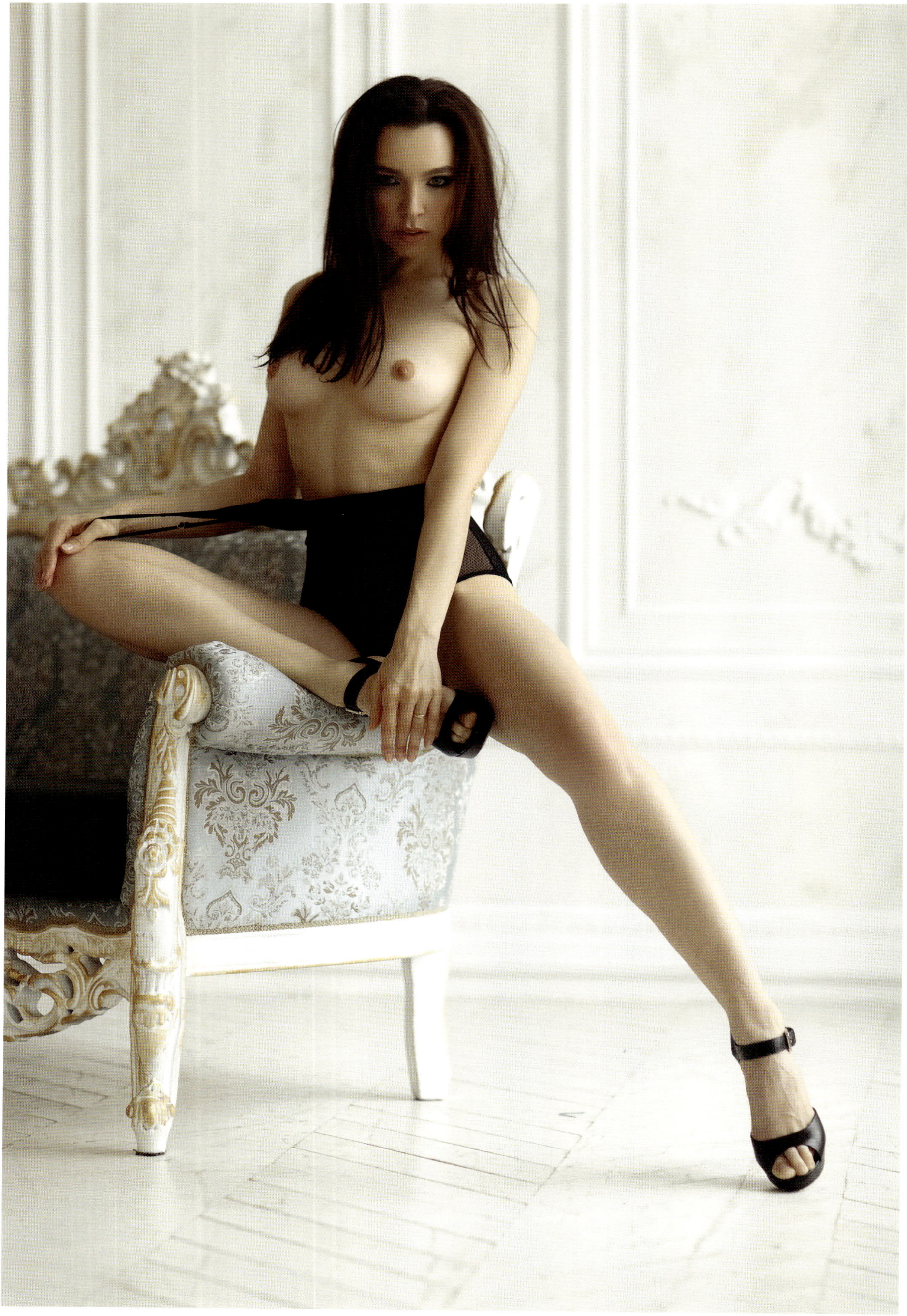

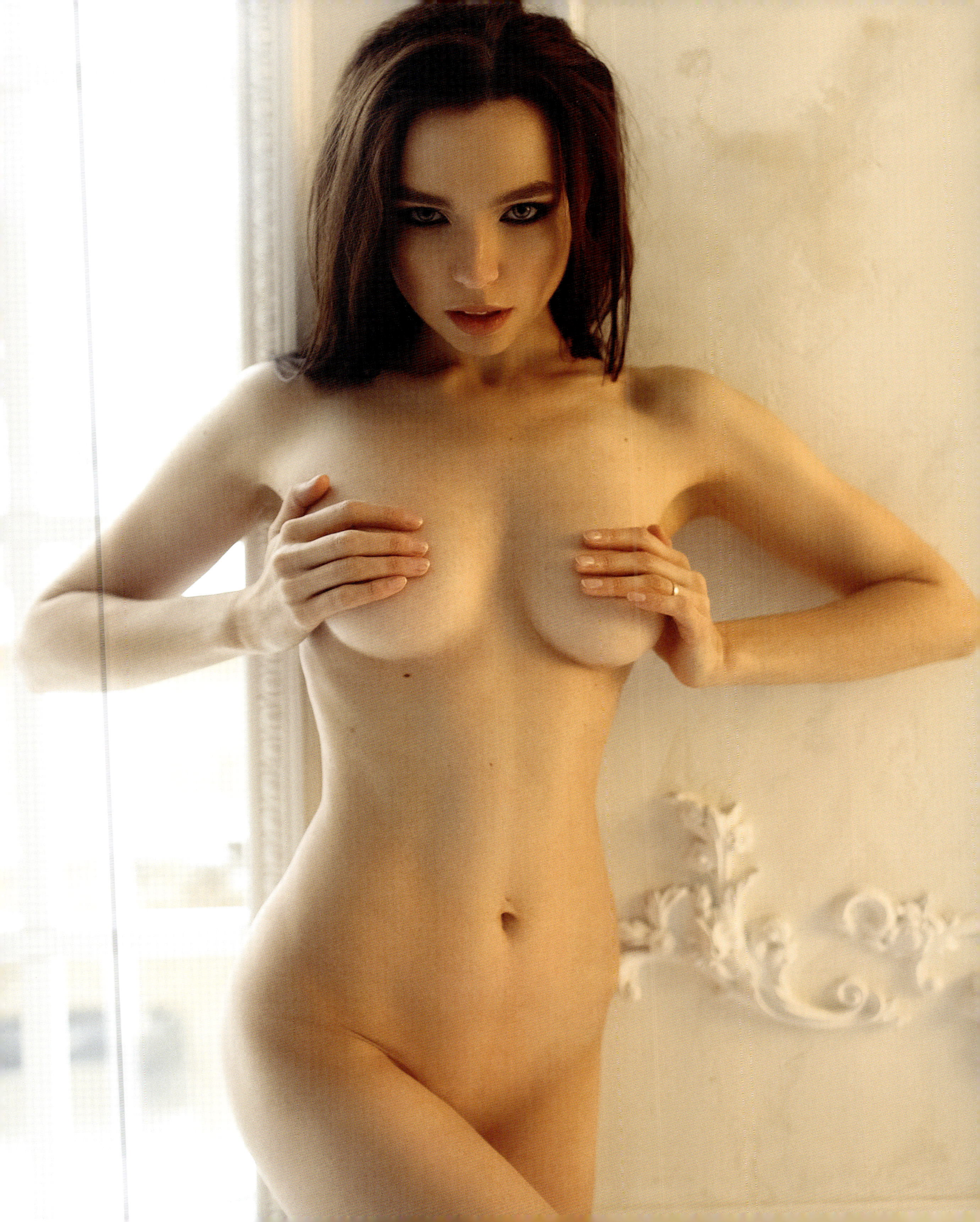

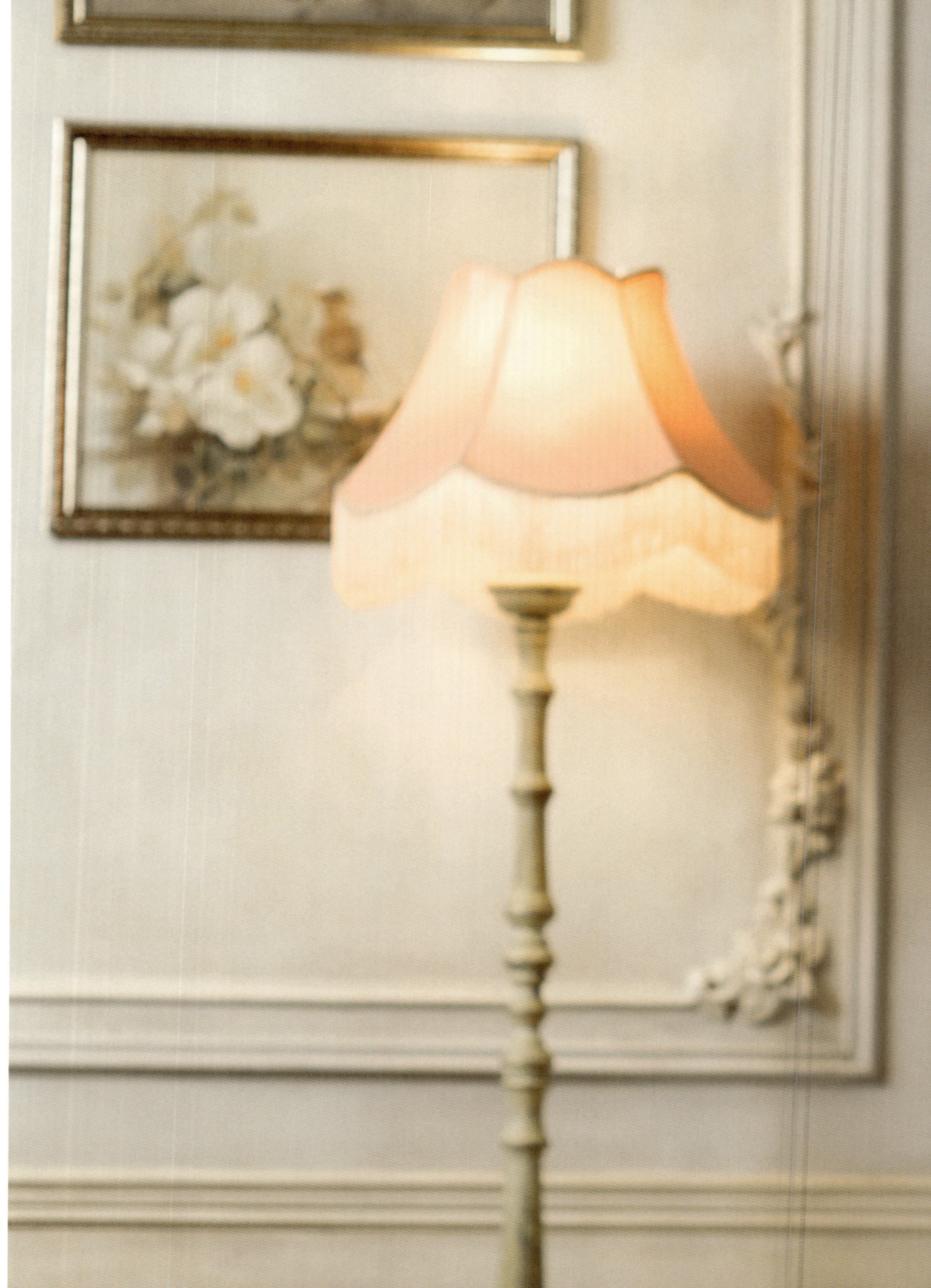

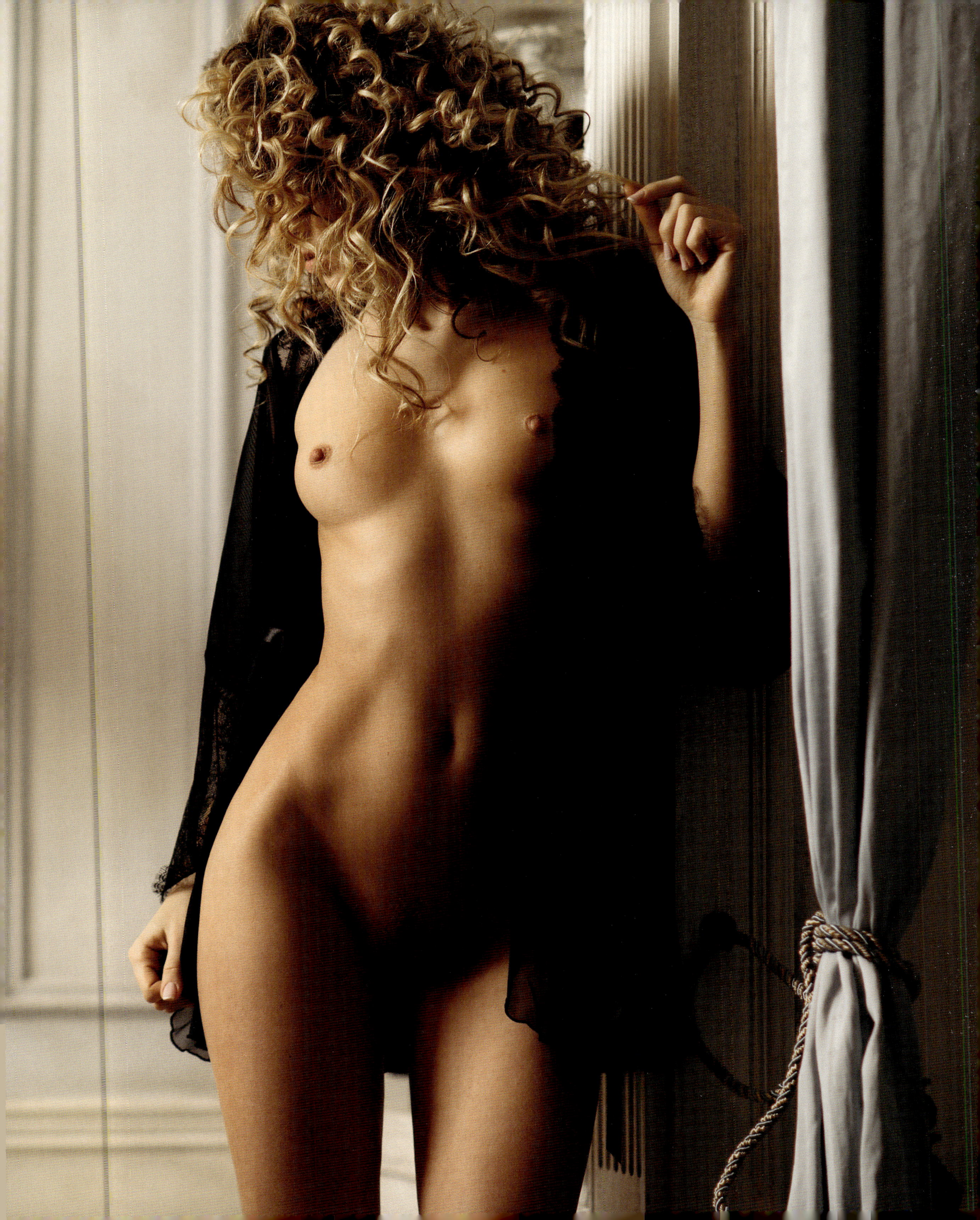

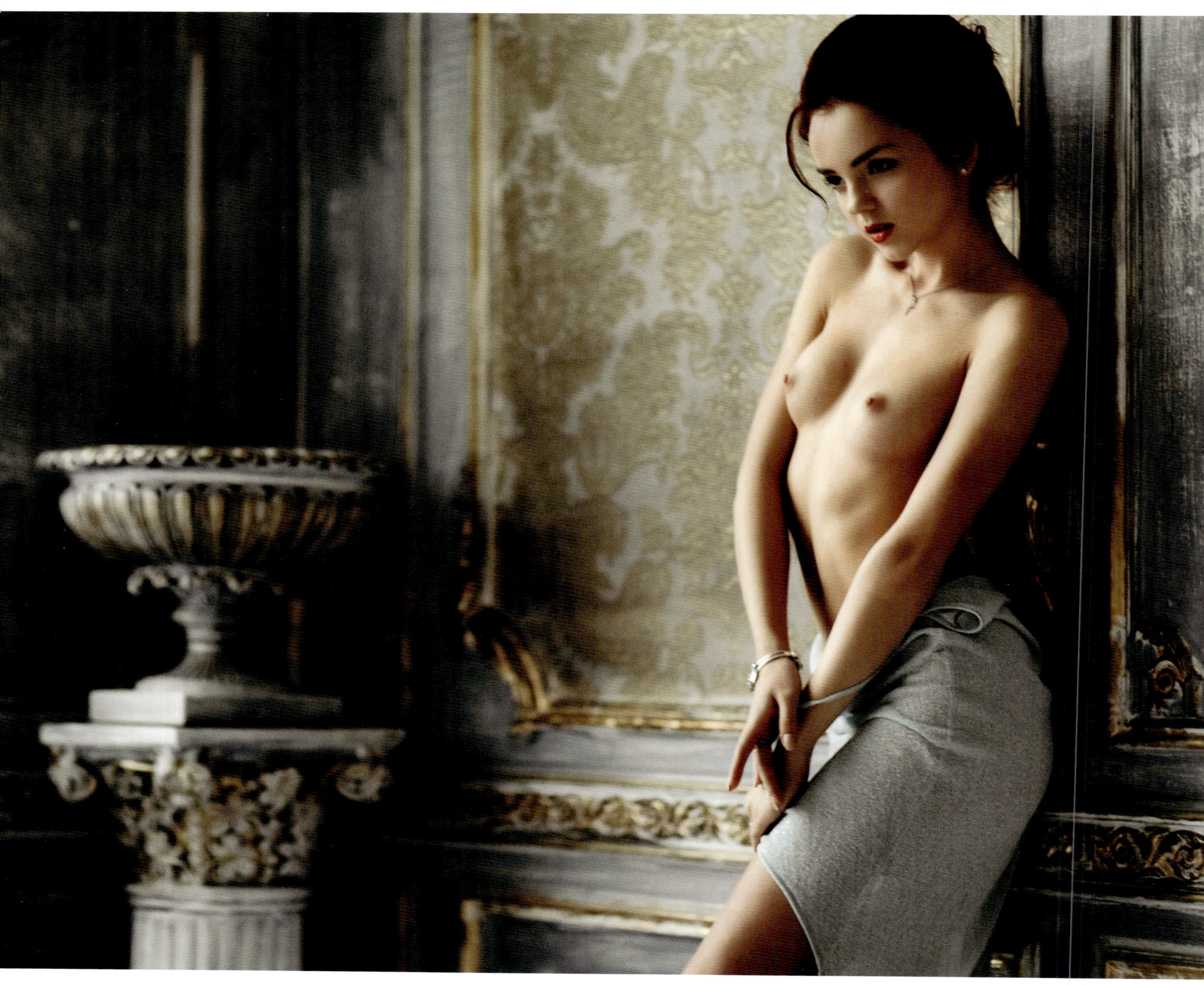

▲ ЕКАТЕРИНА Ш. | EKATERINA SH.

ЕКАТЕРИНА Ш. | EKATERINA SH. ▶

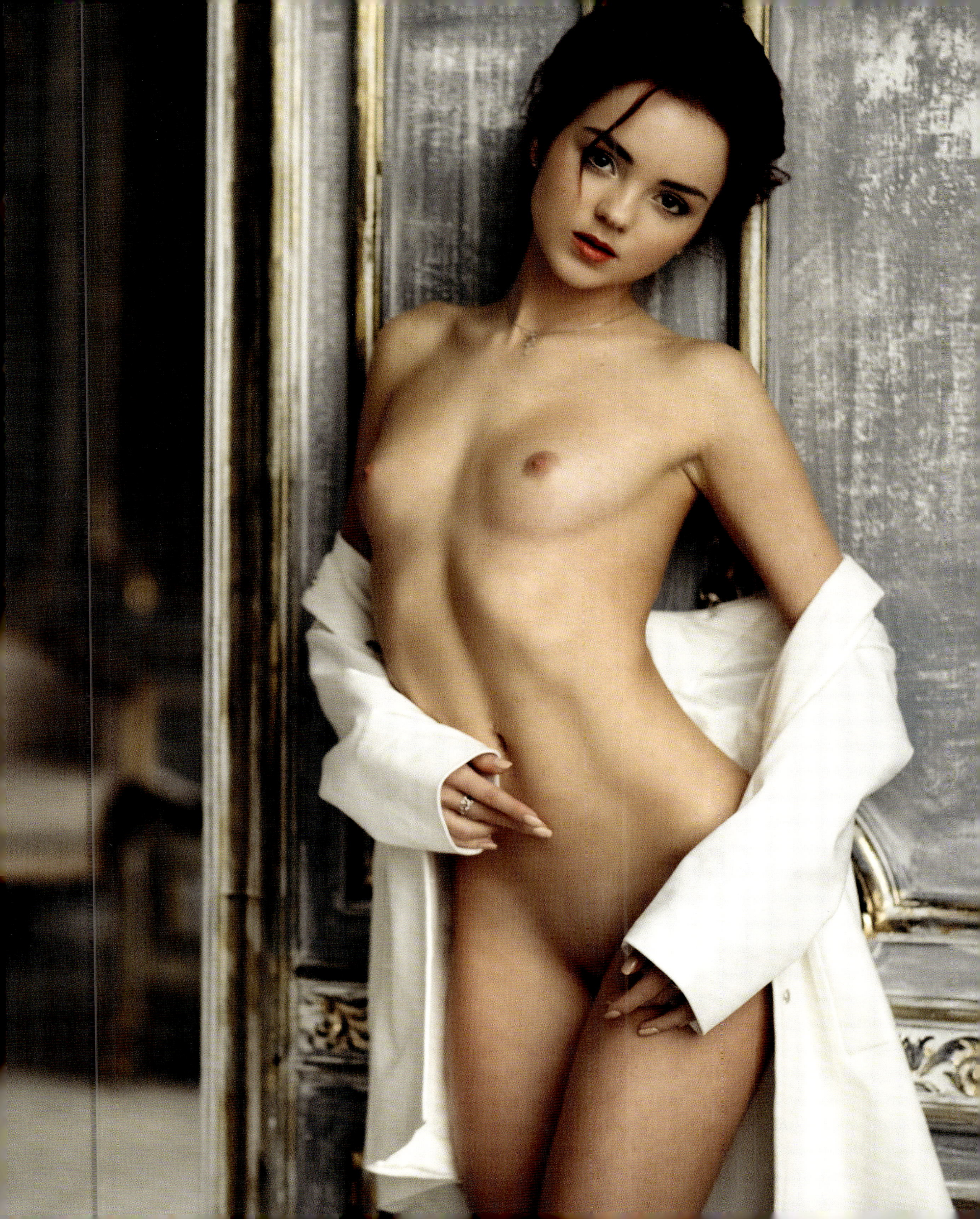

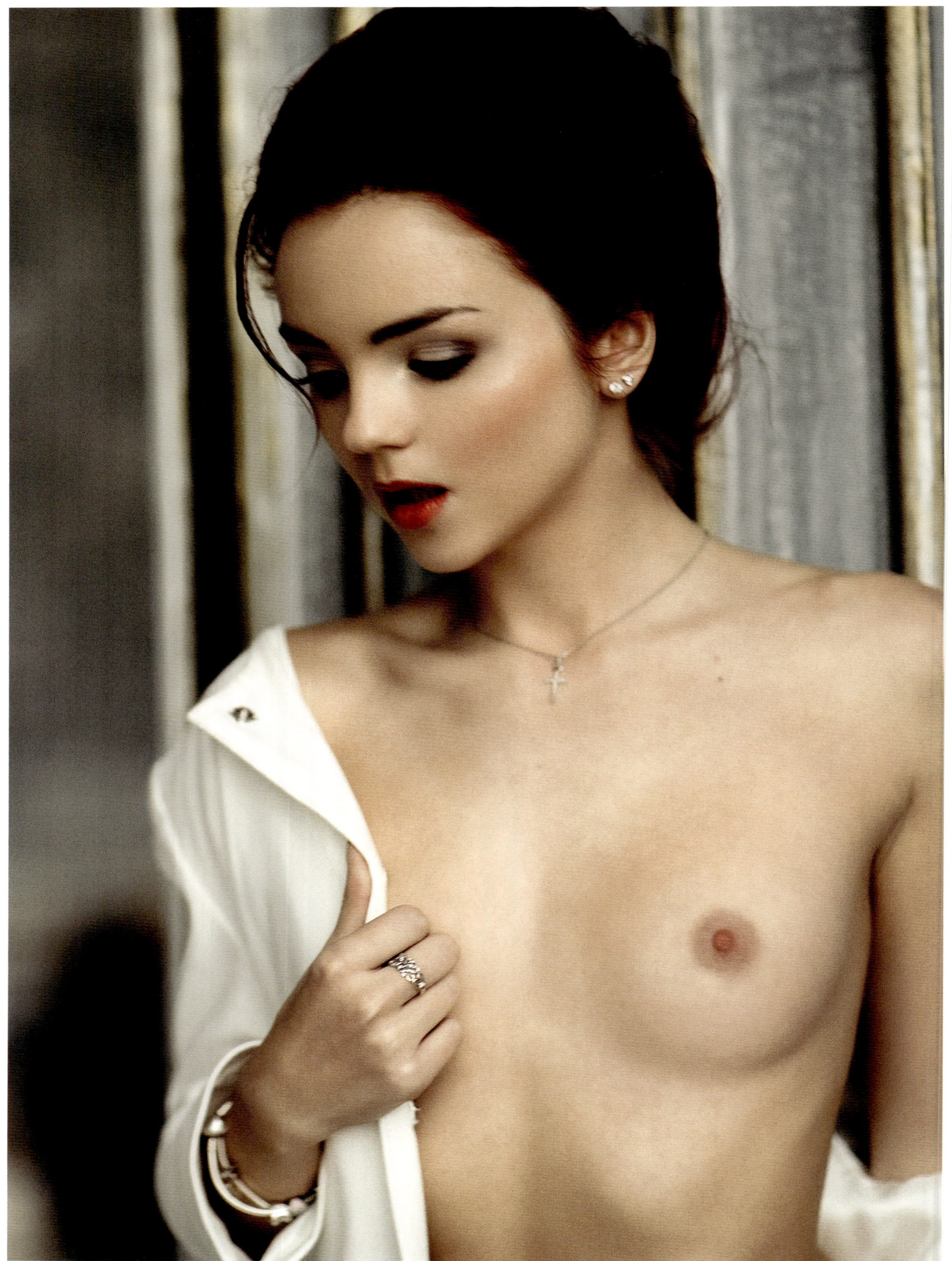

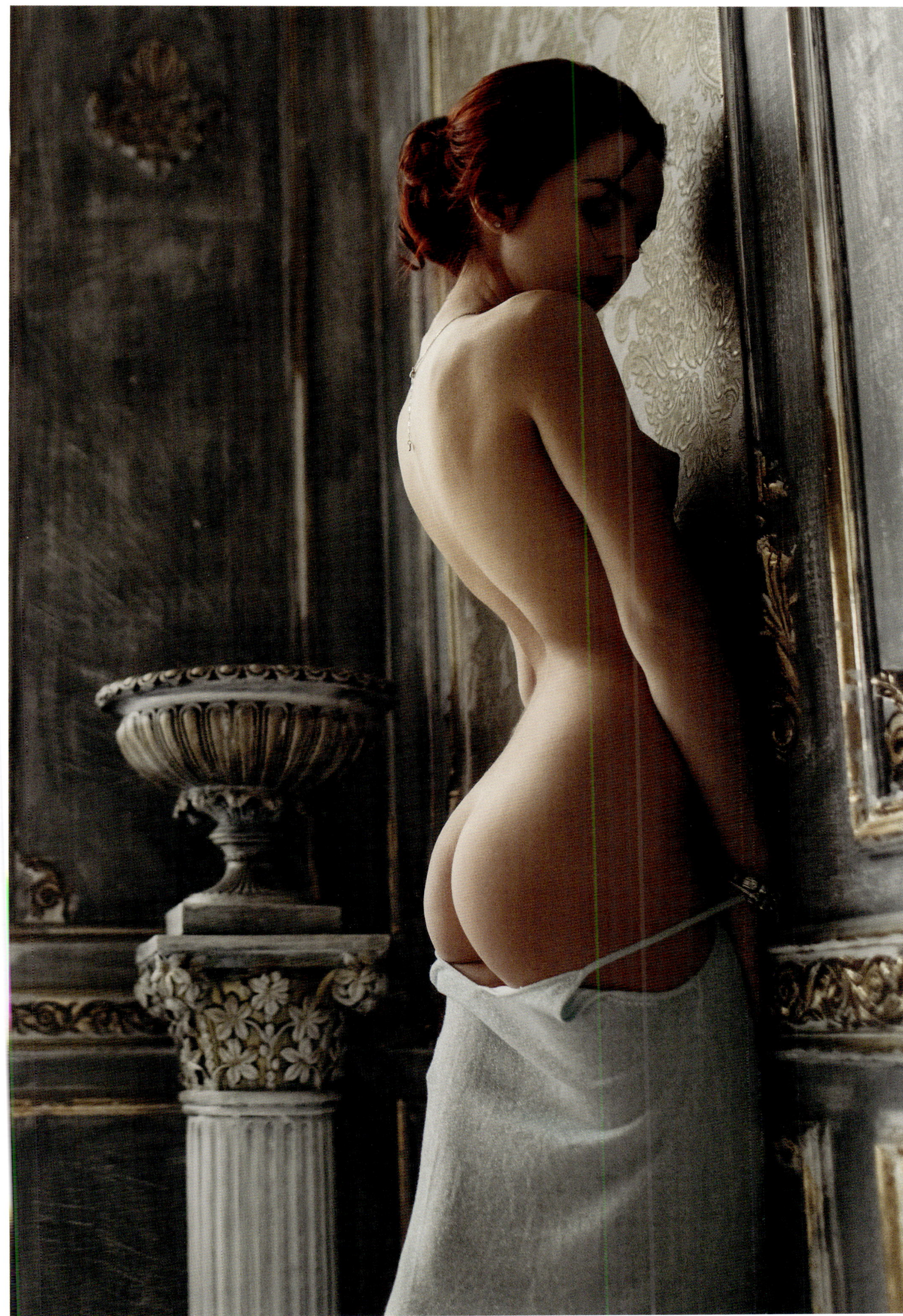

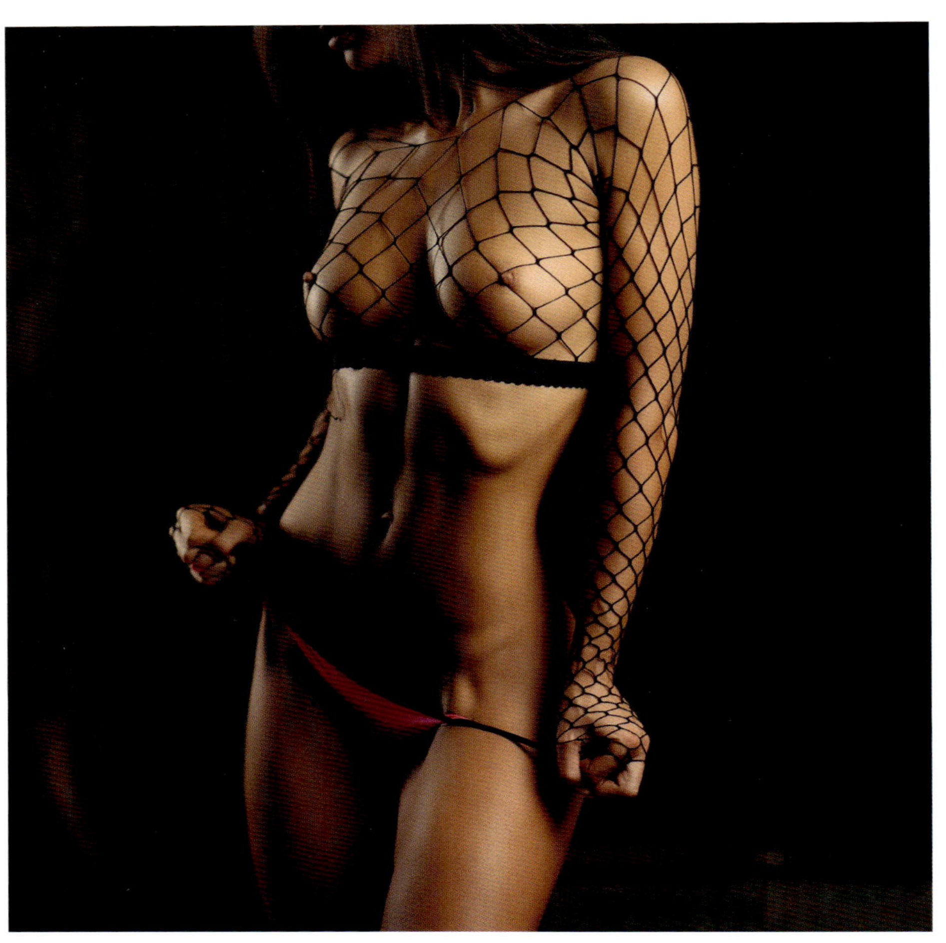

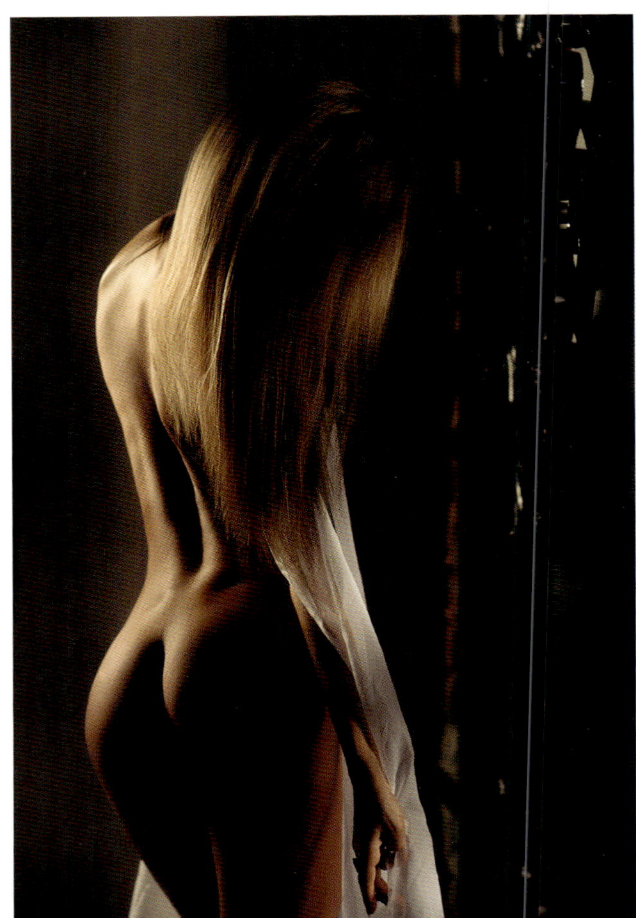

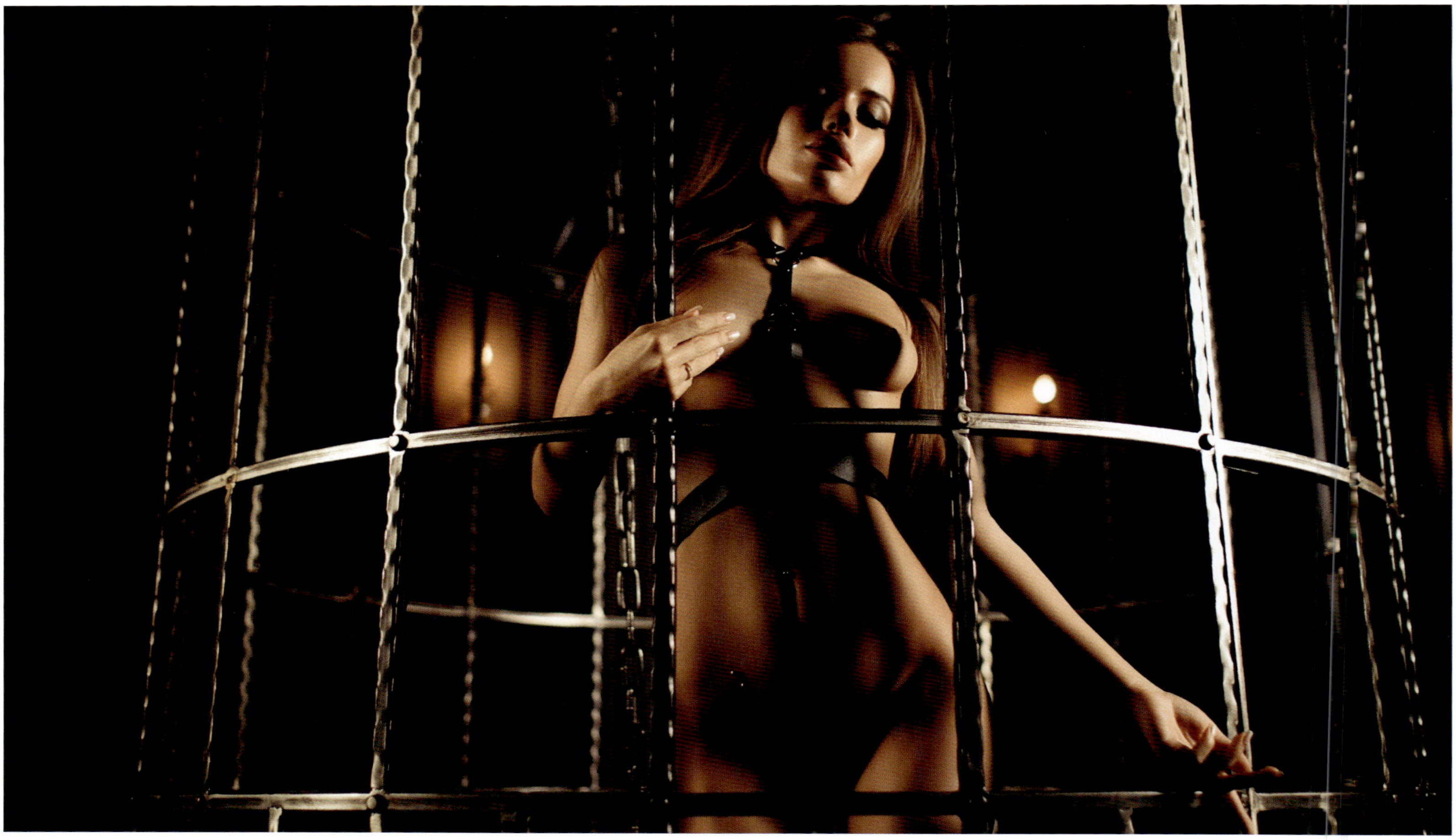

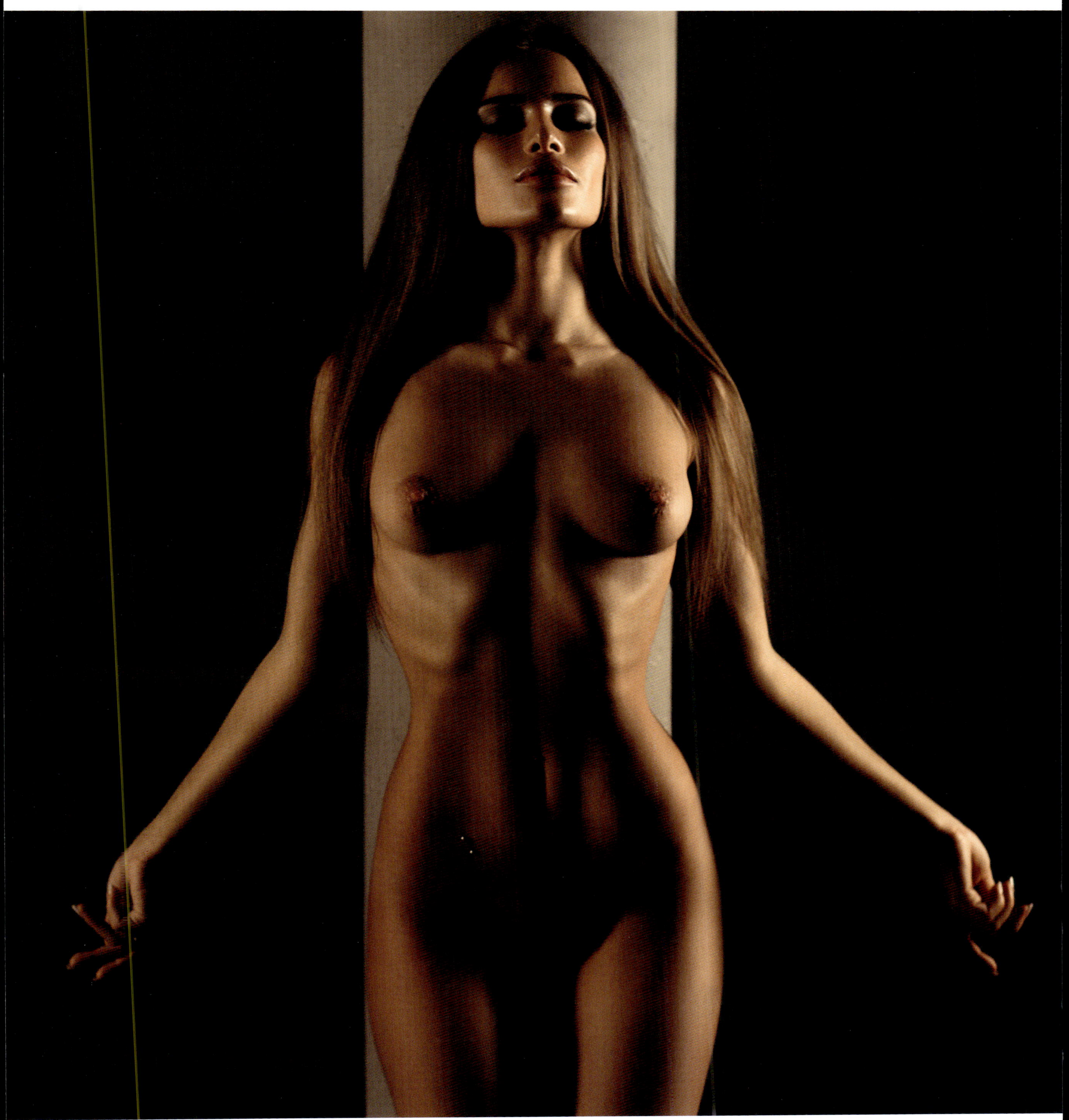

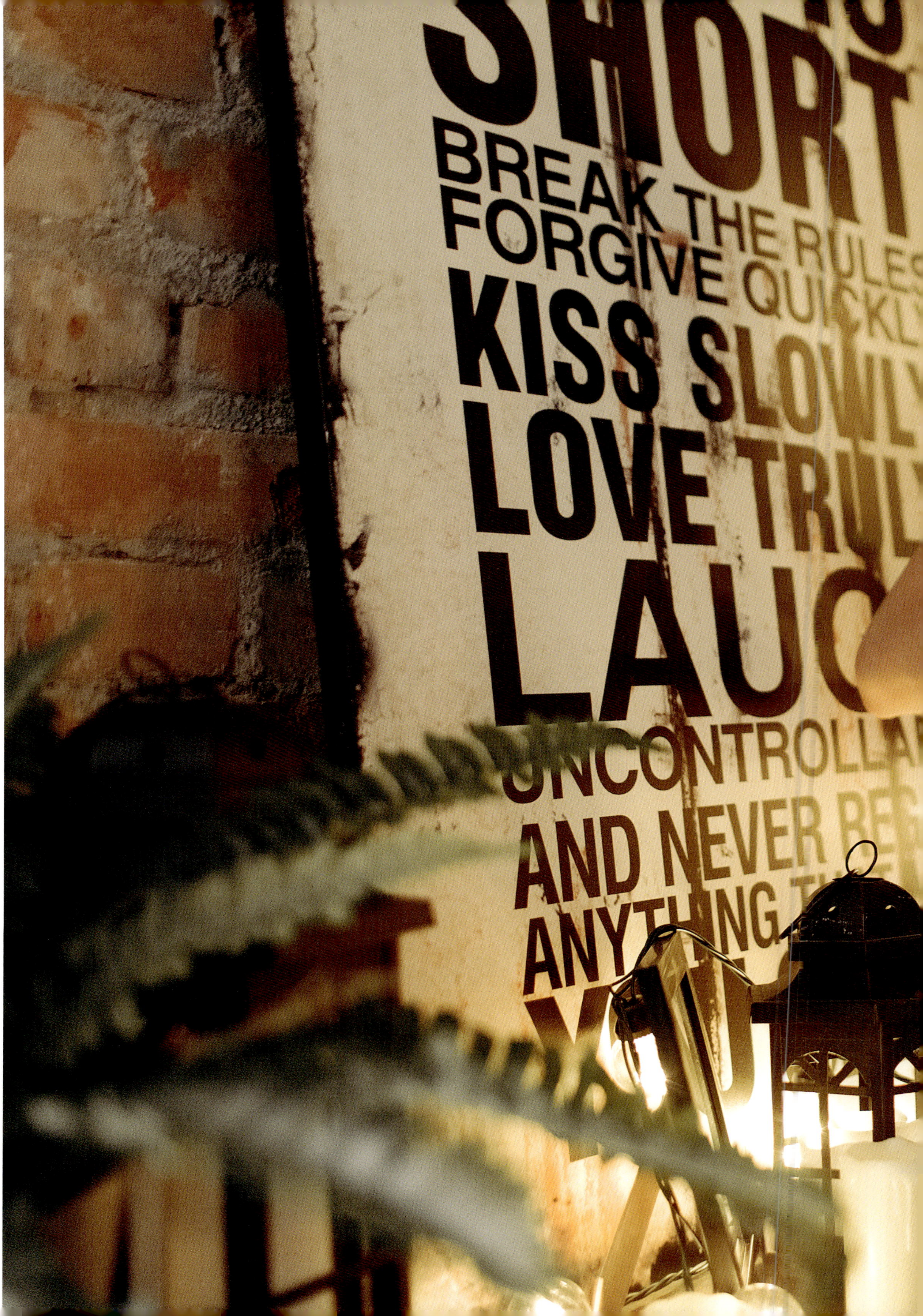
SHORT
BREAK THE RULES
FORGIVE QUICKL
KISS SLOWL
LOVE TRUL
LAUG
UNCONTROLLA
AND NEVER RE
ANYTH NG

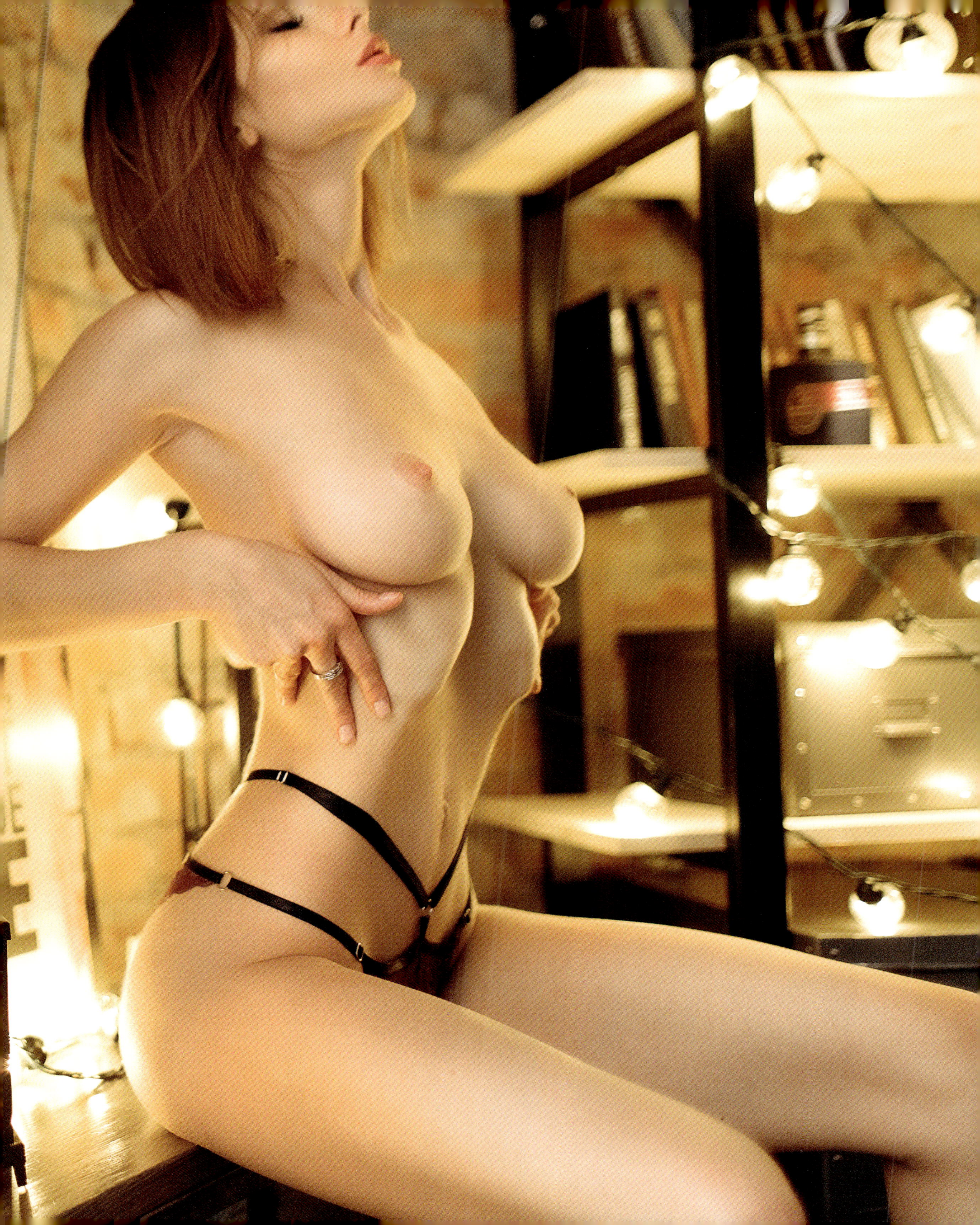

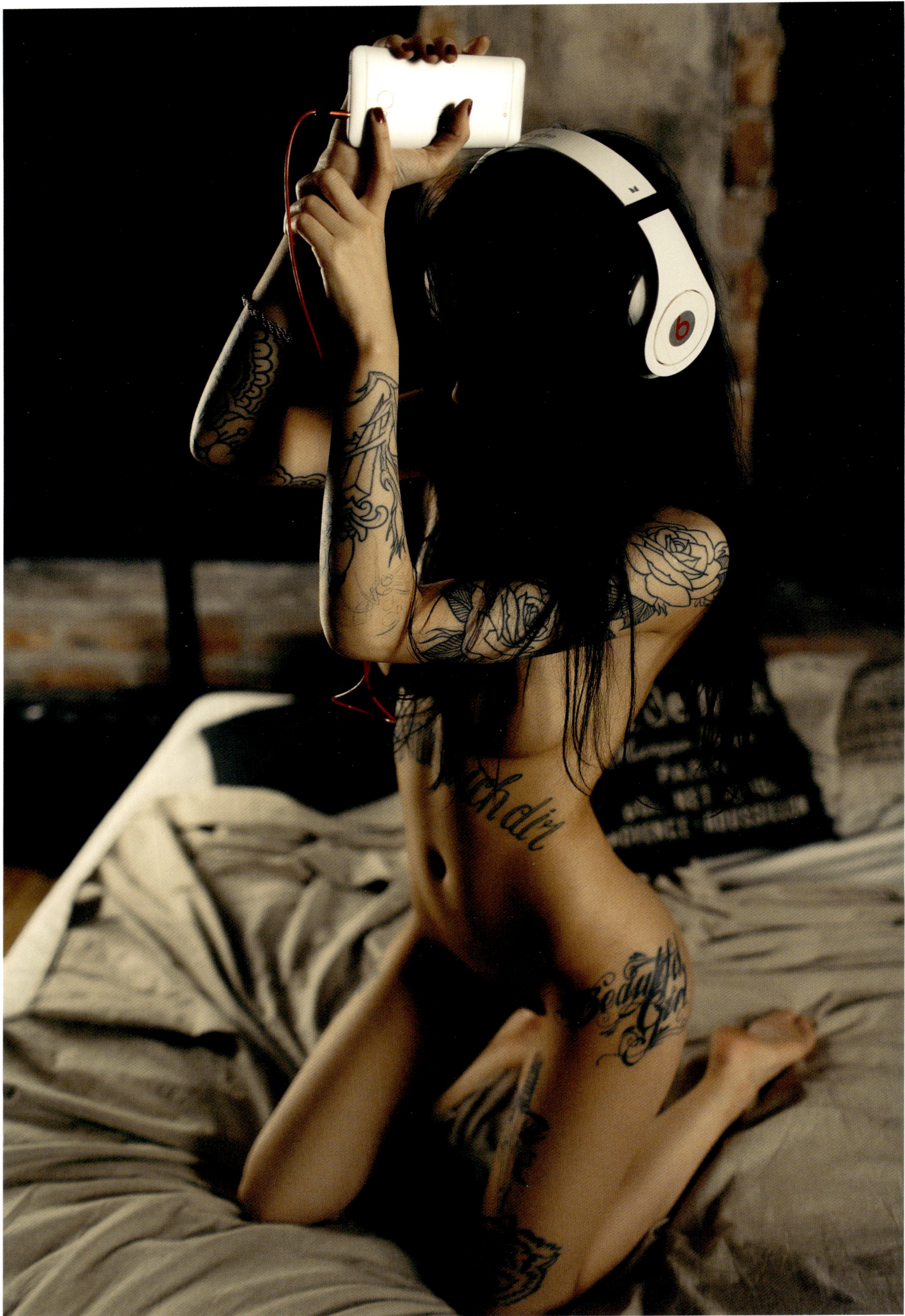

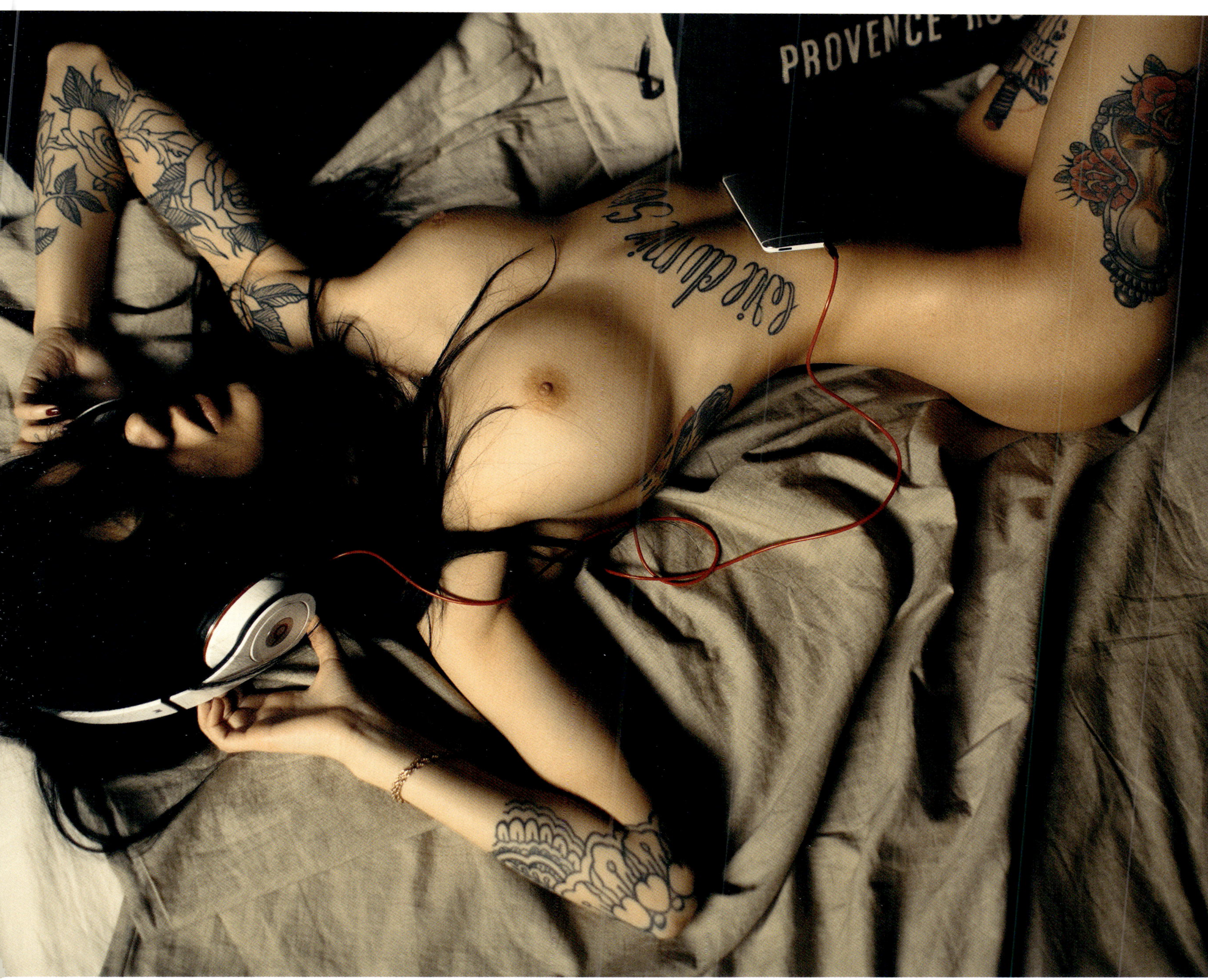
PROVENCE

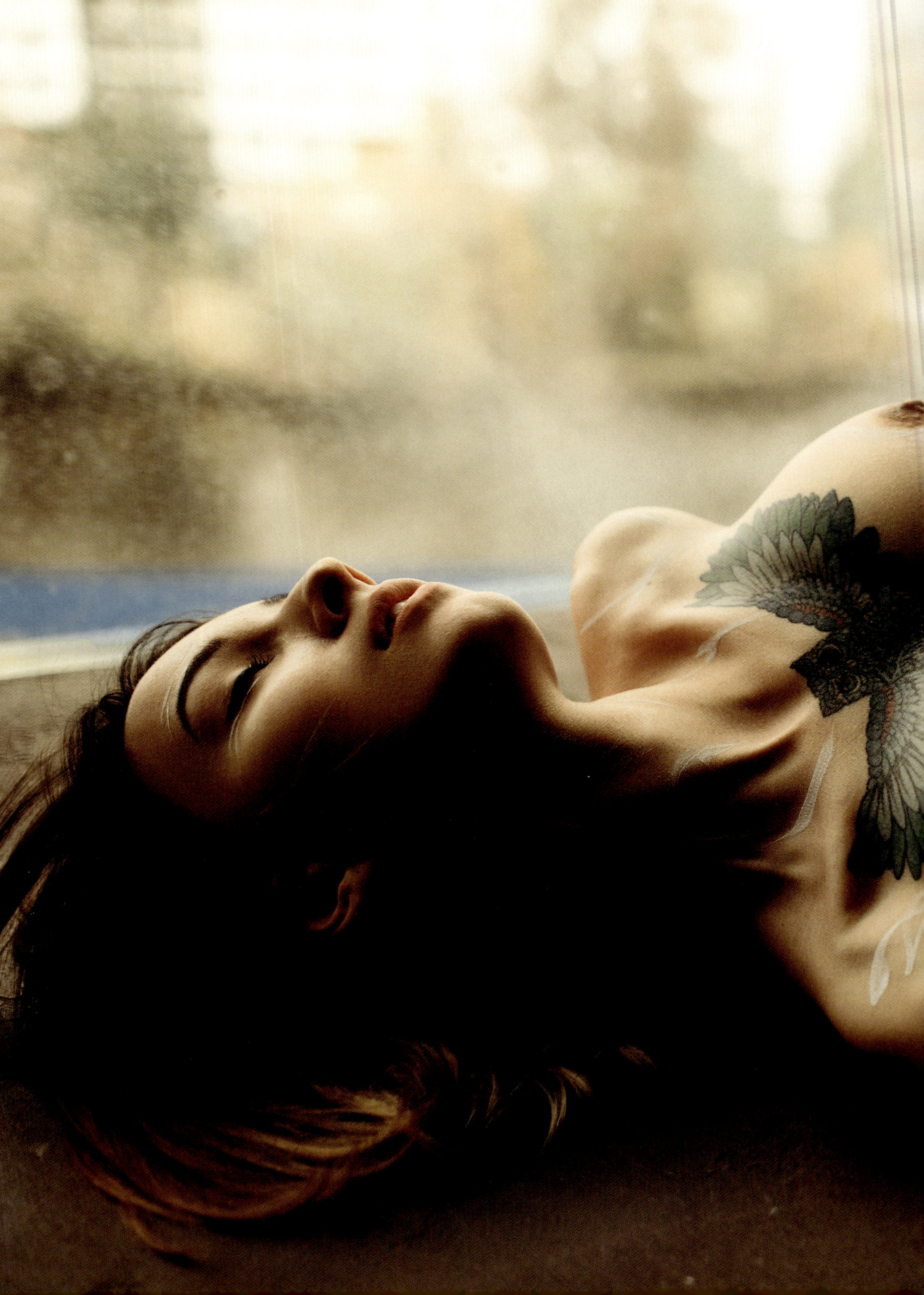

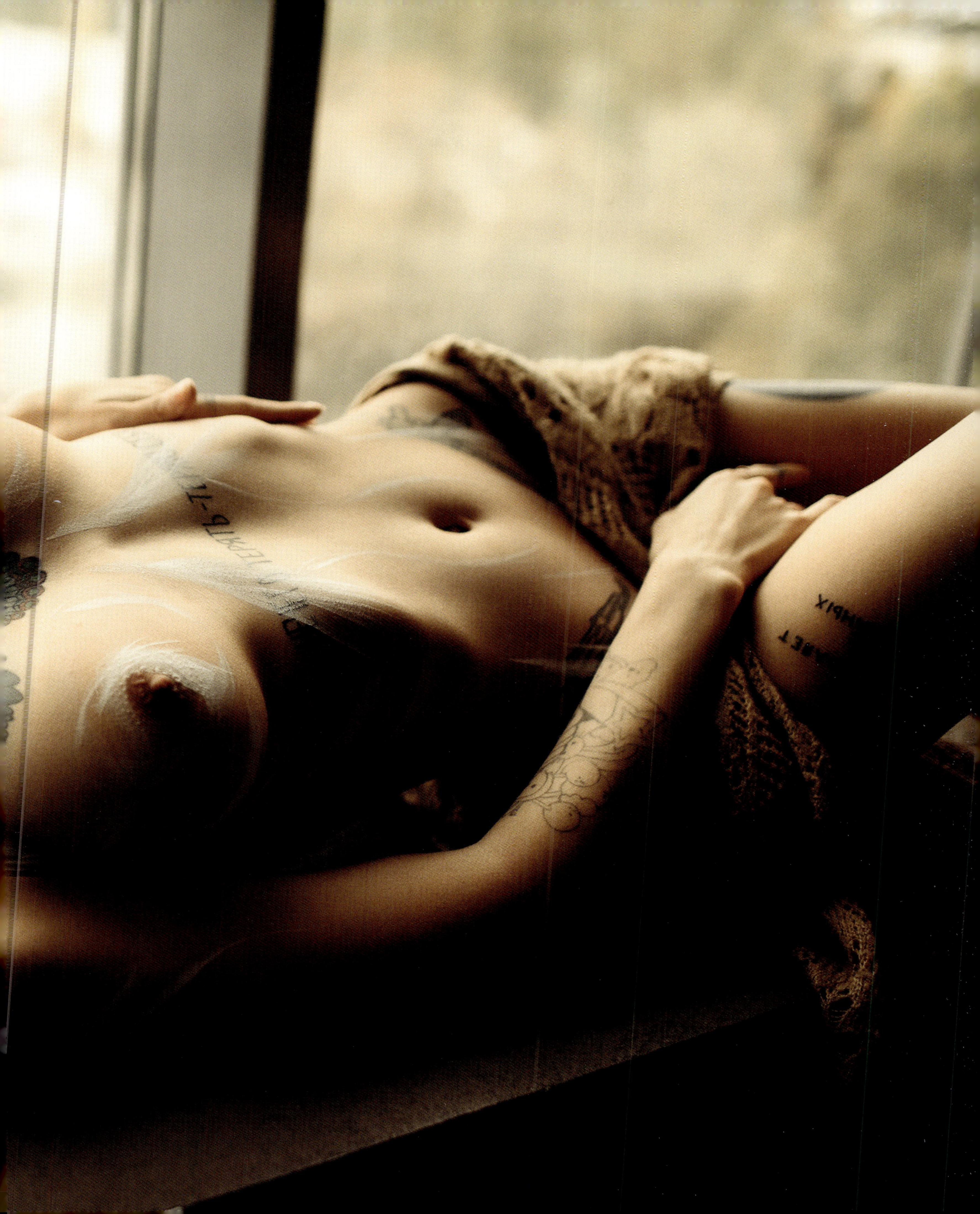

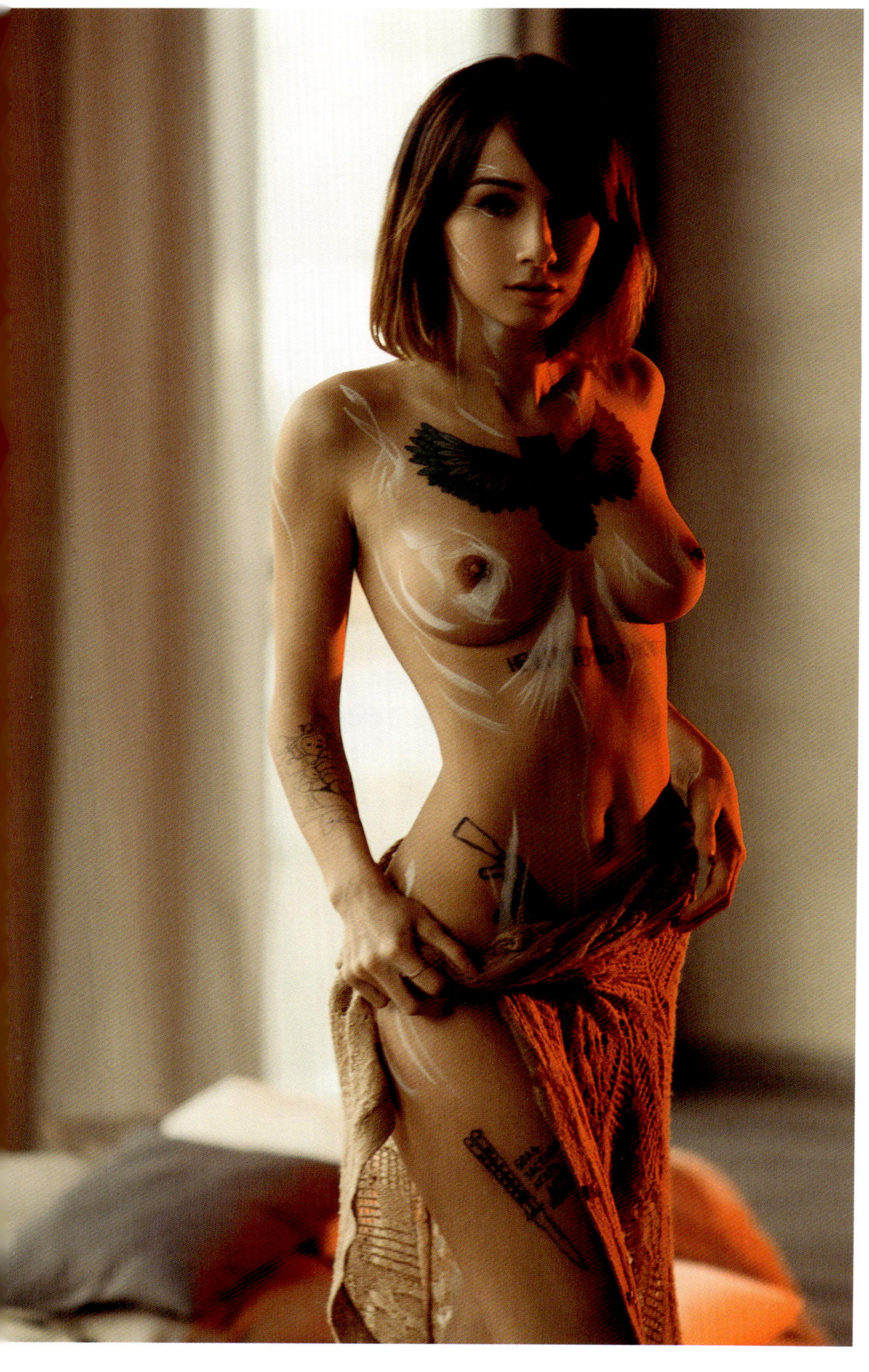

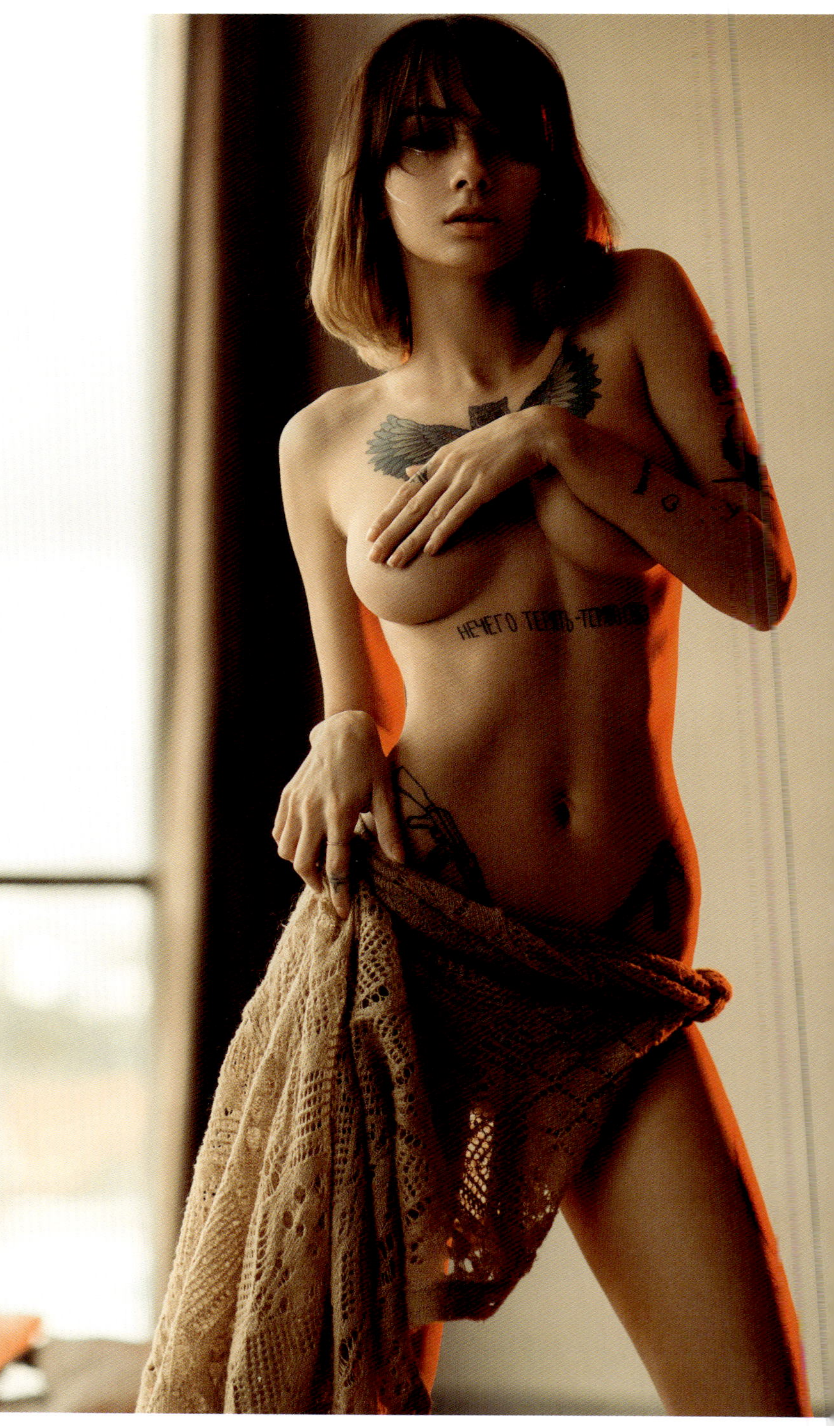

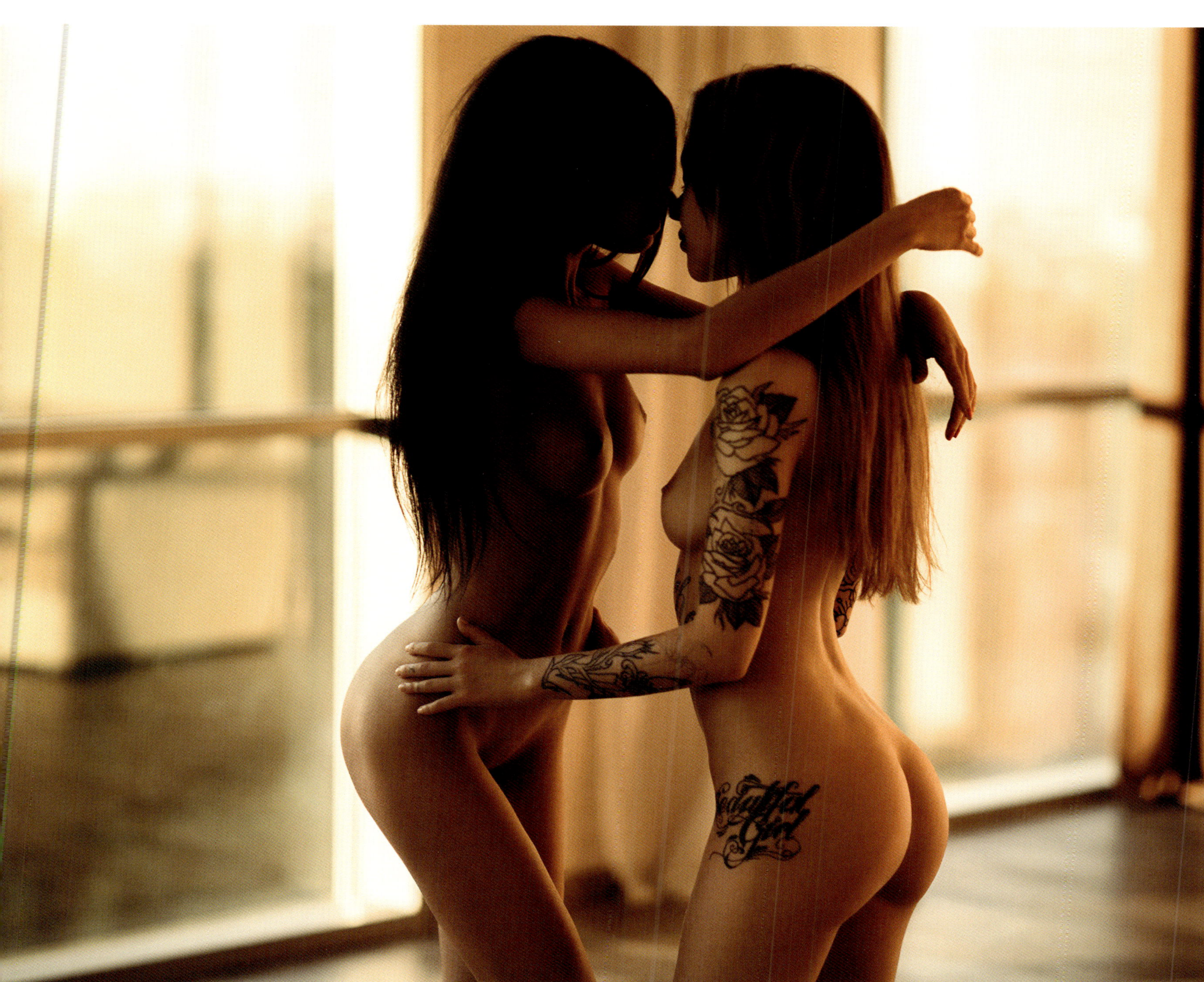

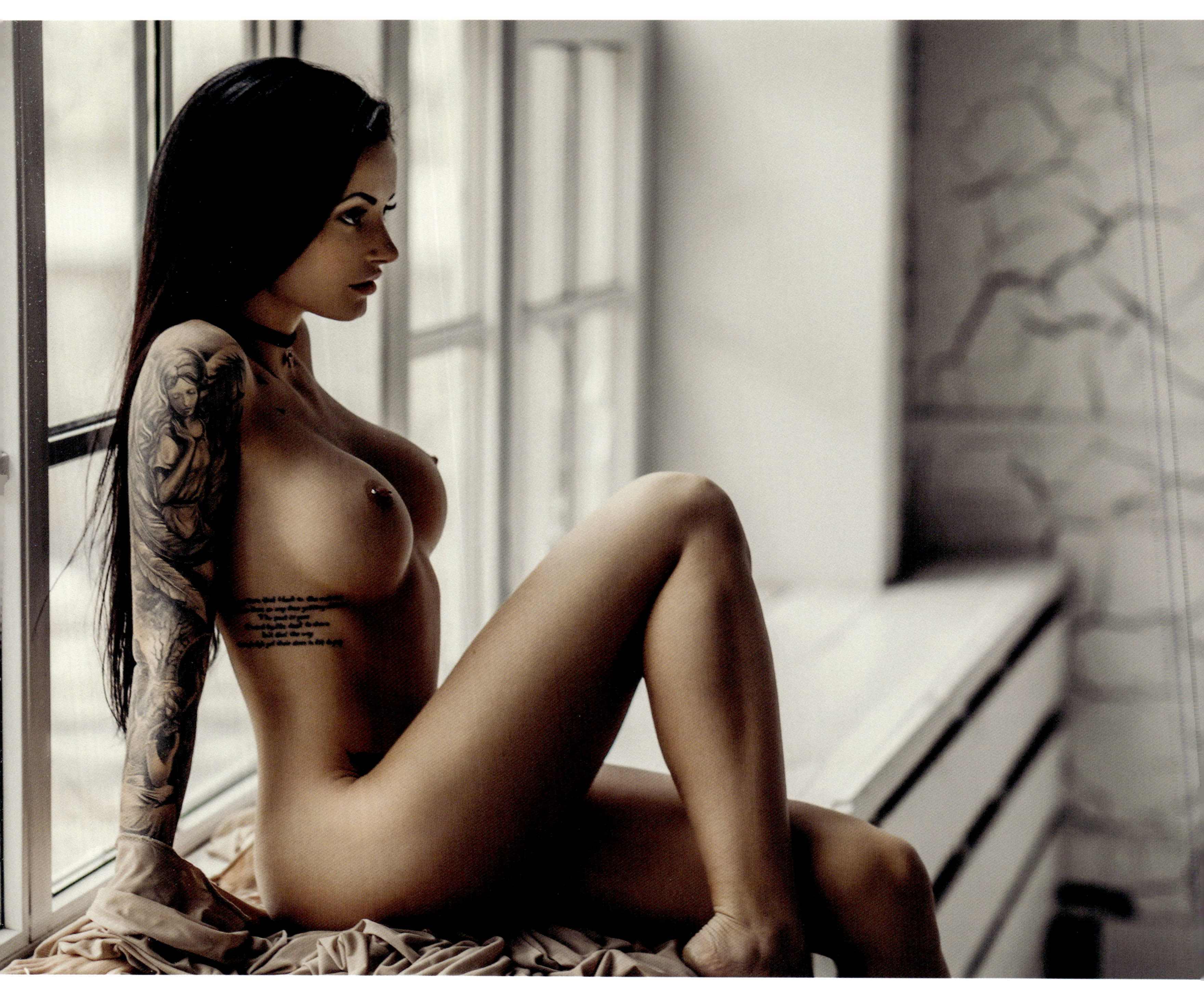

▲ АННА С. | ANNA S.

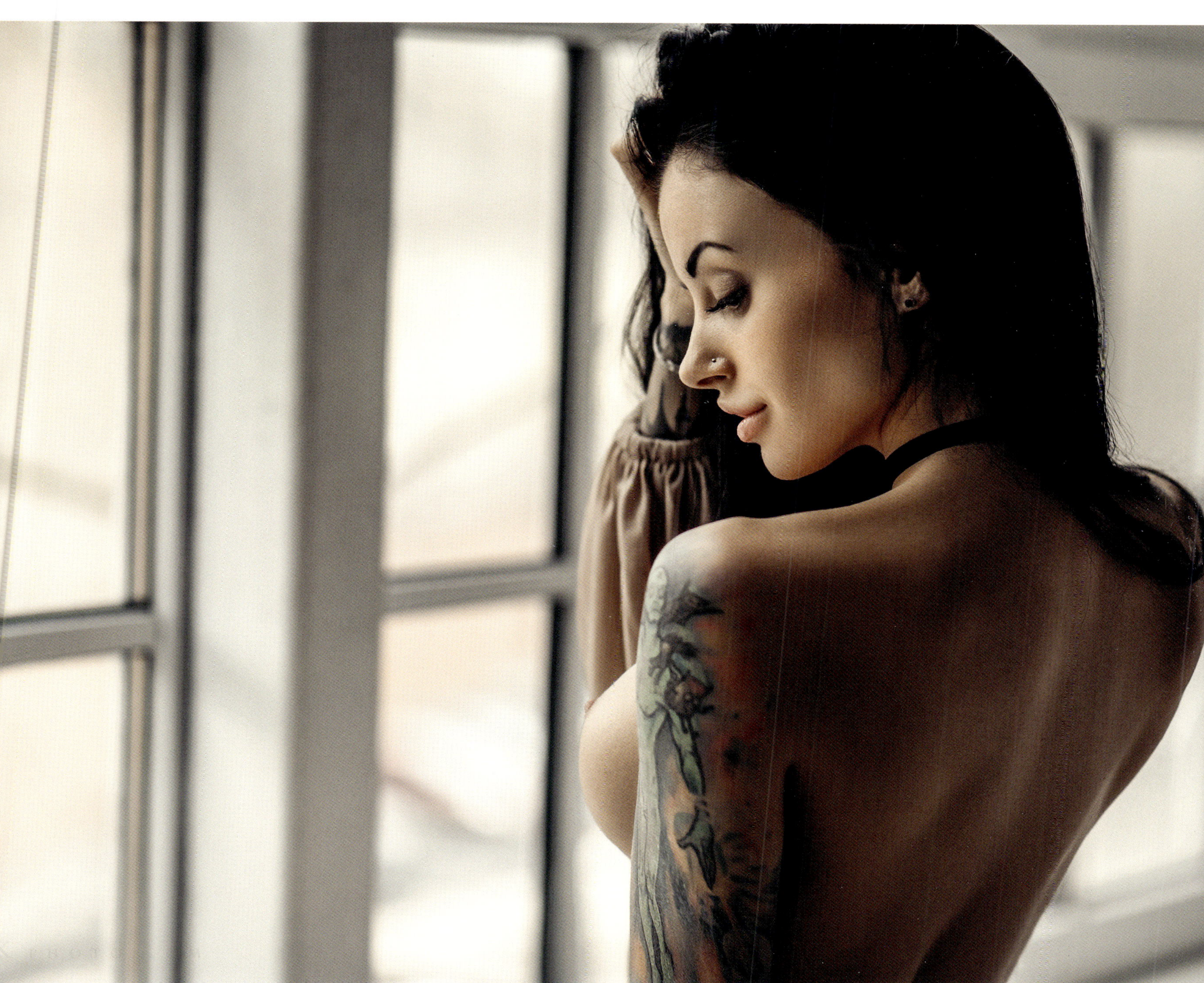

АННА С. | ANNA S. ▲

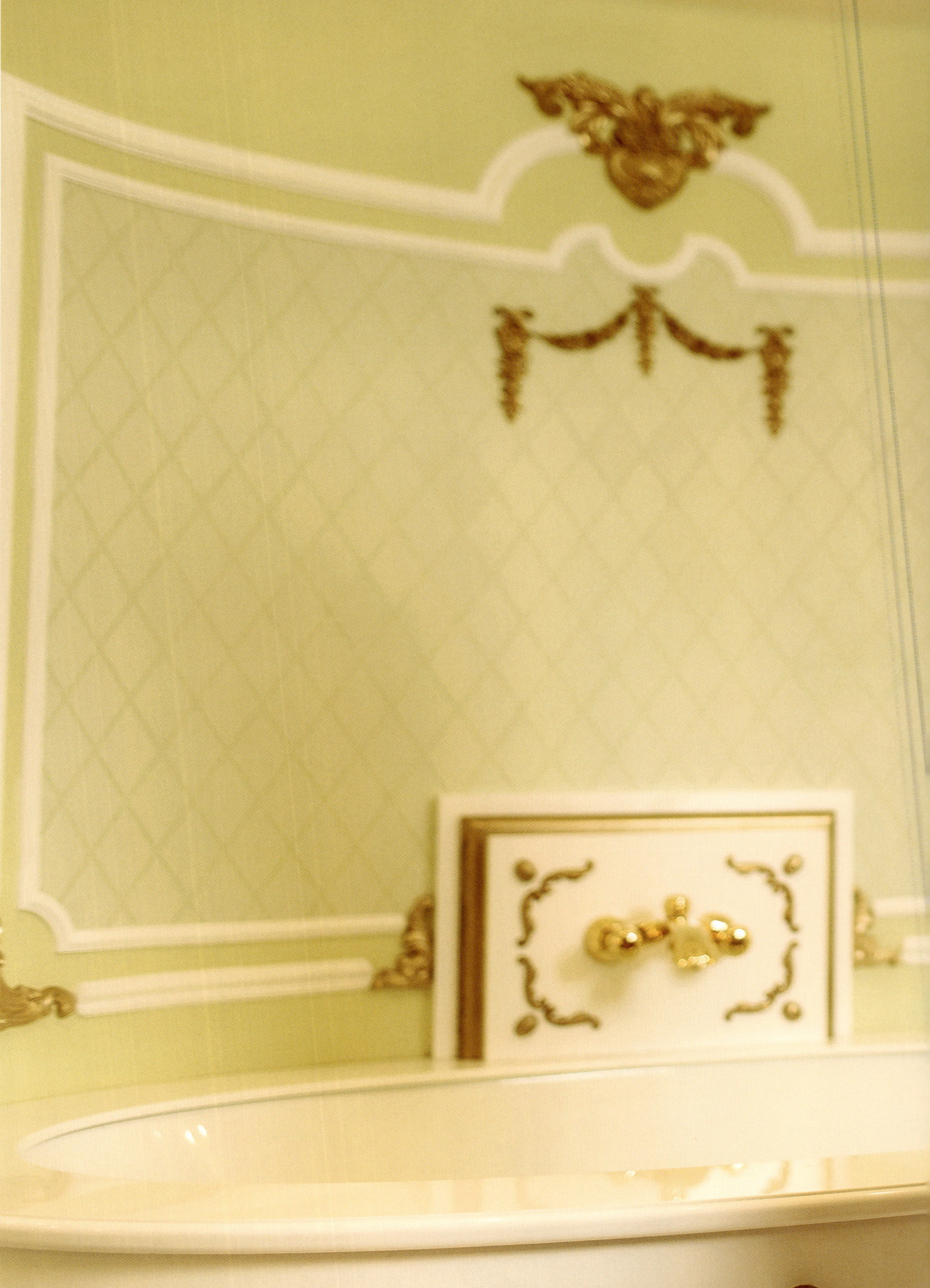

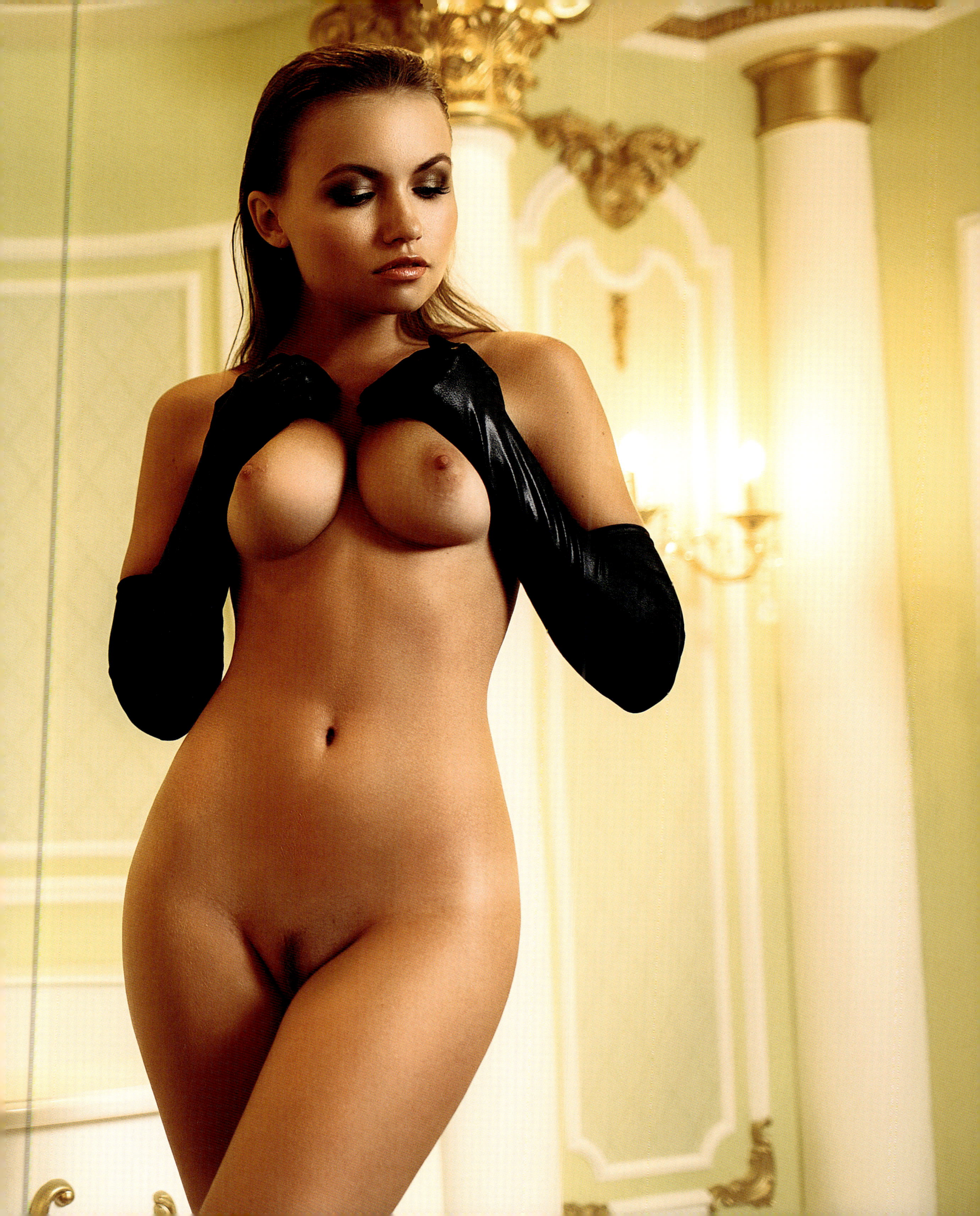

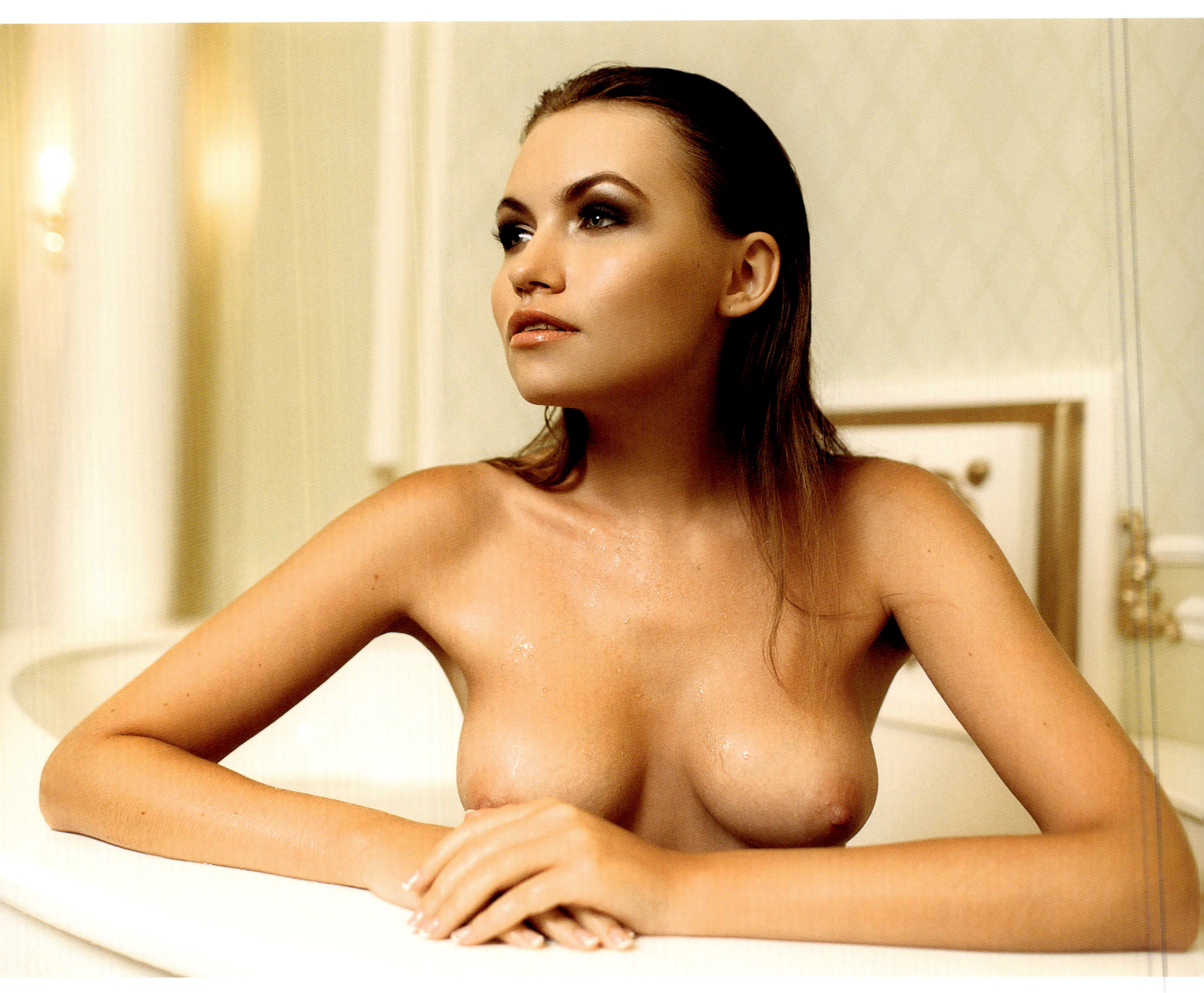

▲ **НИКОЛЬ** | NICOLE

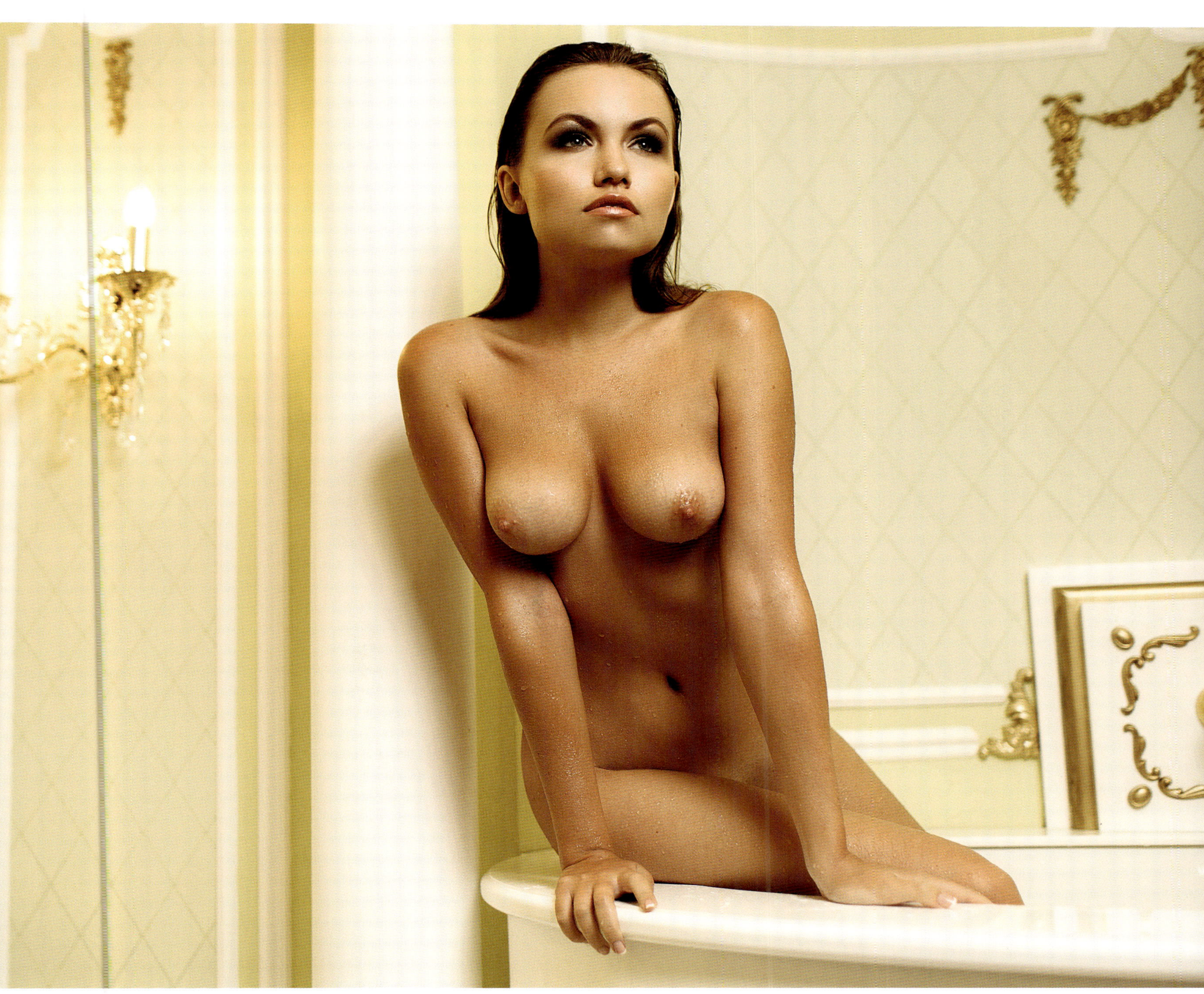

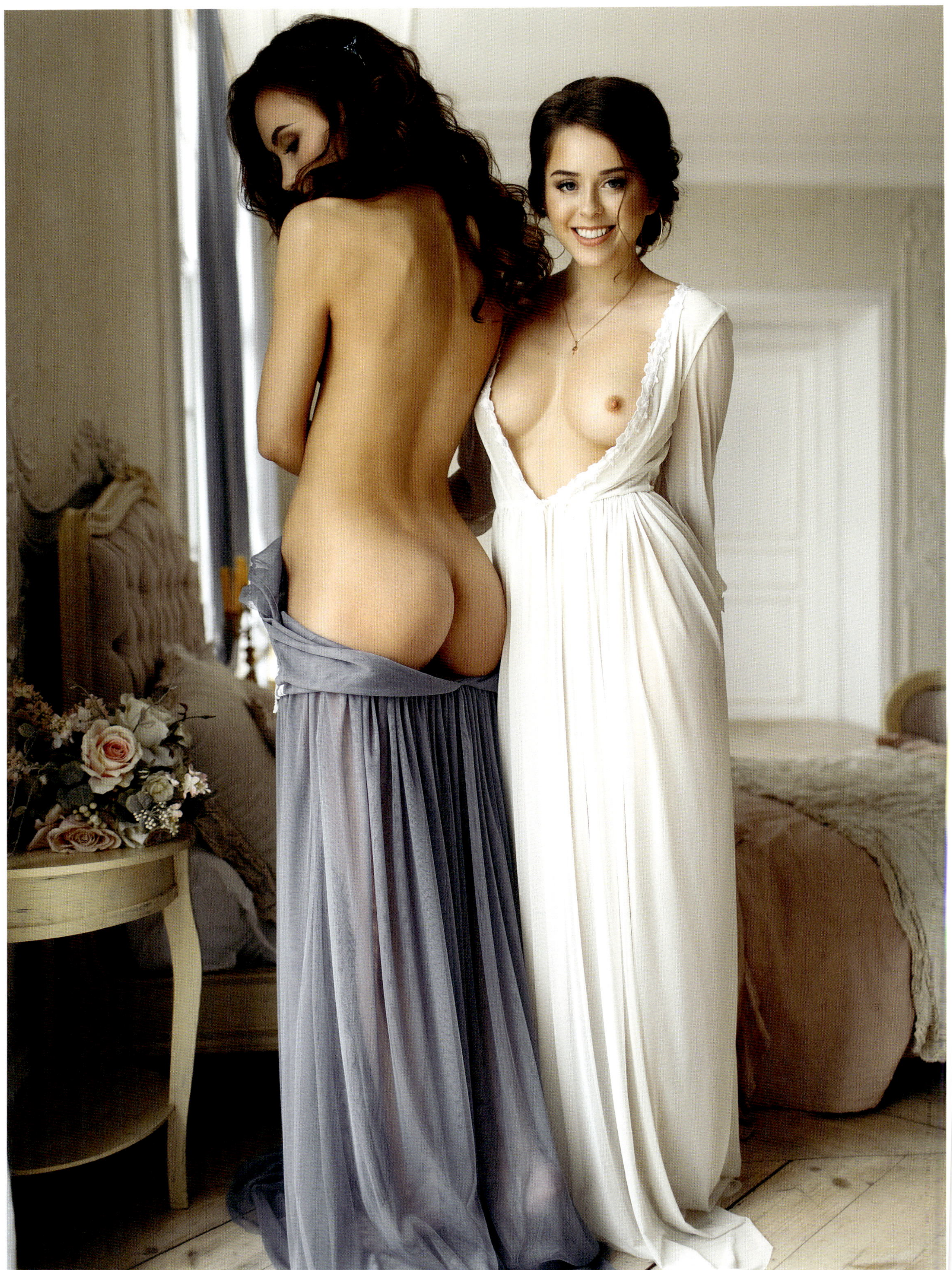

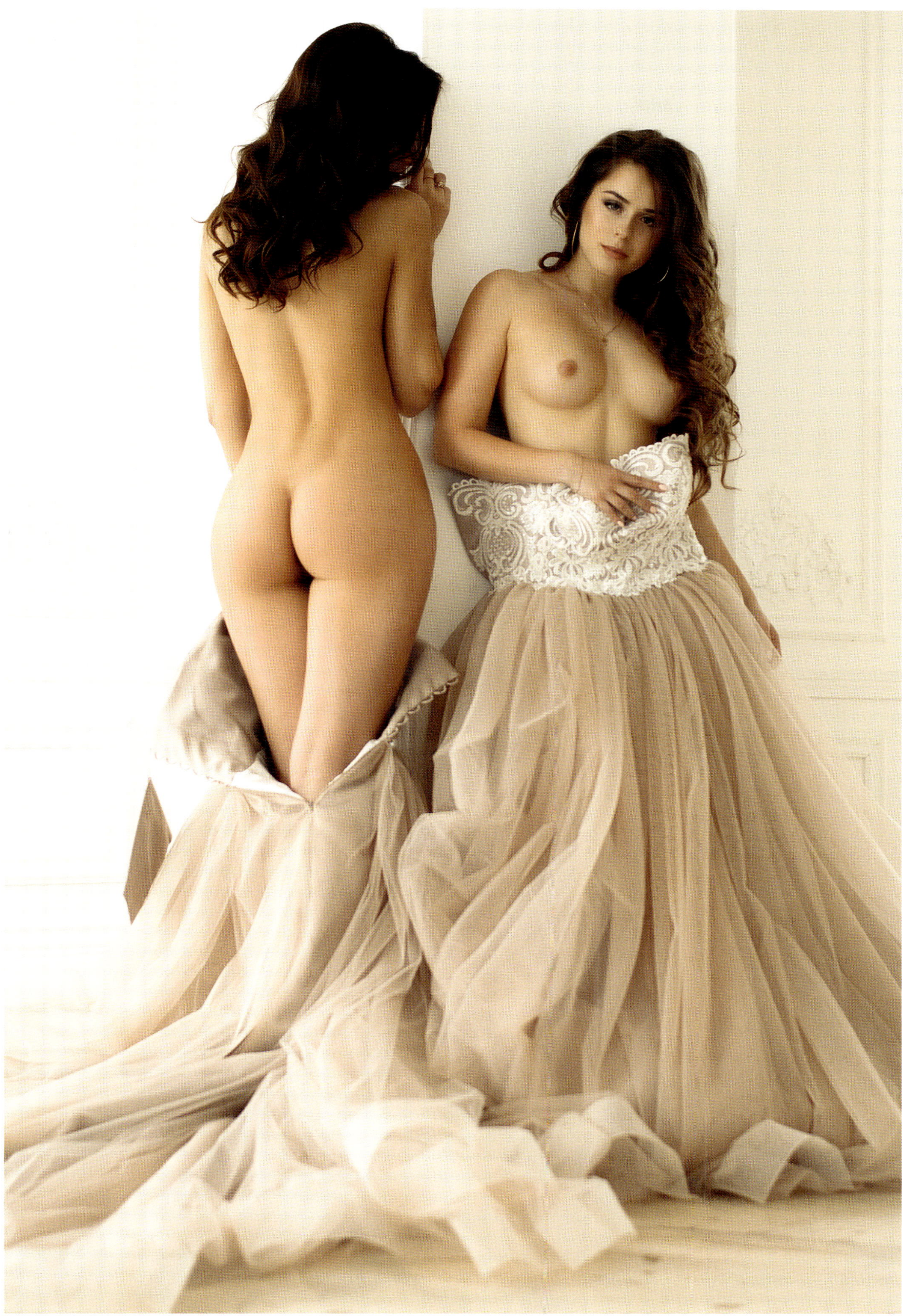

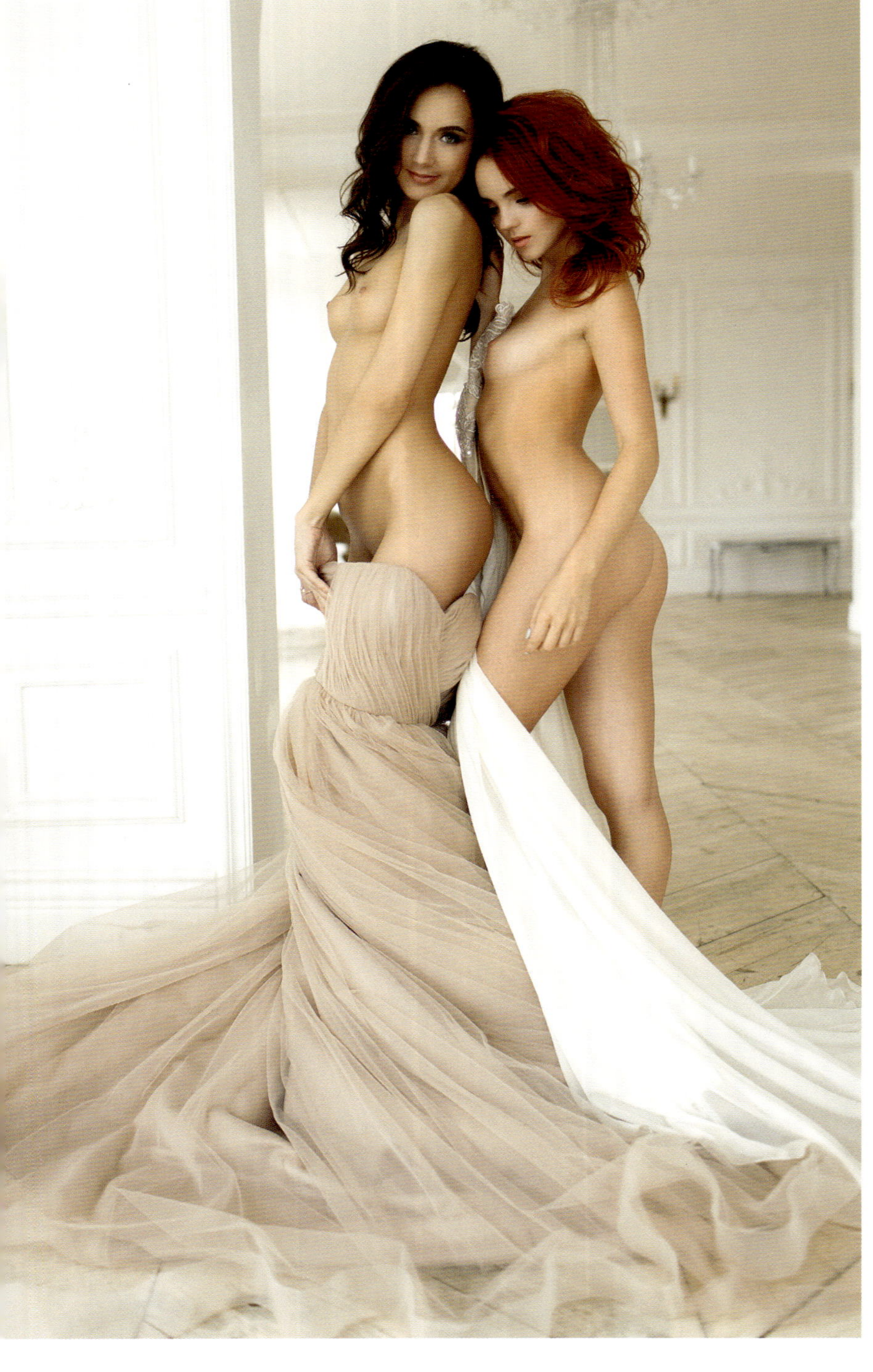

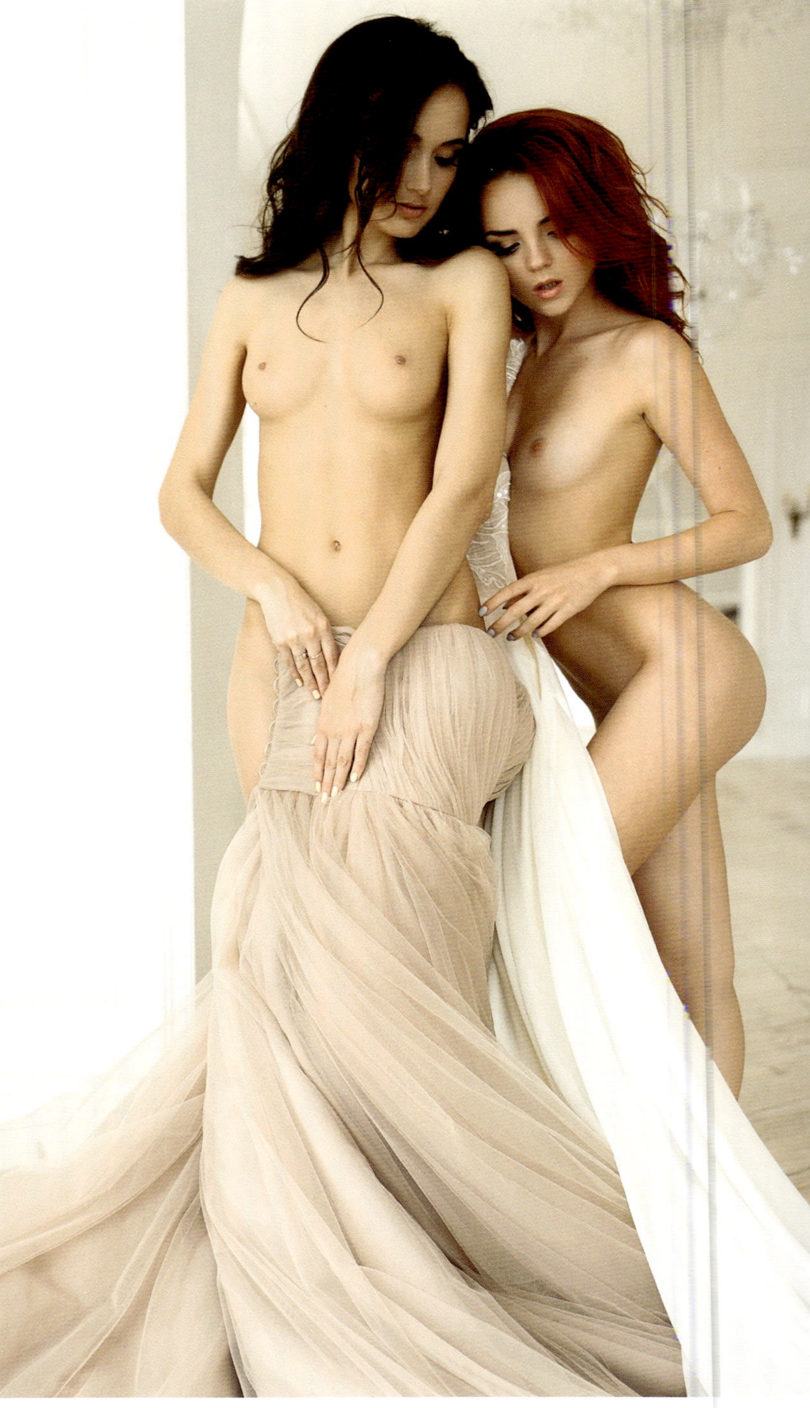

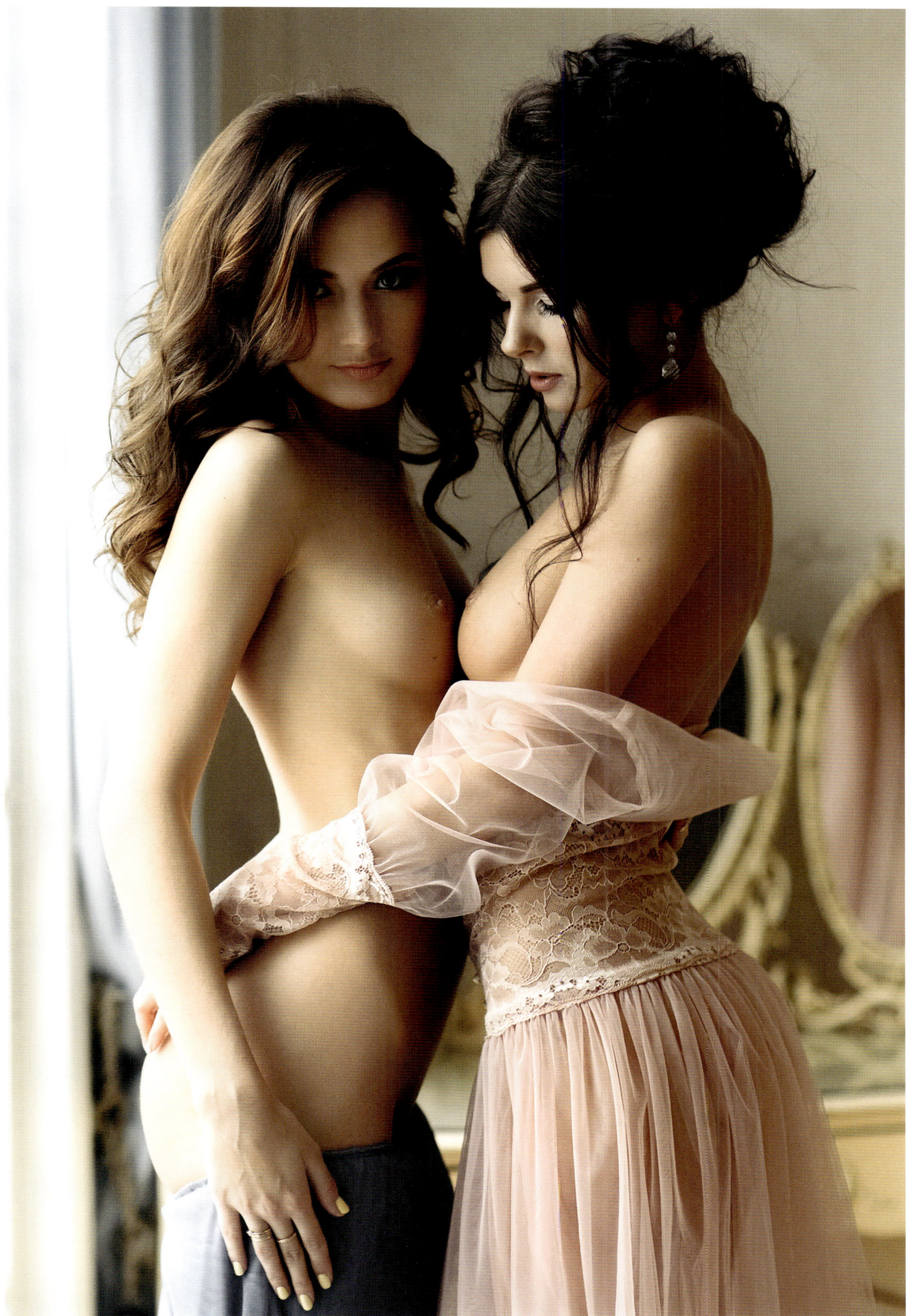

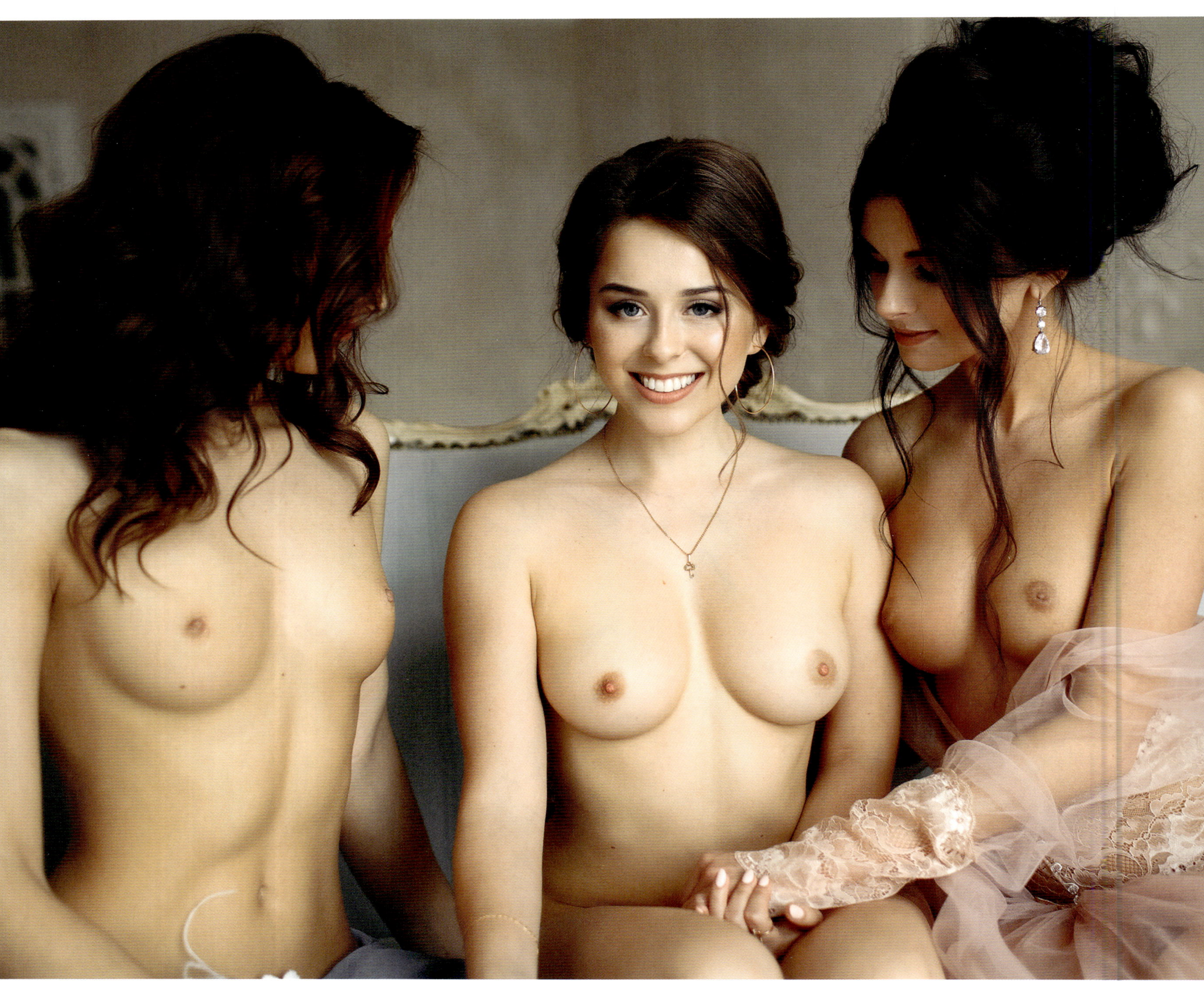

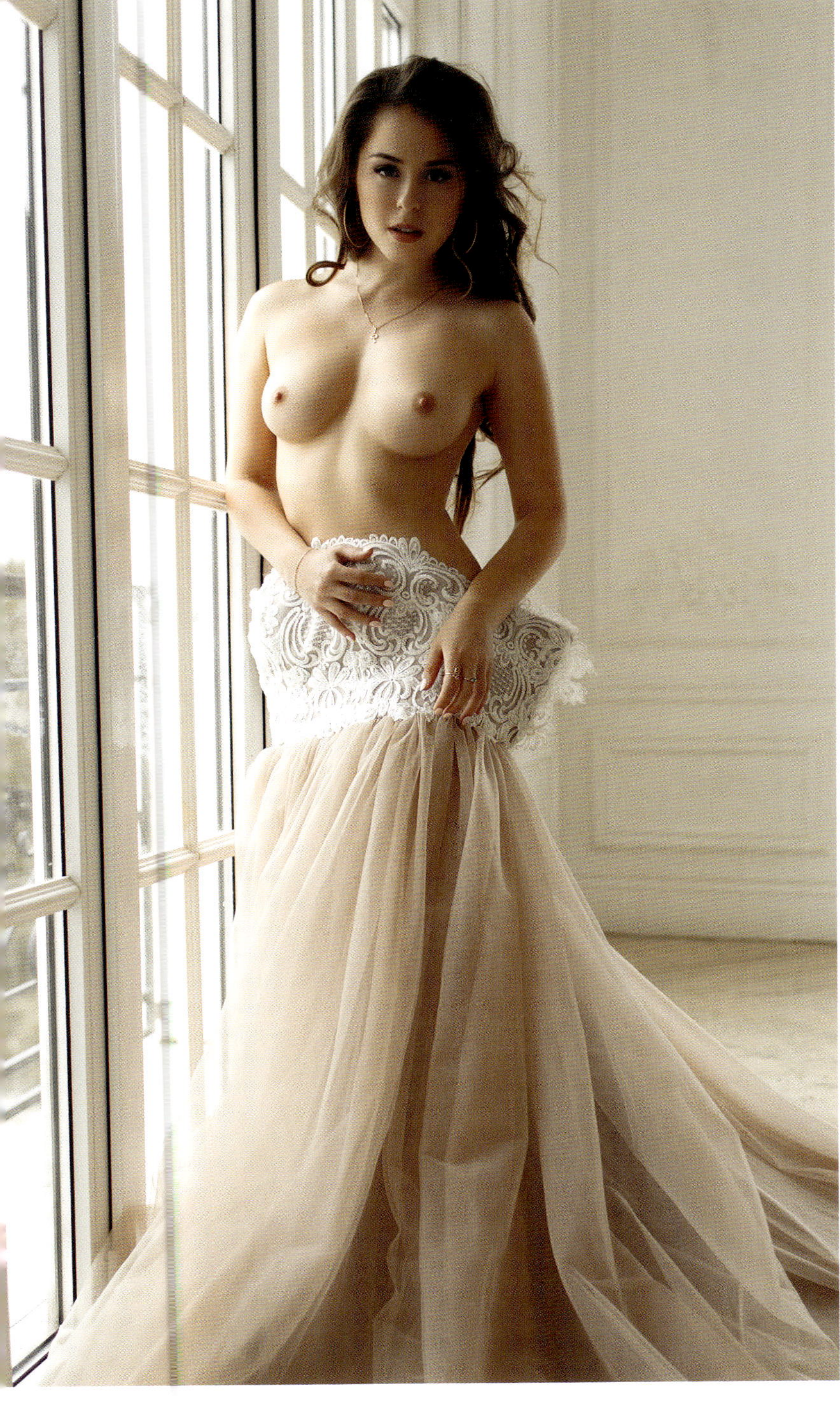

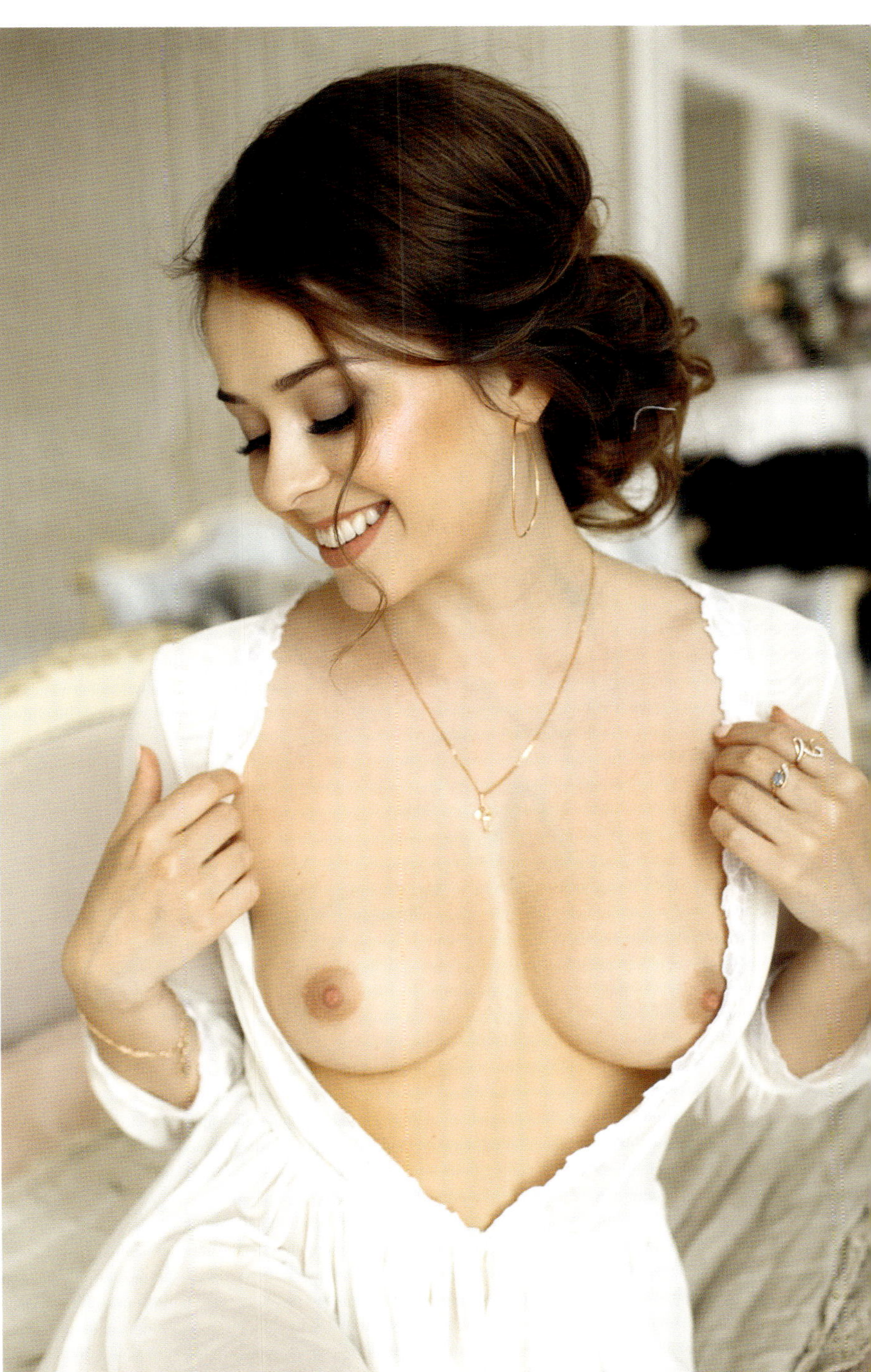

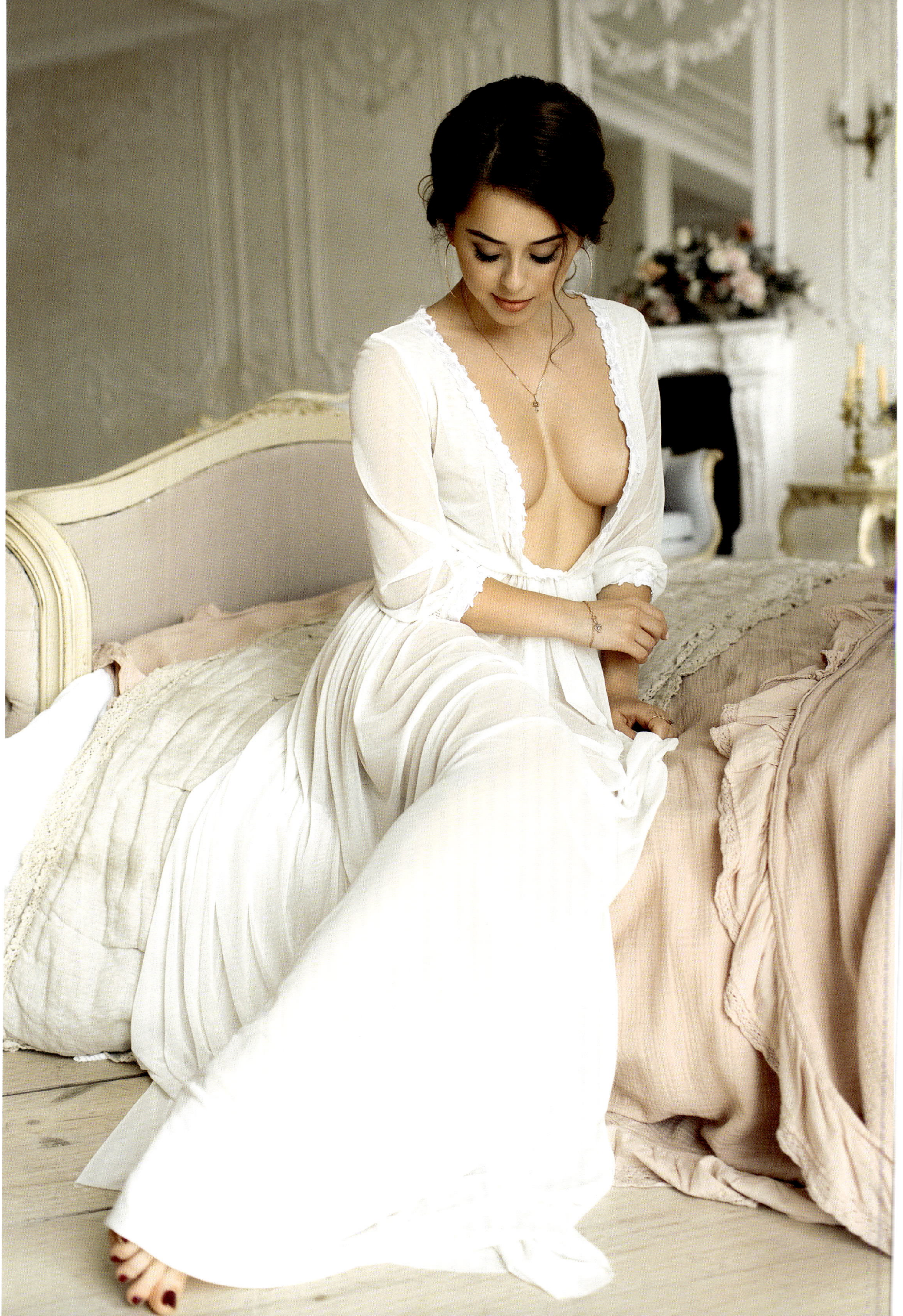

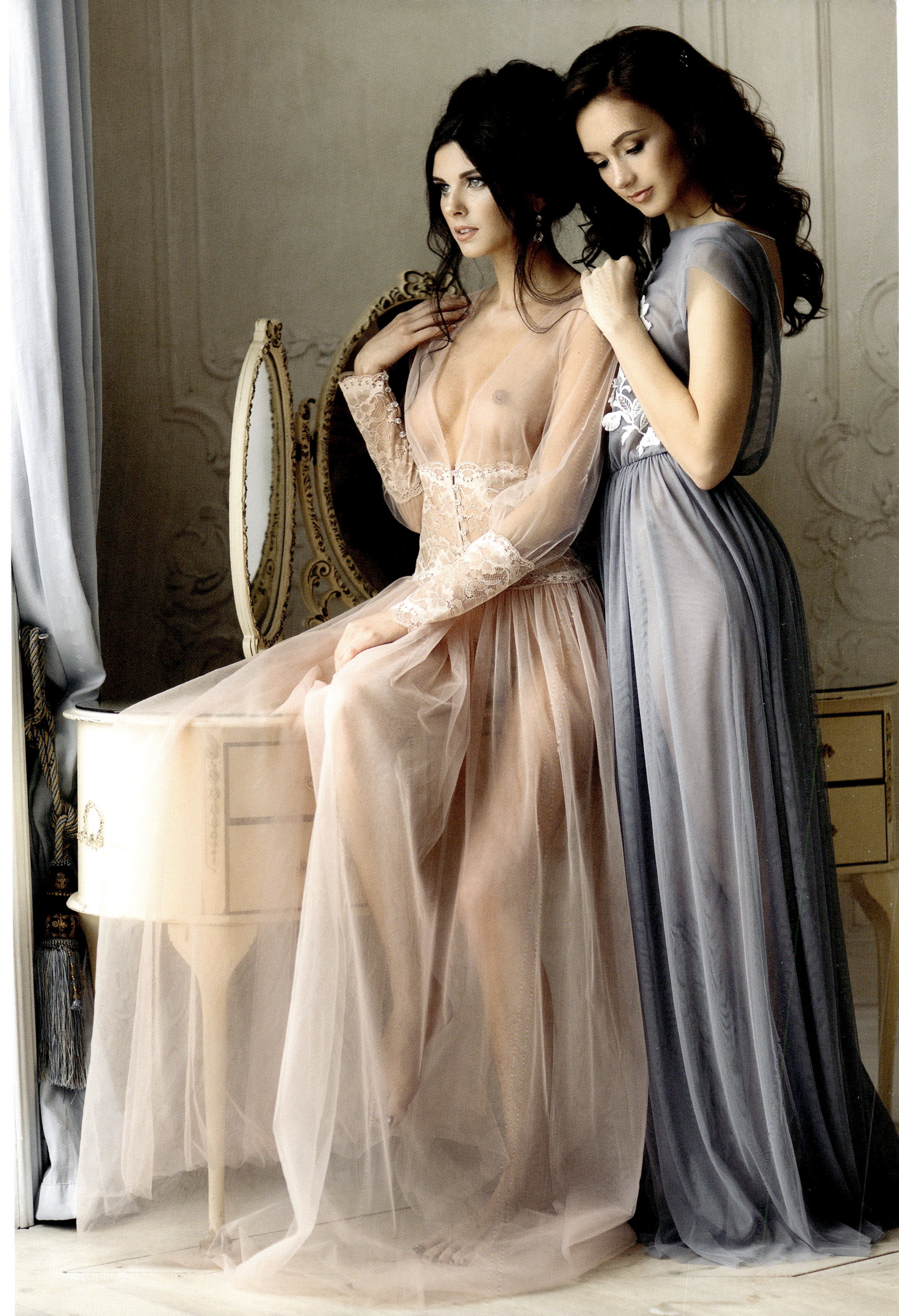

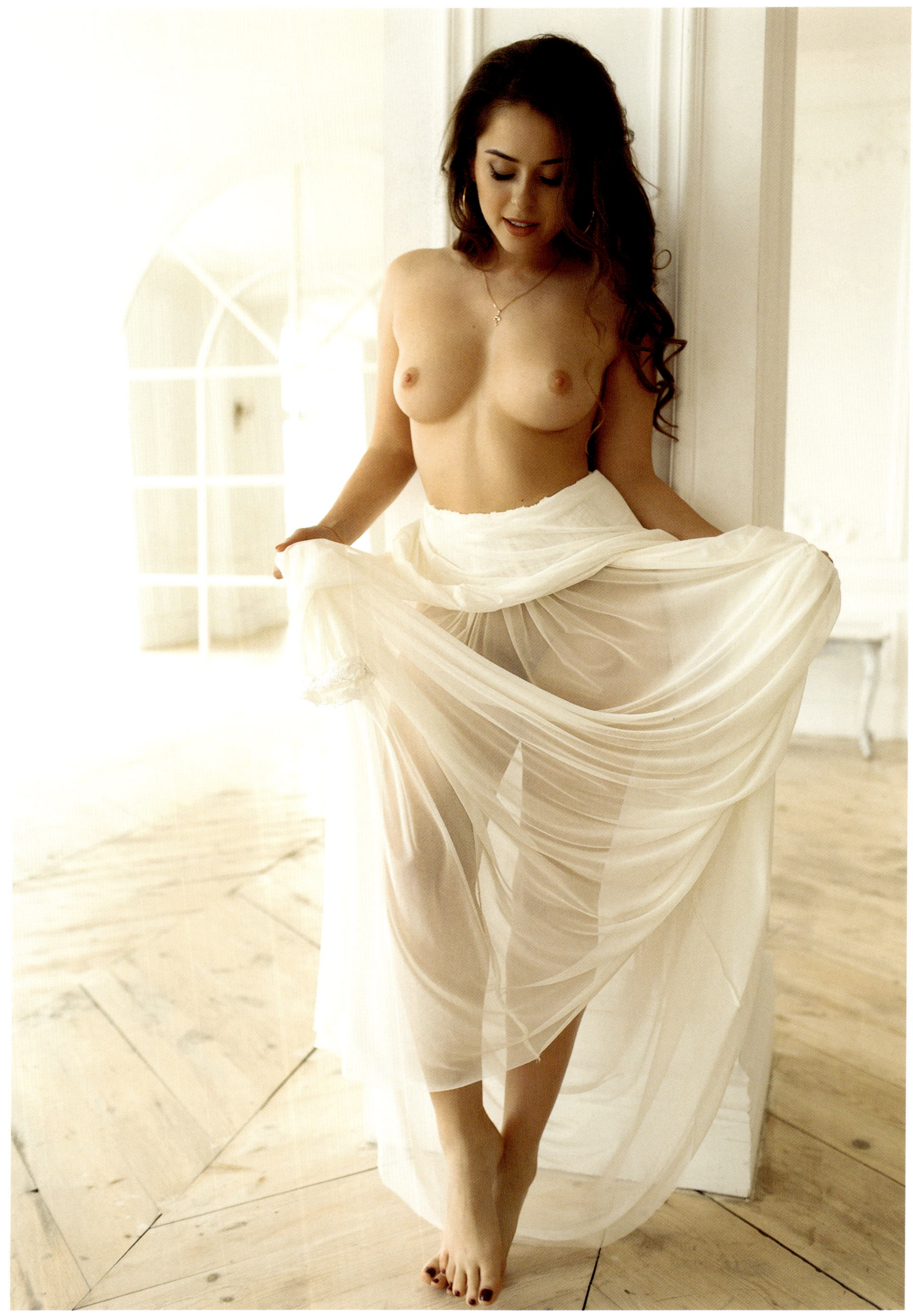

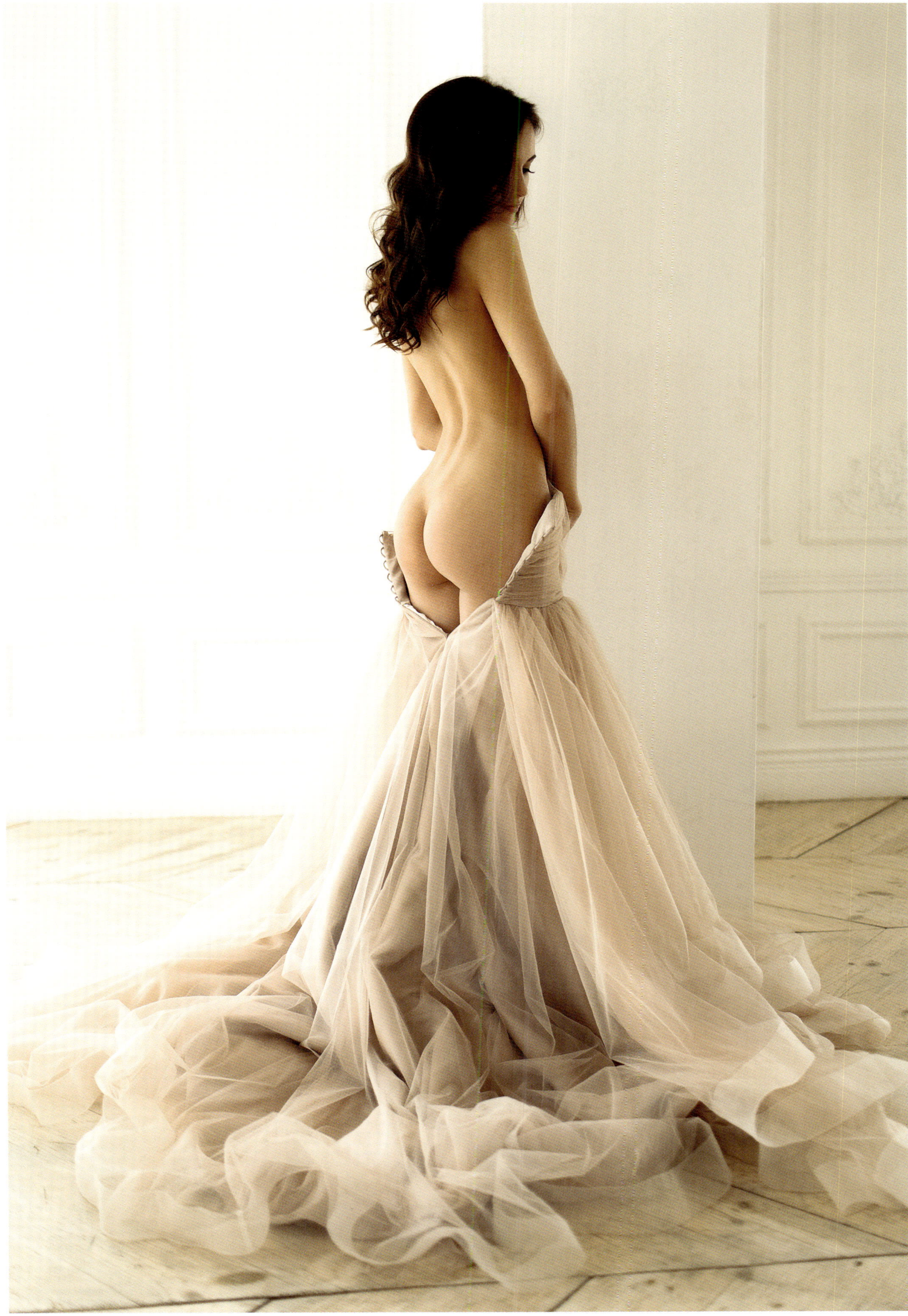

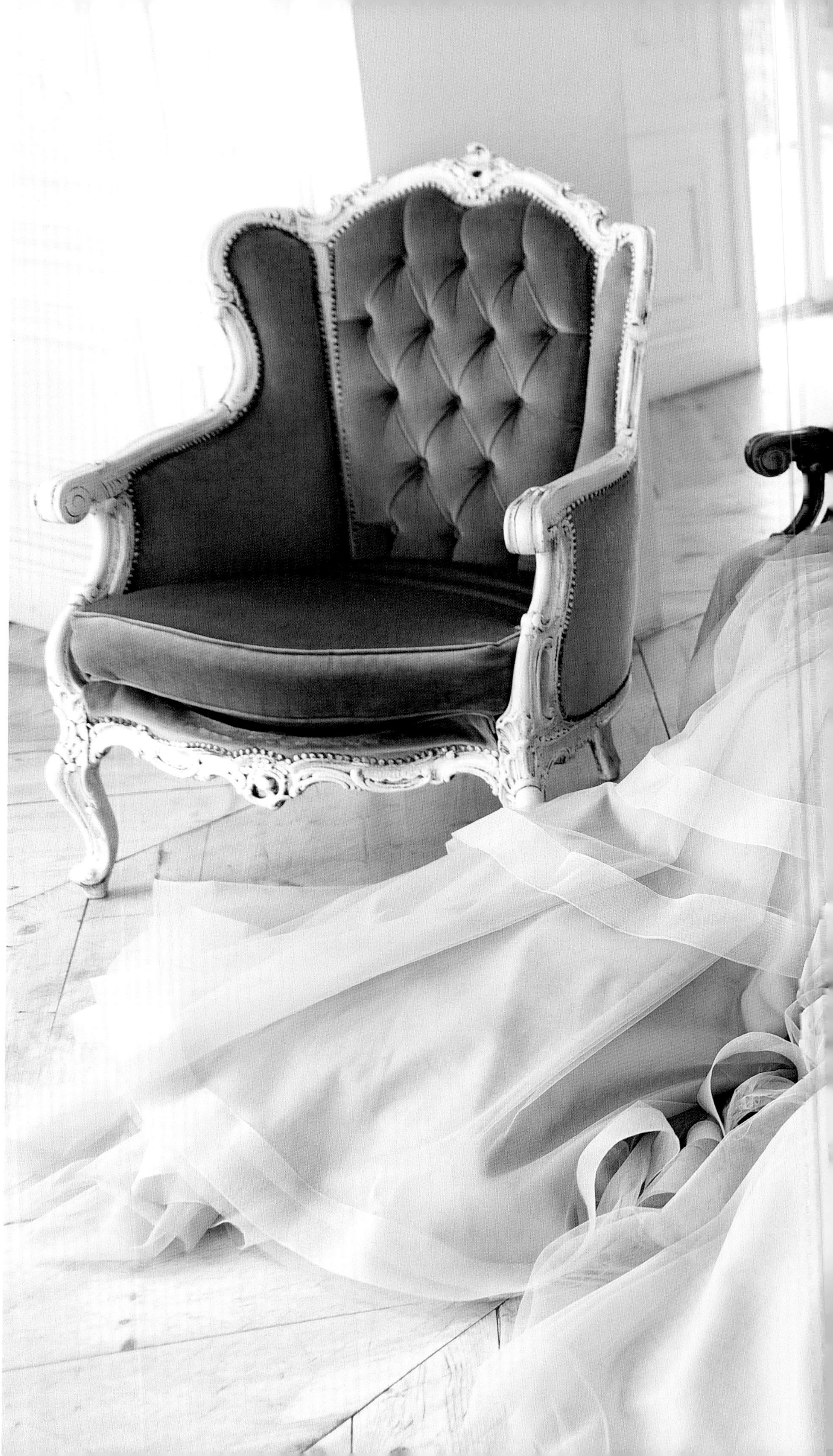

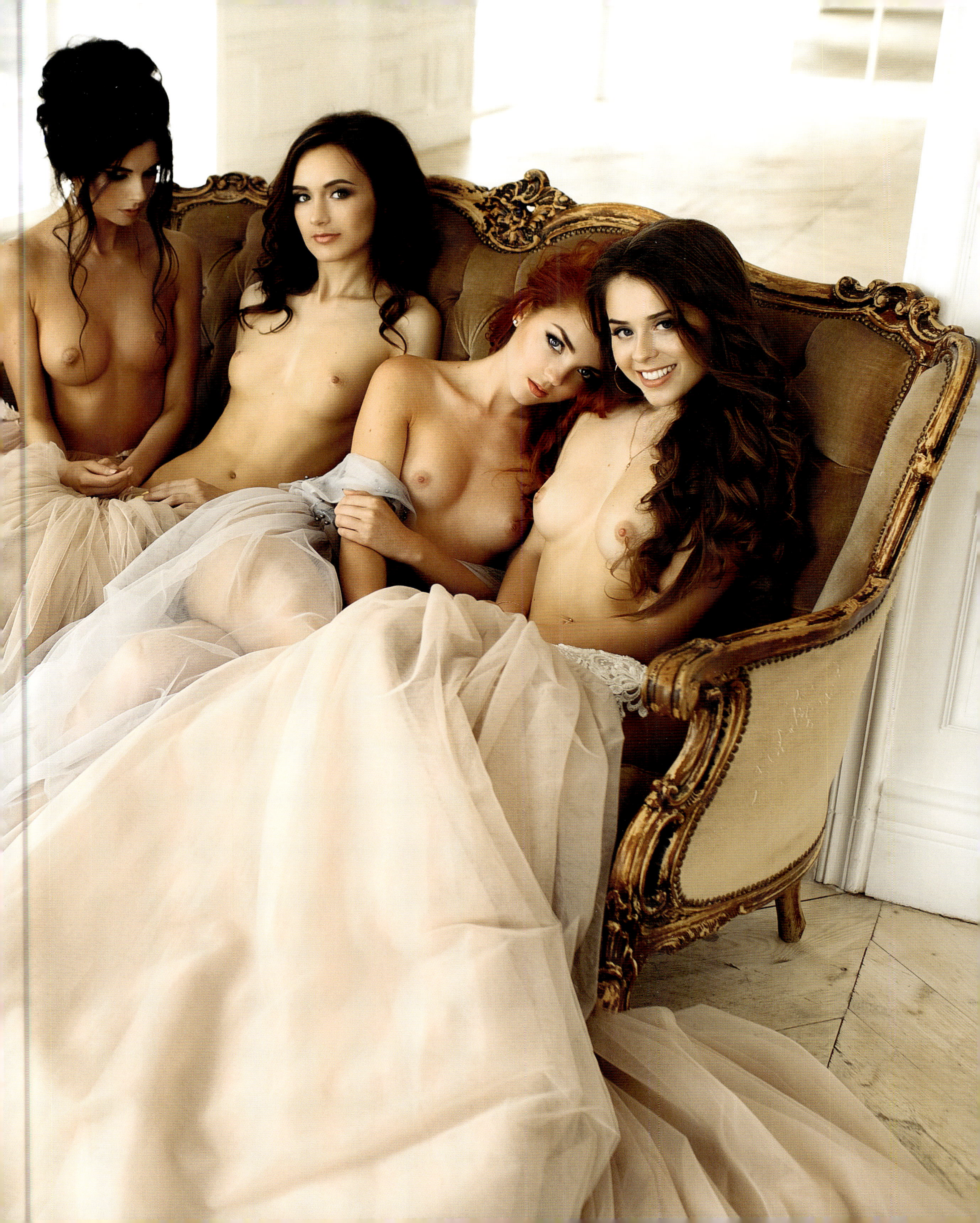

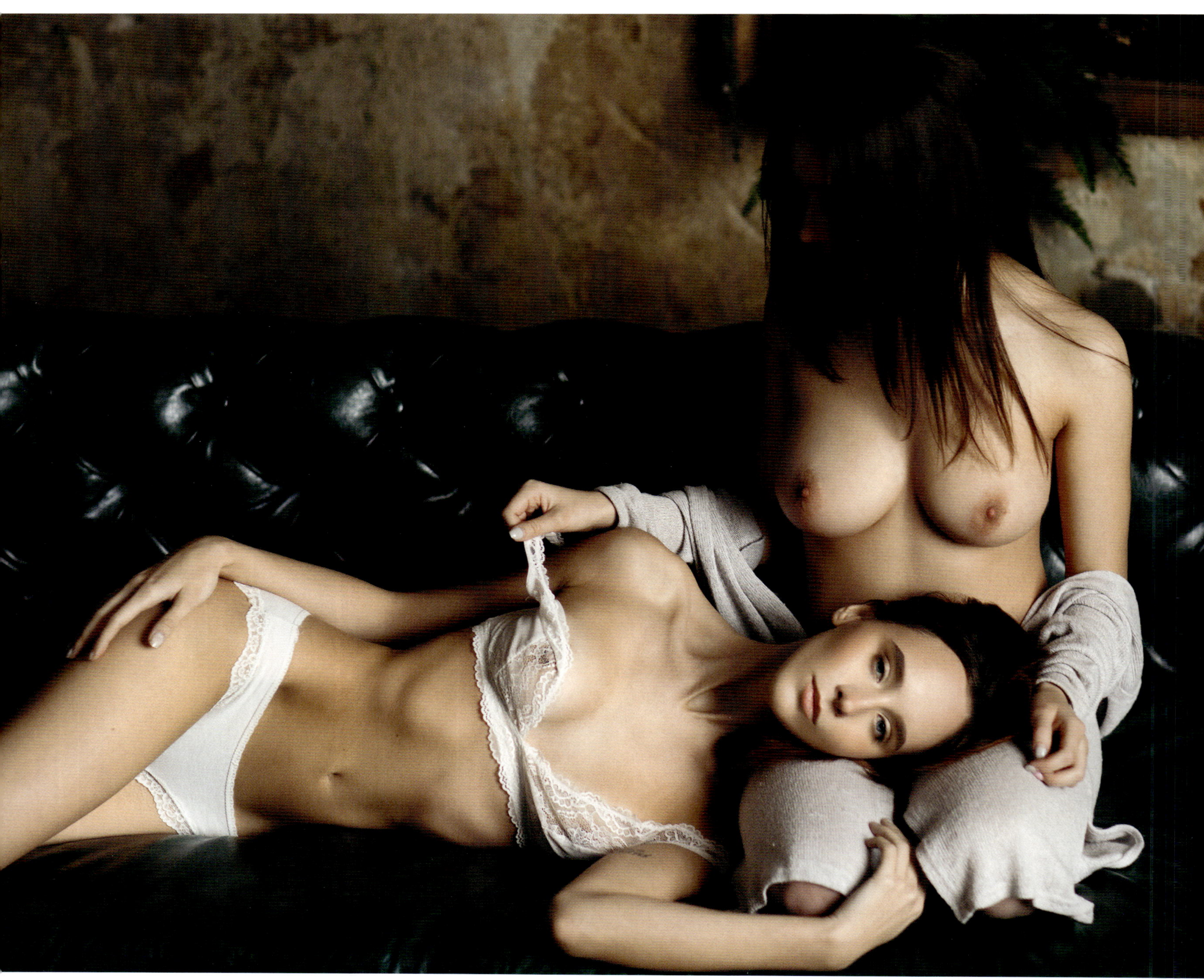

▲ ЛЕРА+ВЕТА | LERA+VETA

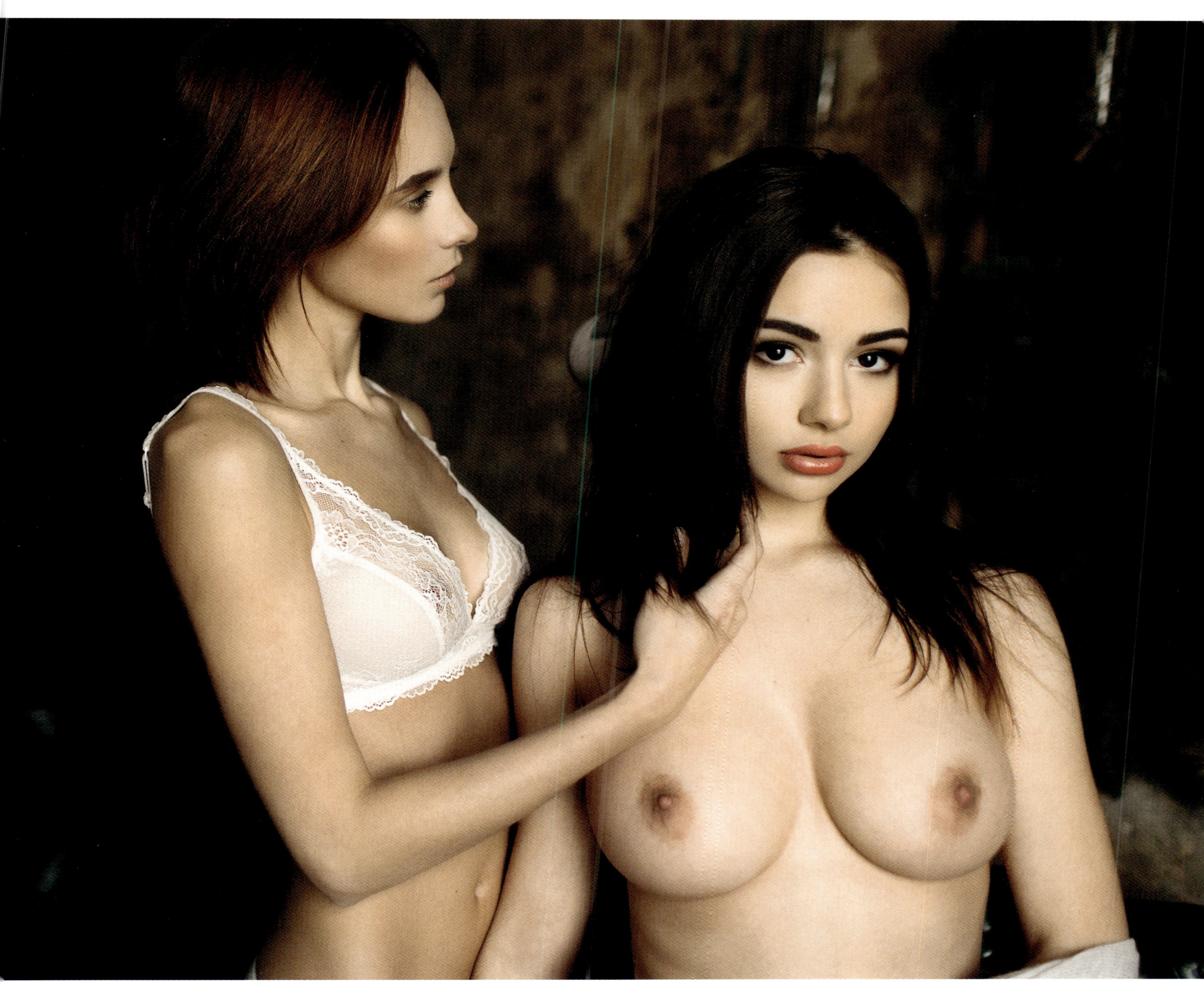

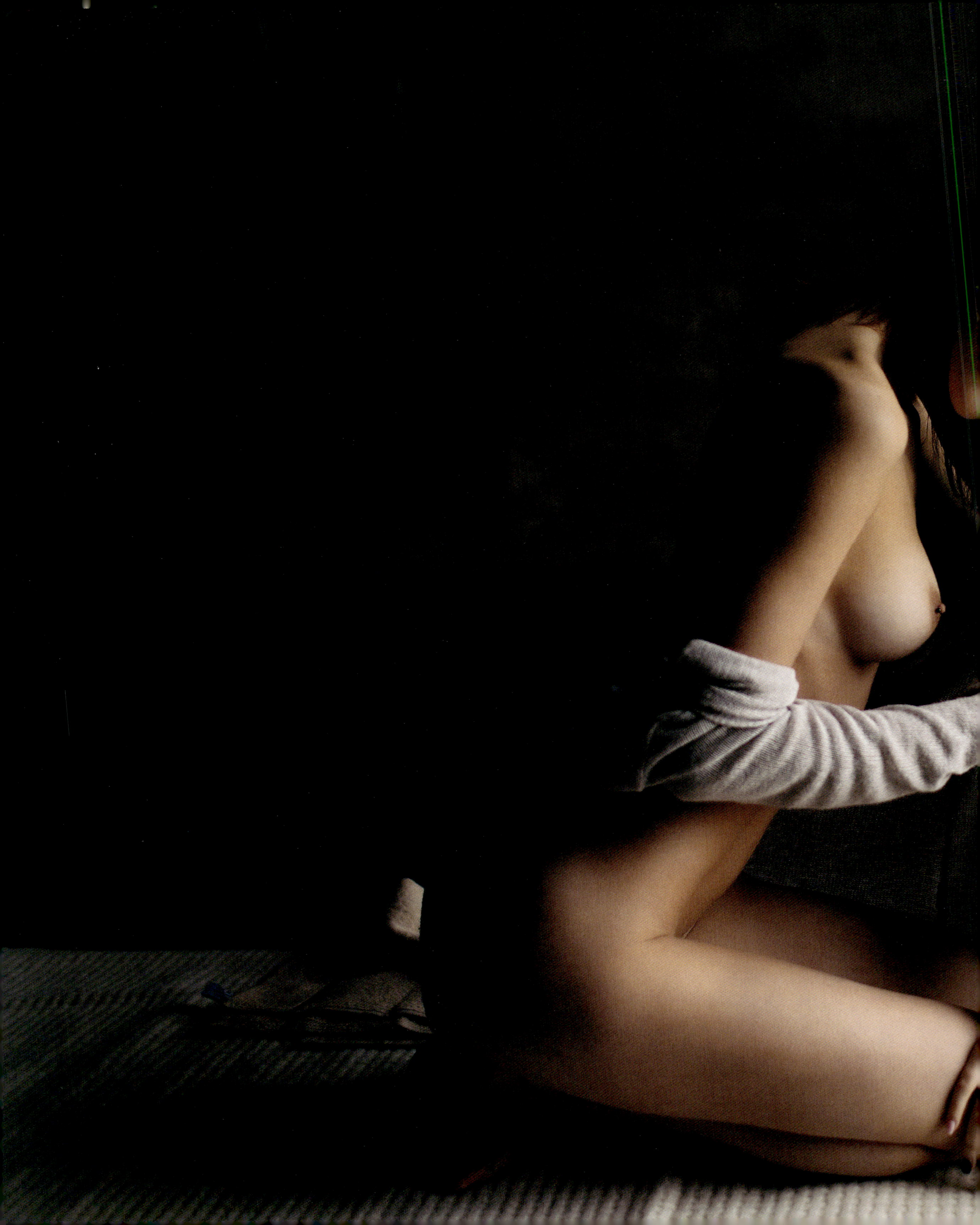

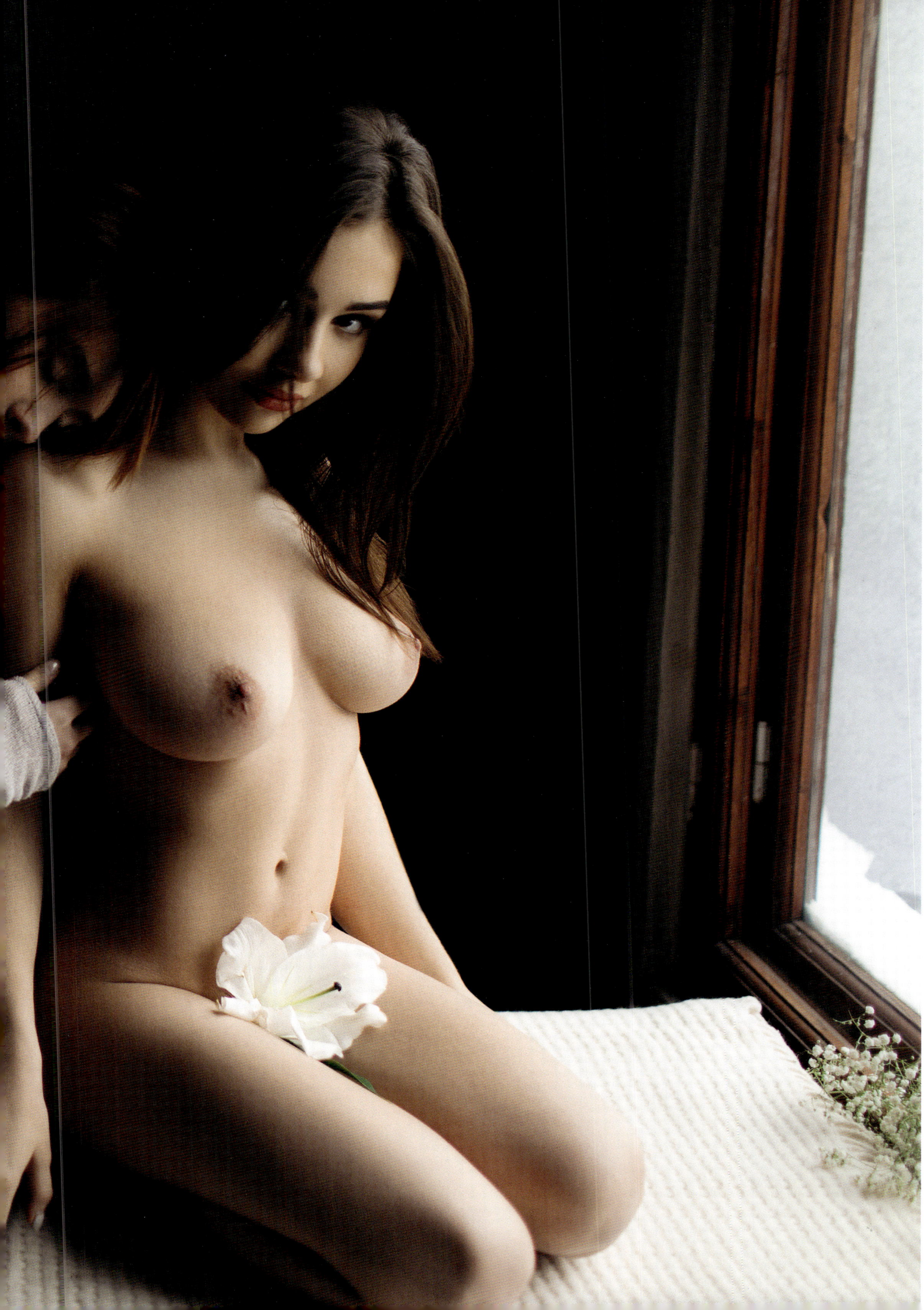

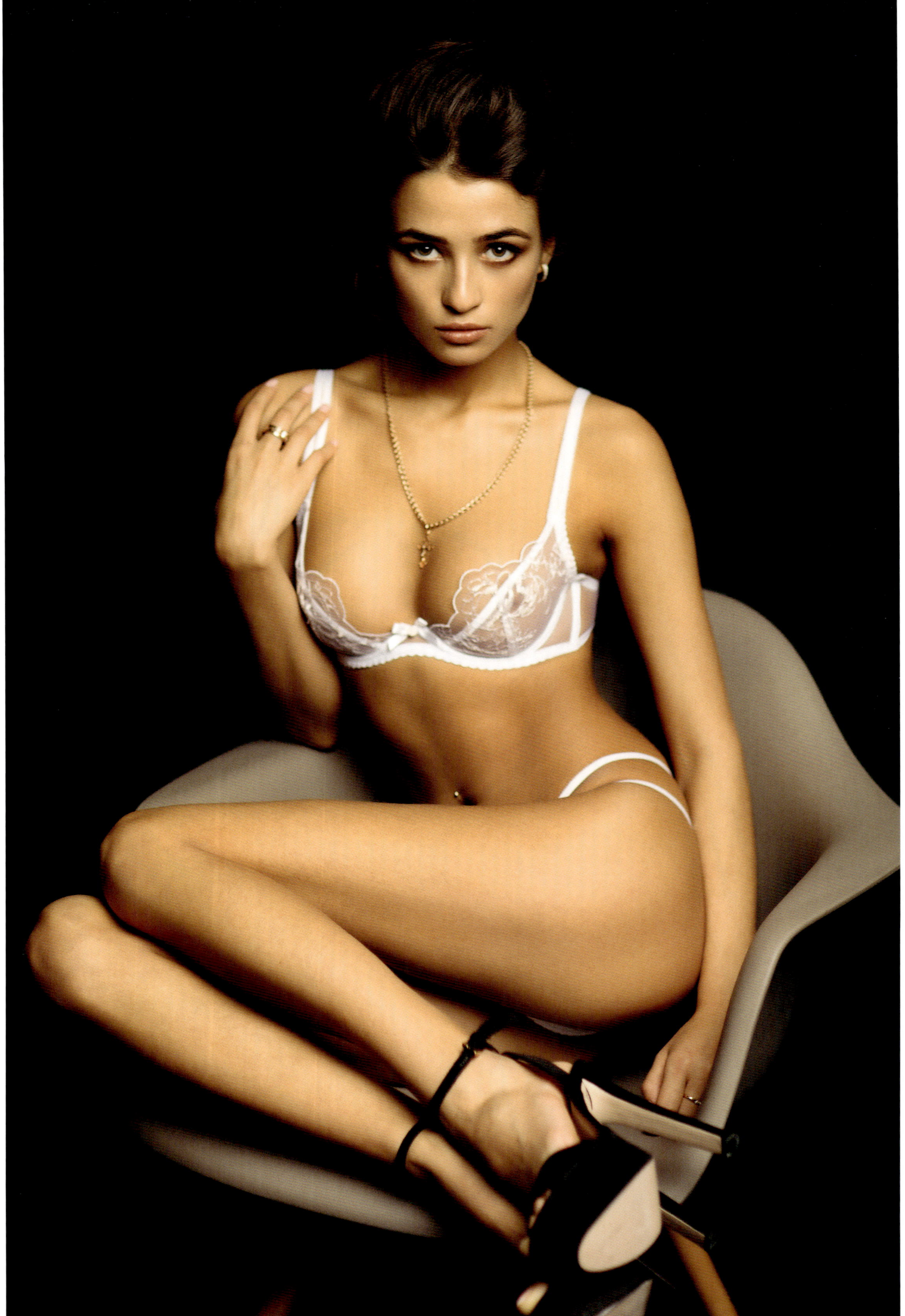

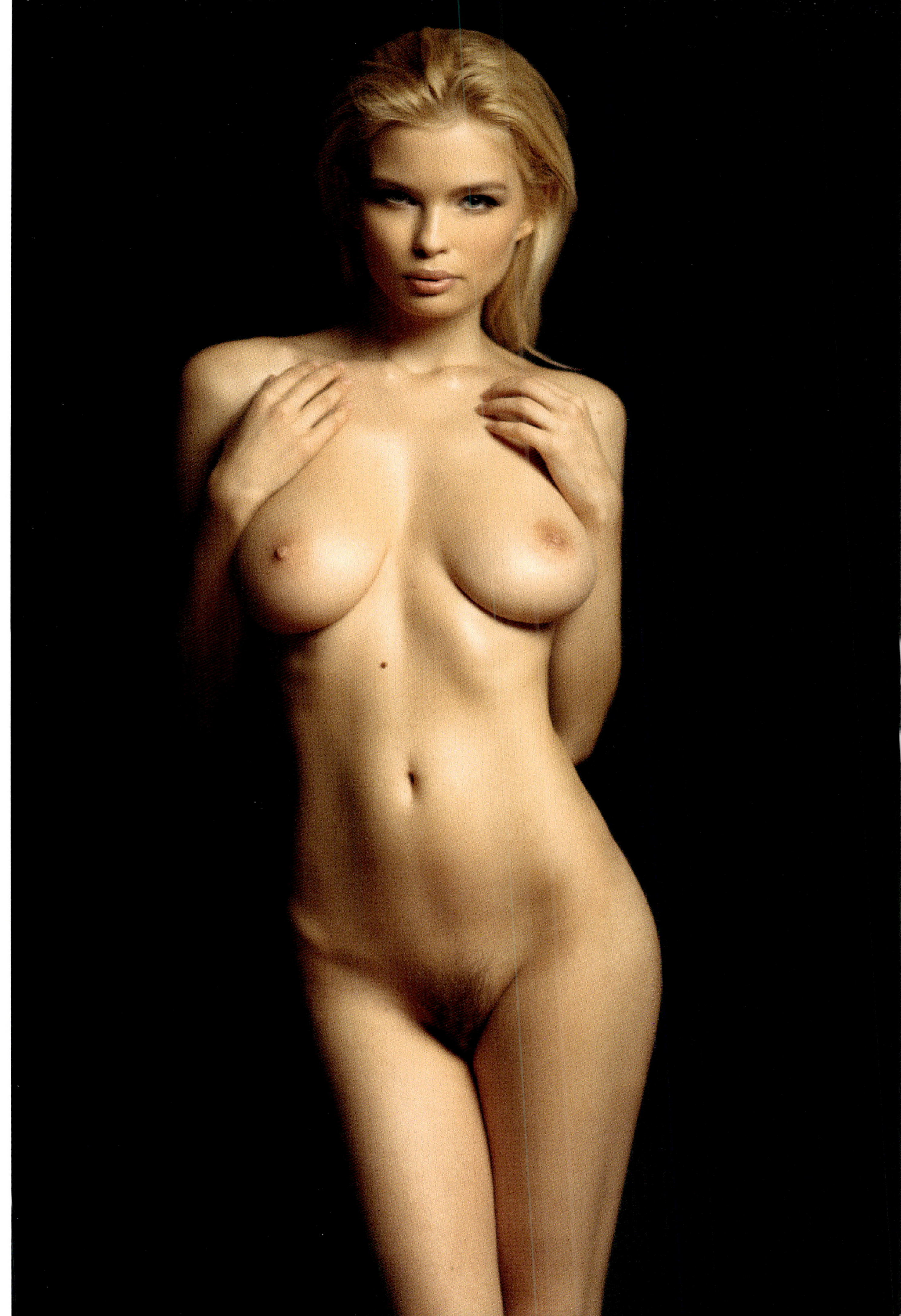

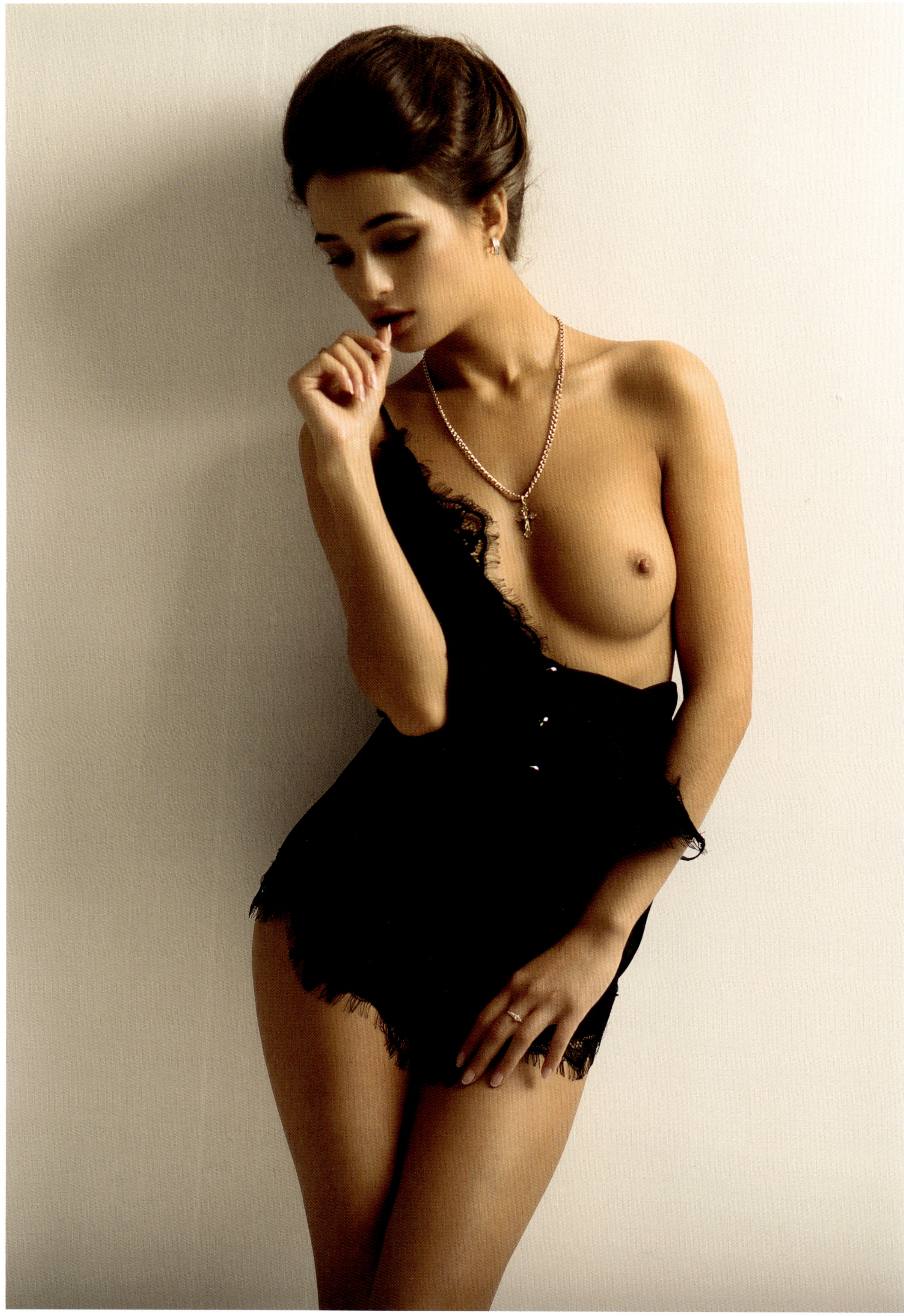

СВЕТЛАНА | SVETLANA

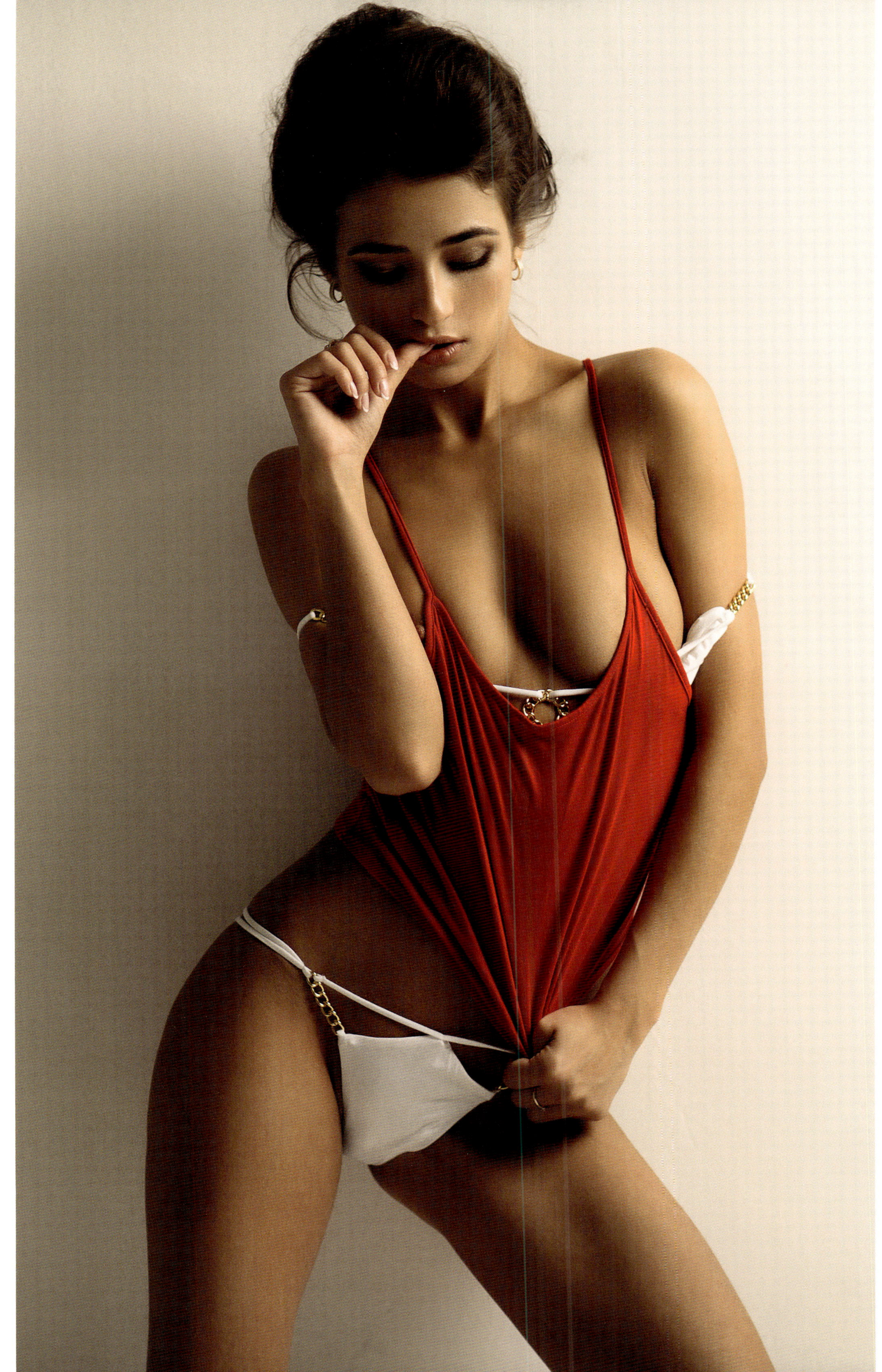

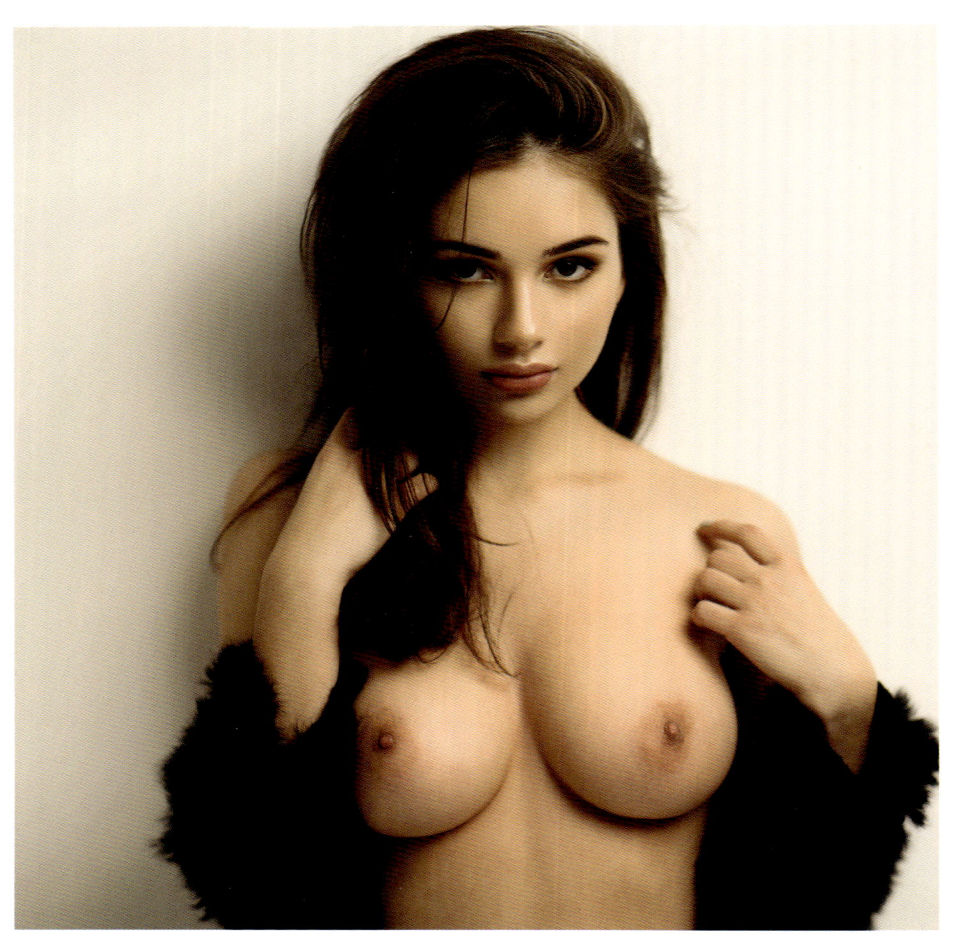
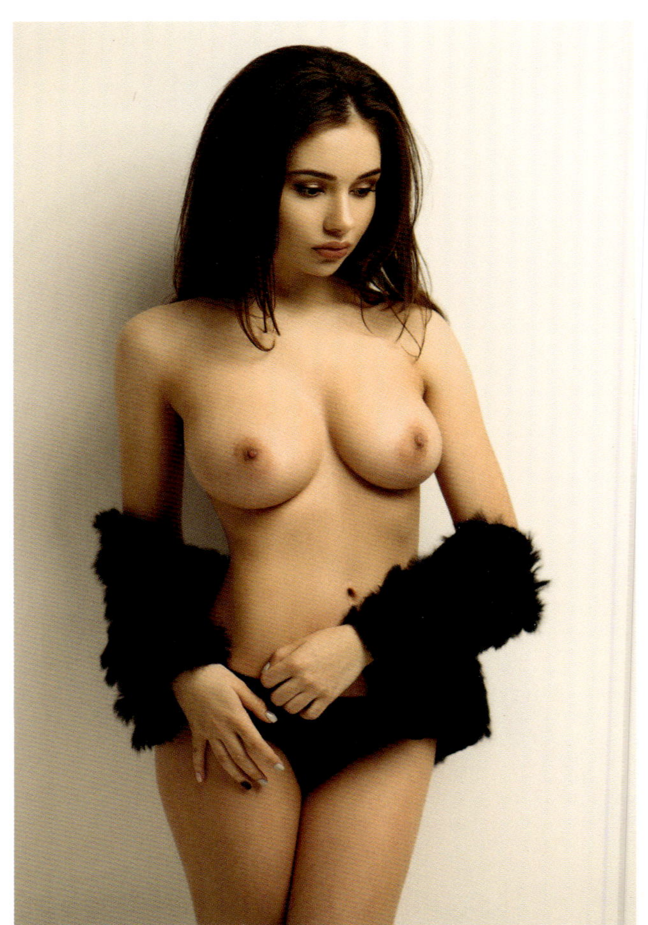
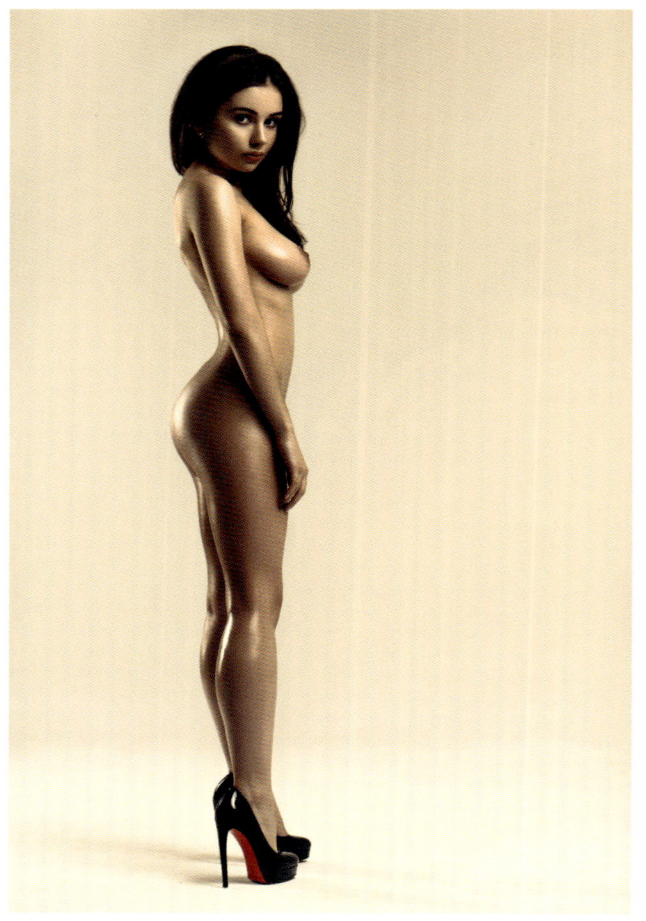
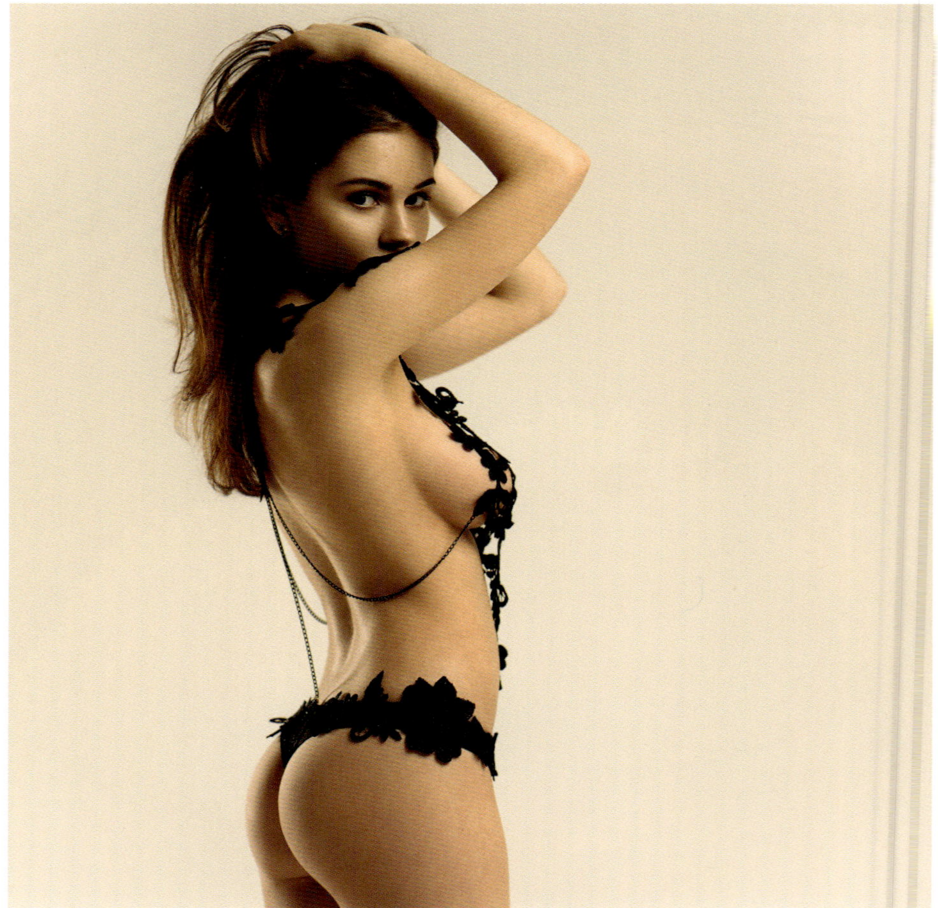

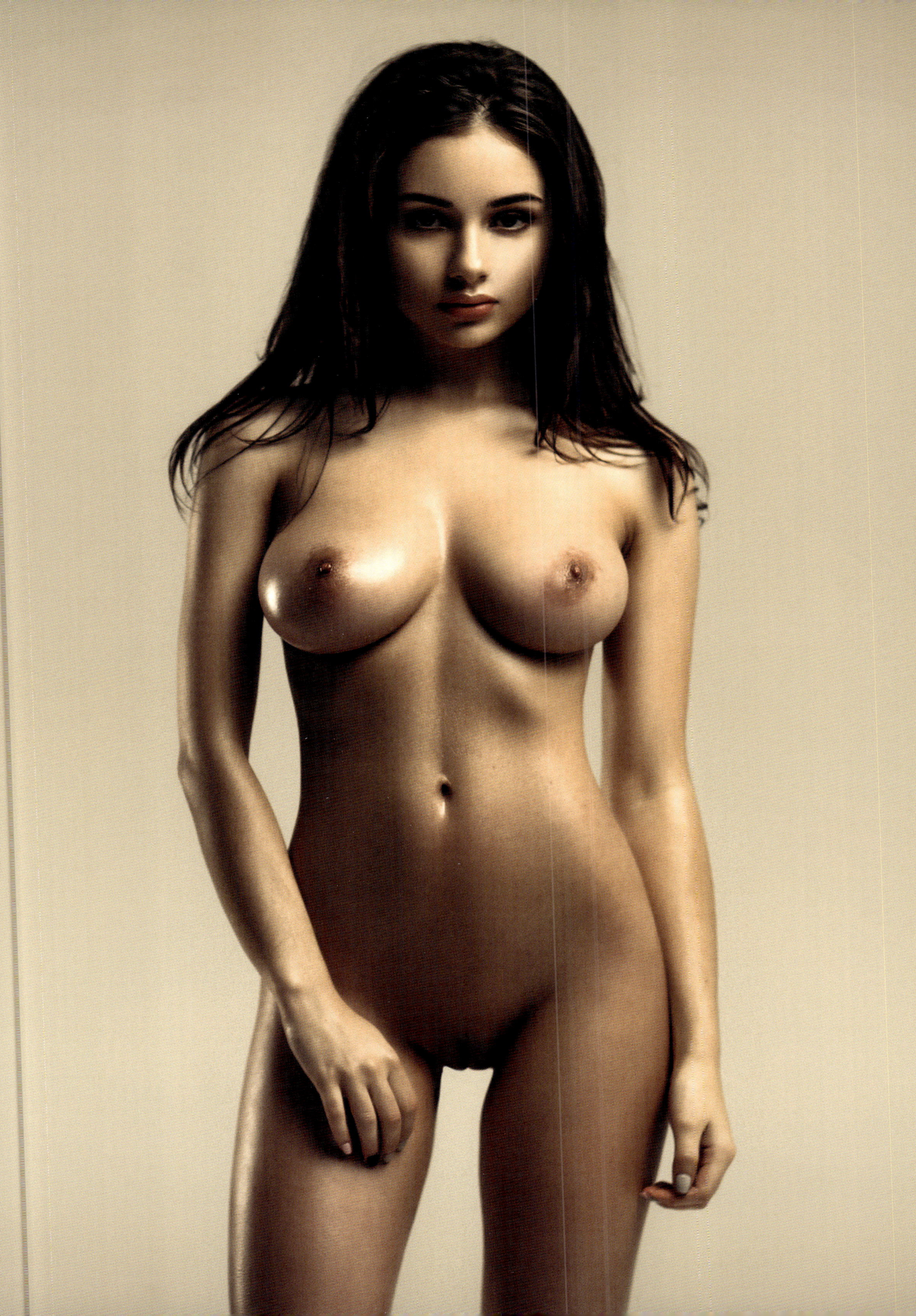

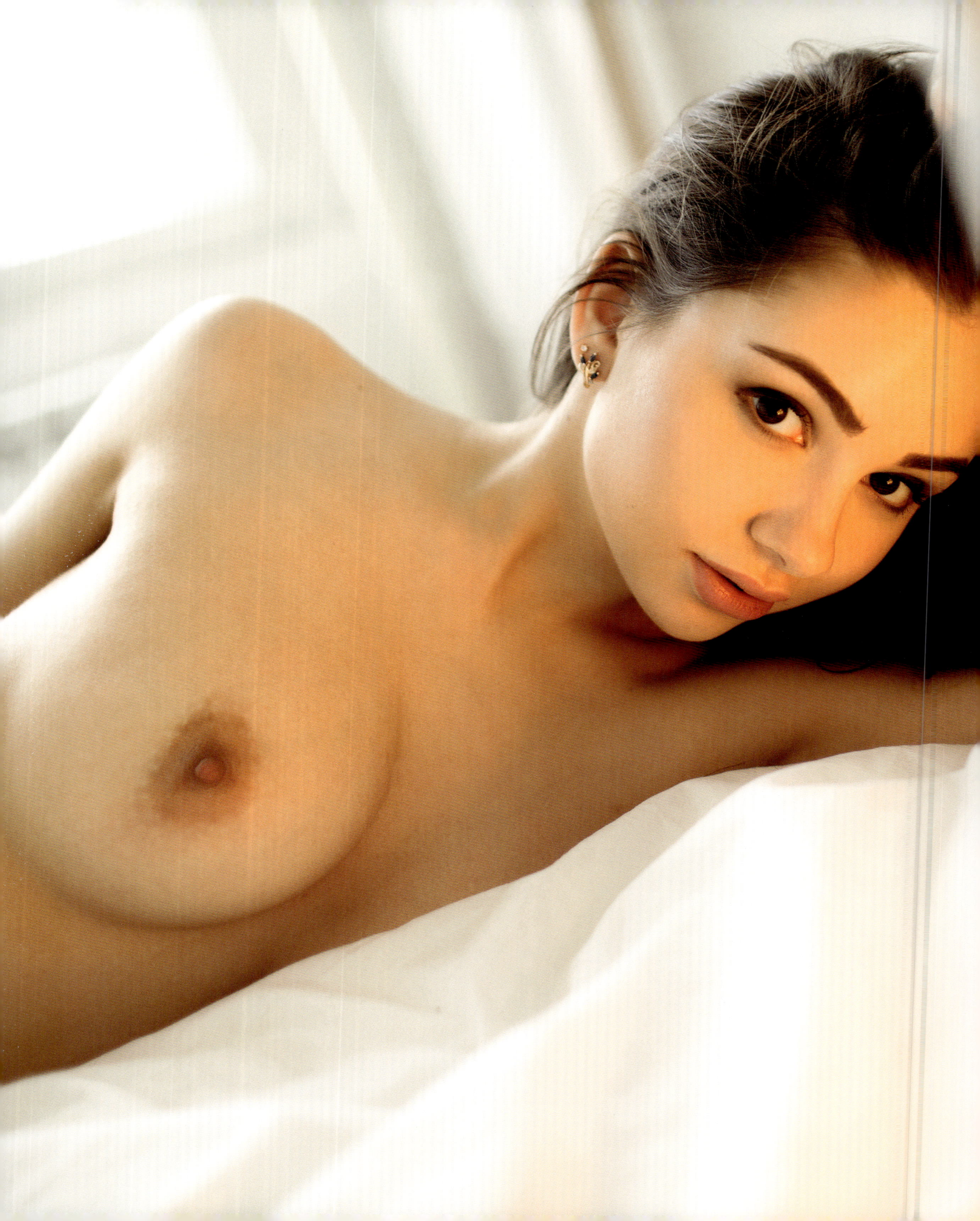

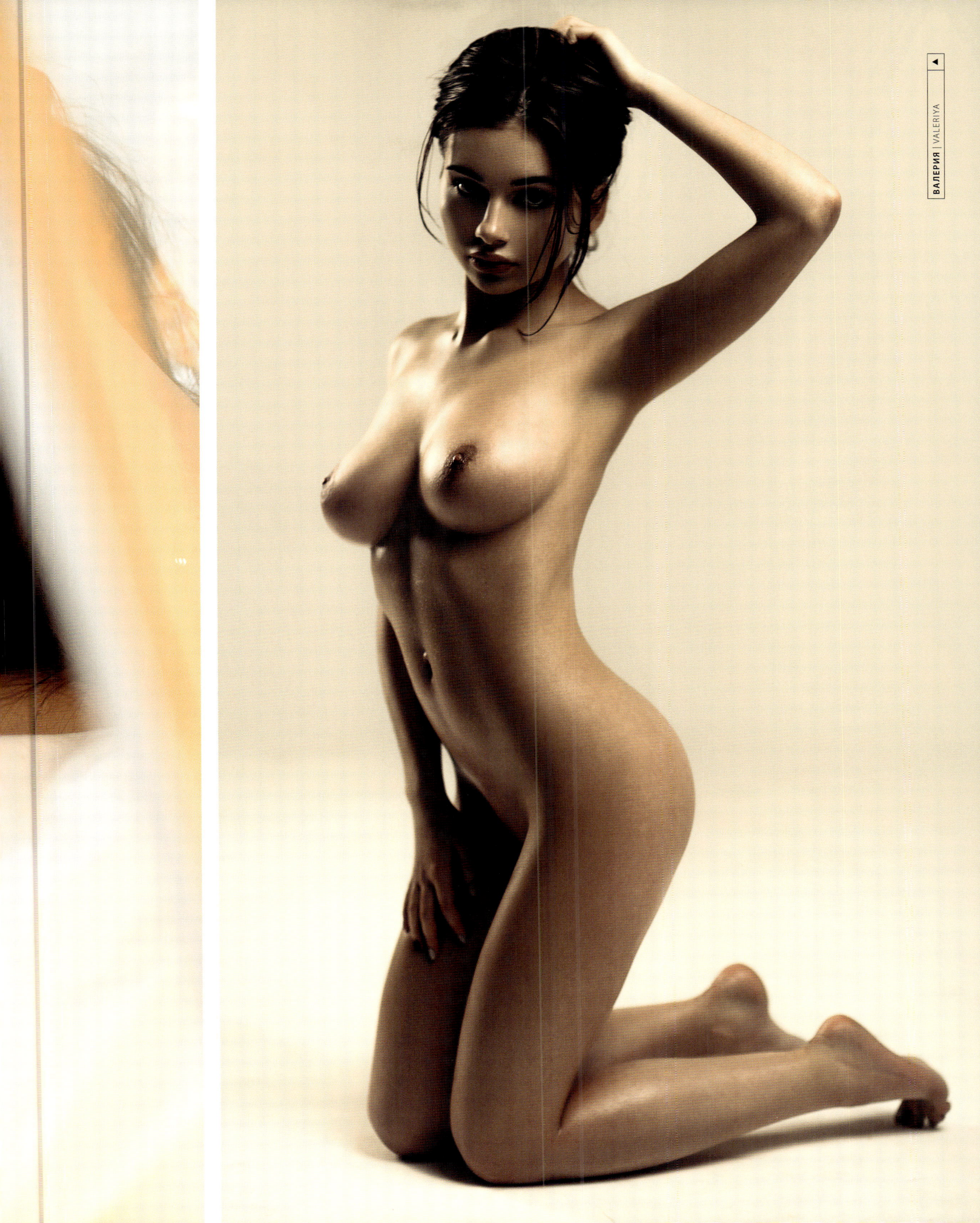

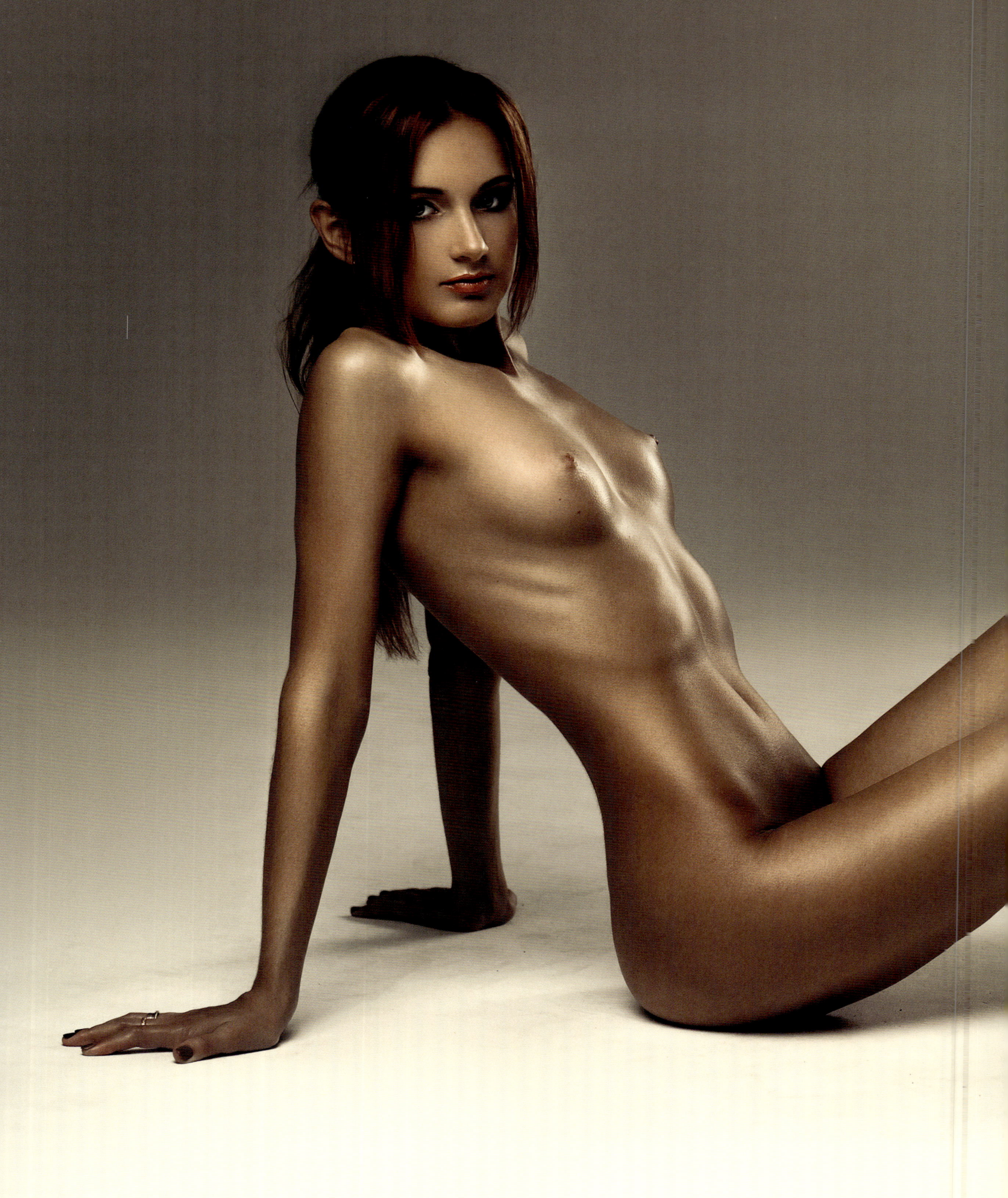

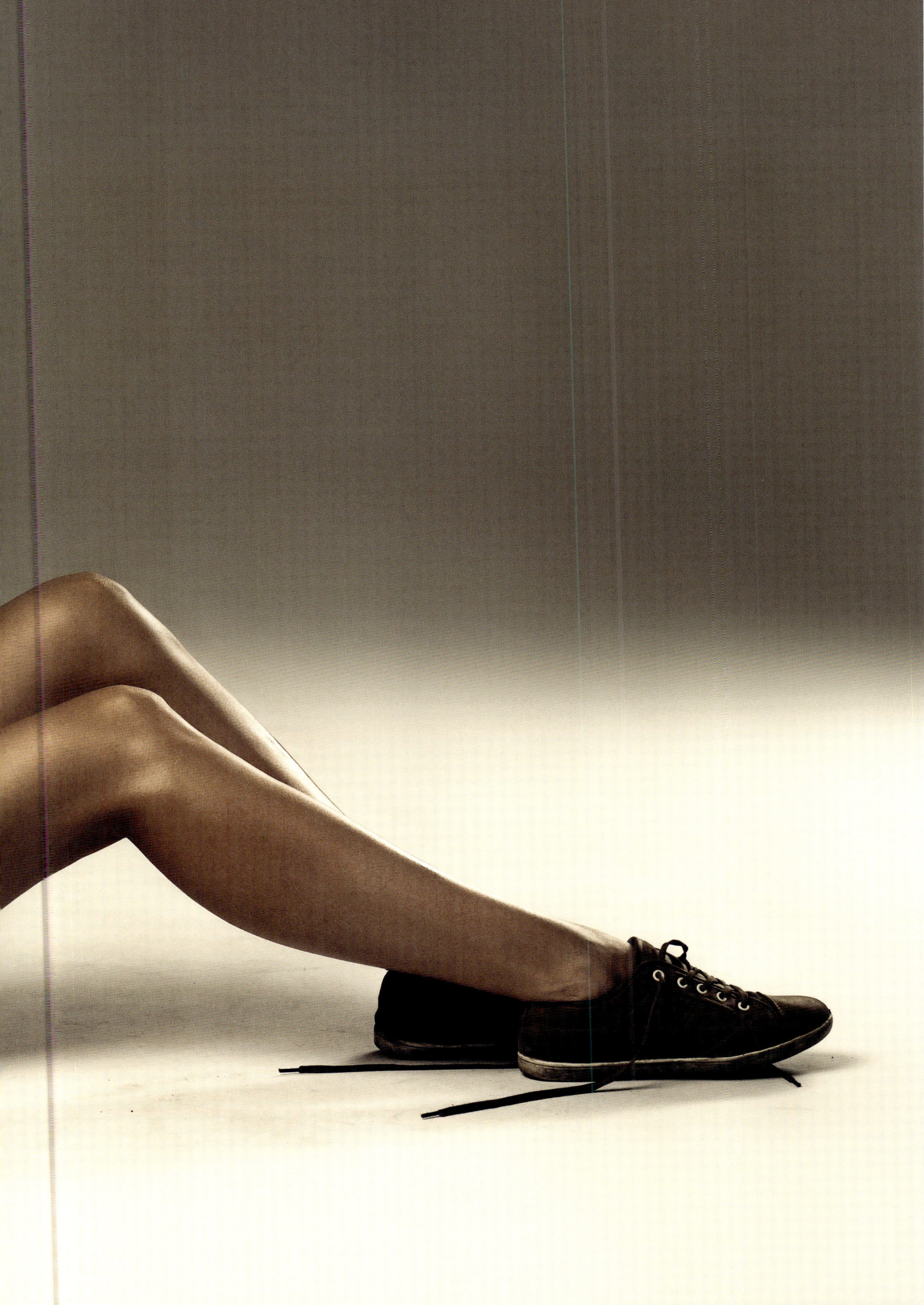

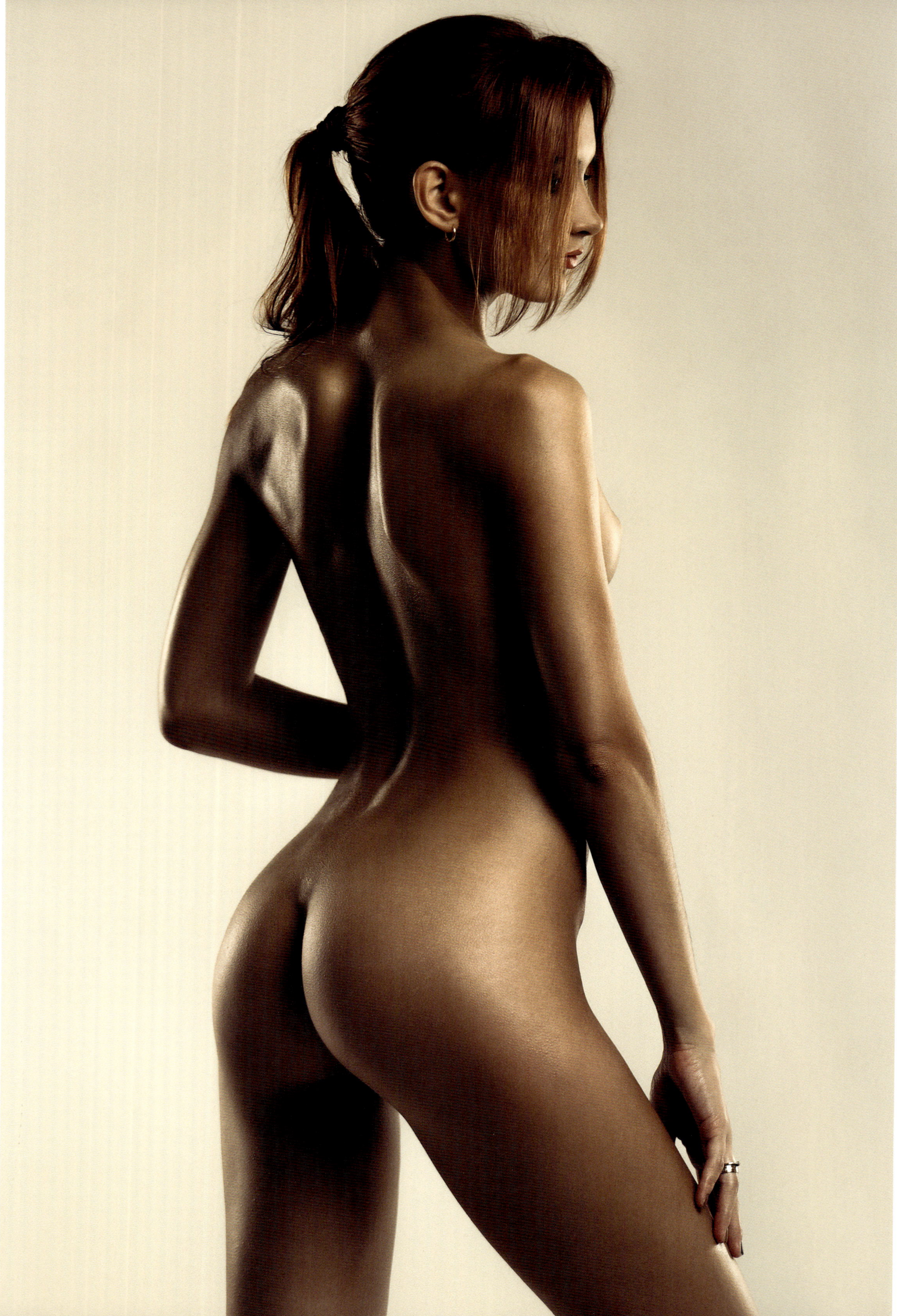

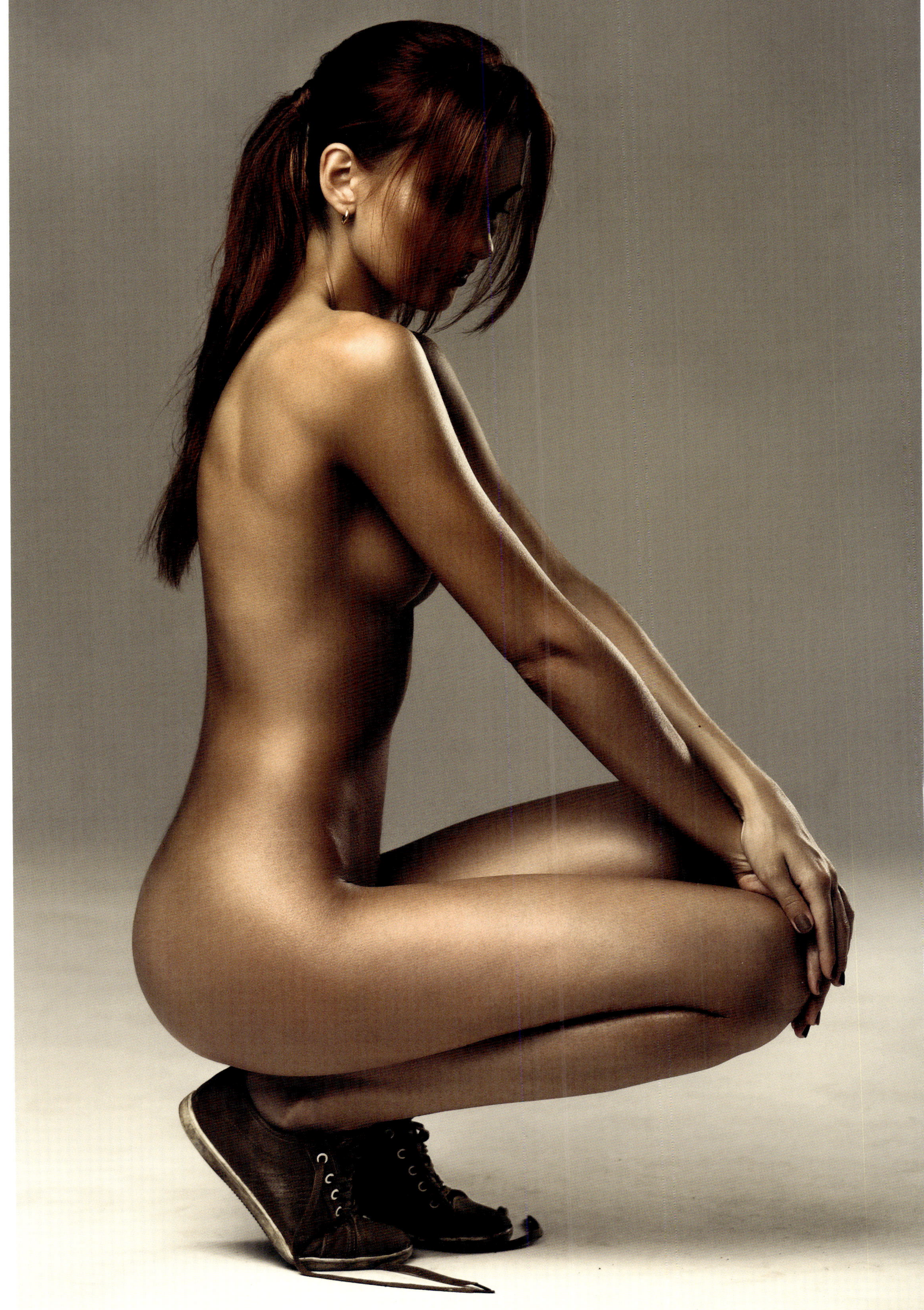

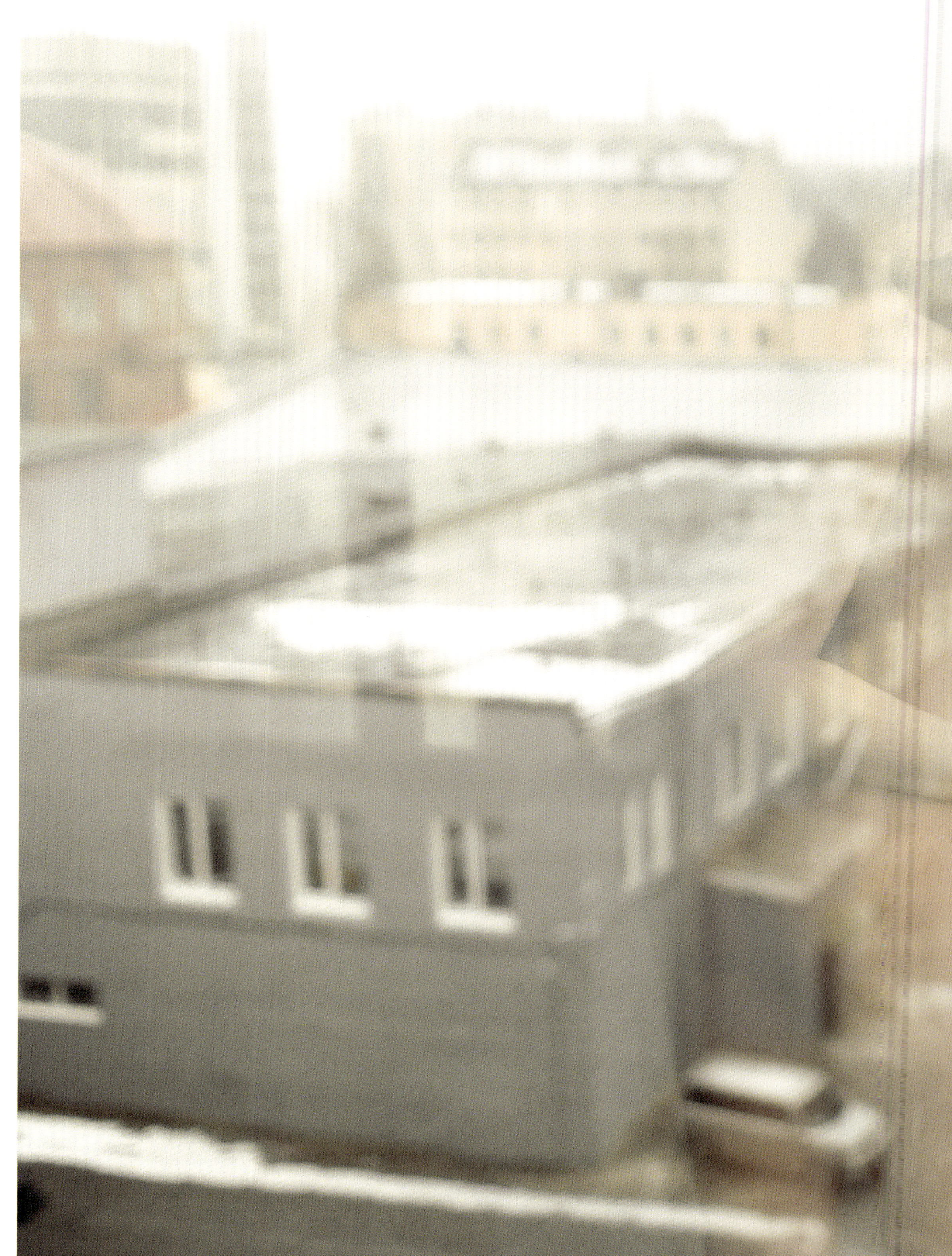

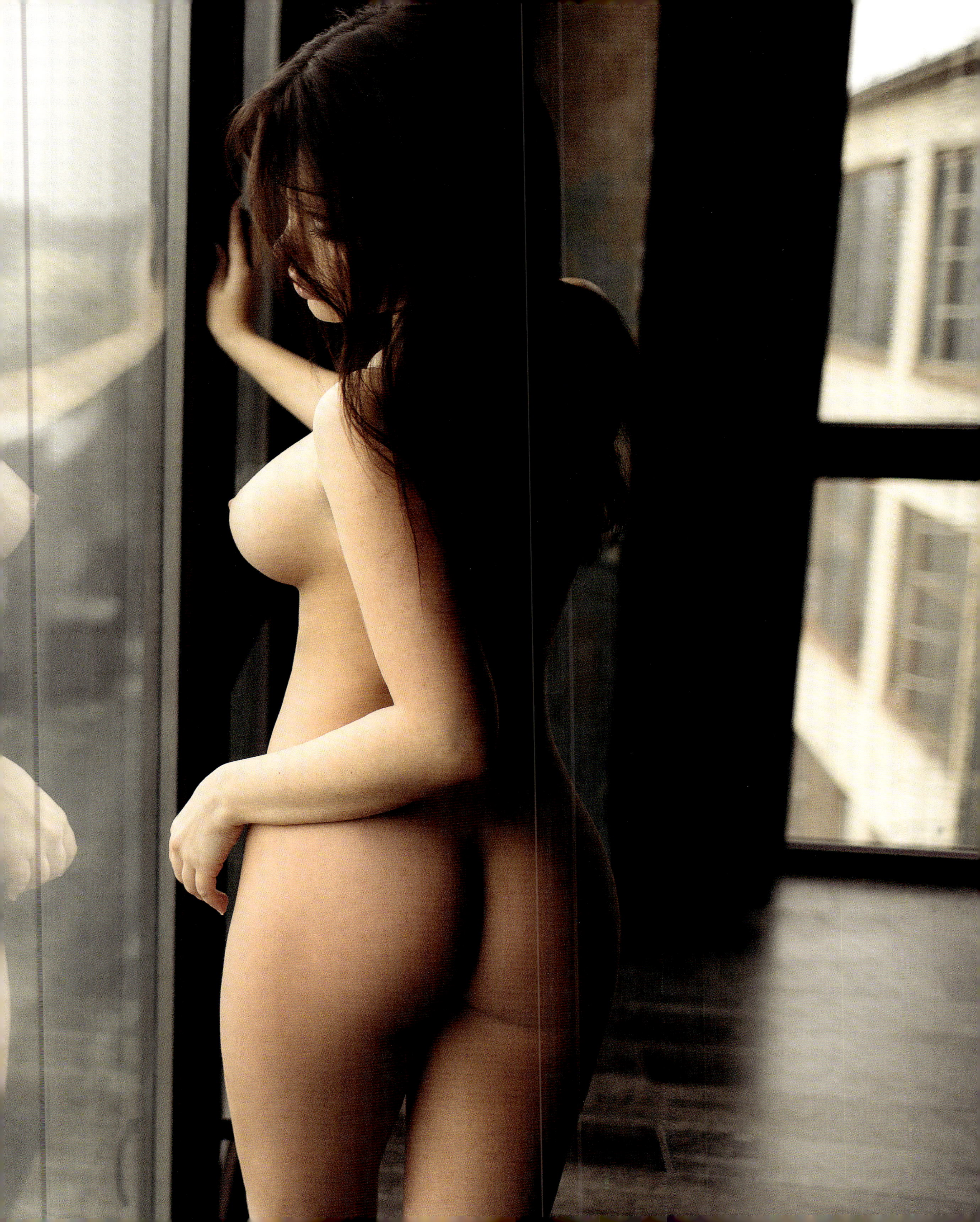

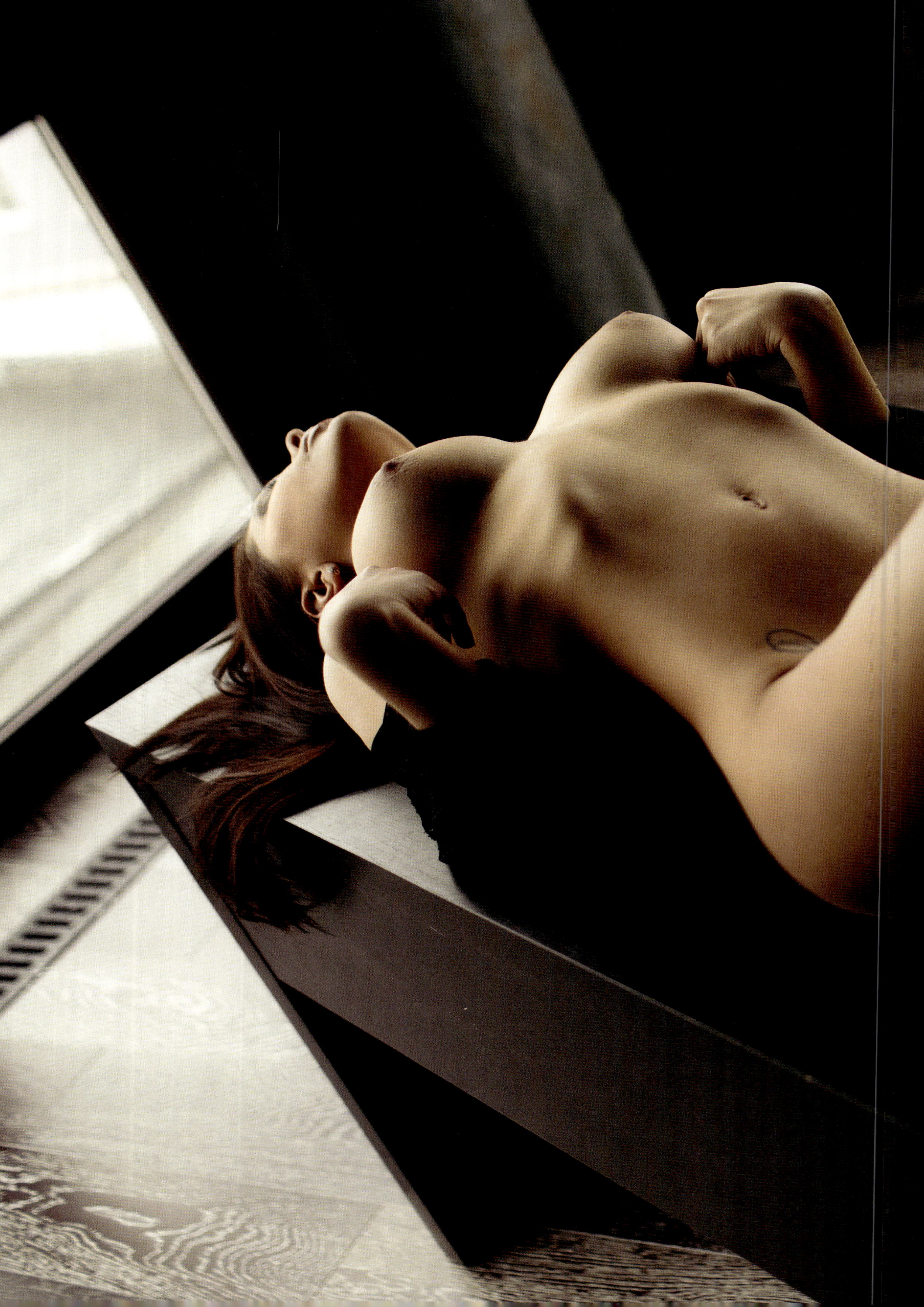

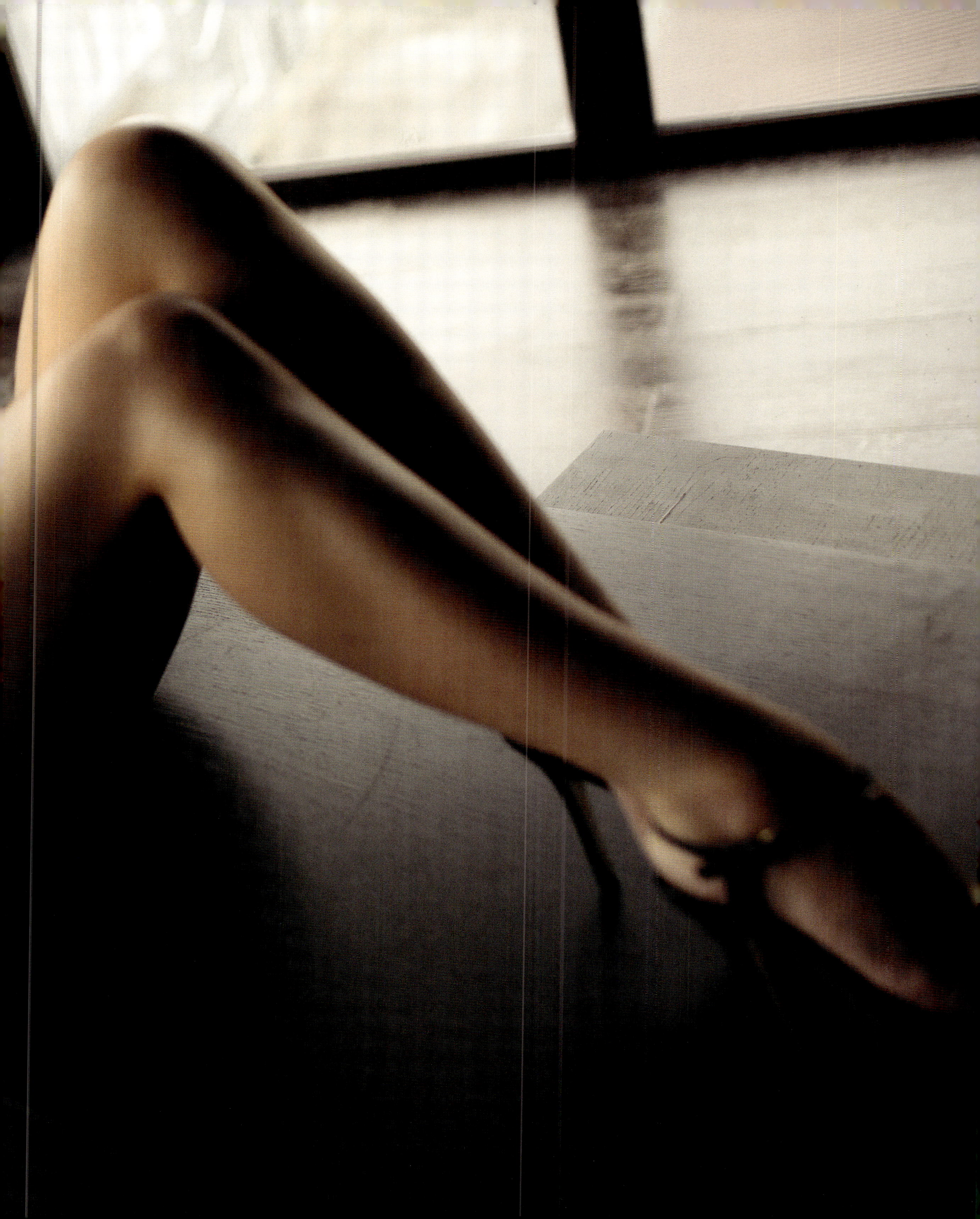

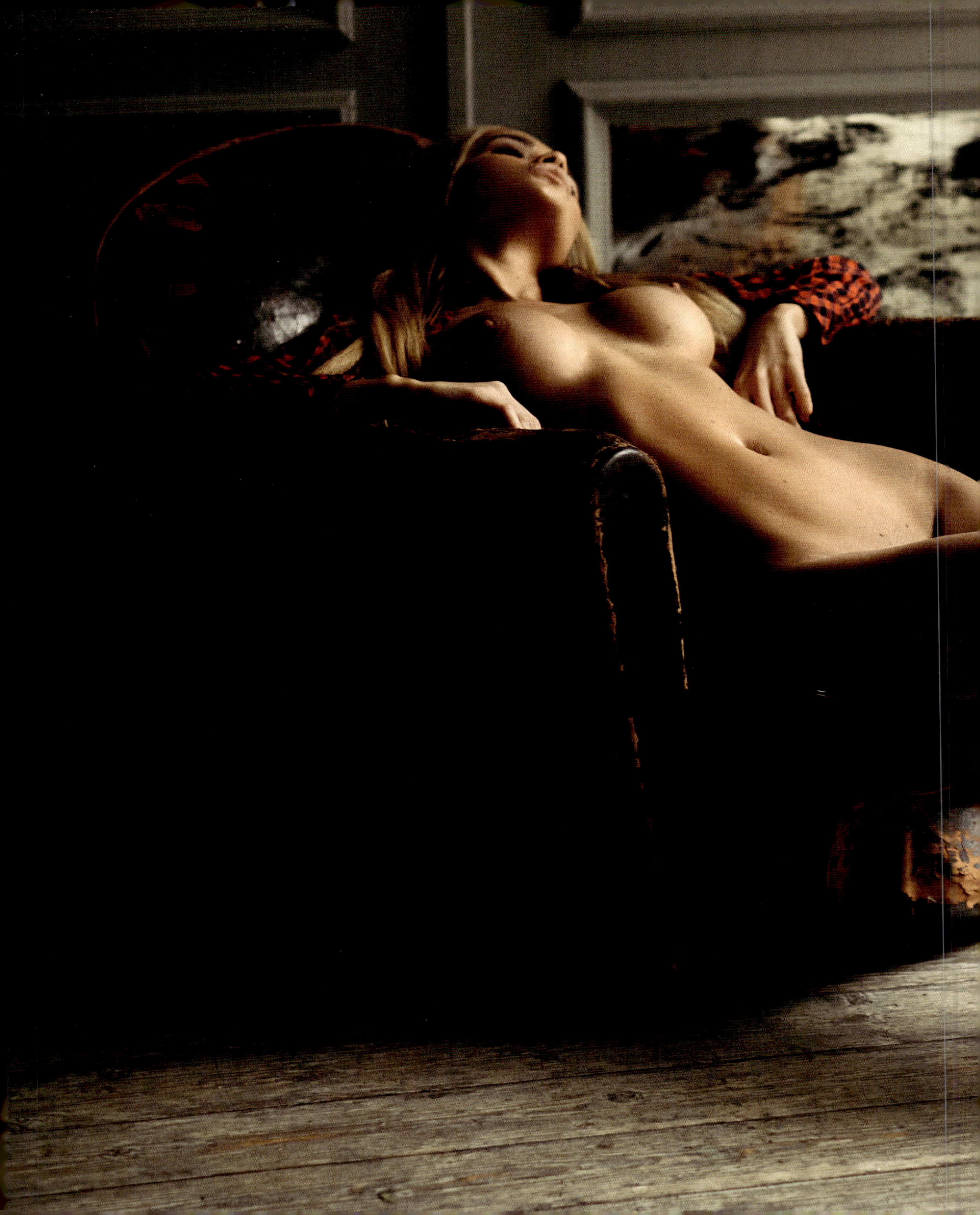

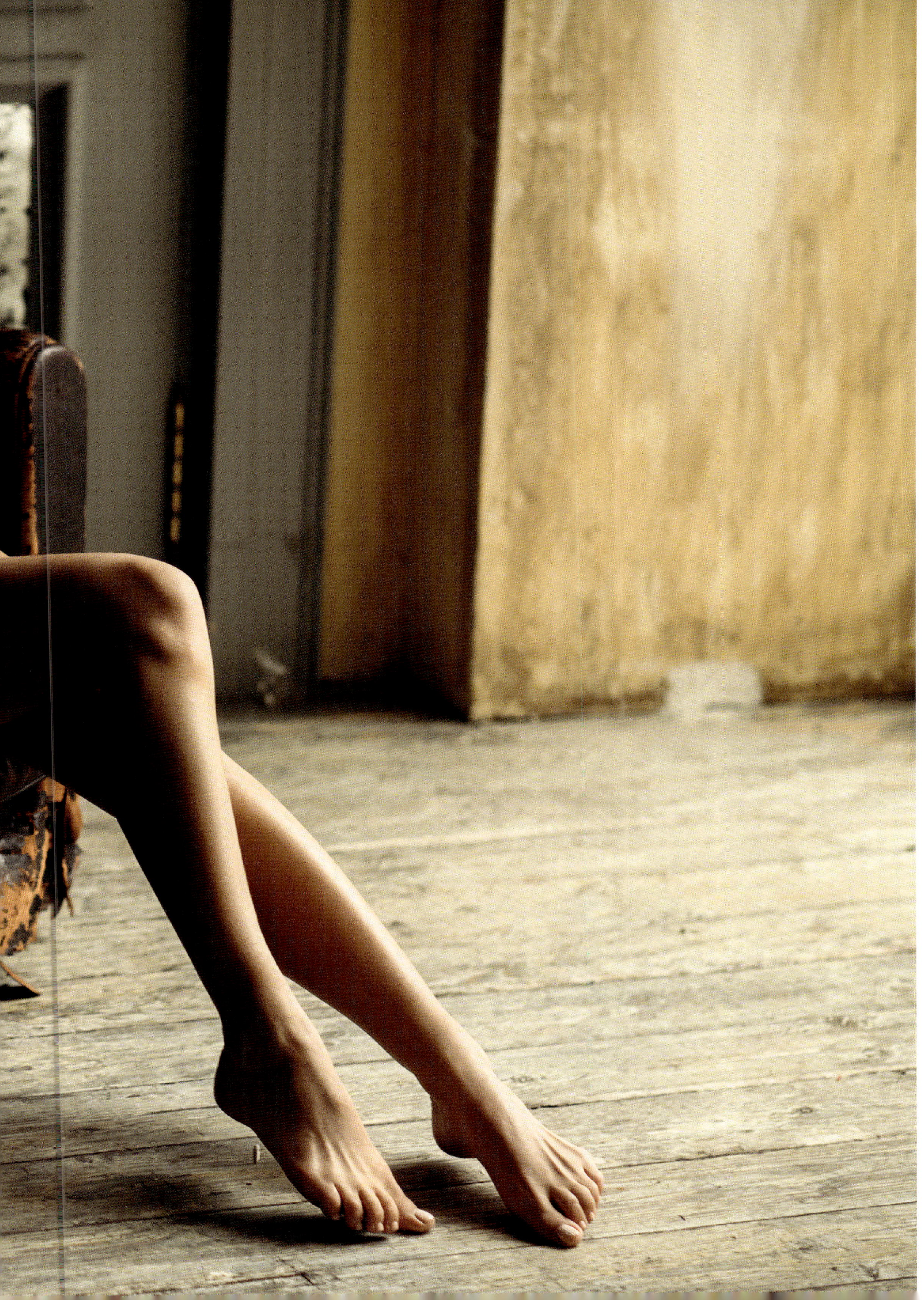

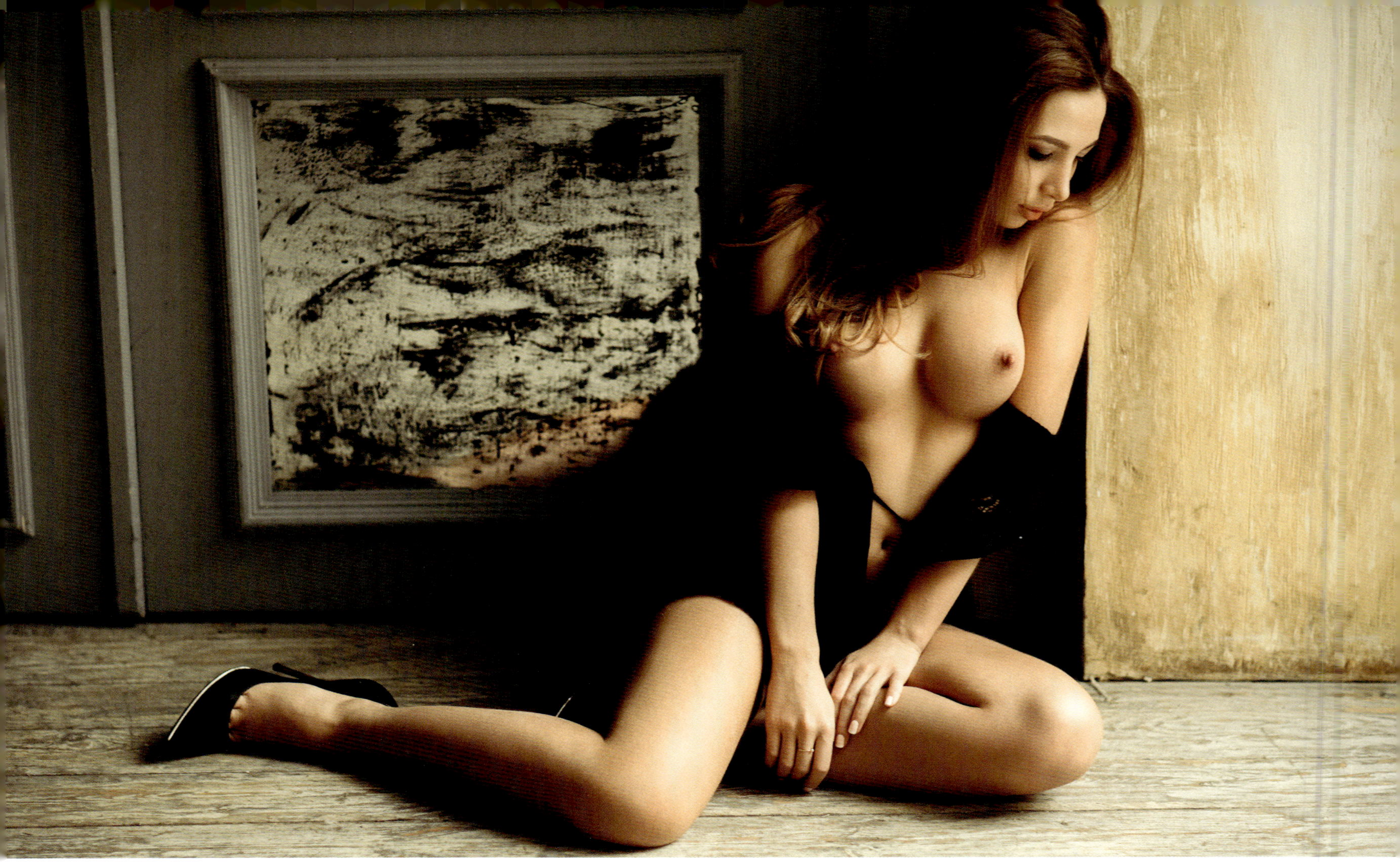

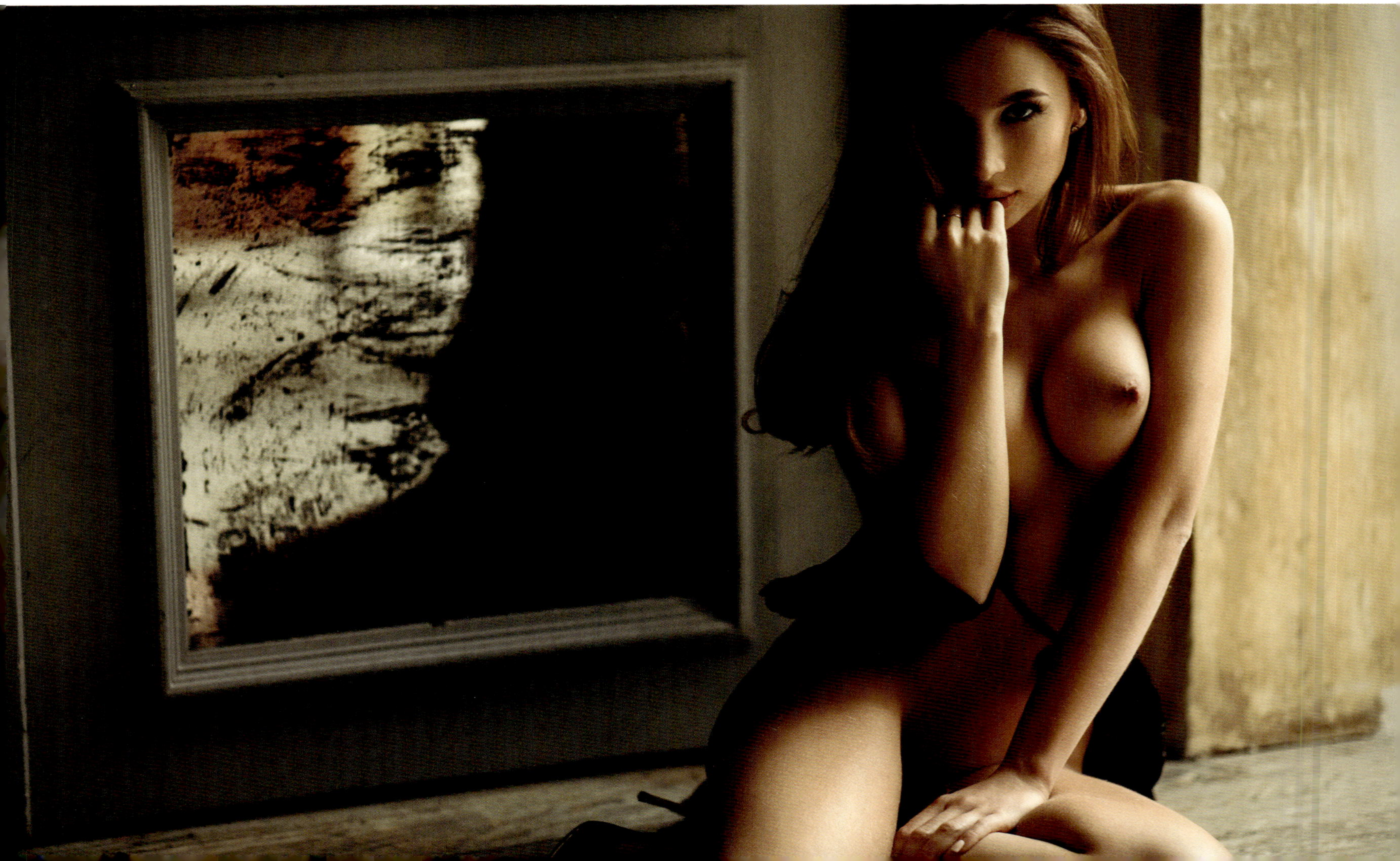

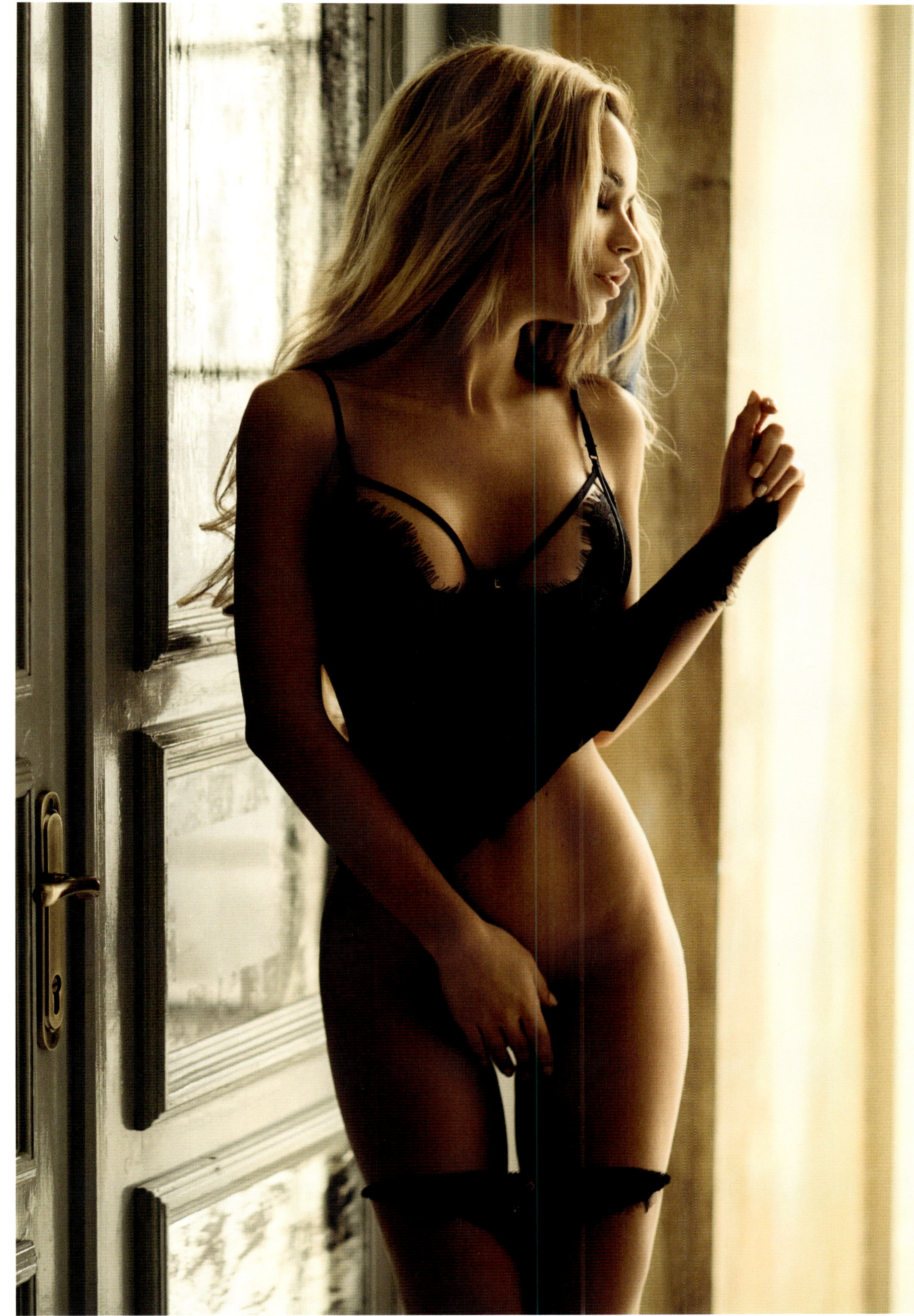

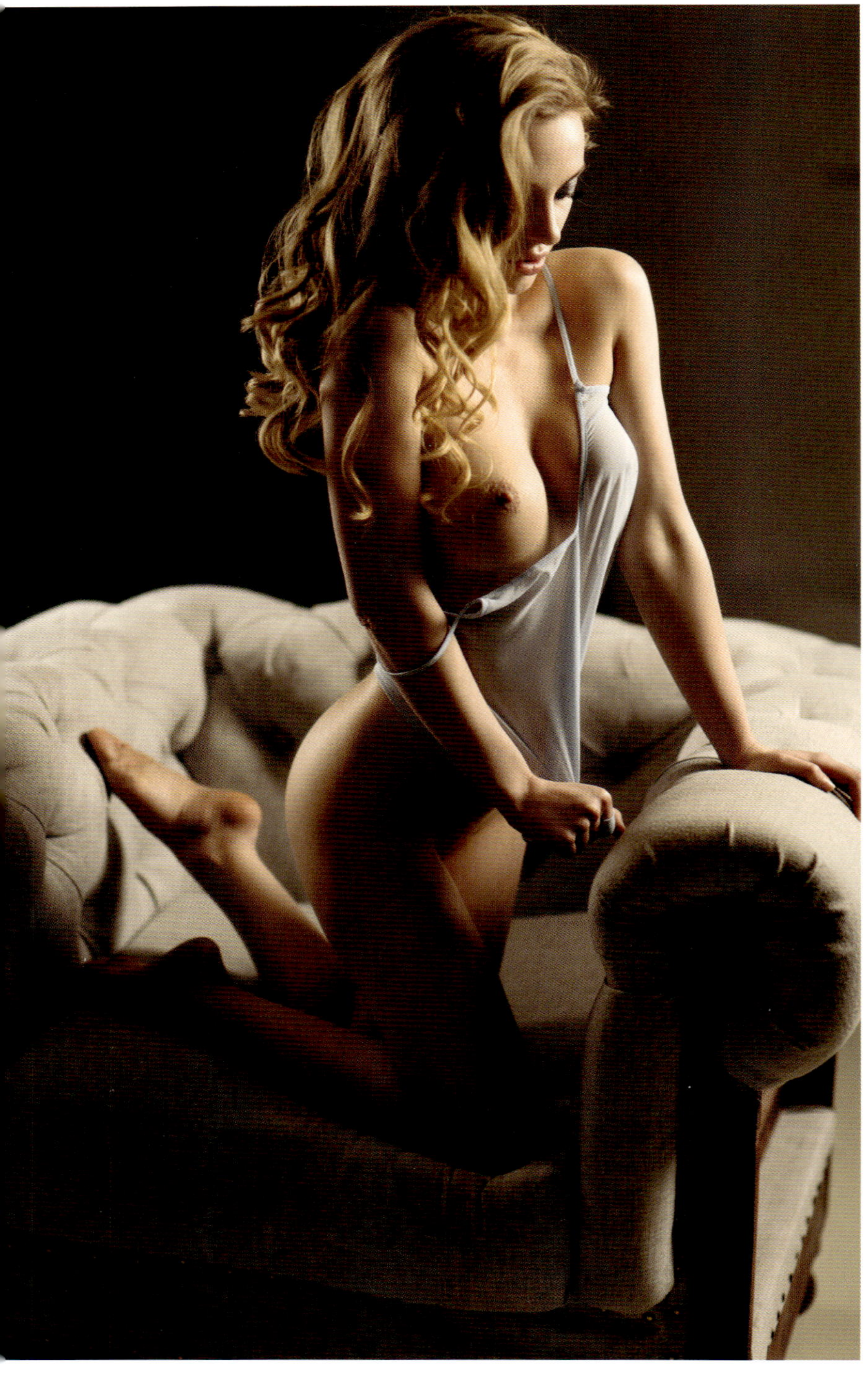

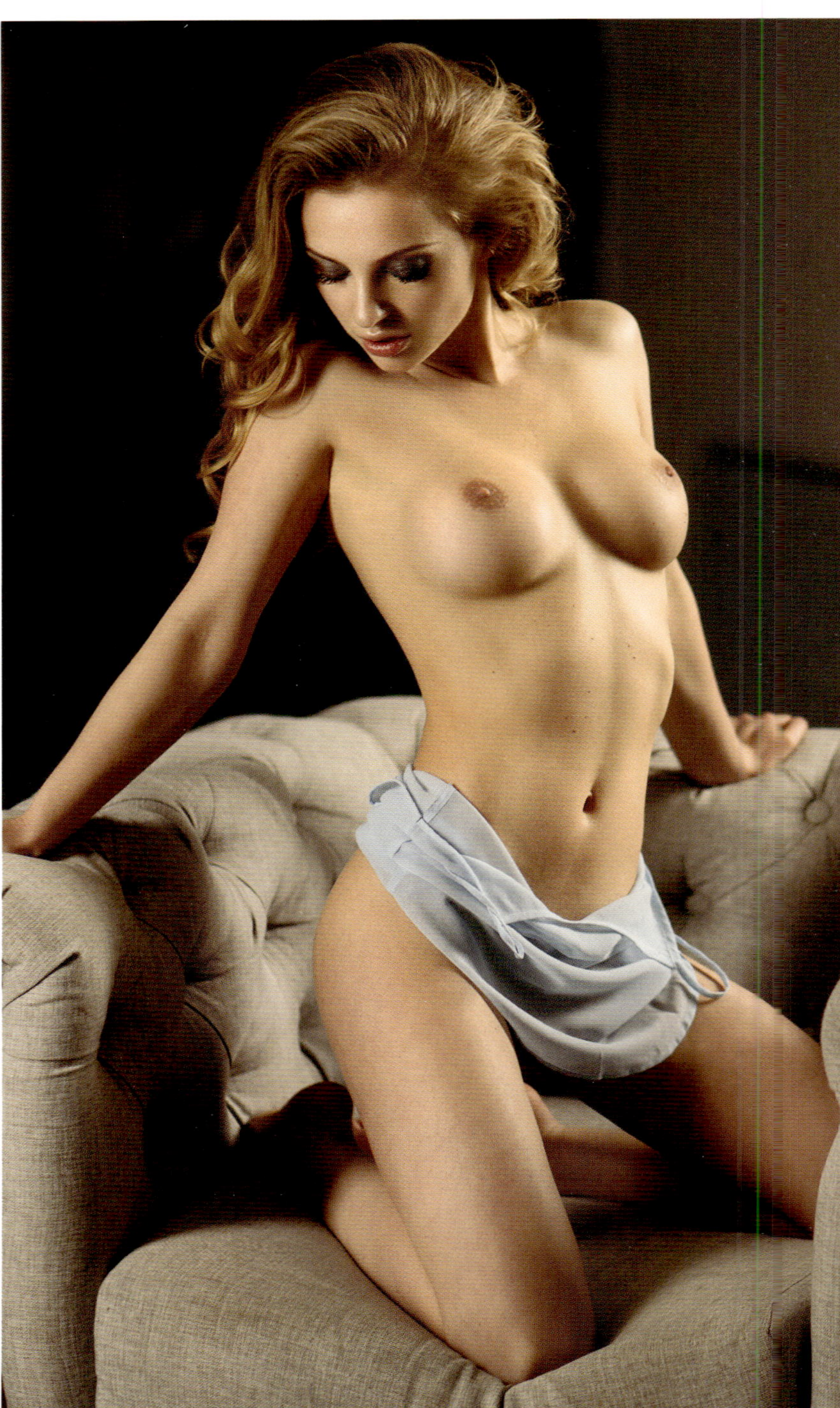

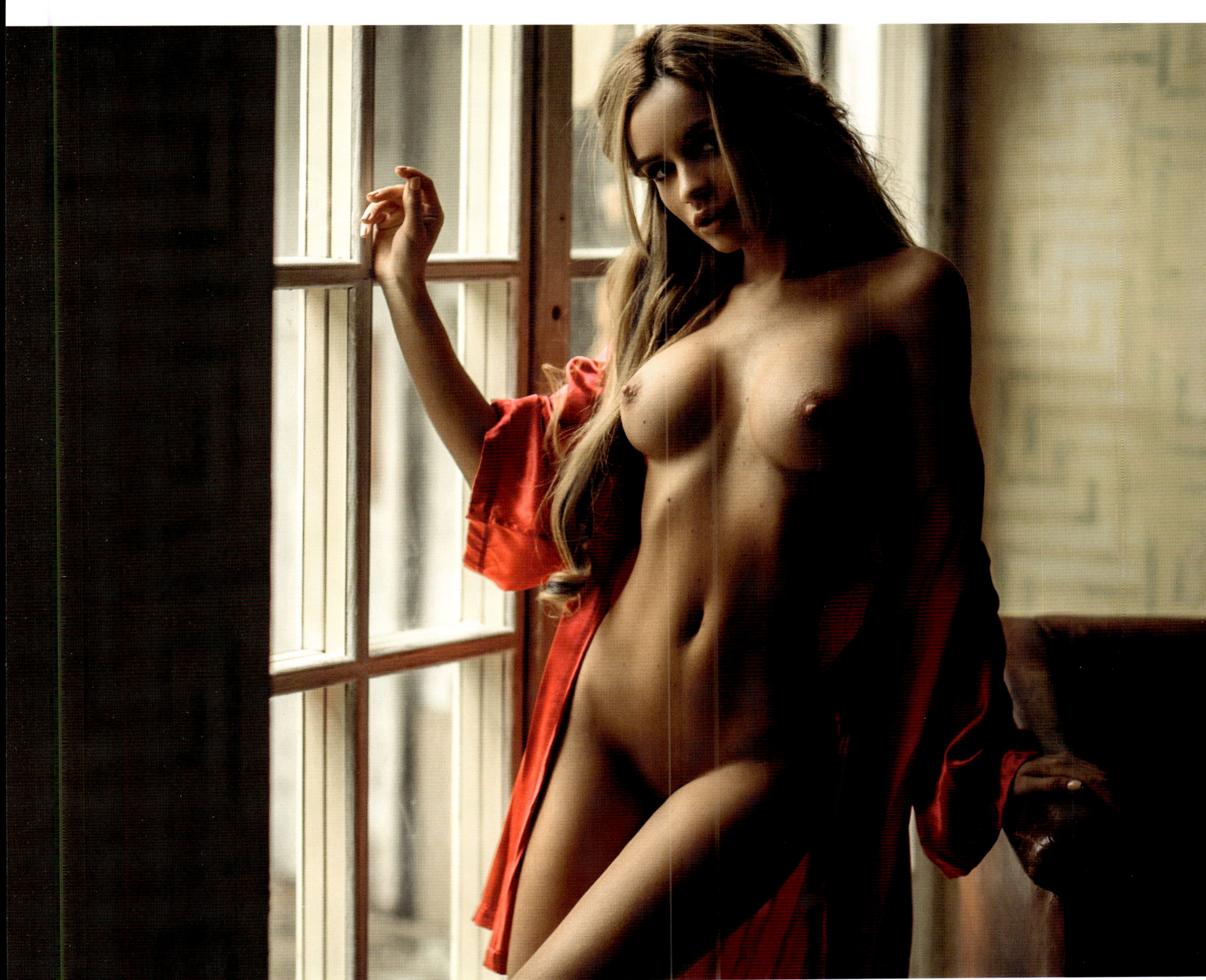

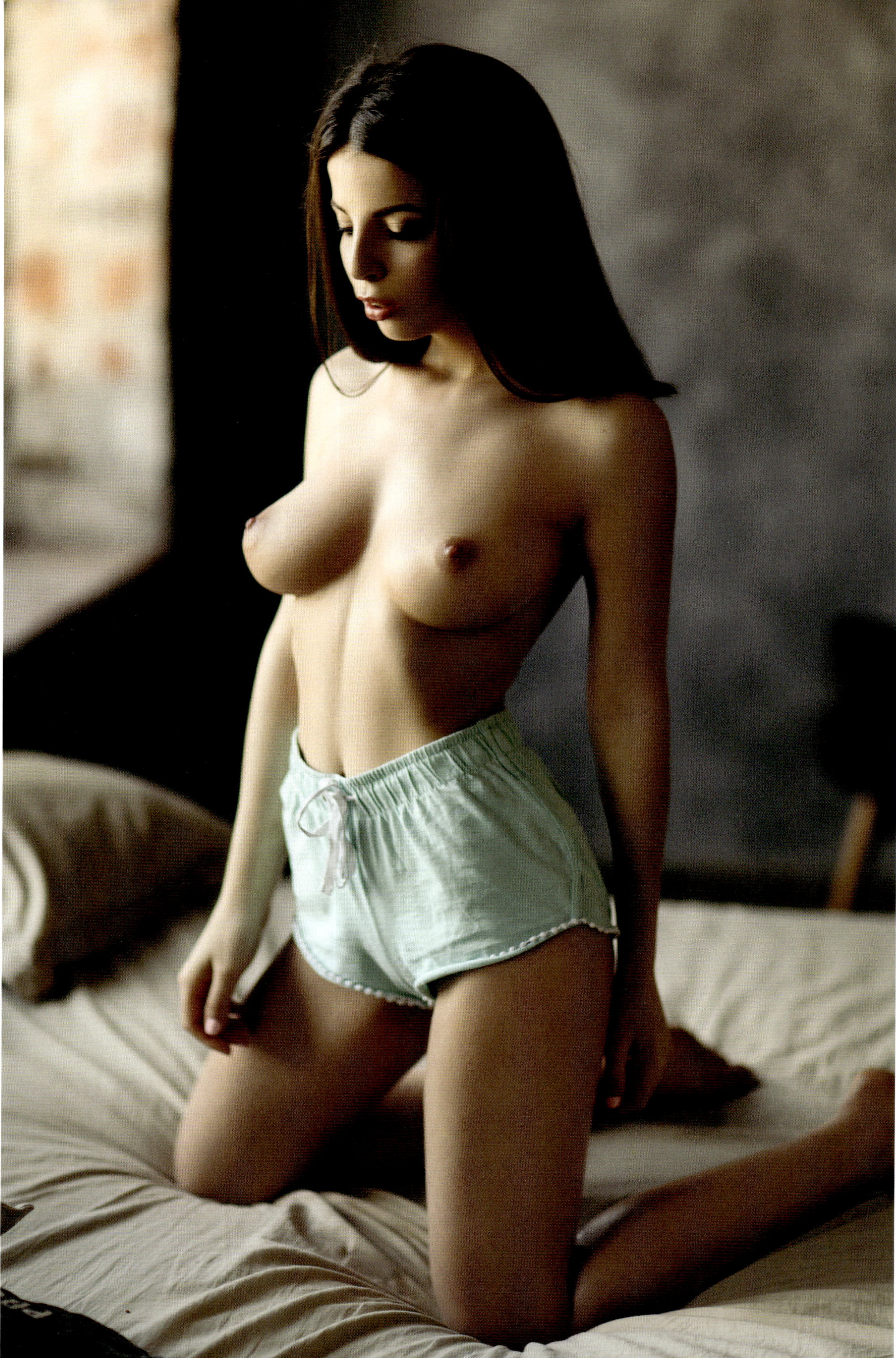

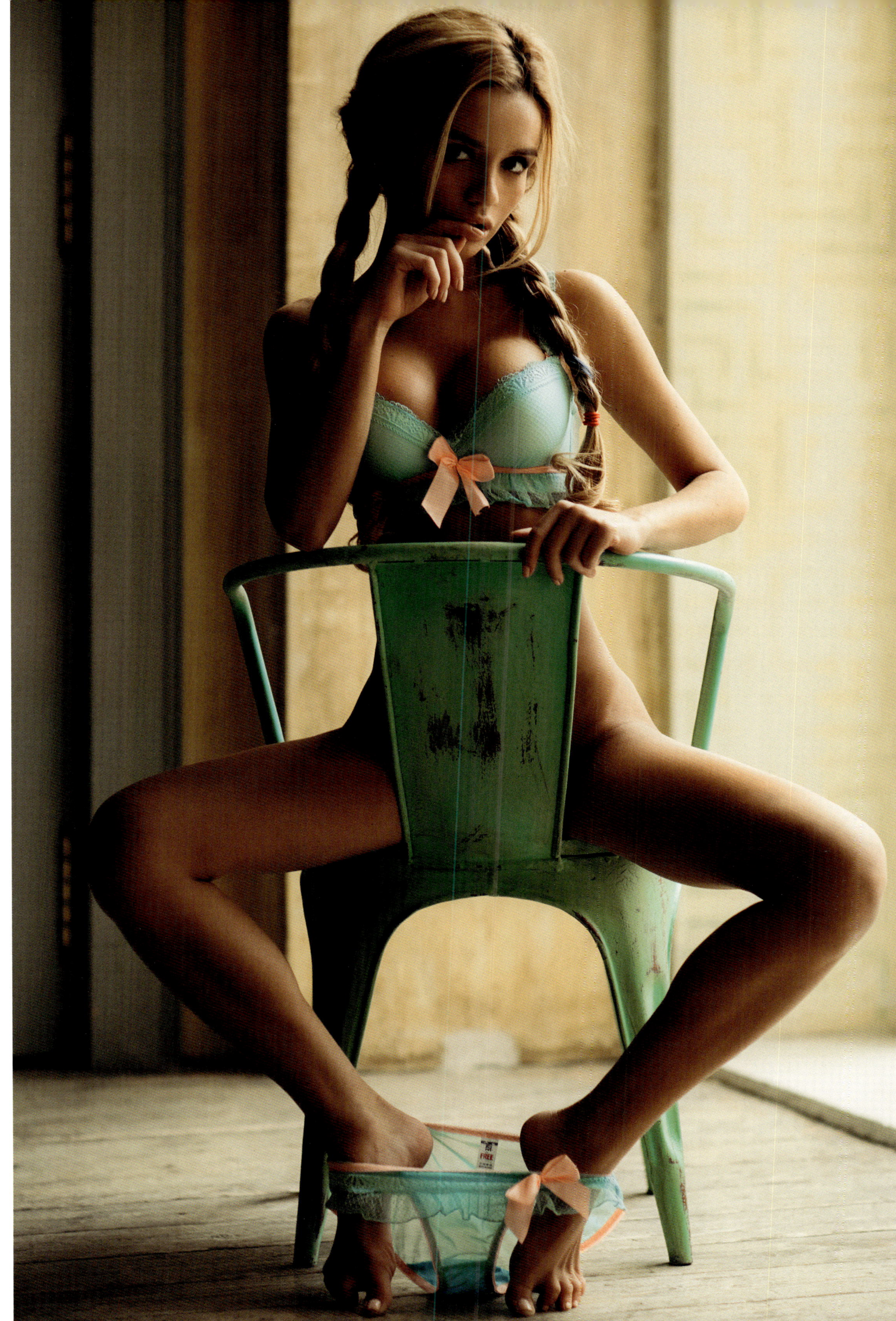

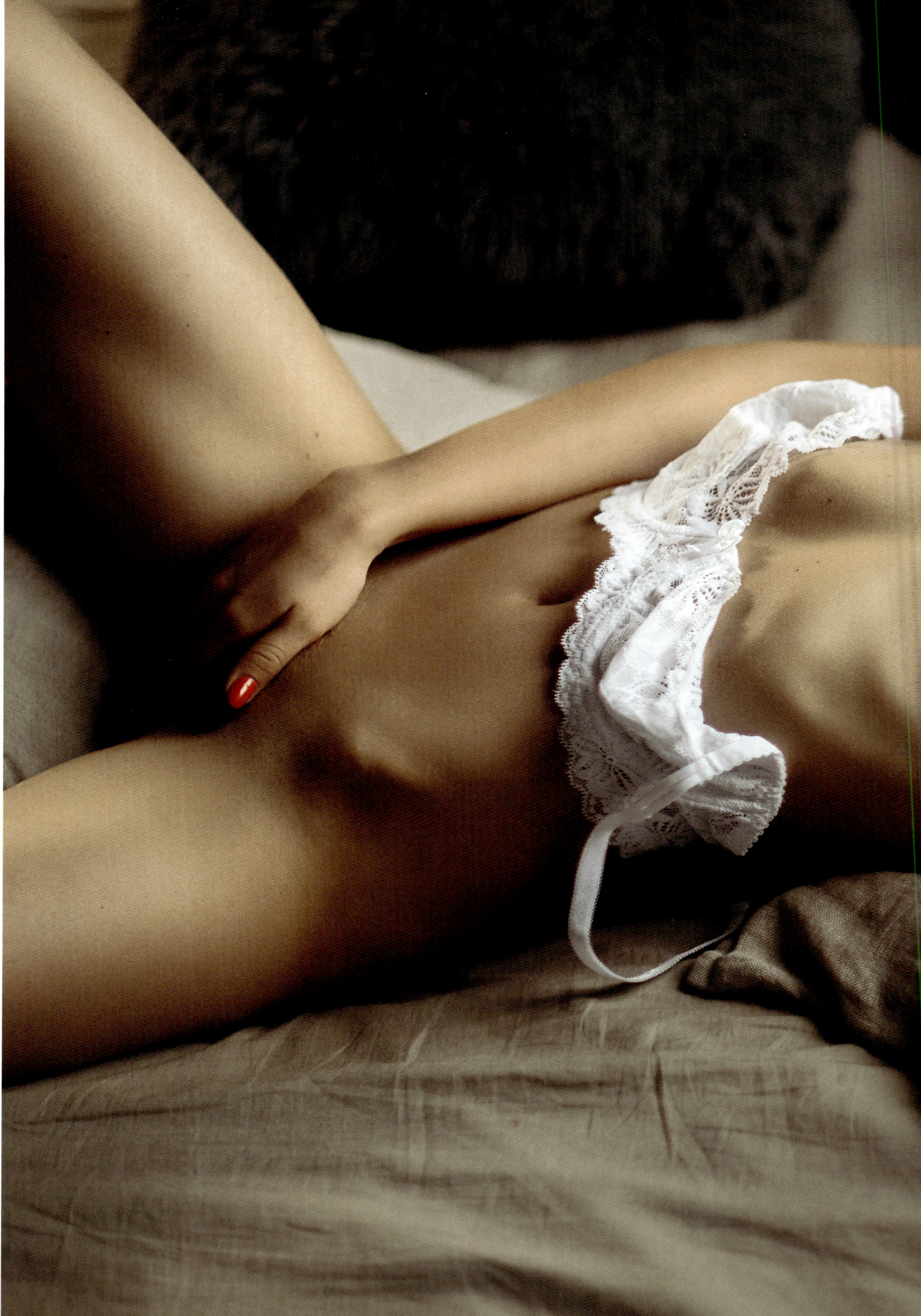

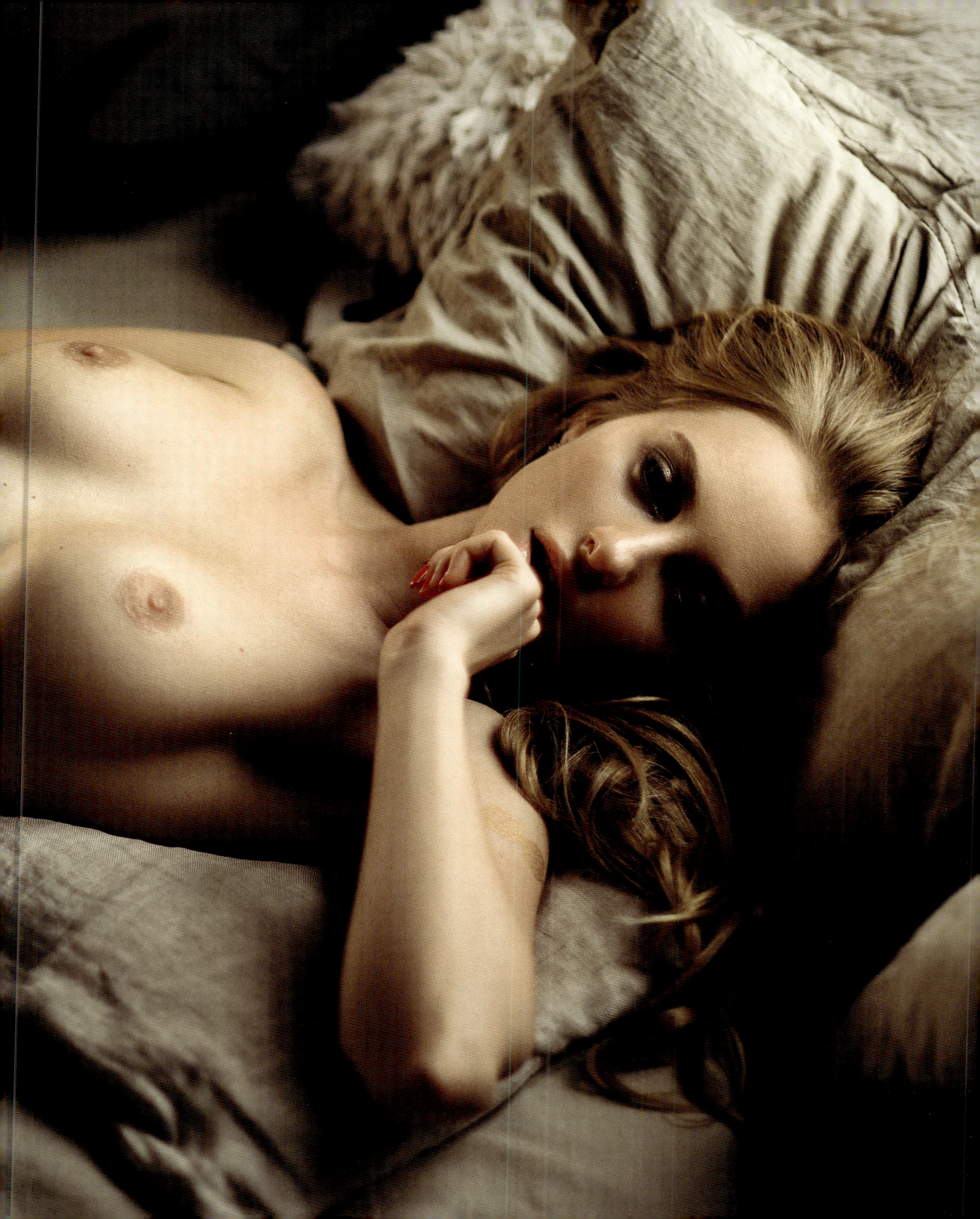

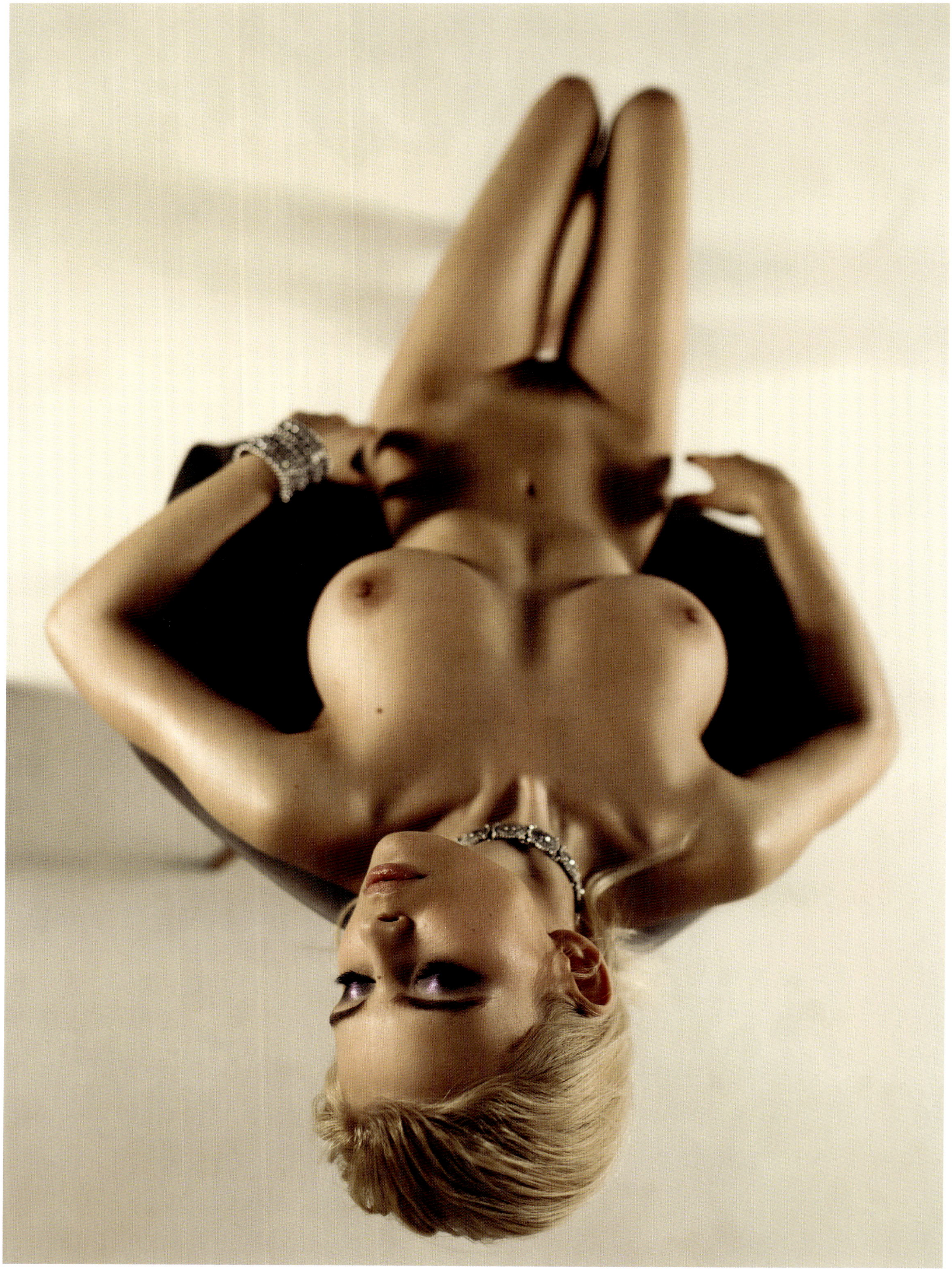

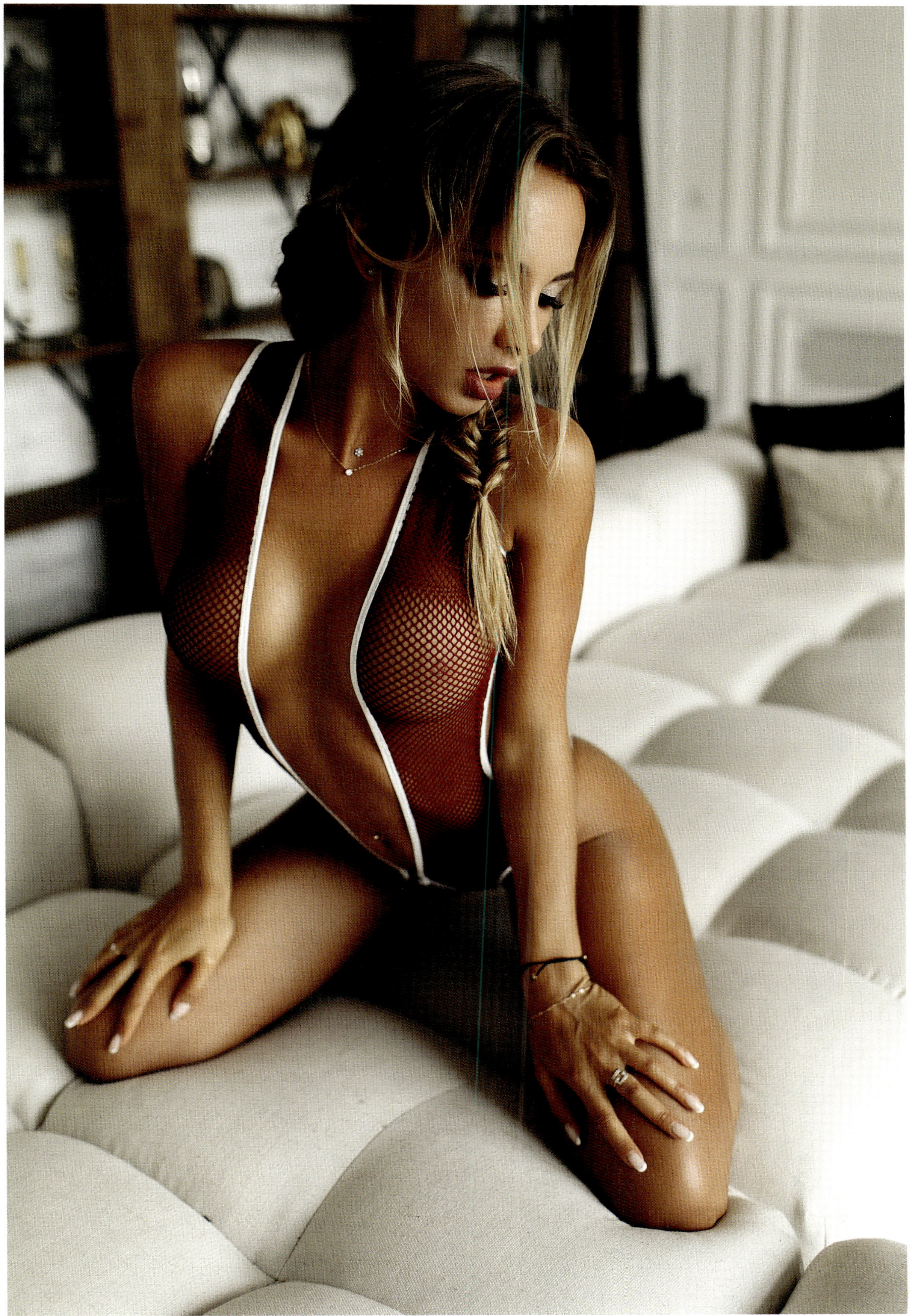

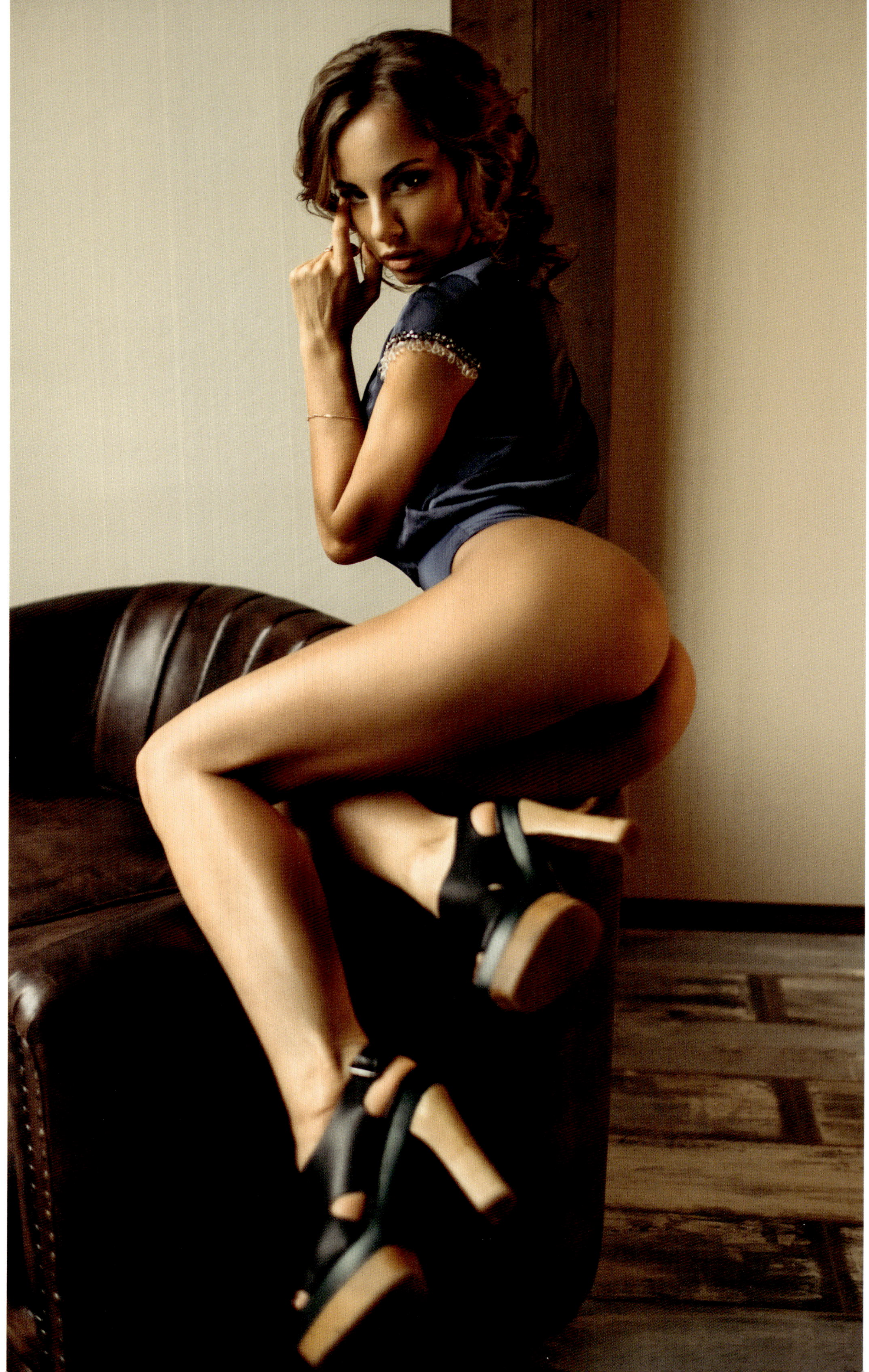

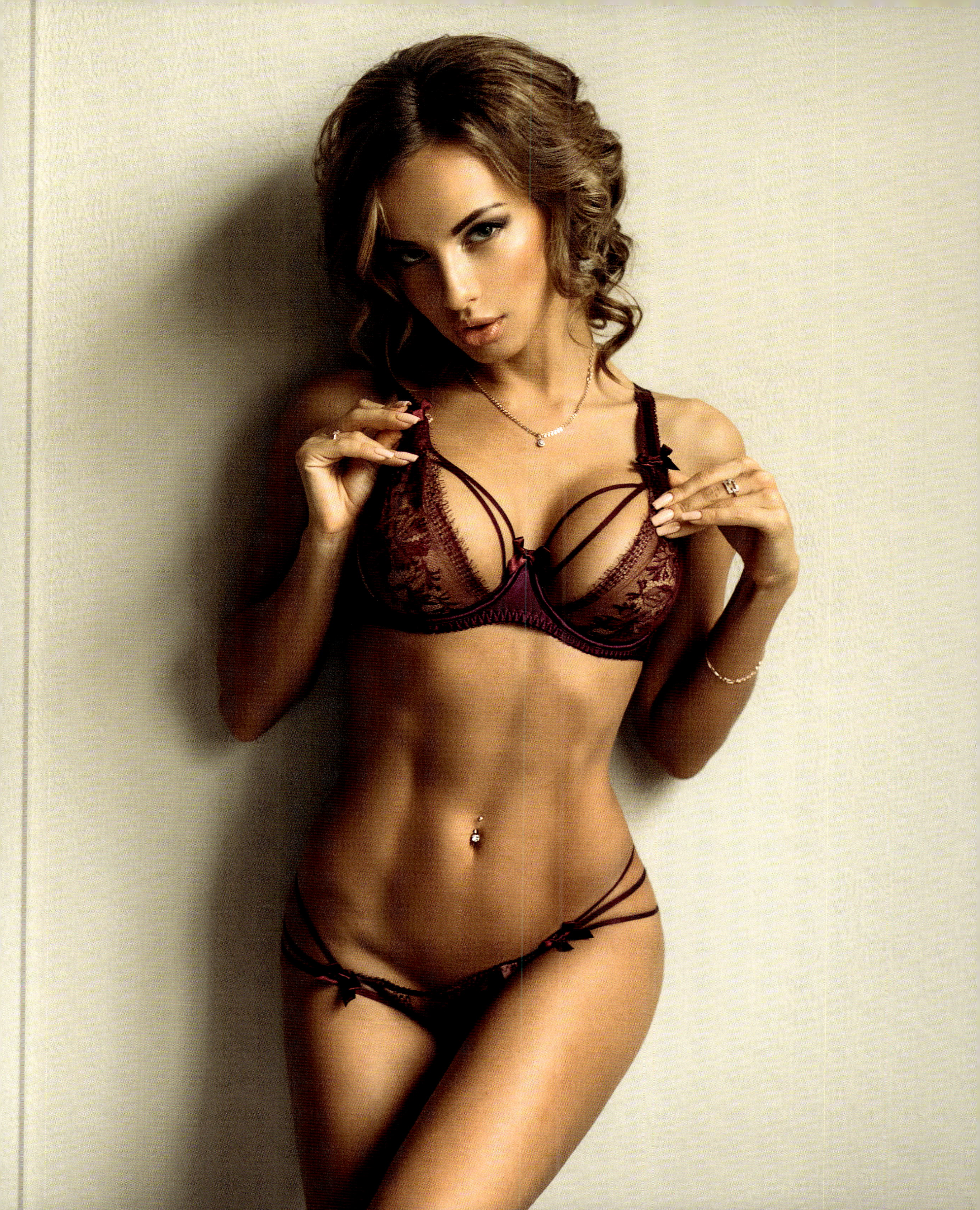

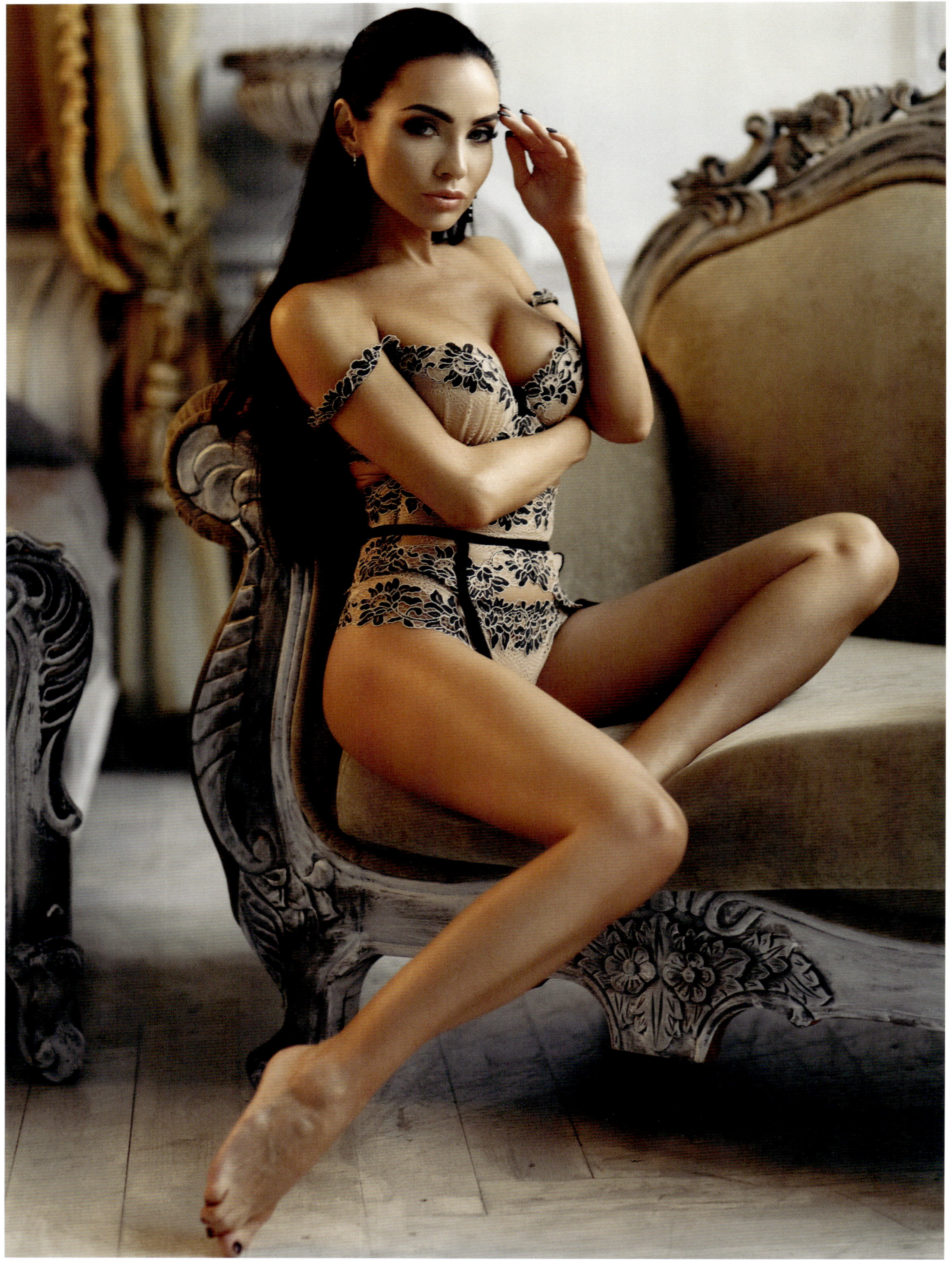

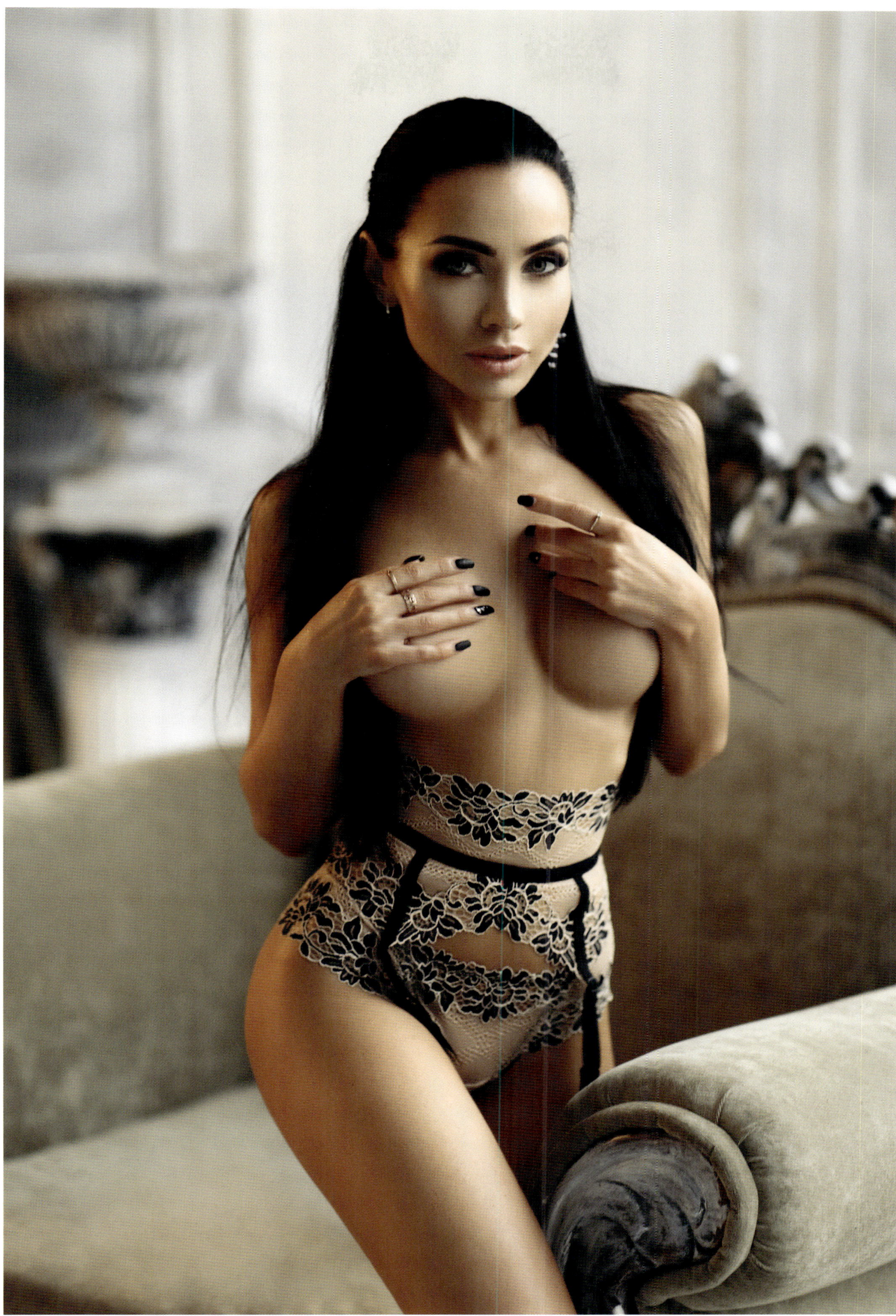

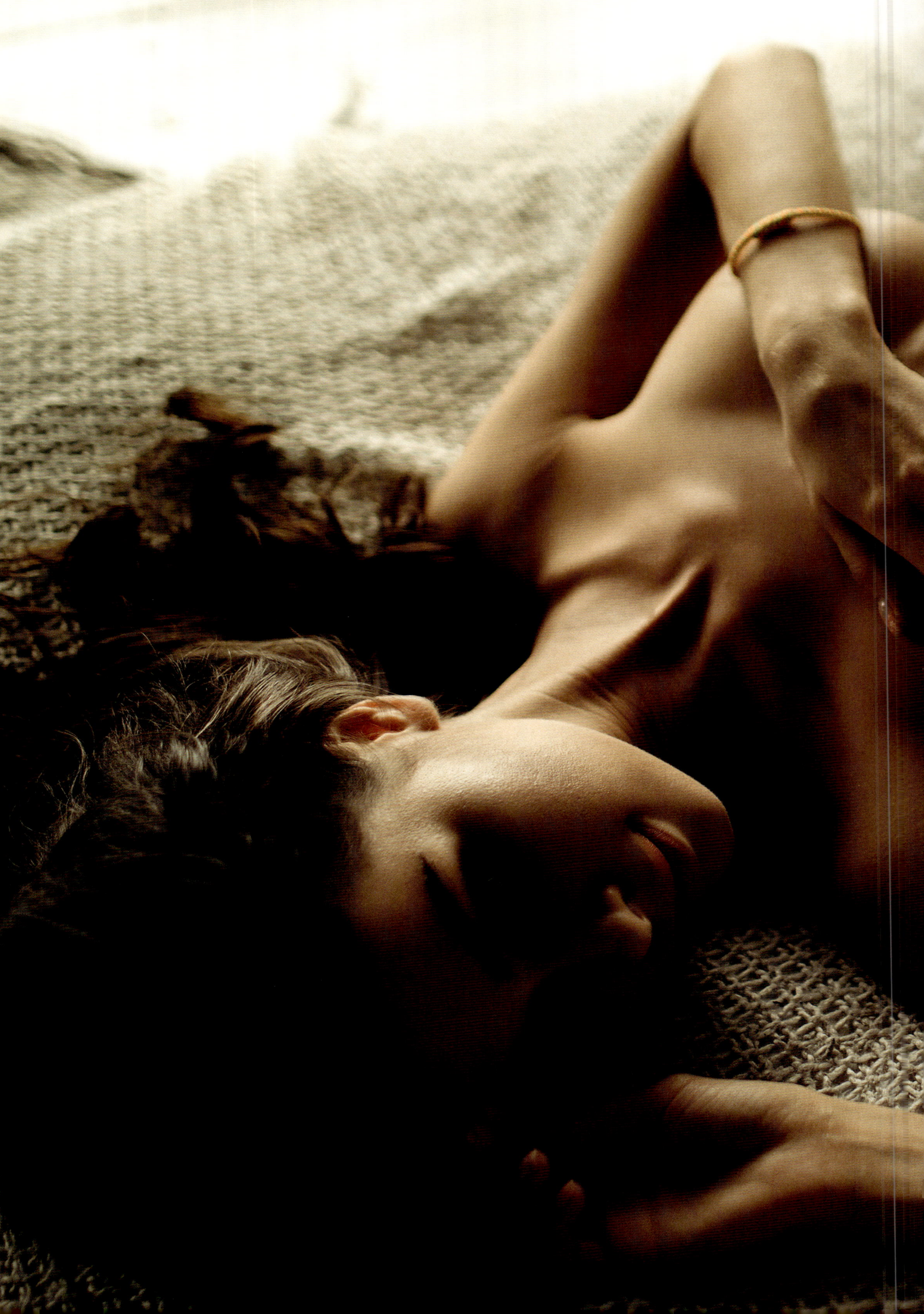

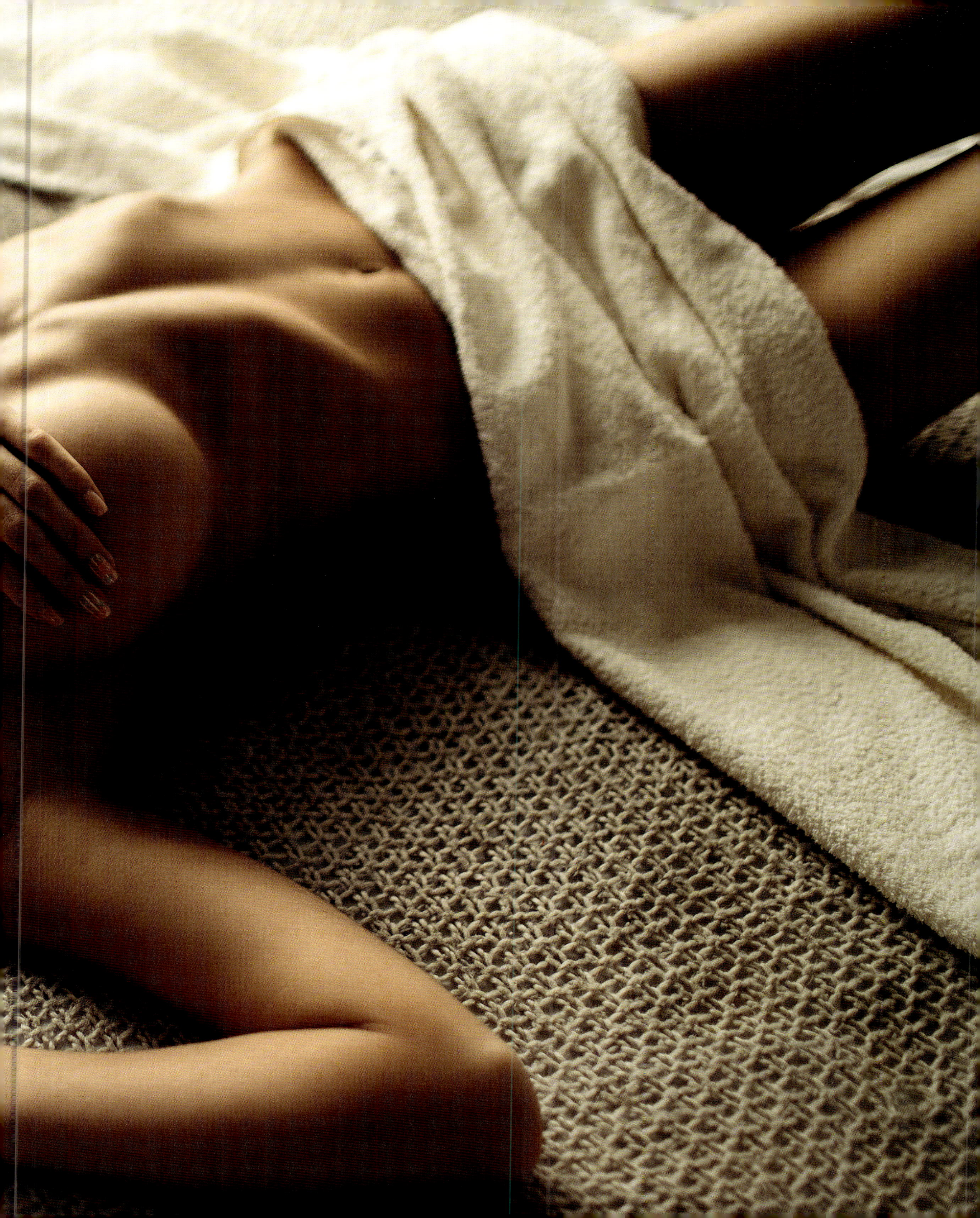

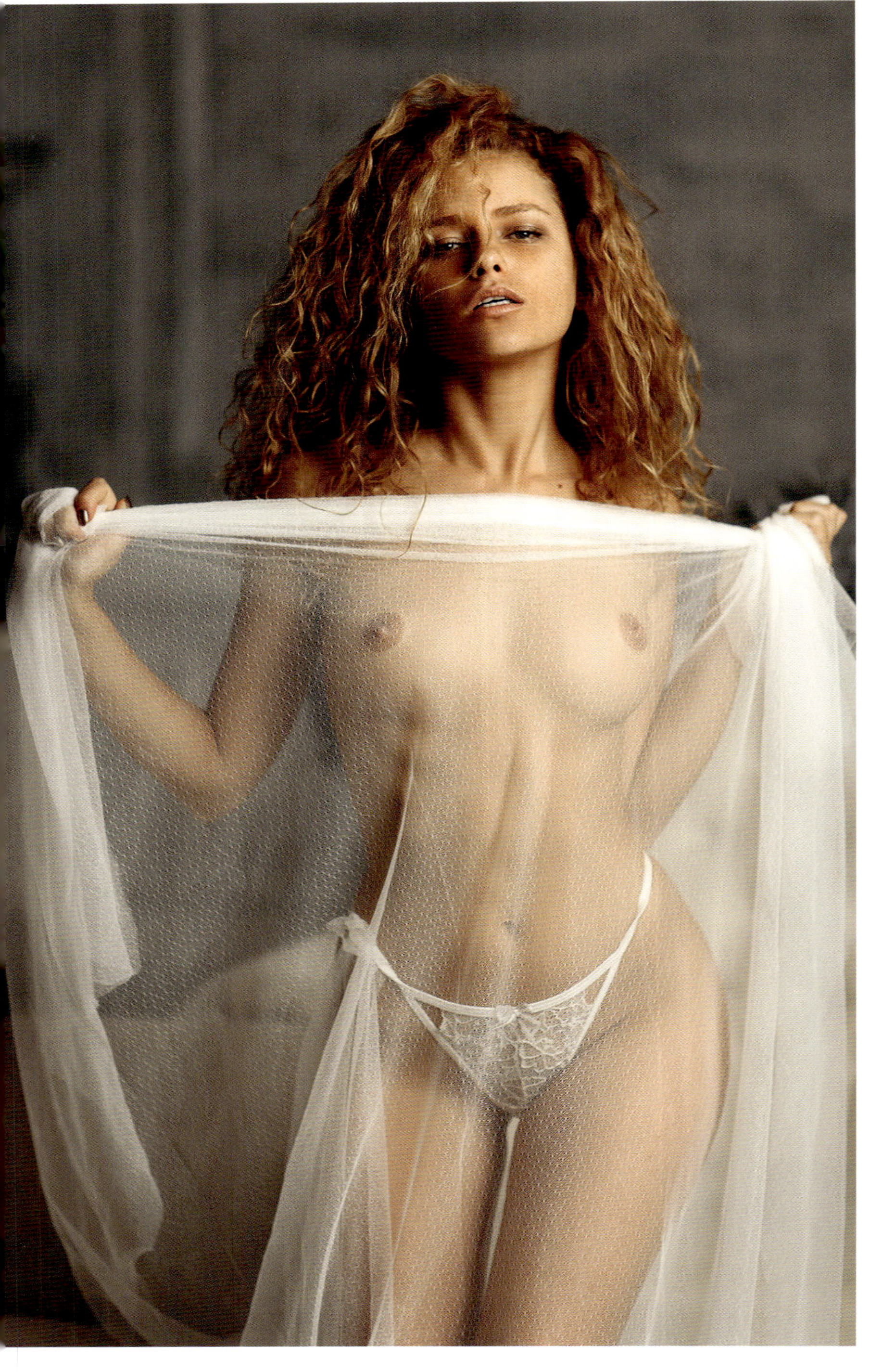

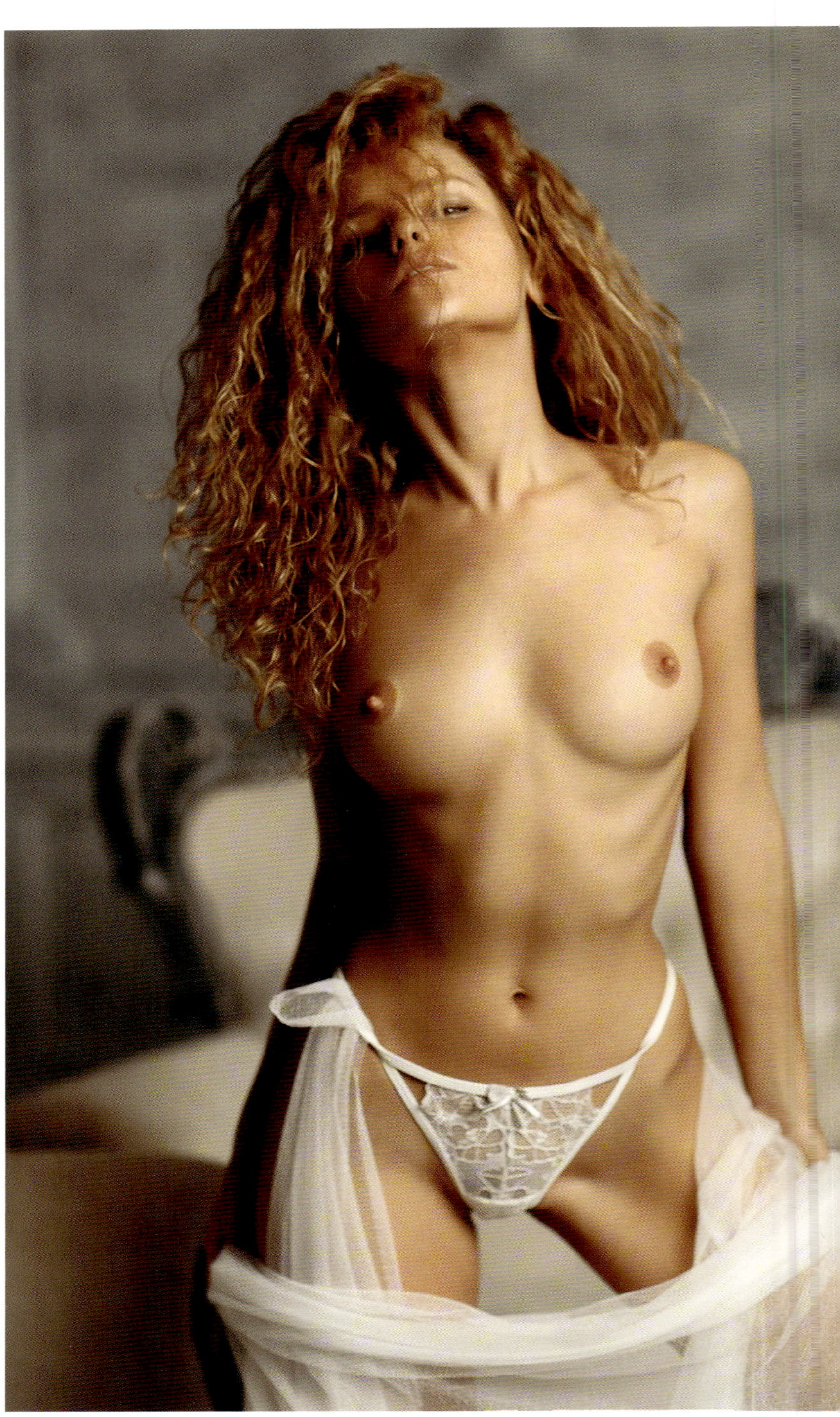

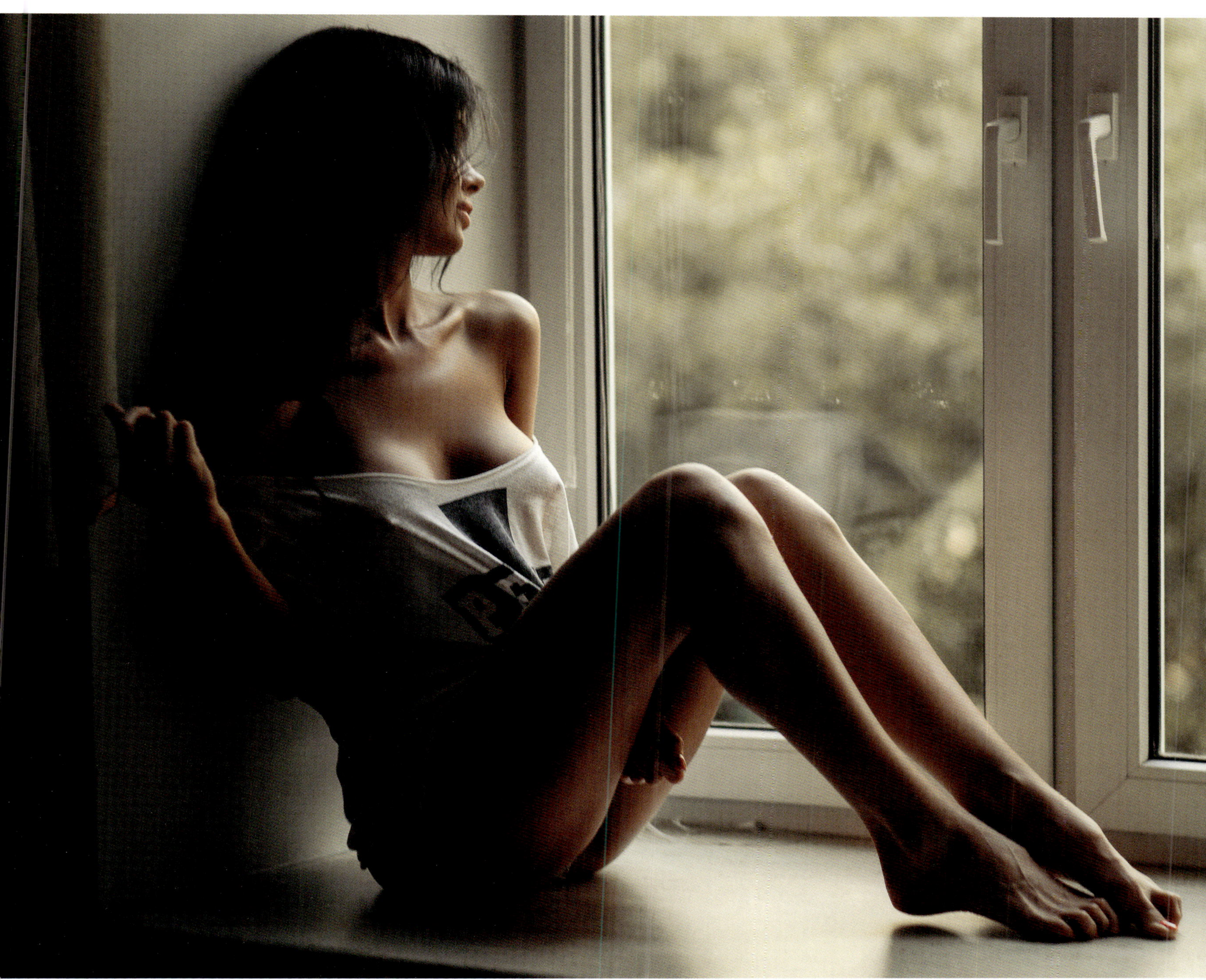

ВИКТОРИЯ | VIKTORIA ▲

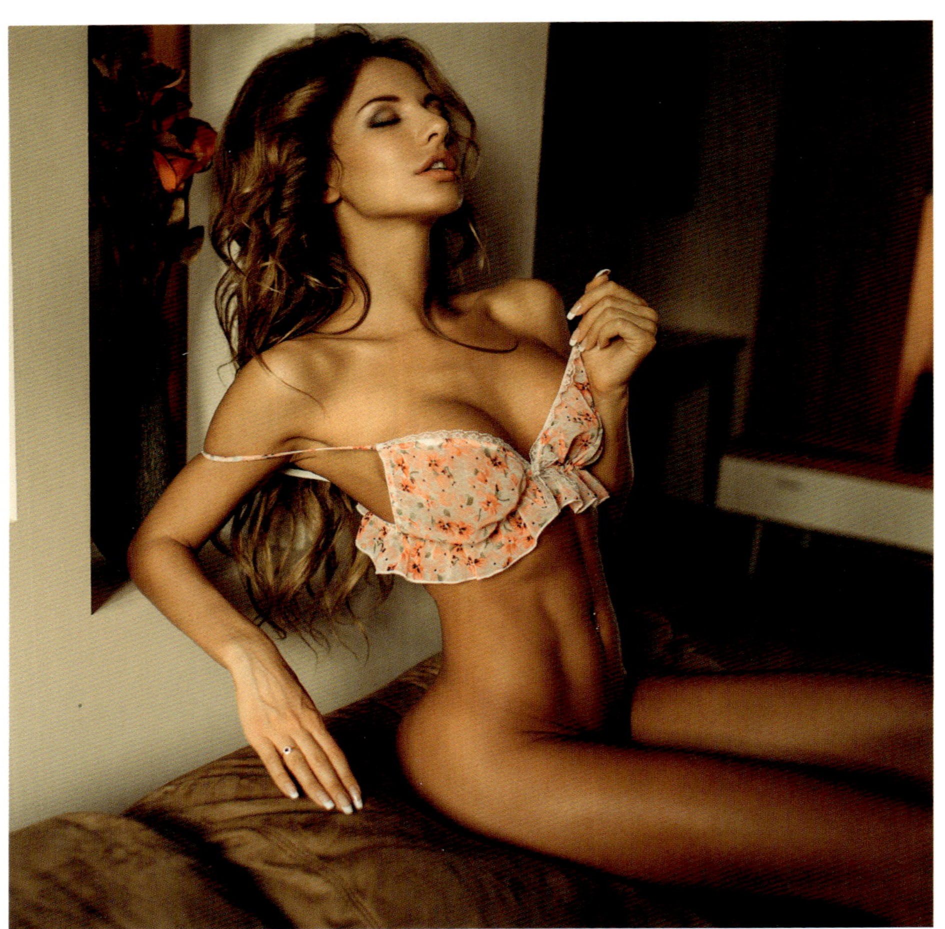

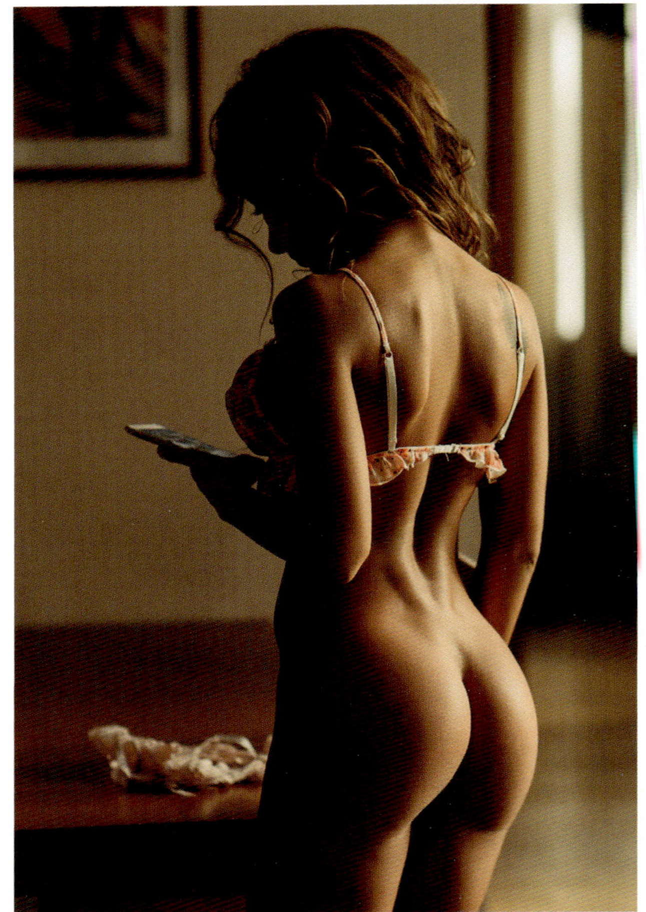

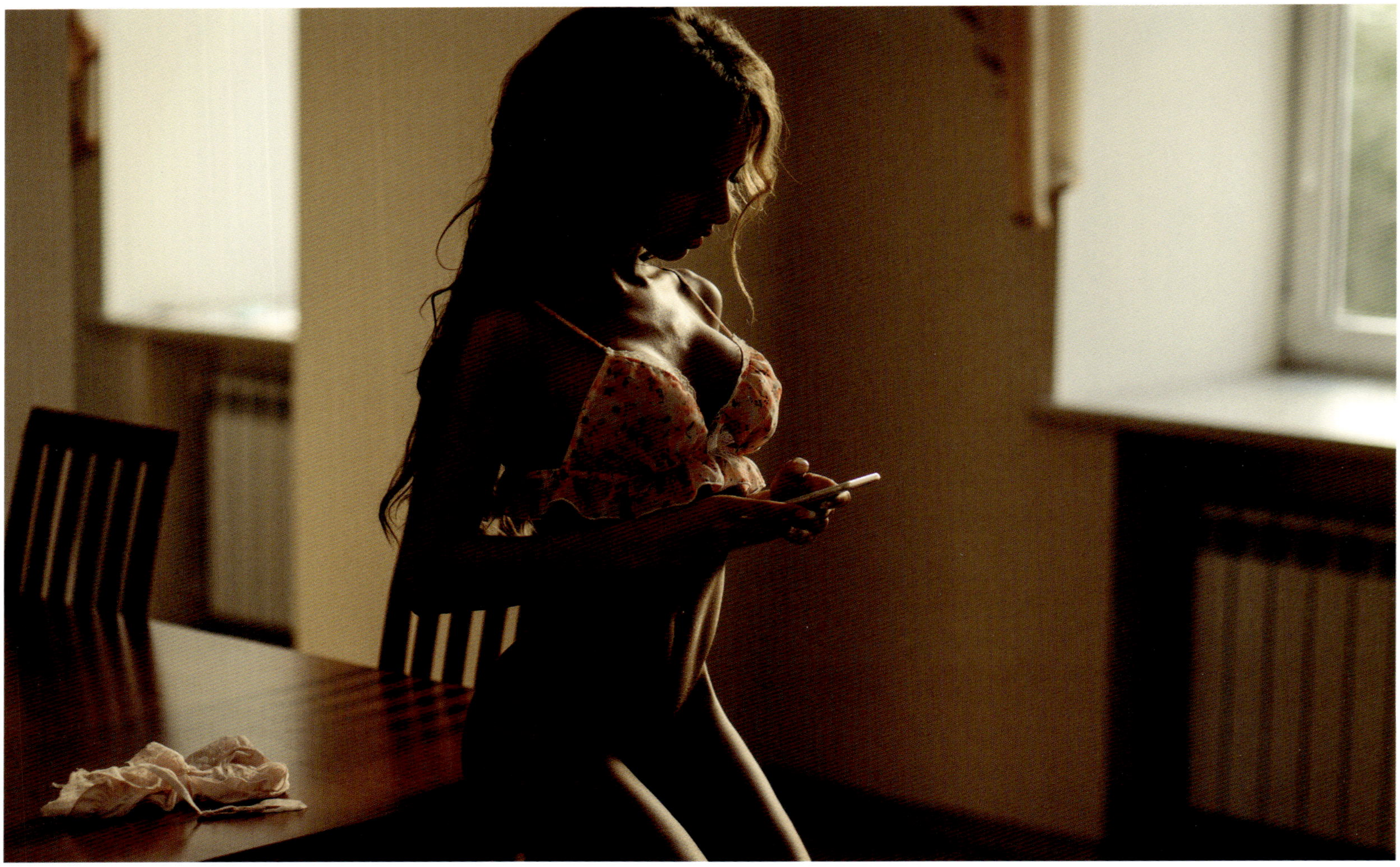

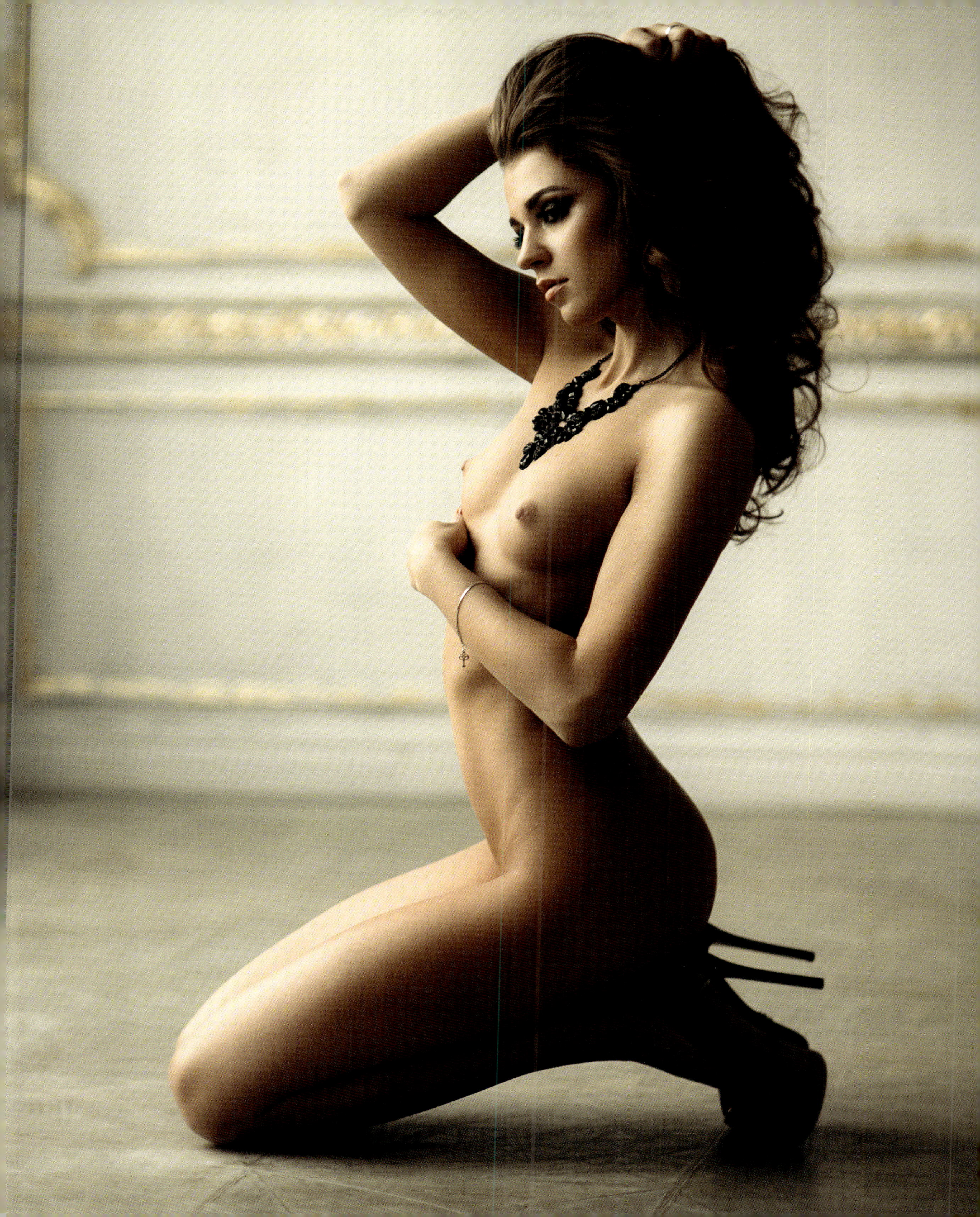

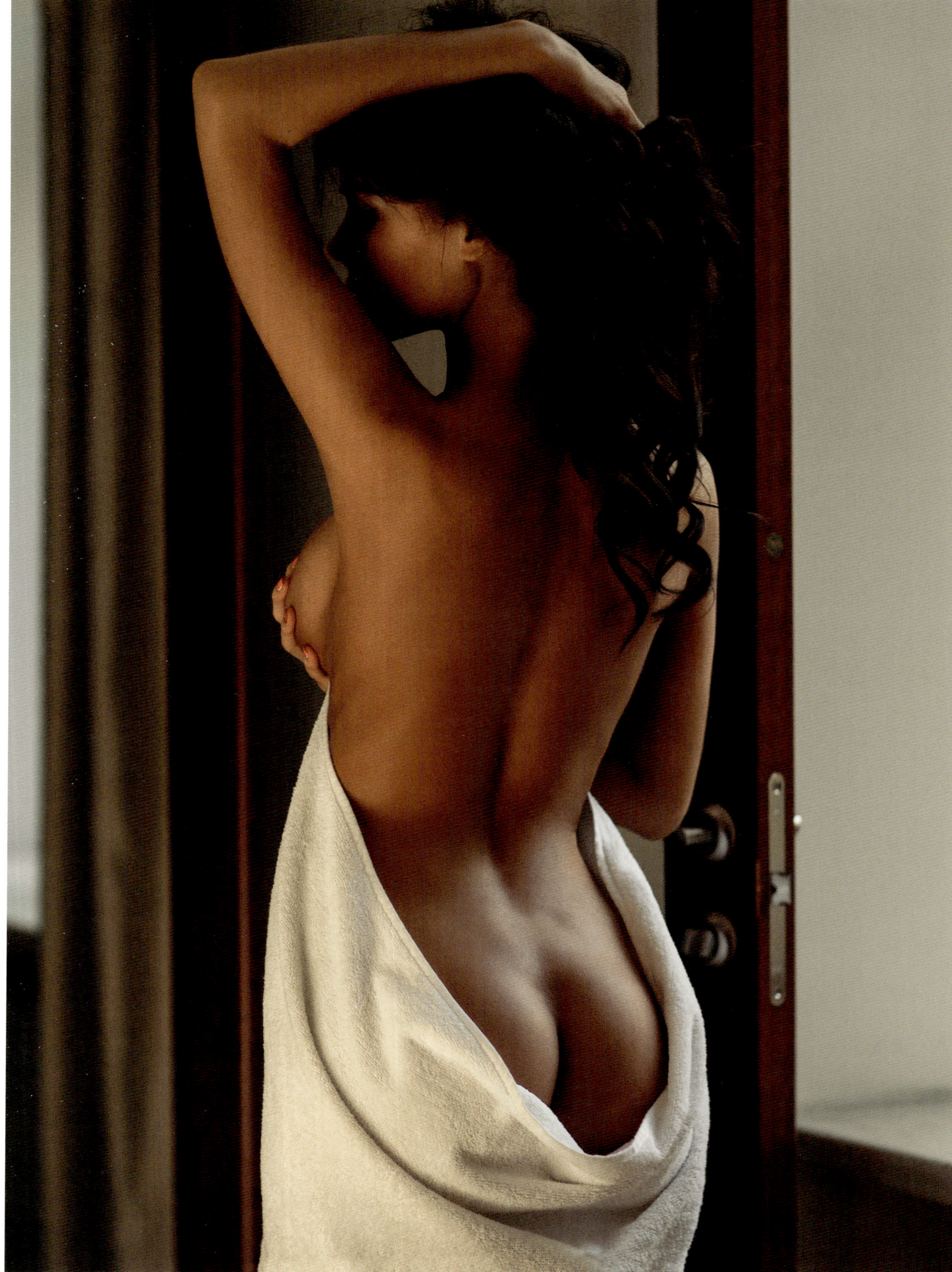

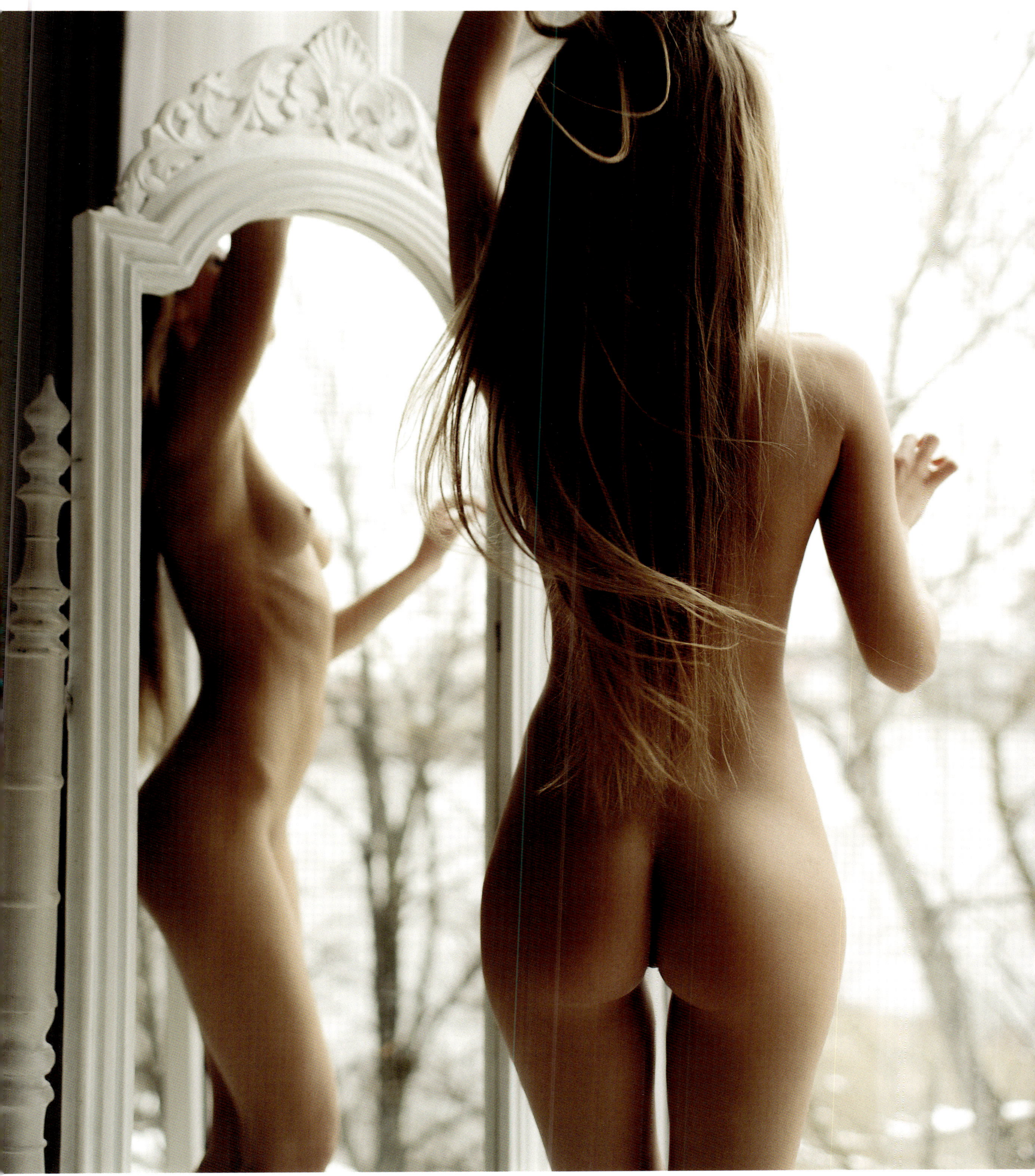

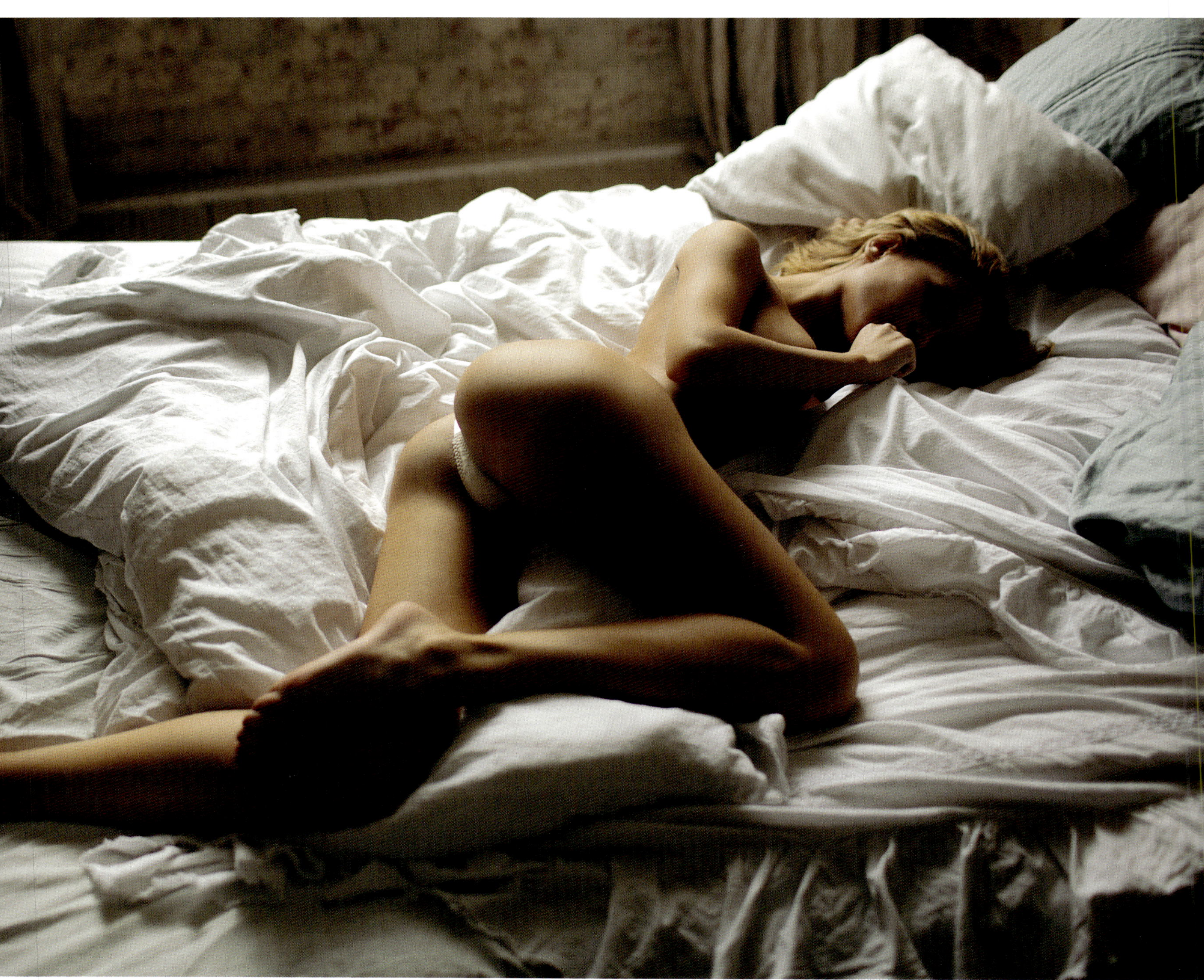

▲ ЕКАТЕРИНА З. | EKATERINA Z.

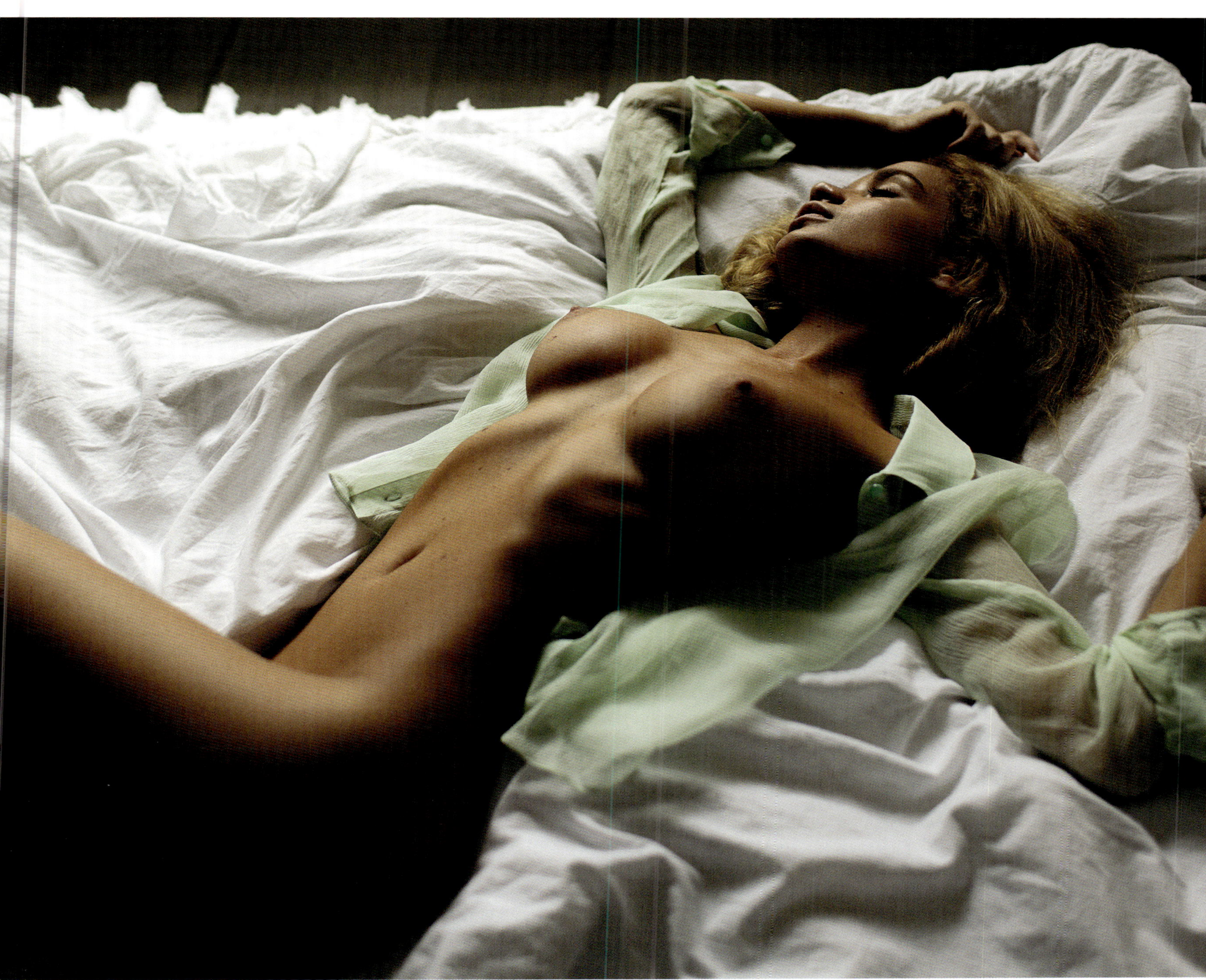

ЕКАТЕРИНА З. | EKATERINA Z. ▲

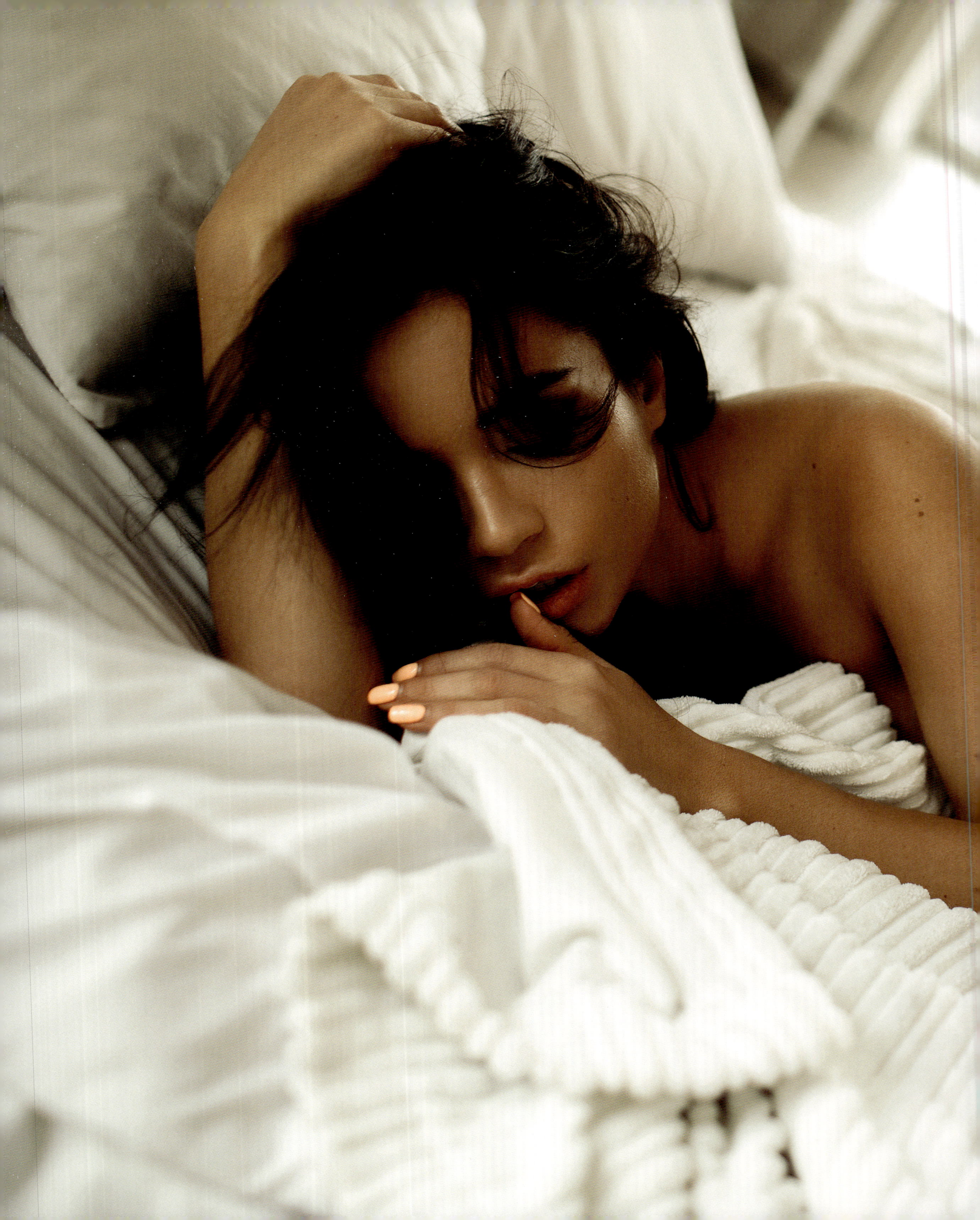

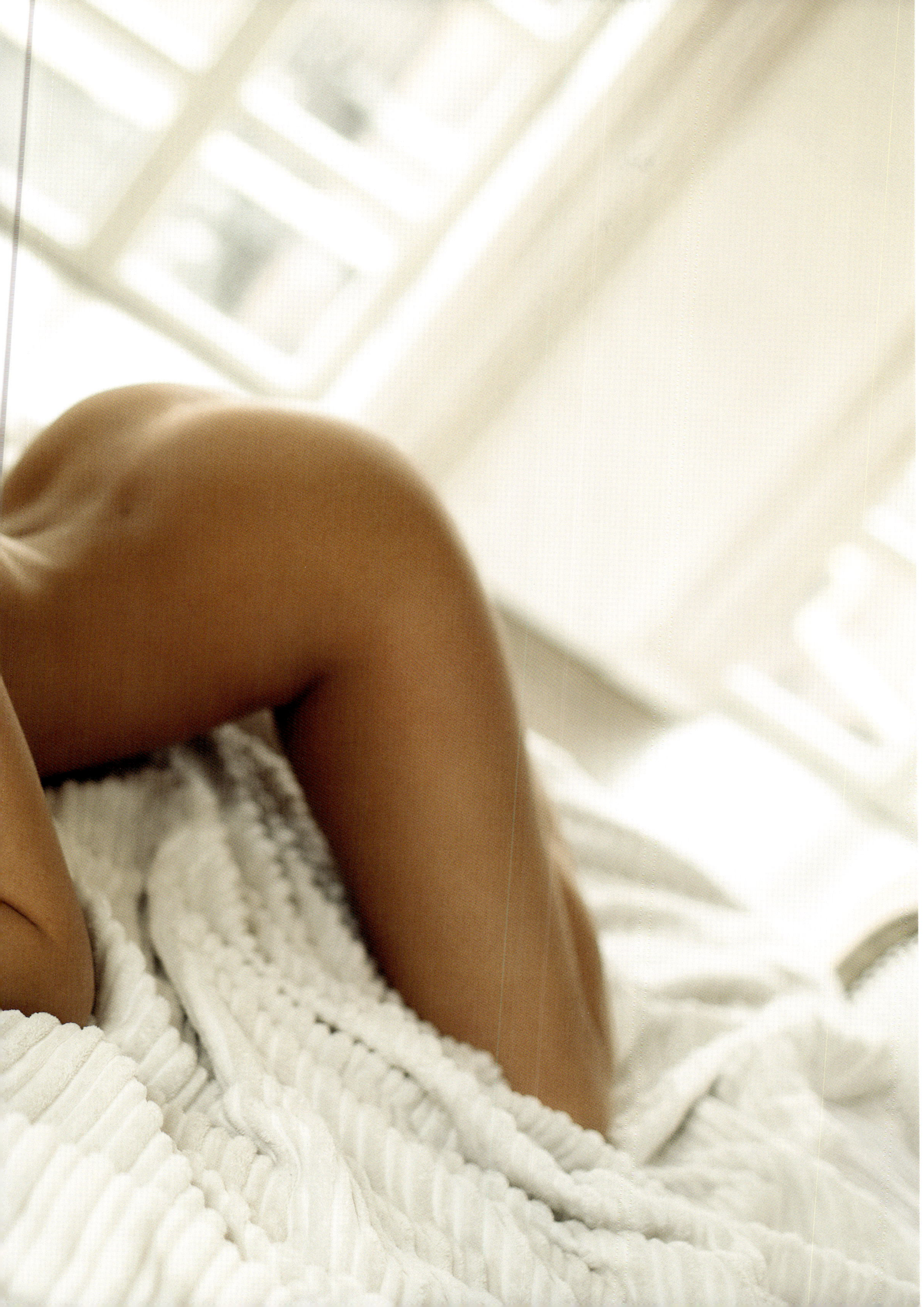

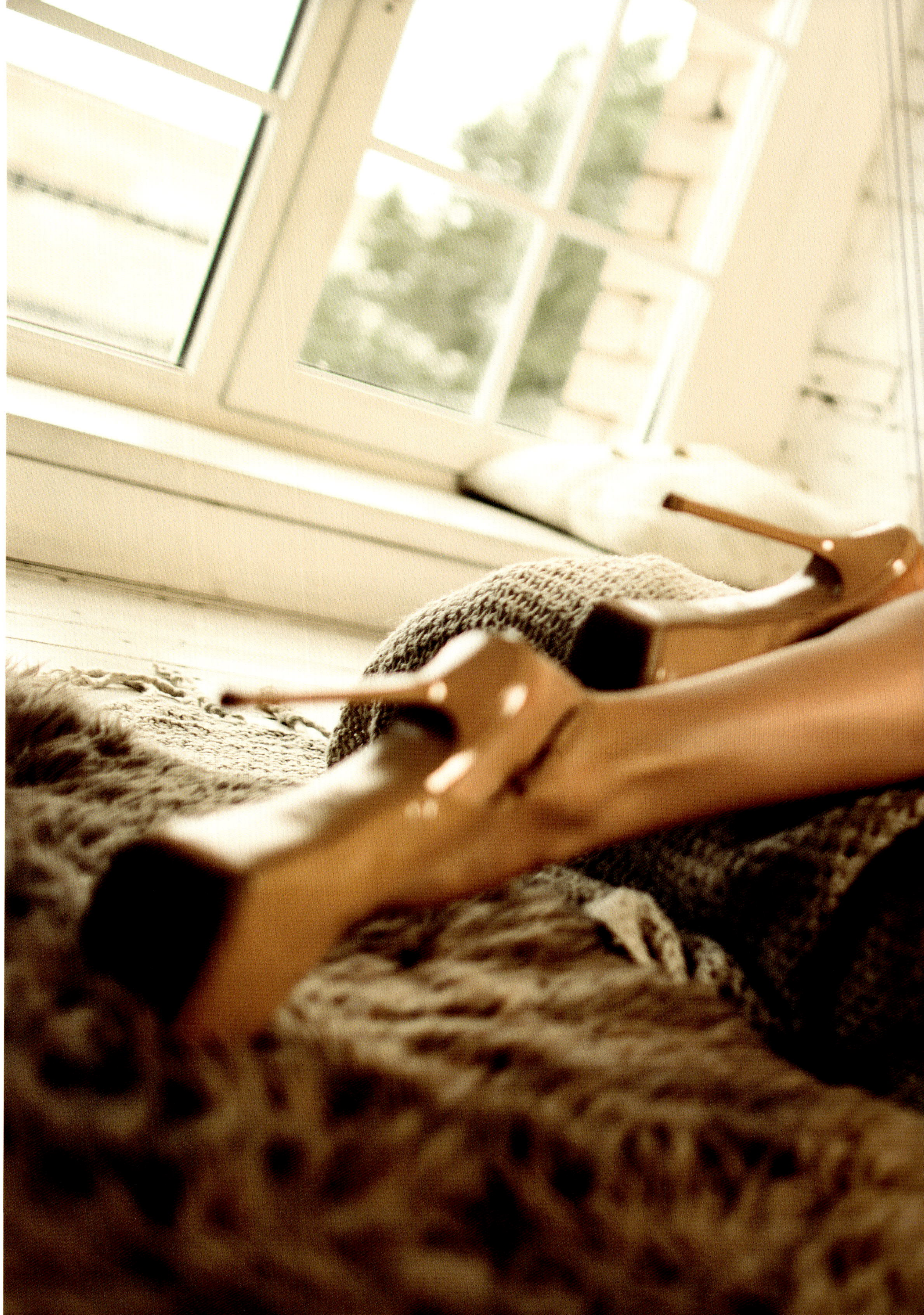

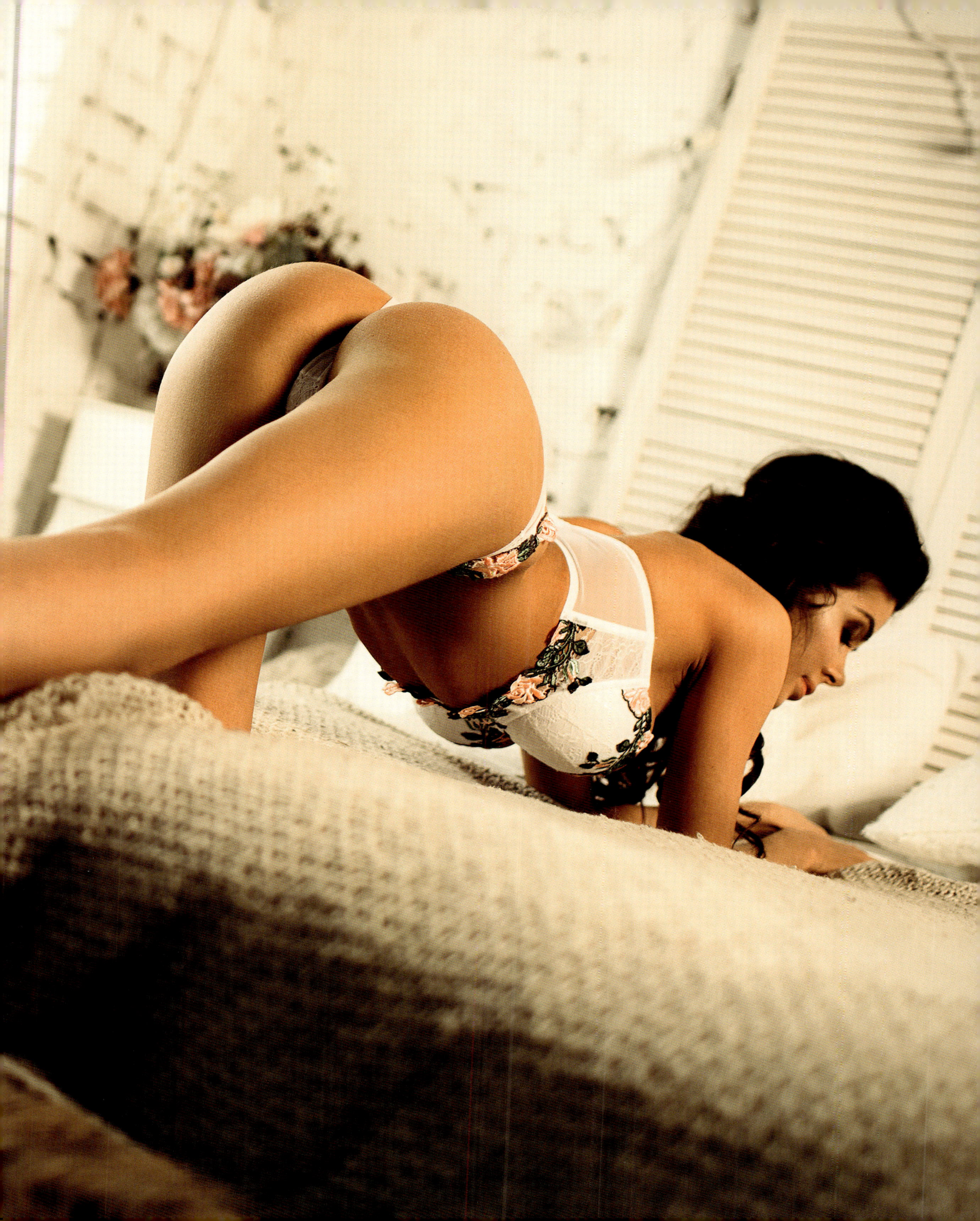

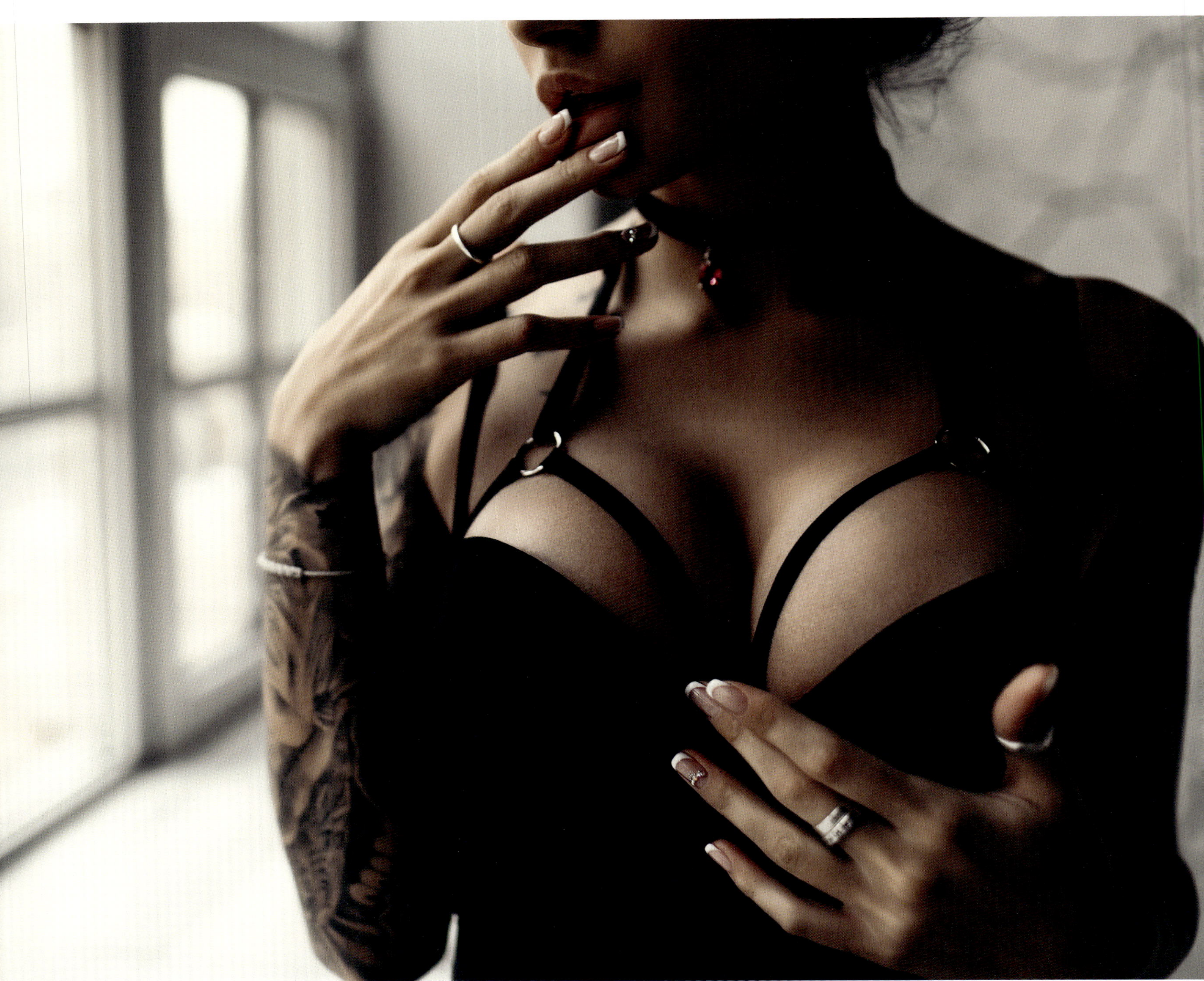

▲ АННА С. | ANNA S.

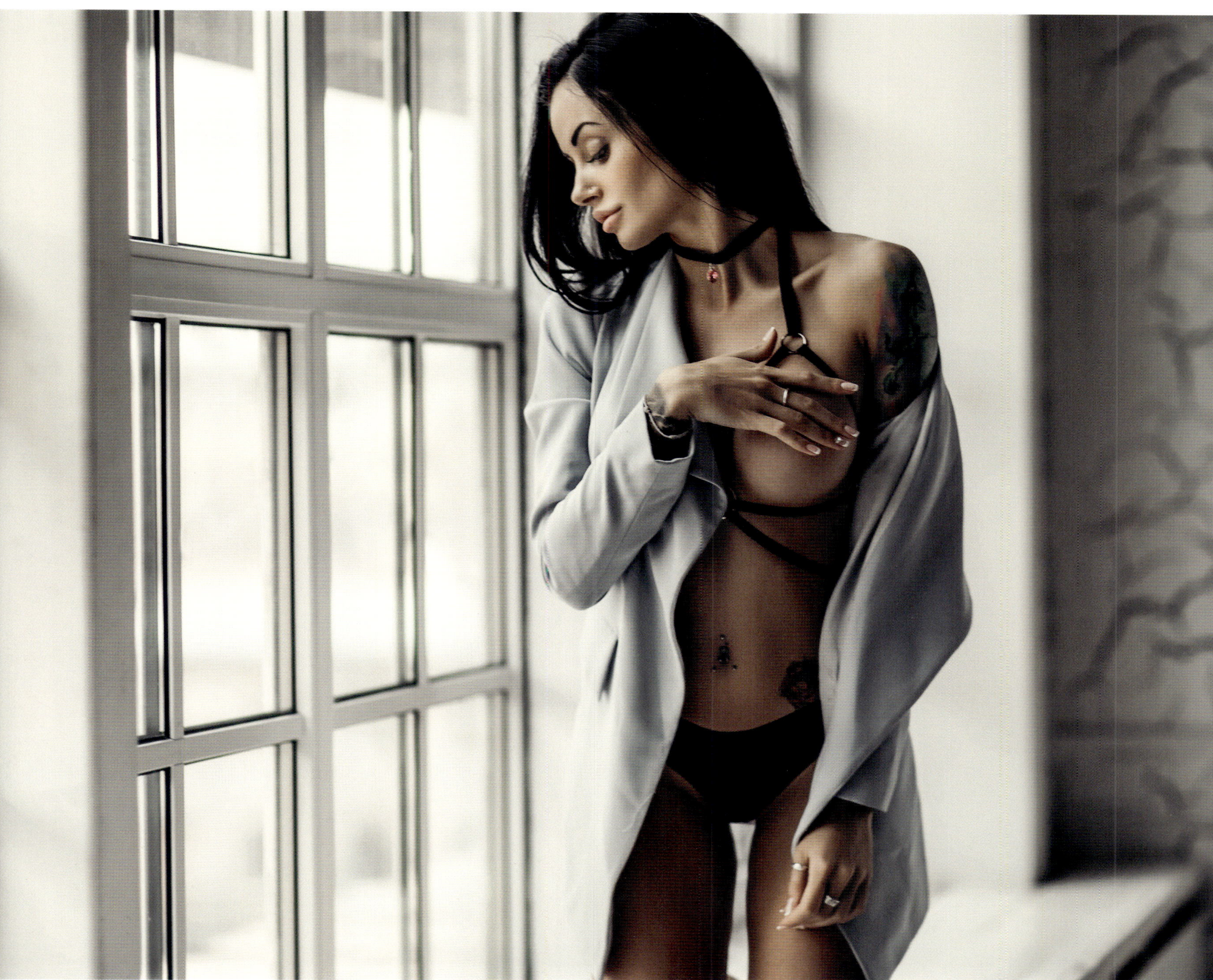

АННА С. | ANNA S. ▲

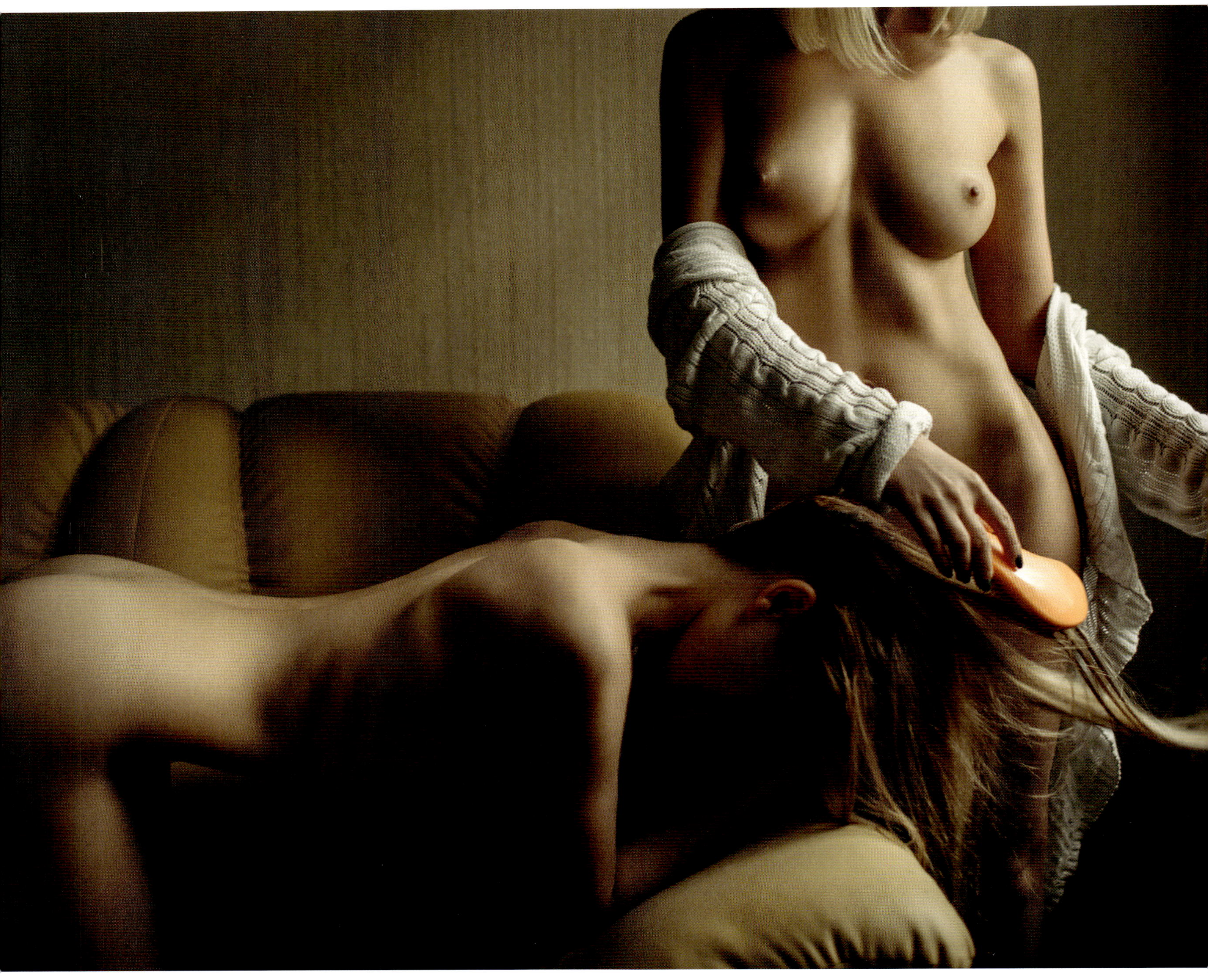

▲ АННА+КСЕНИЯ | ANNA+KSENIA

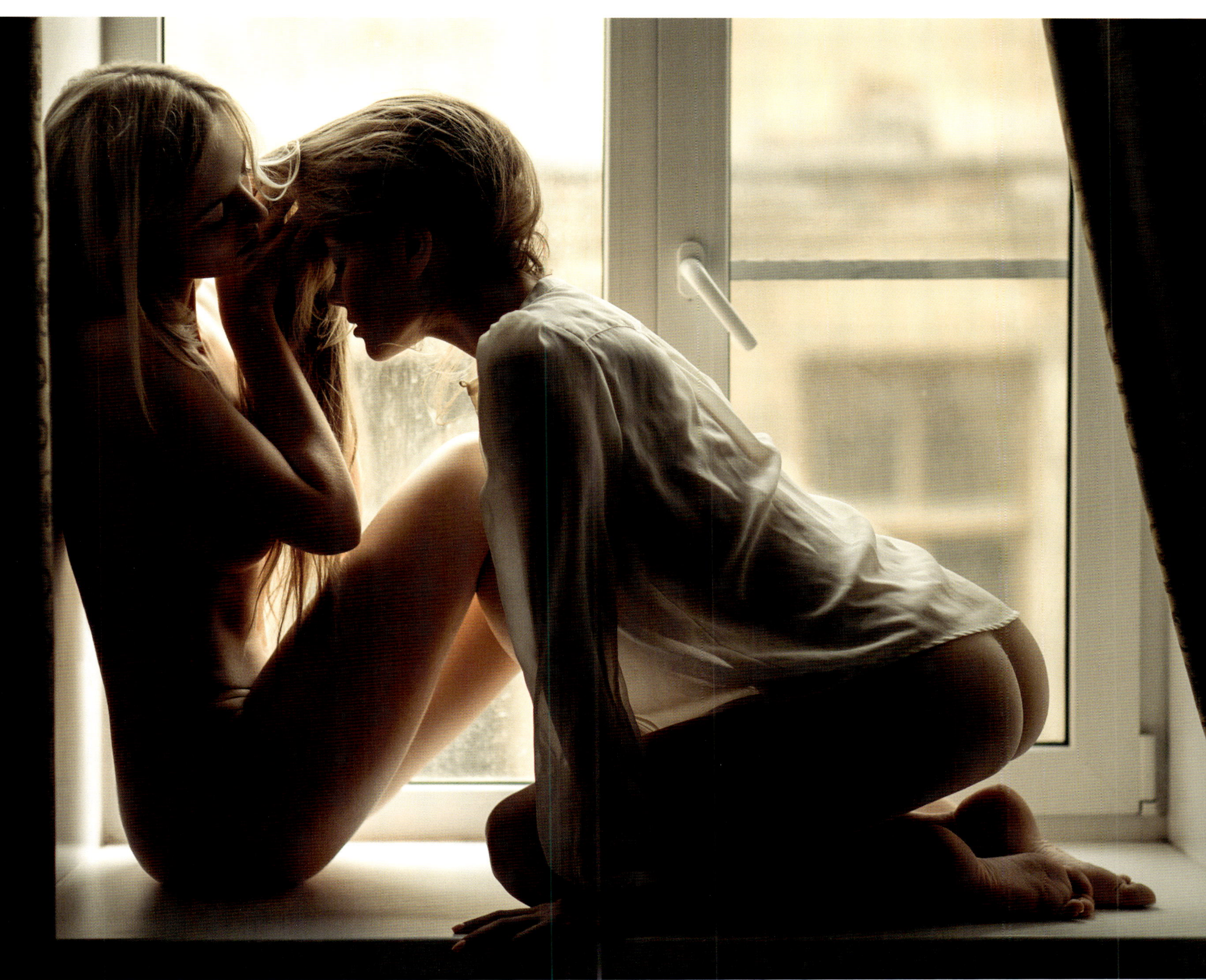

АННА+КСЕНИЯ | ANNA+KSENIA ▲

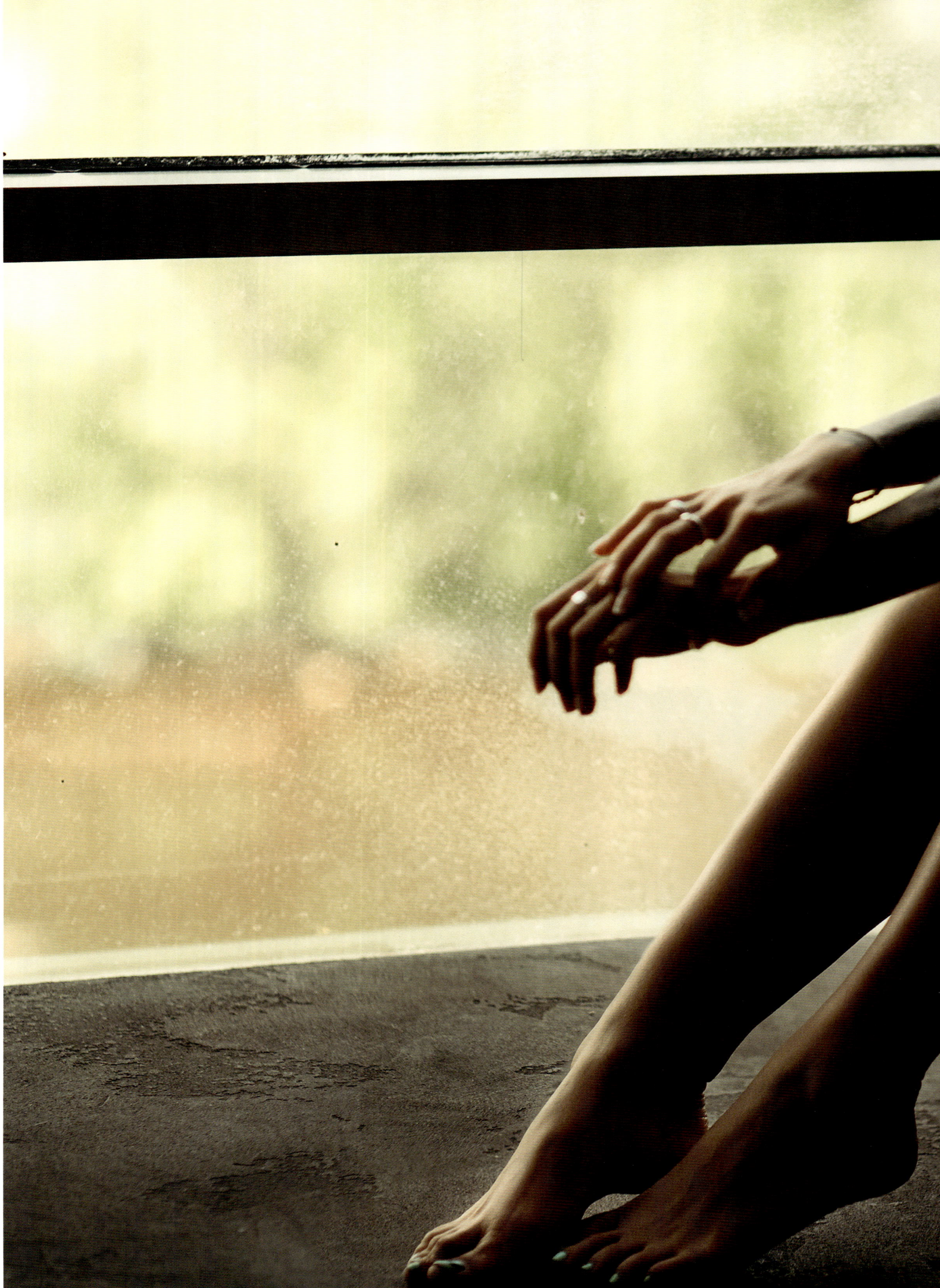

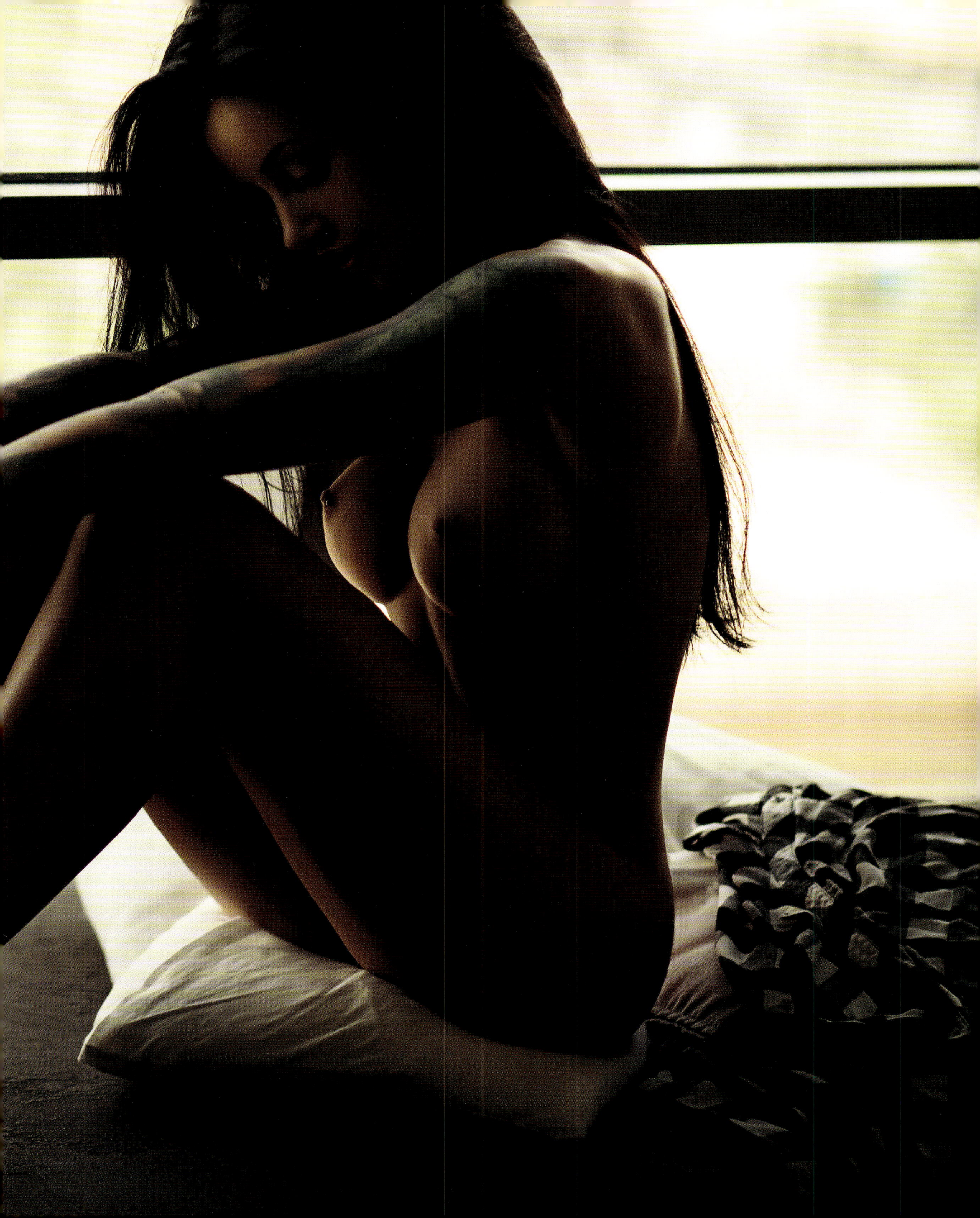

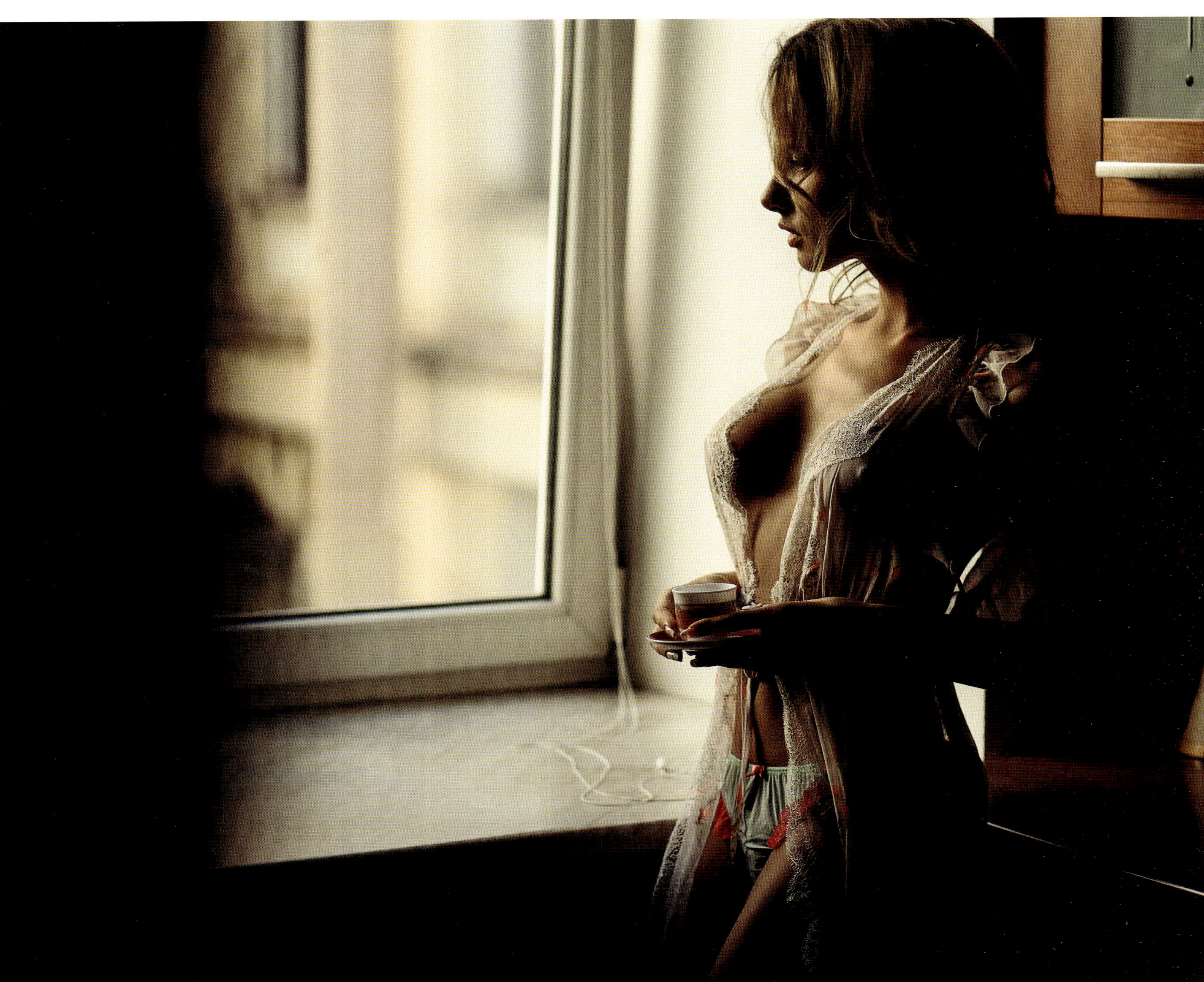

ЕКАТЕРИНА Р. | EKATERINA R. ▲

▶ МАРИАННА | MARIANNA

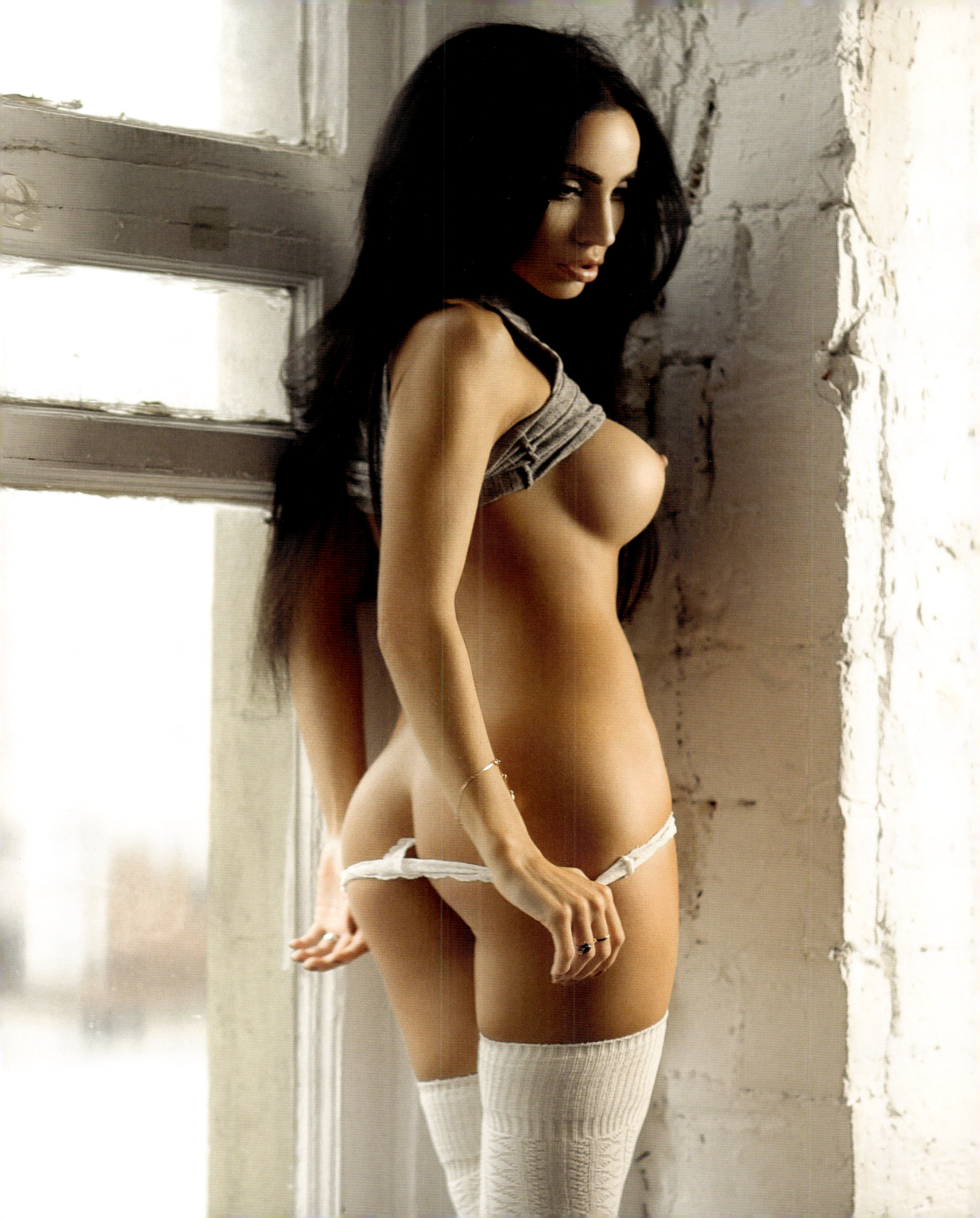

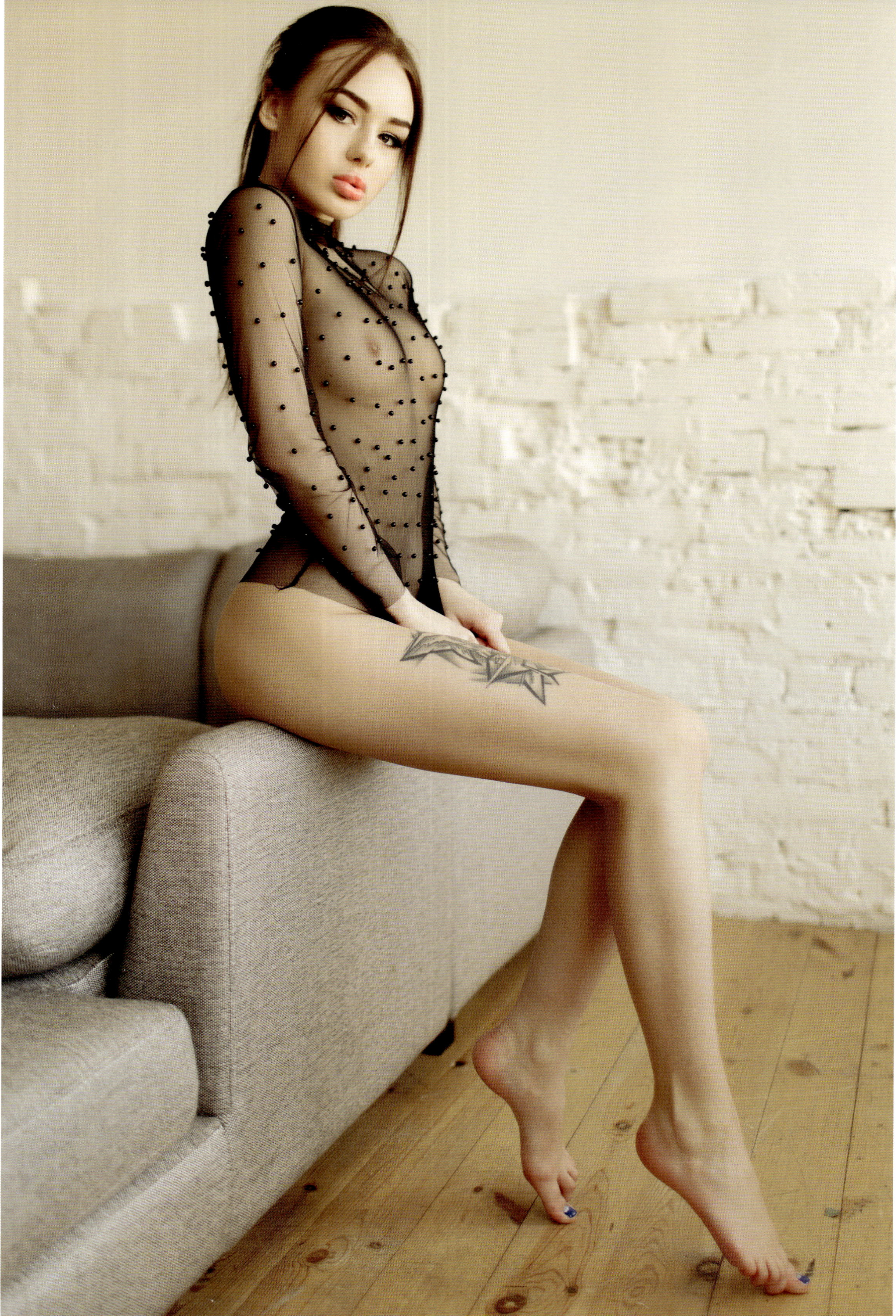

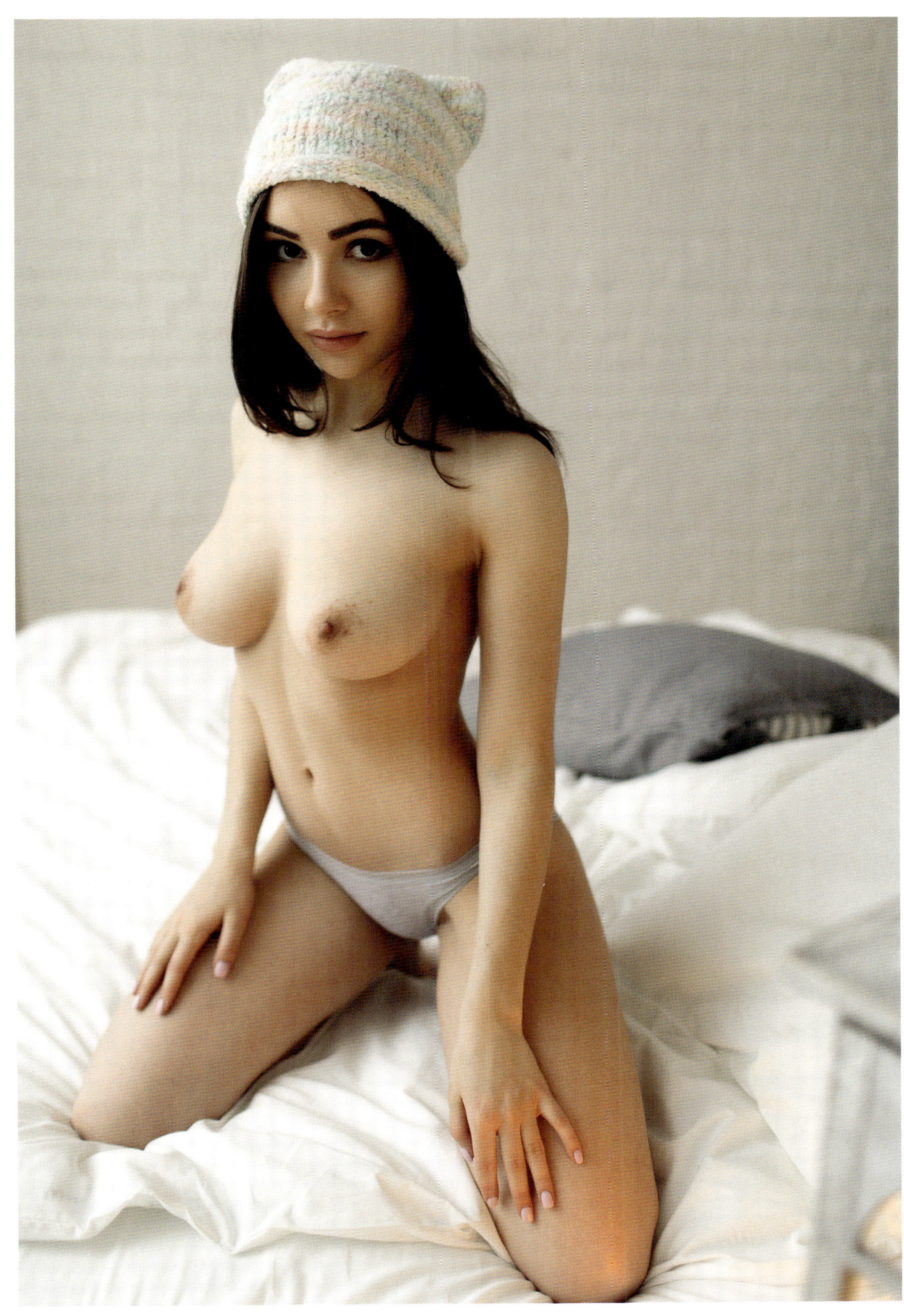

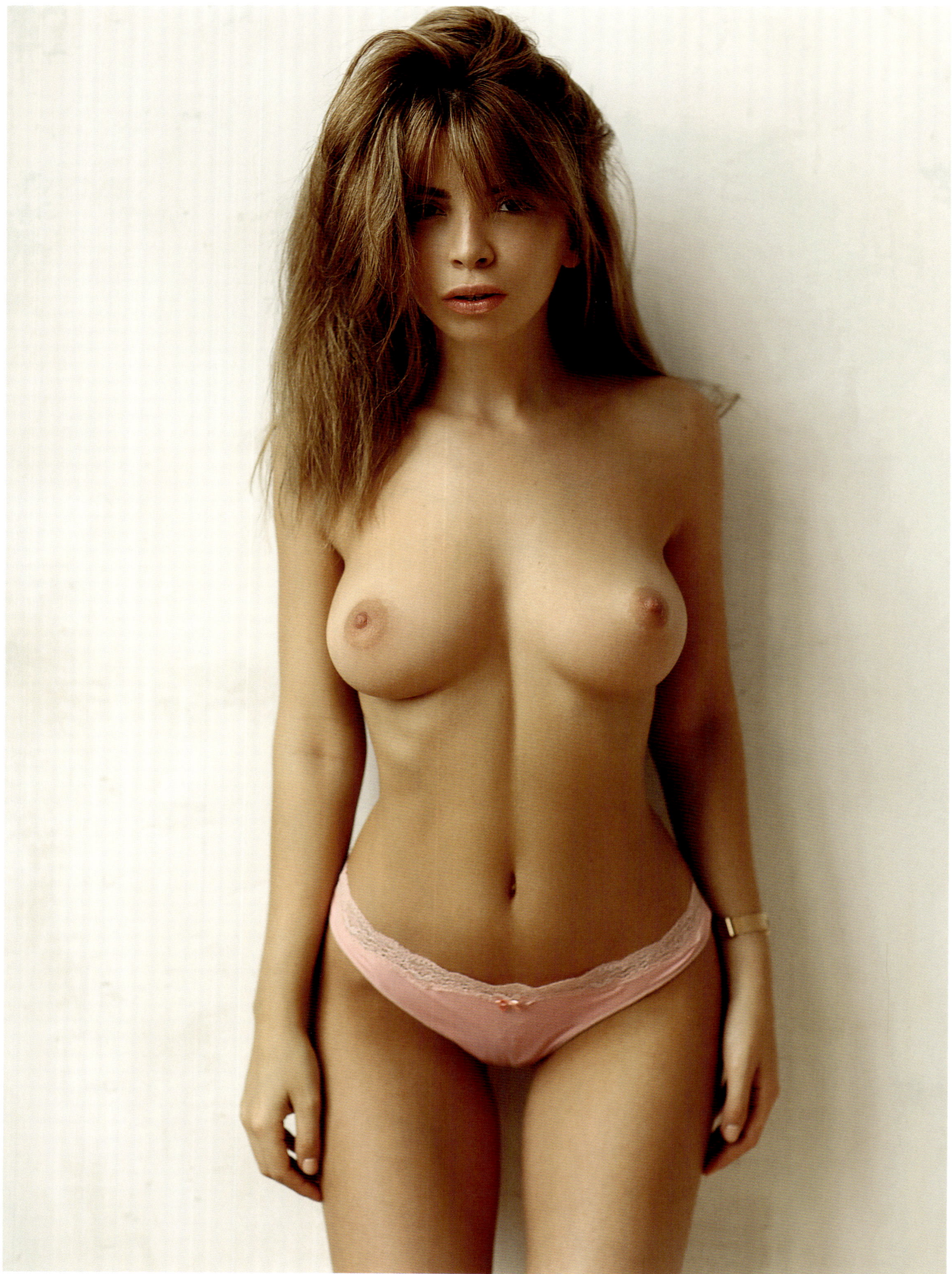

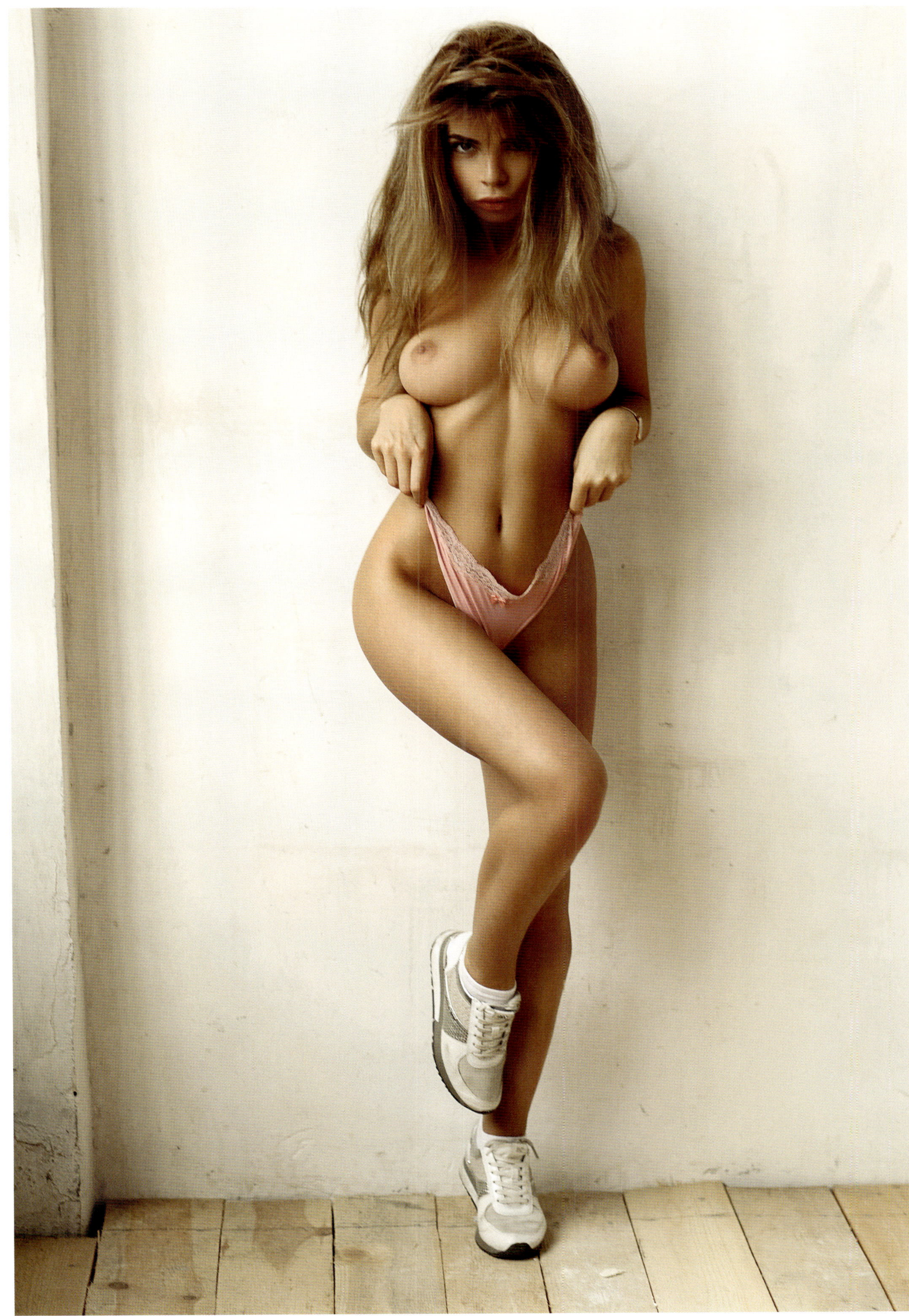

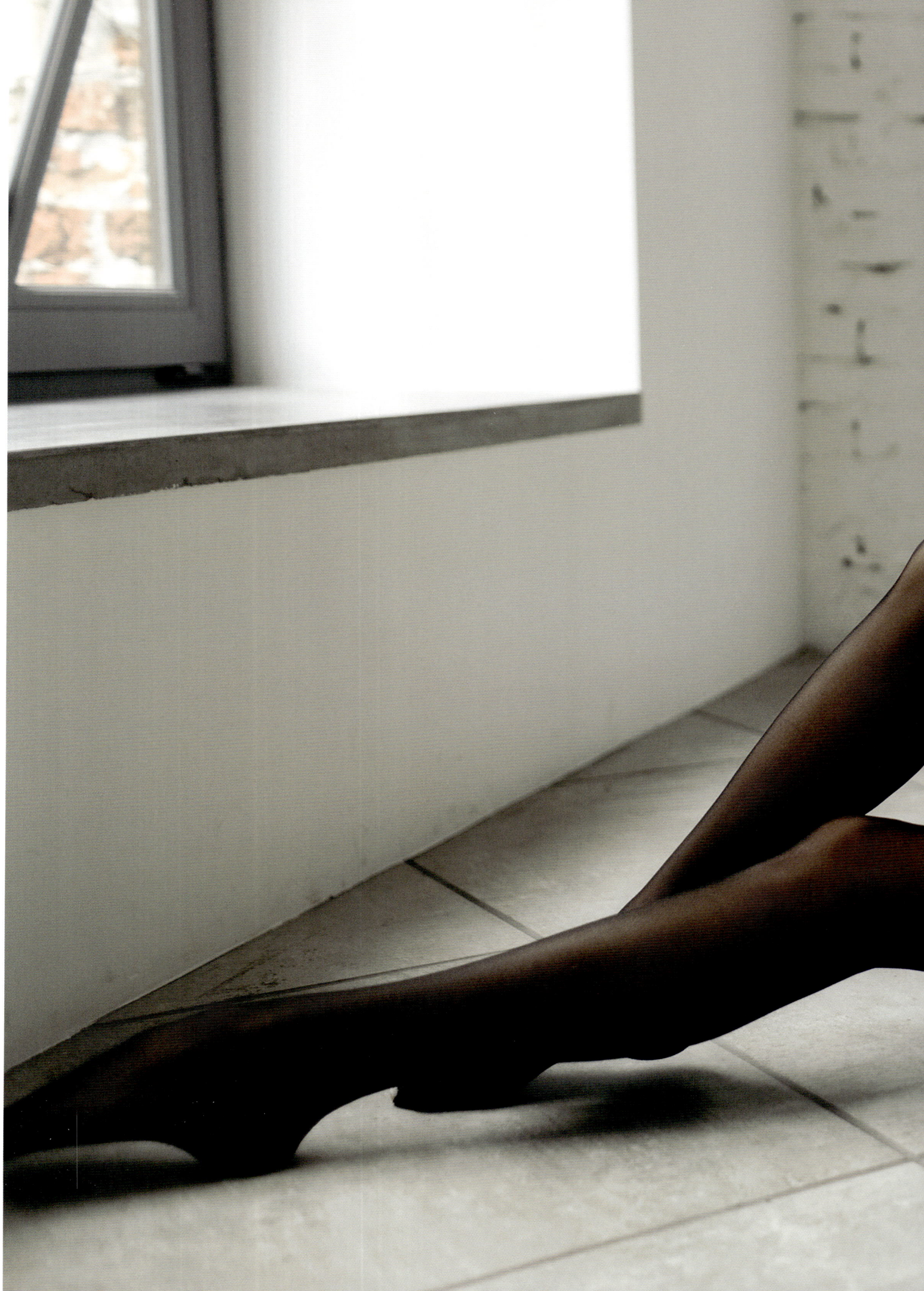

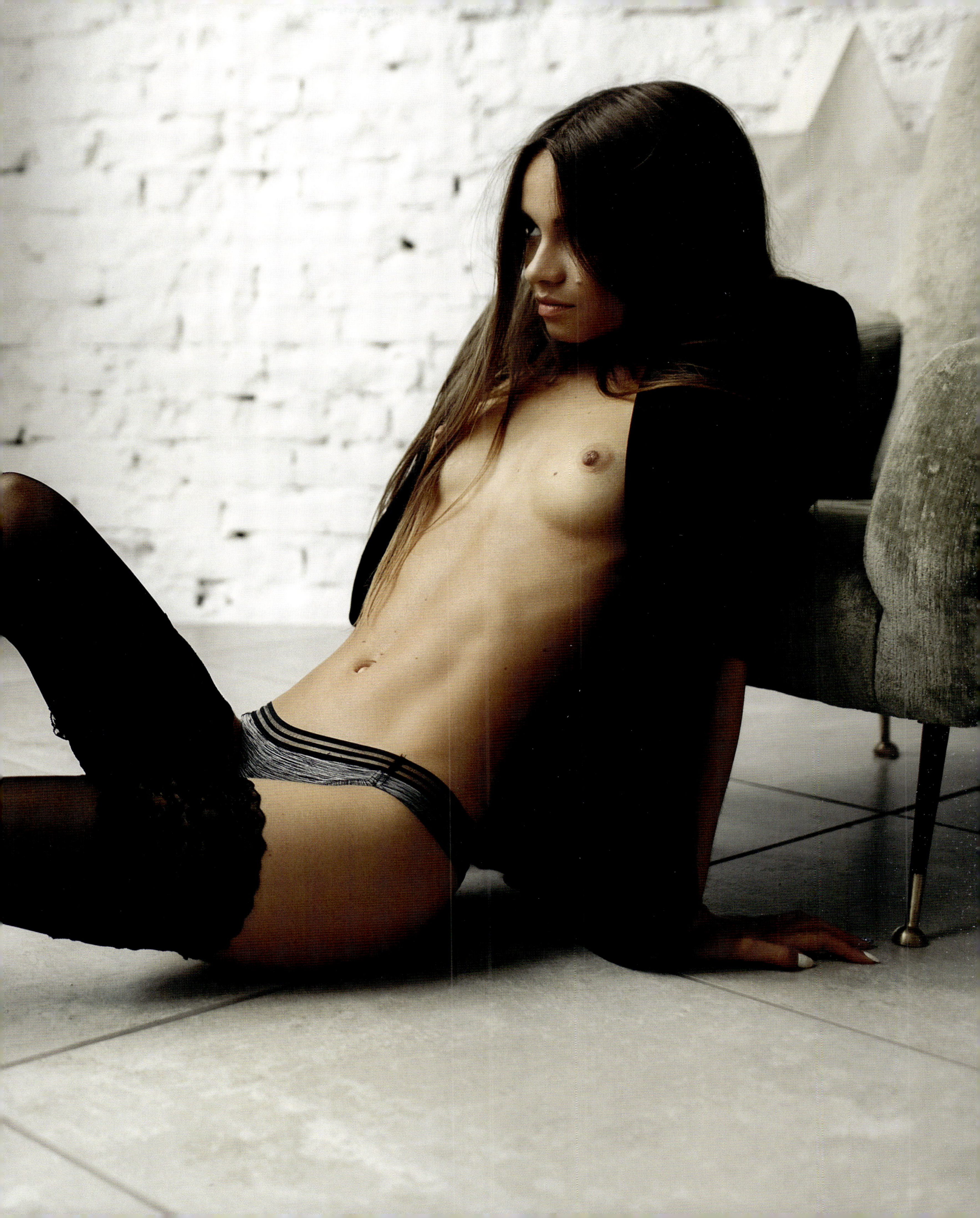

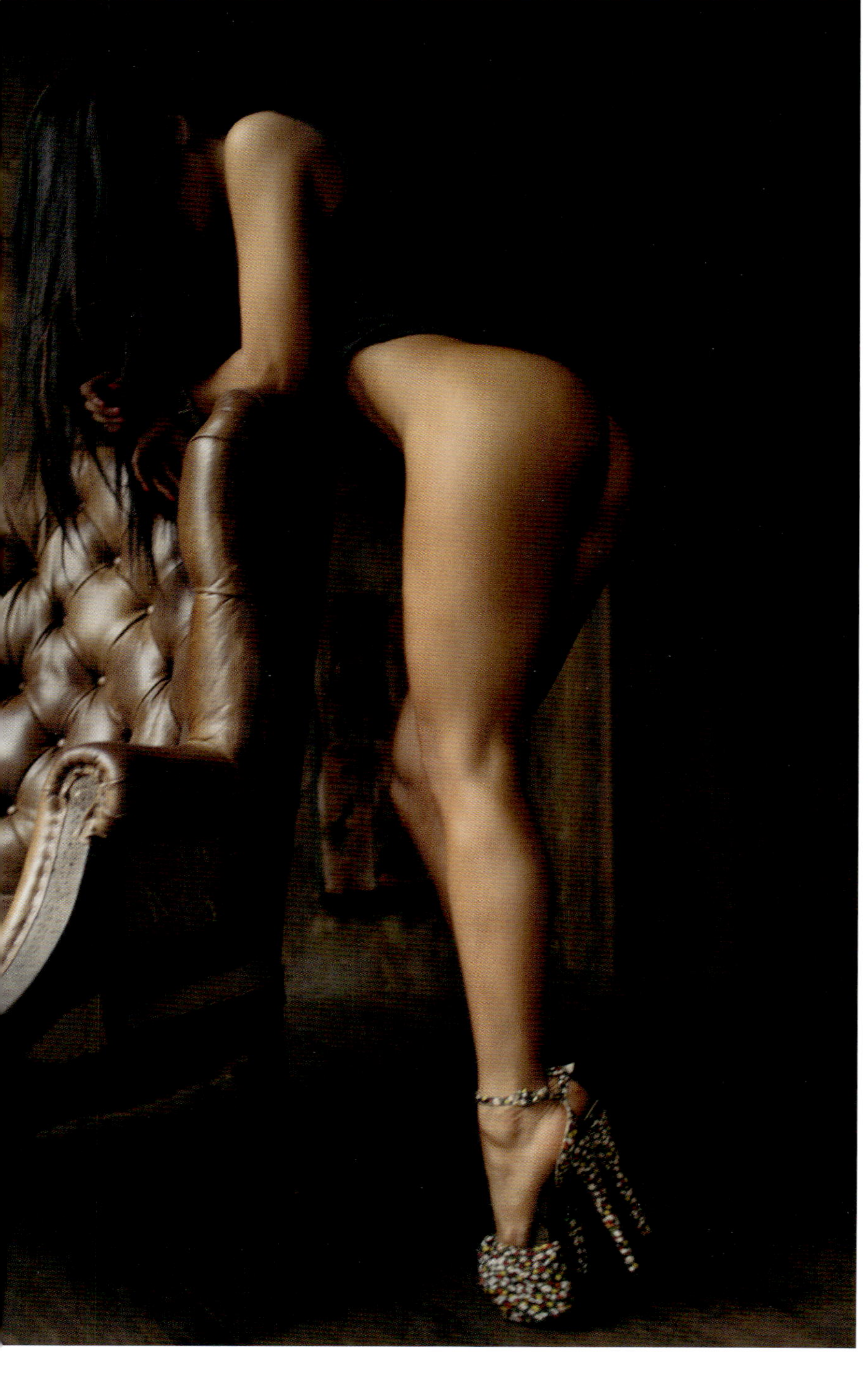

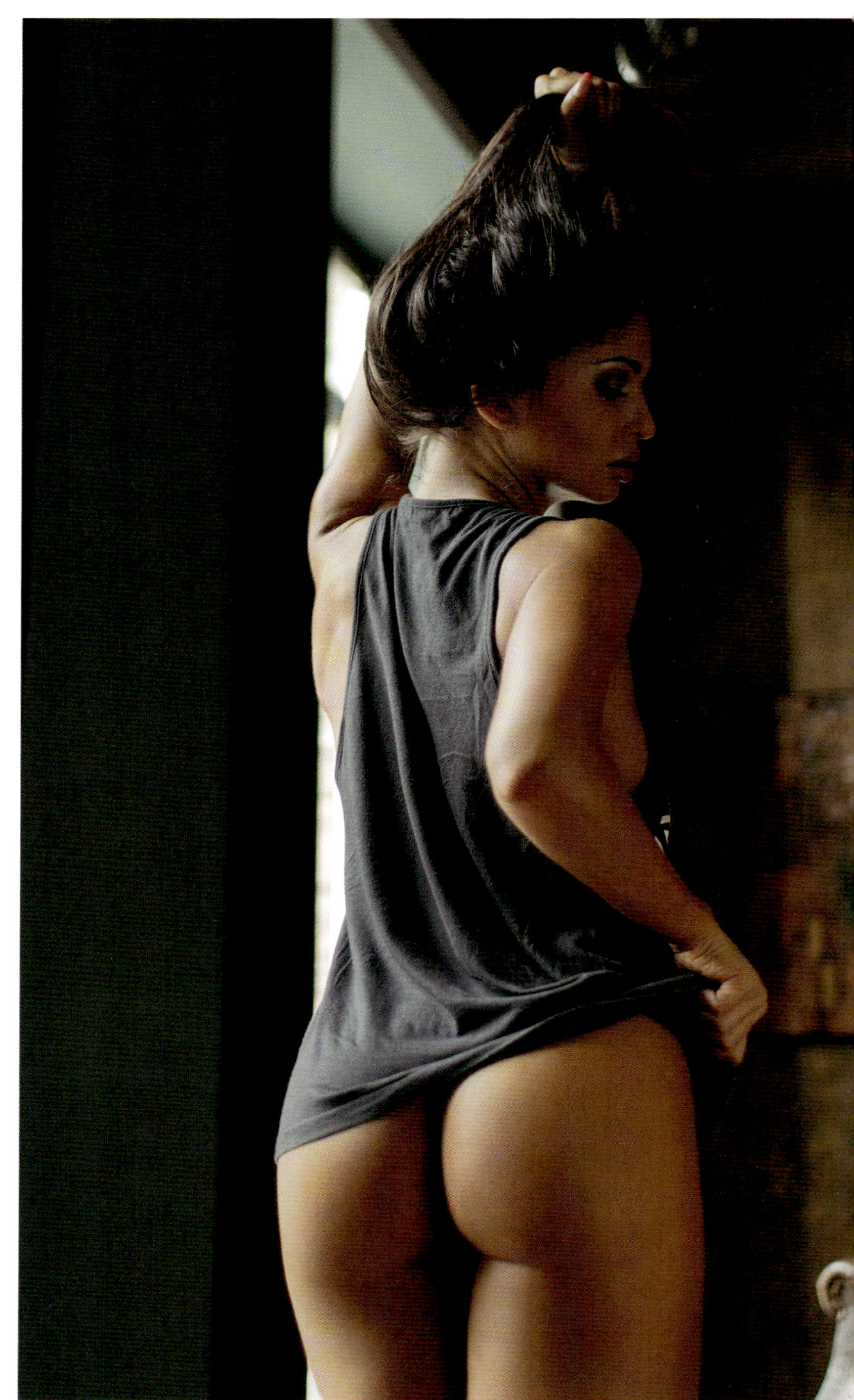

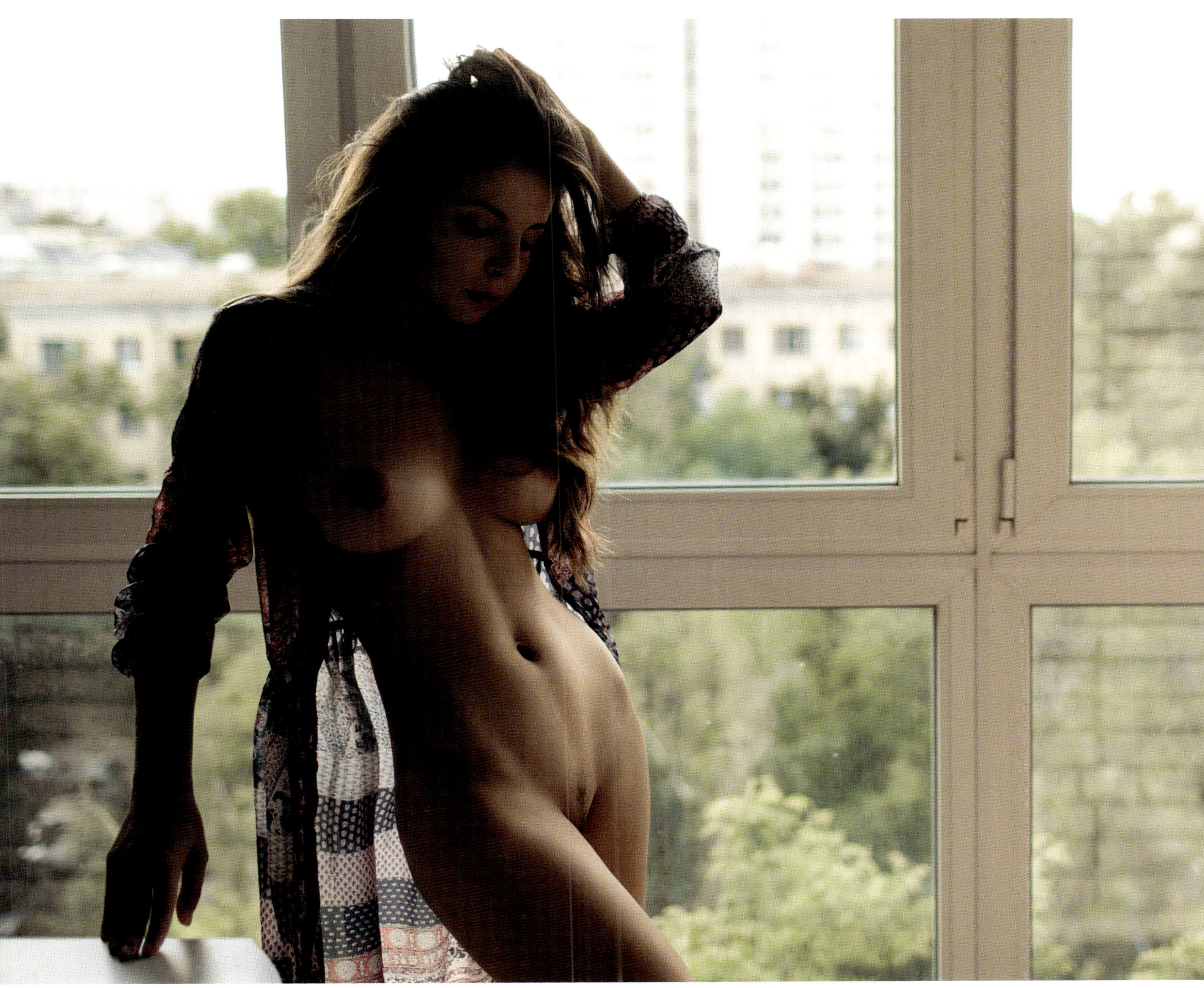

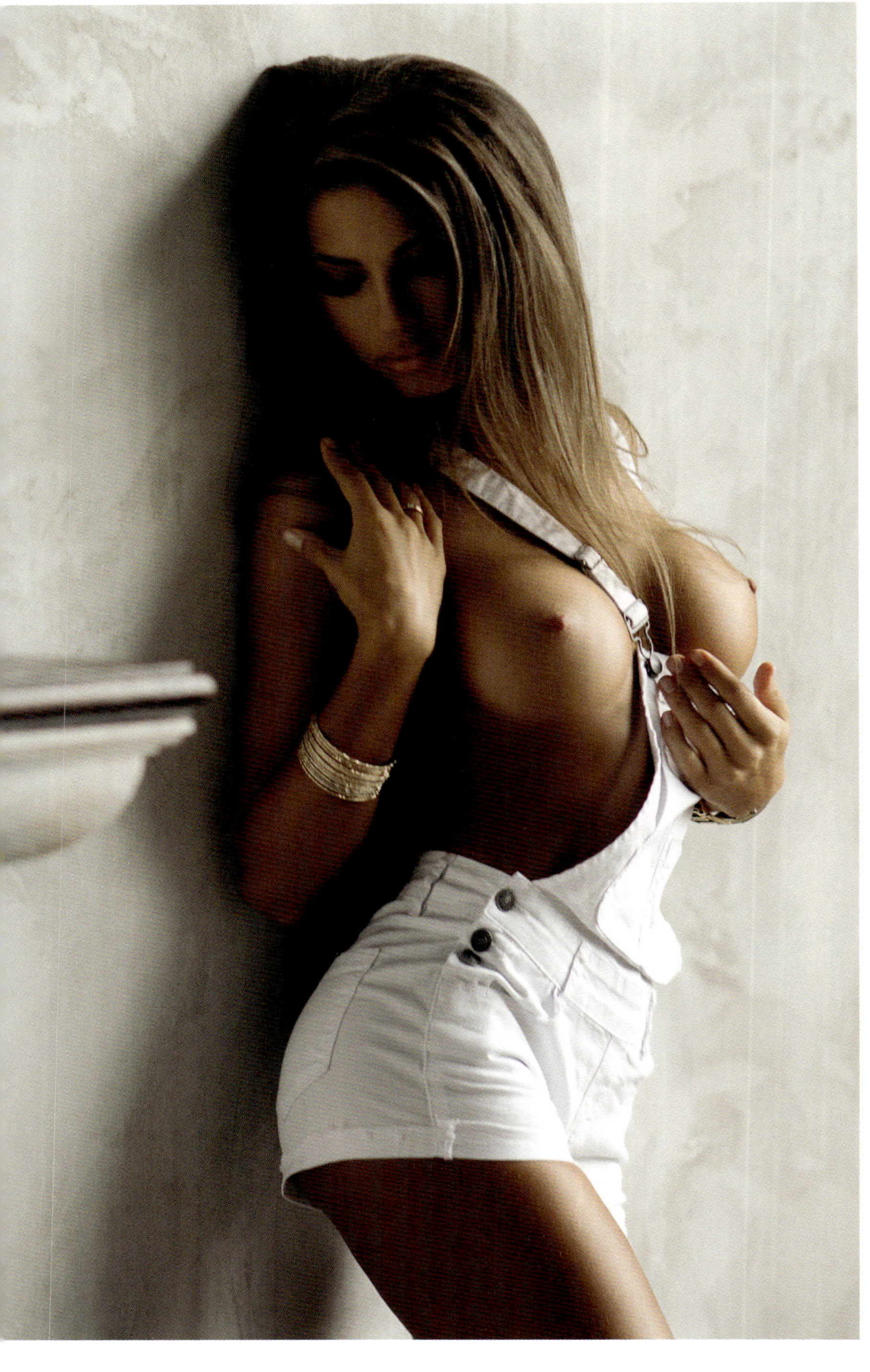

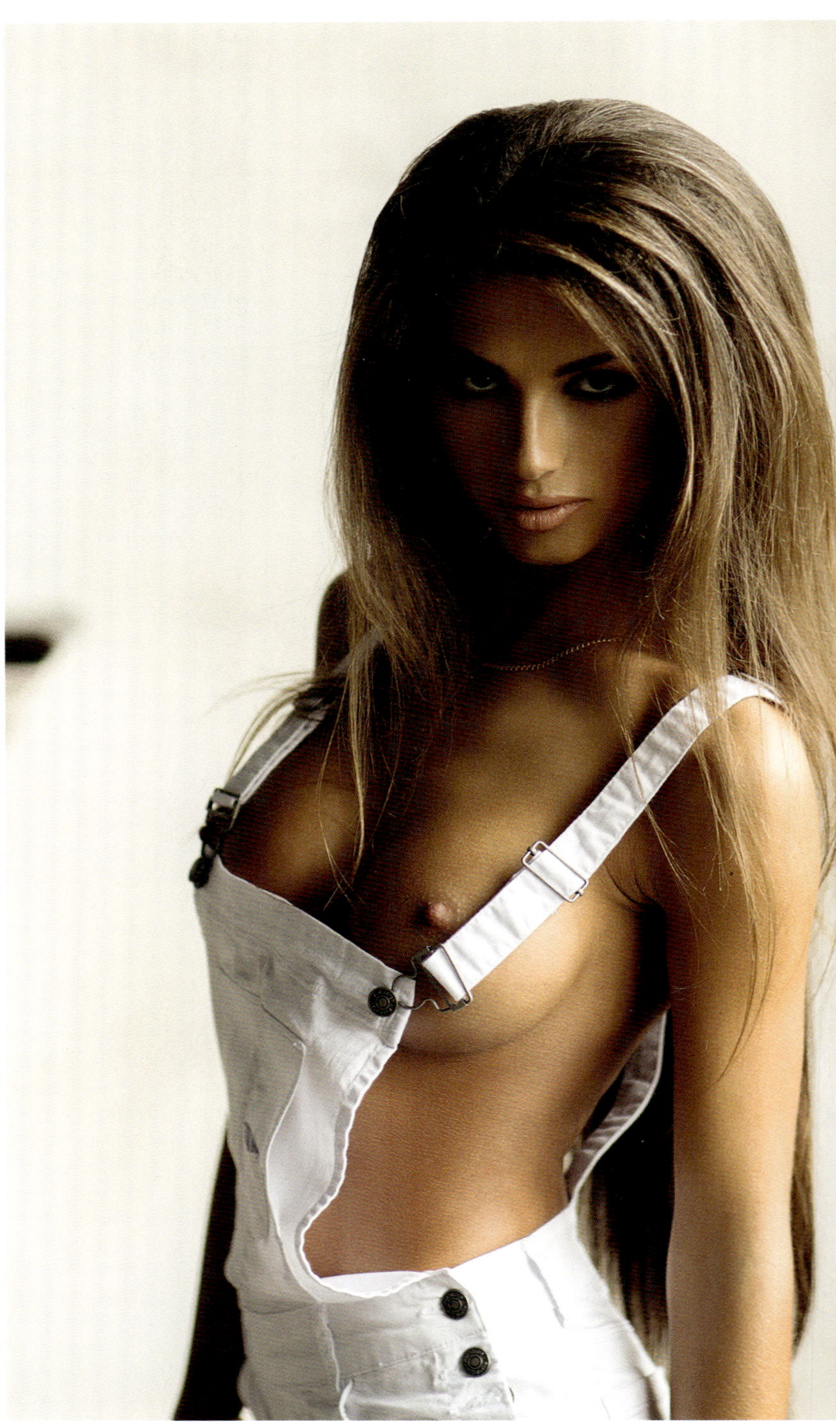

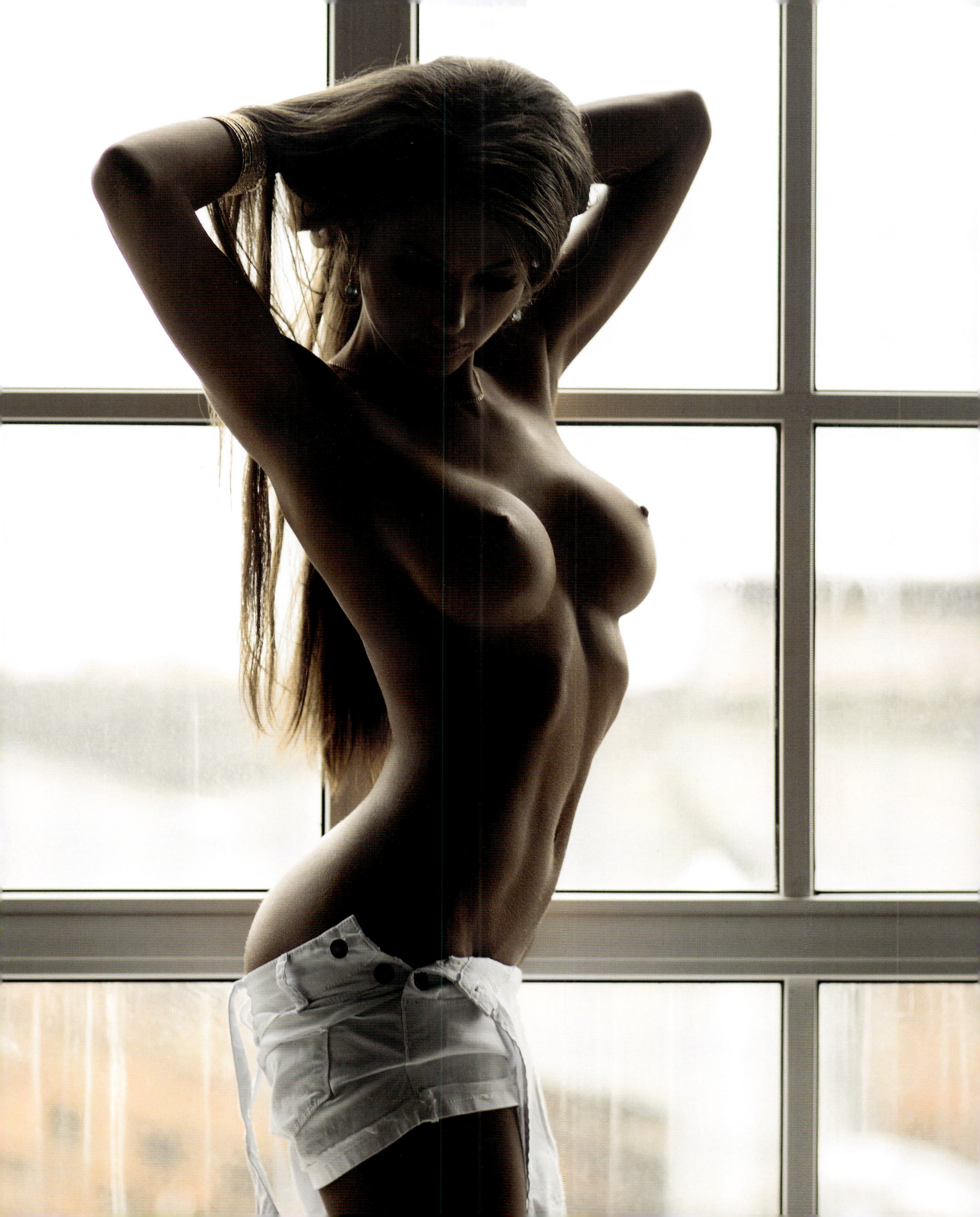

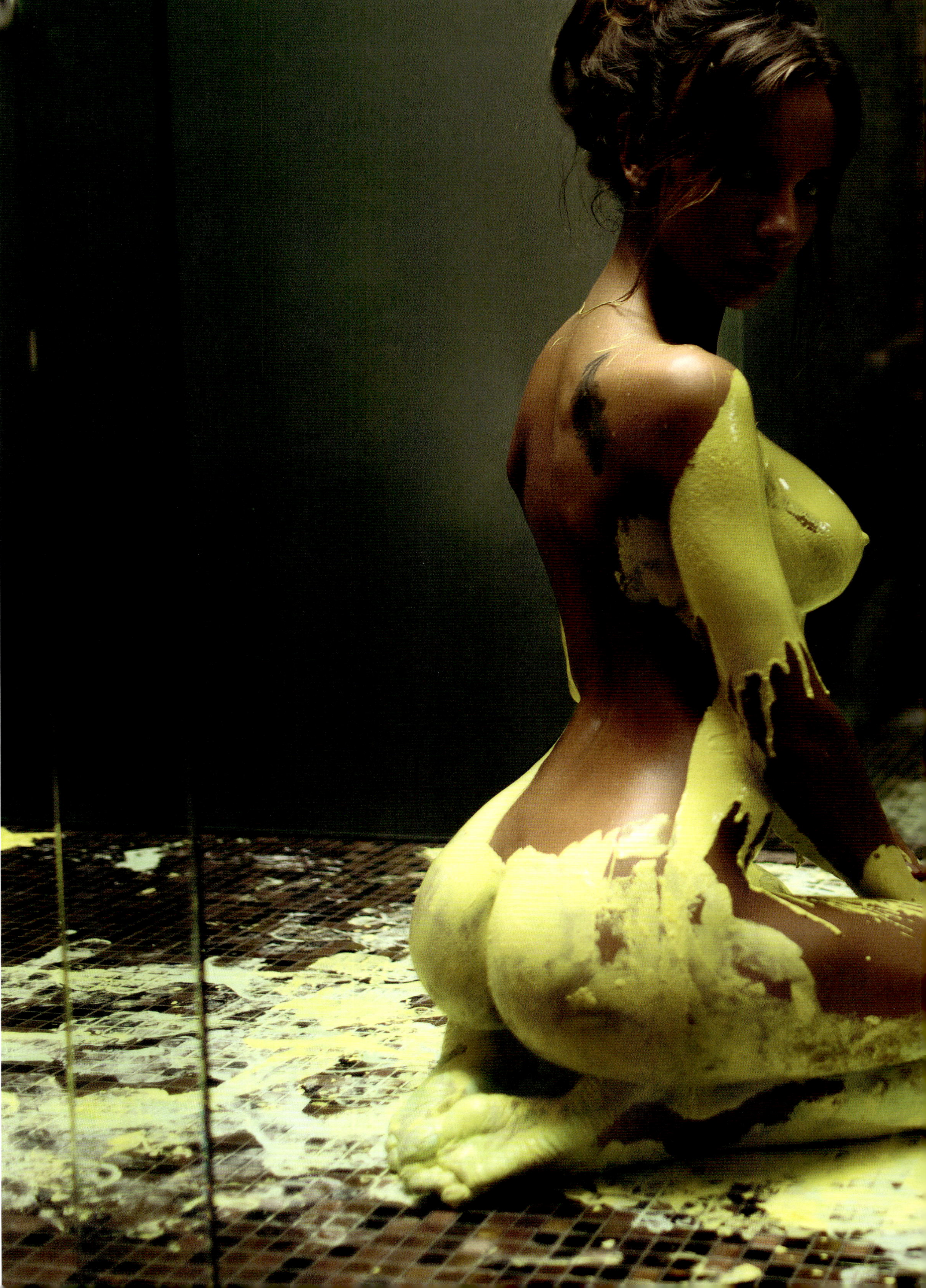

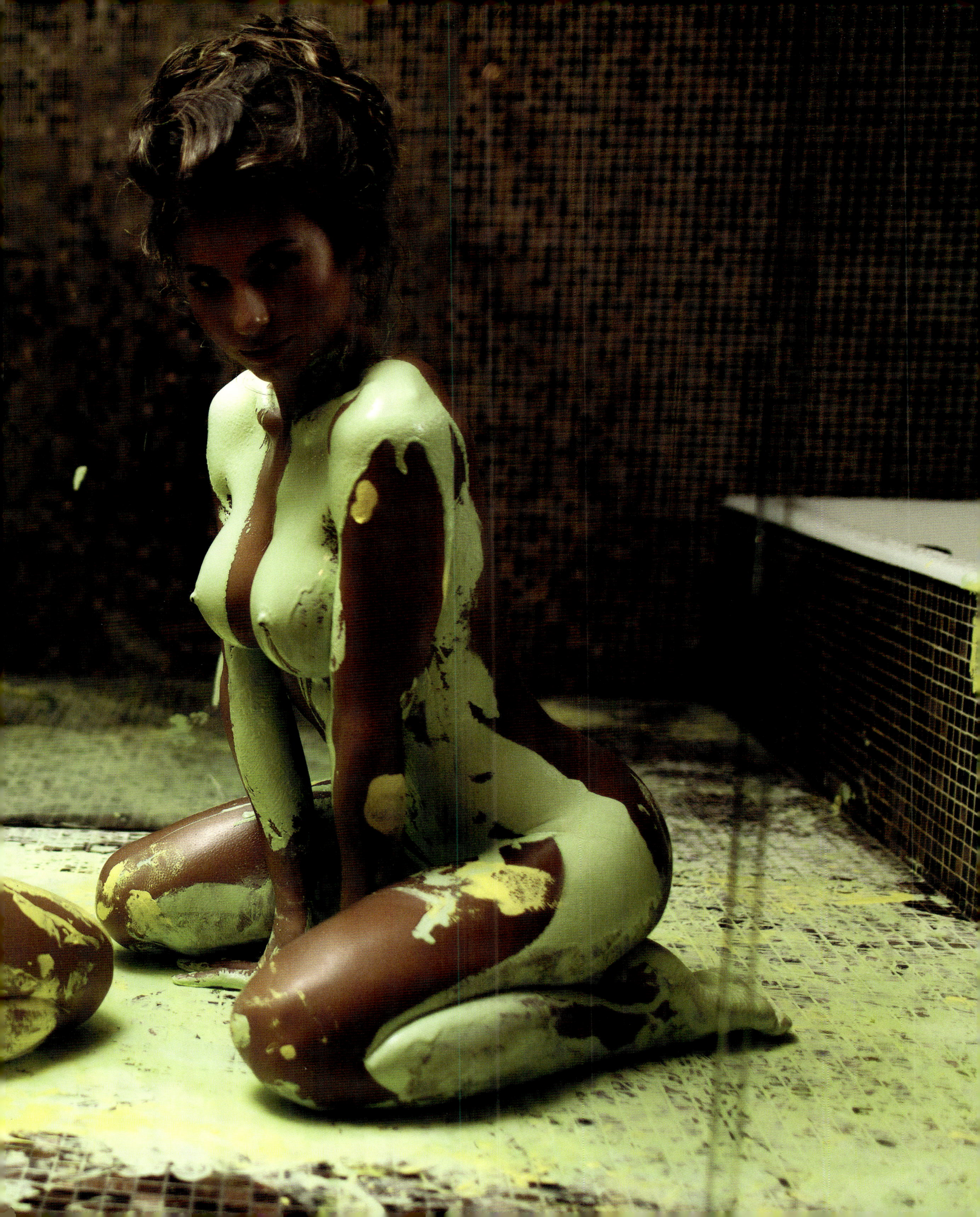

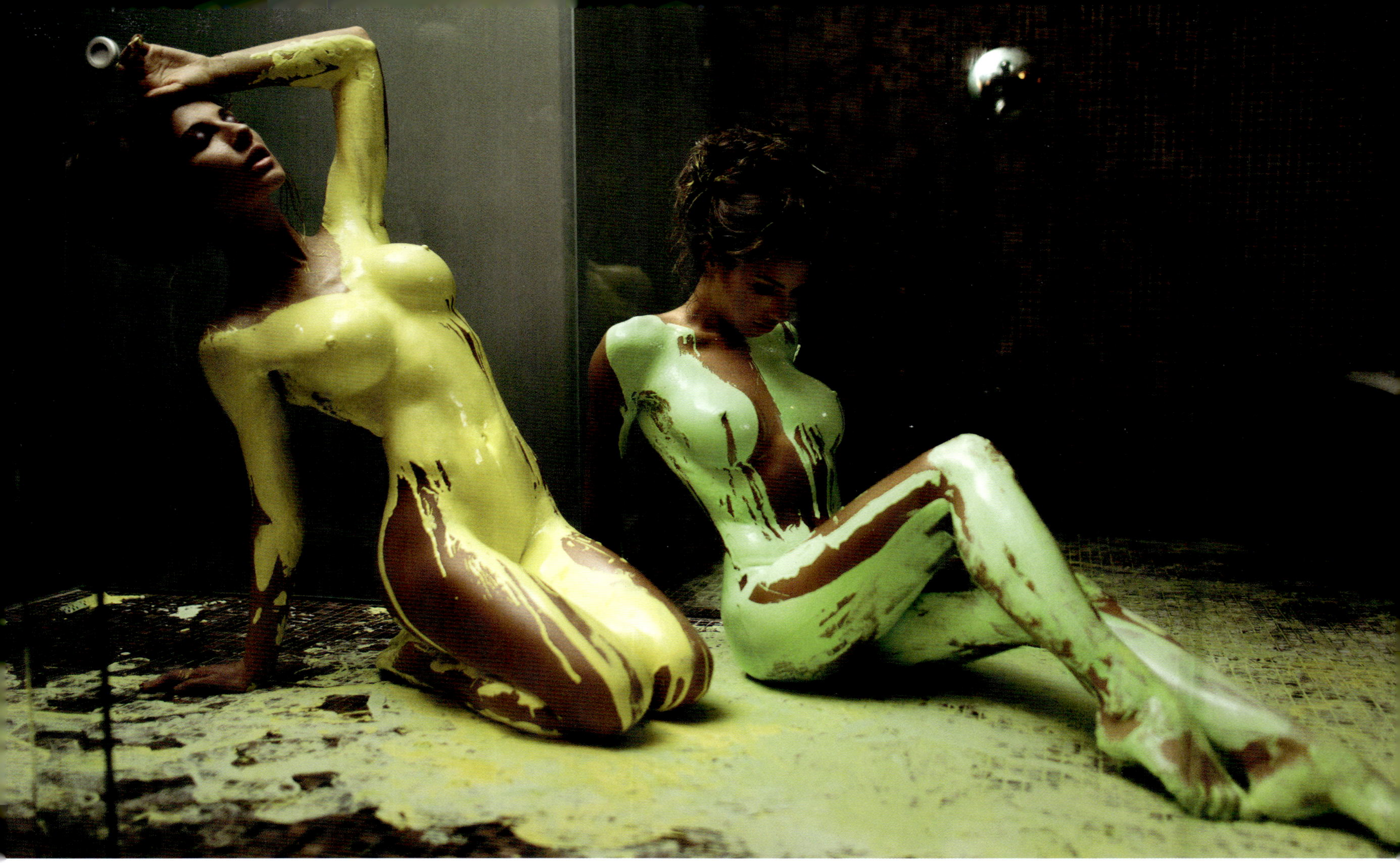

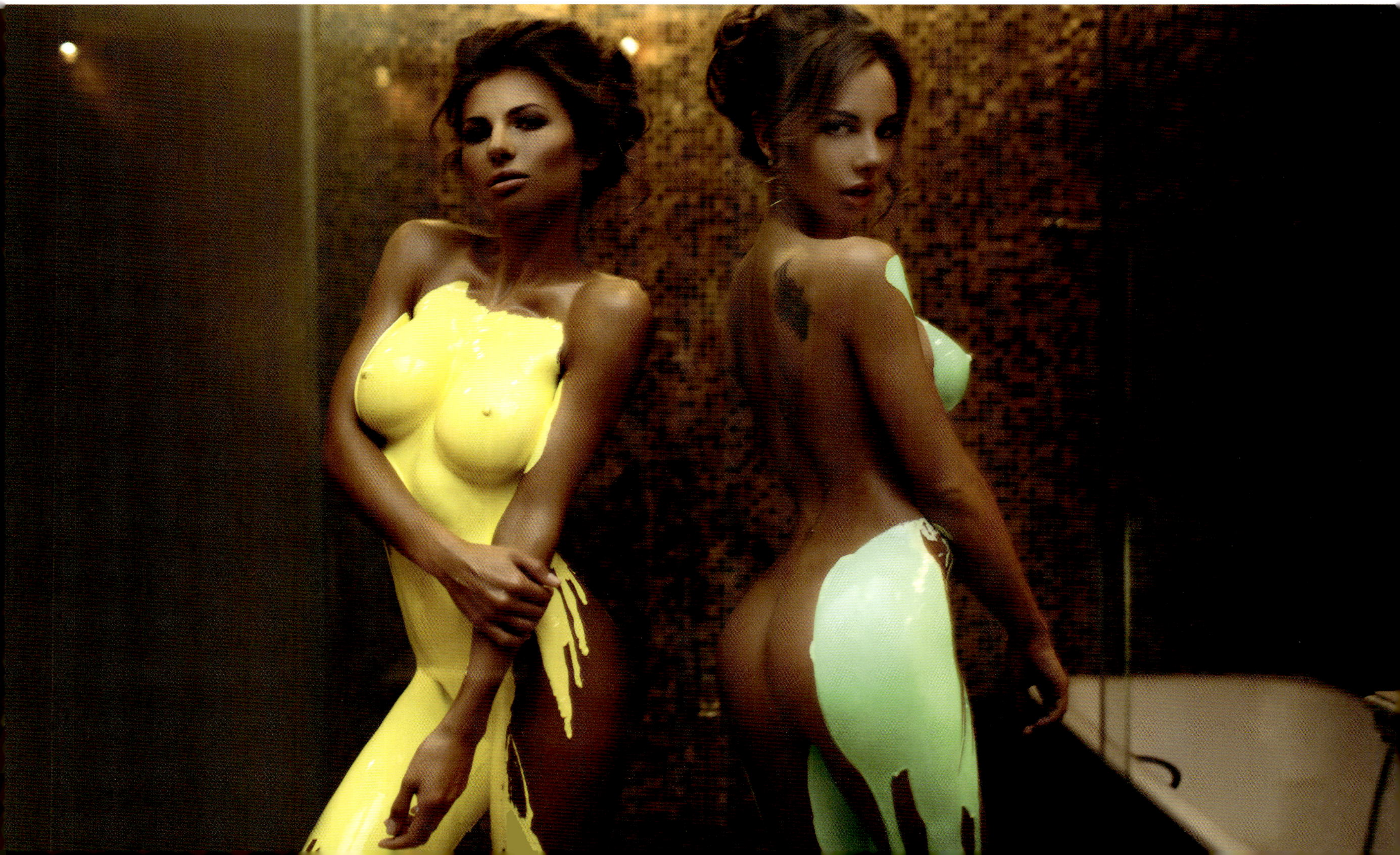

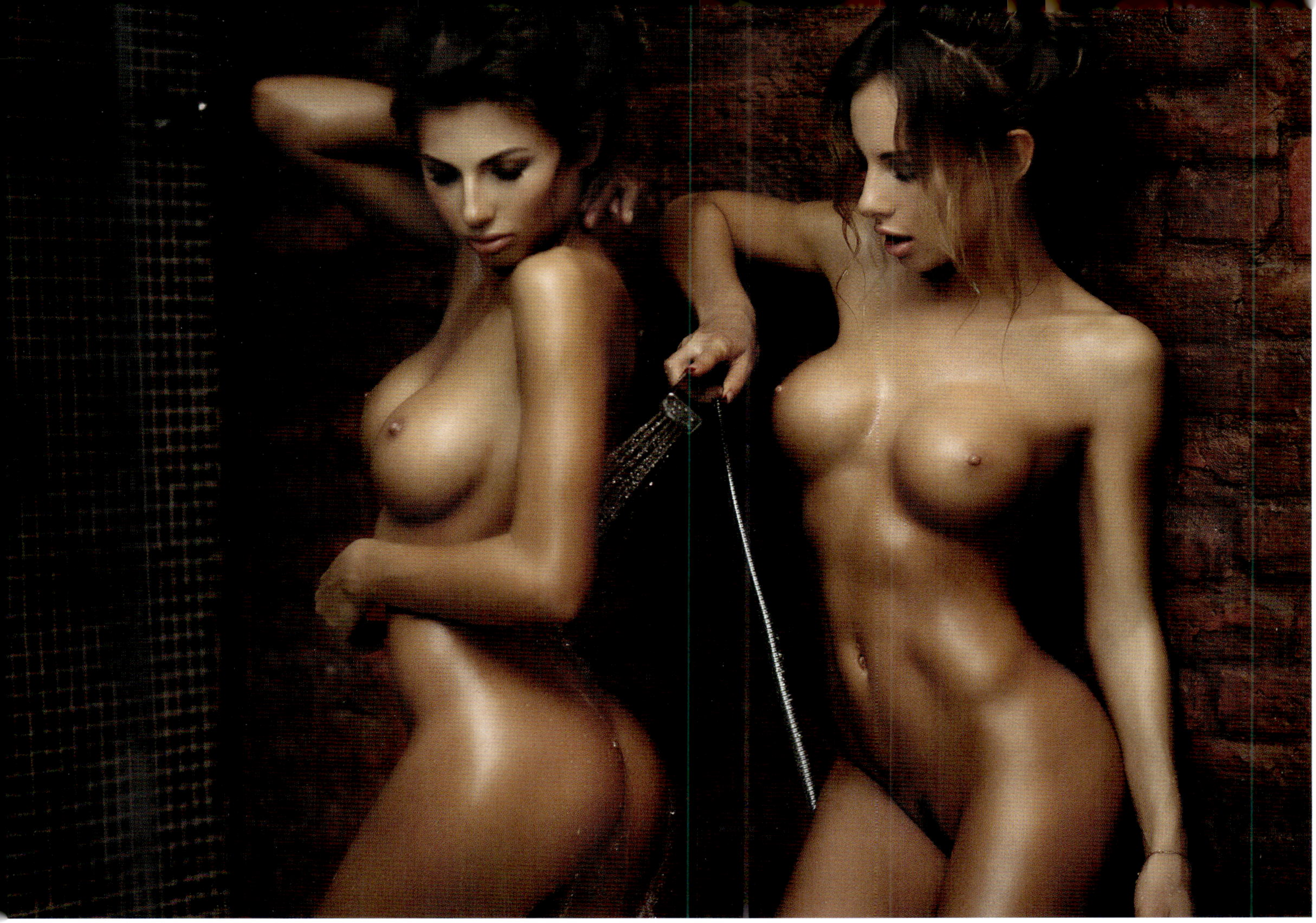

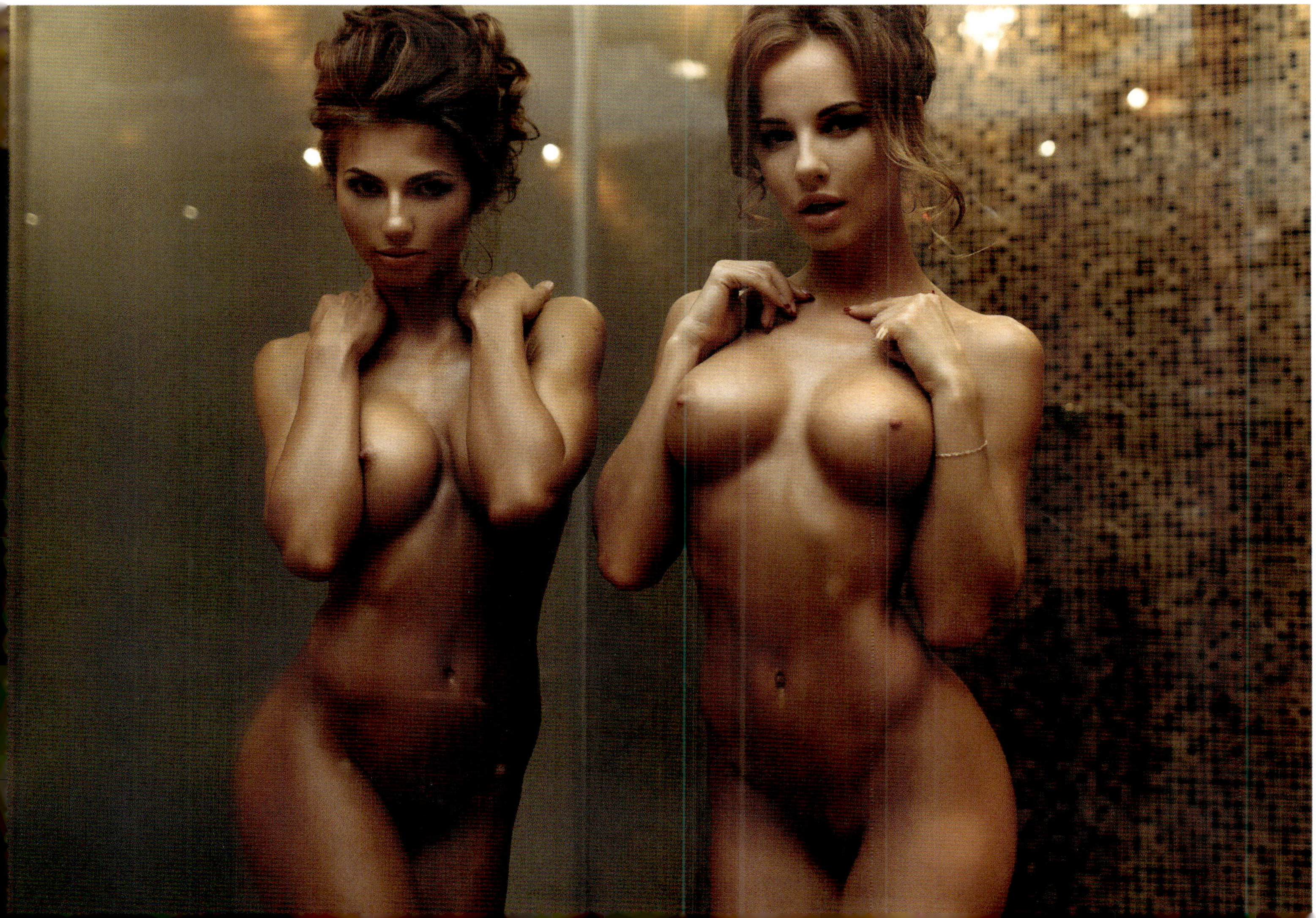

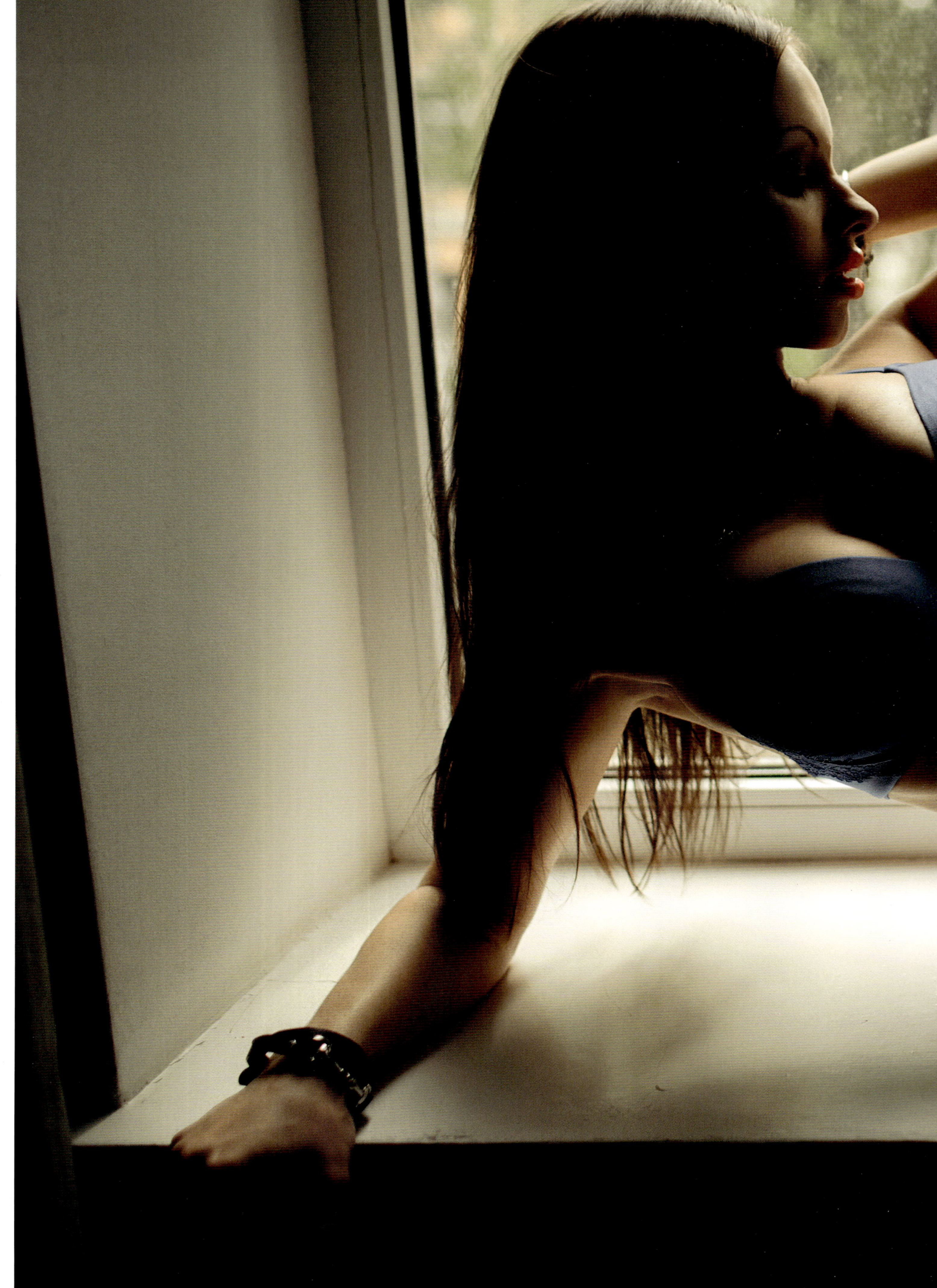

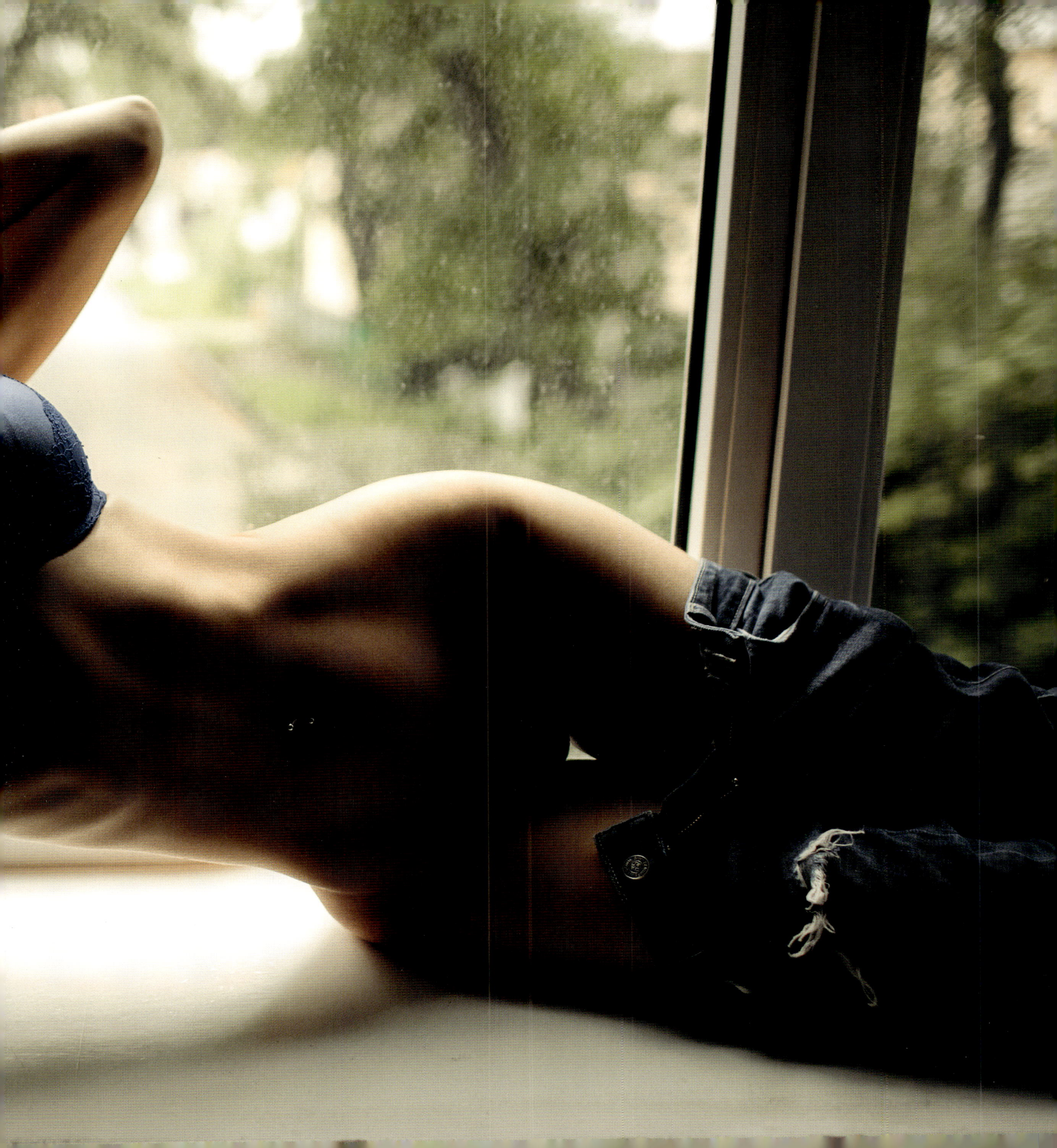

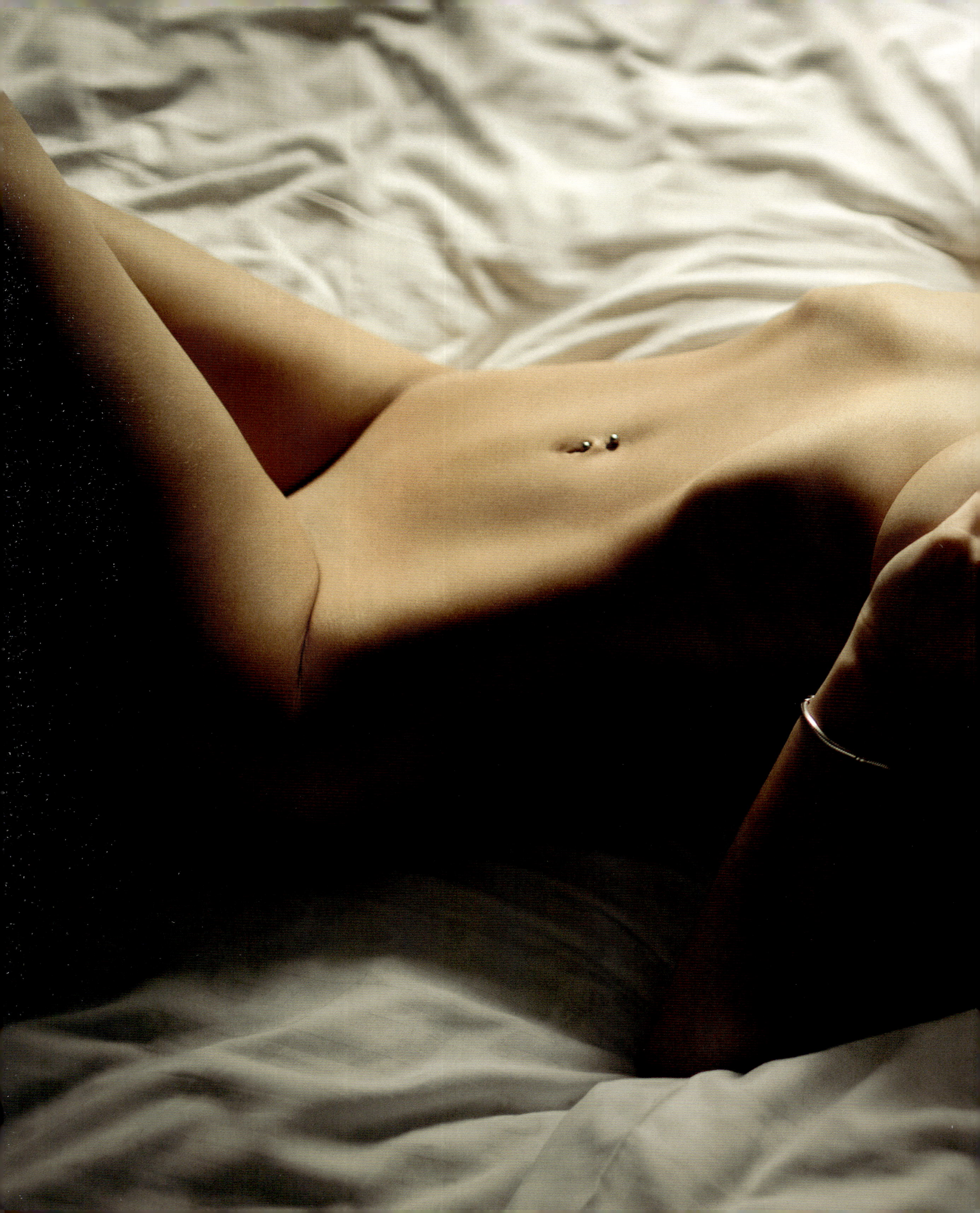

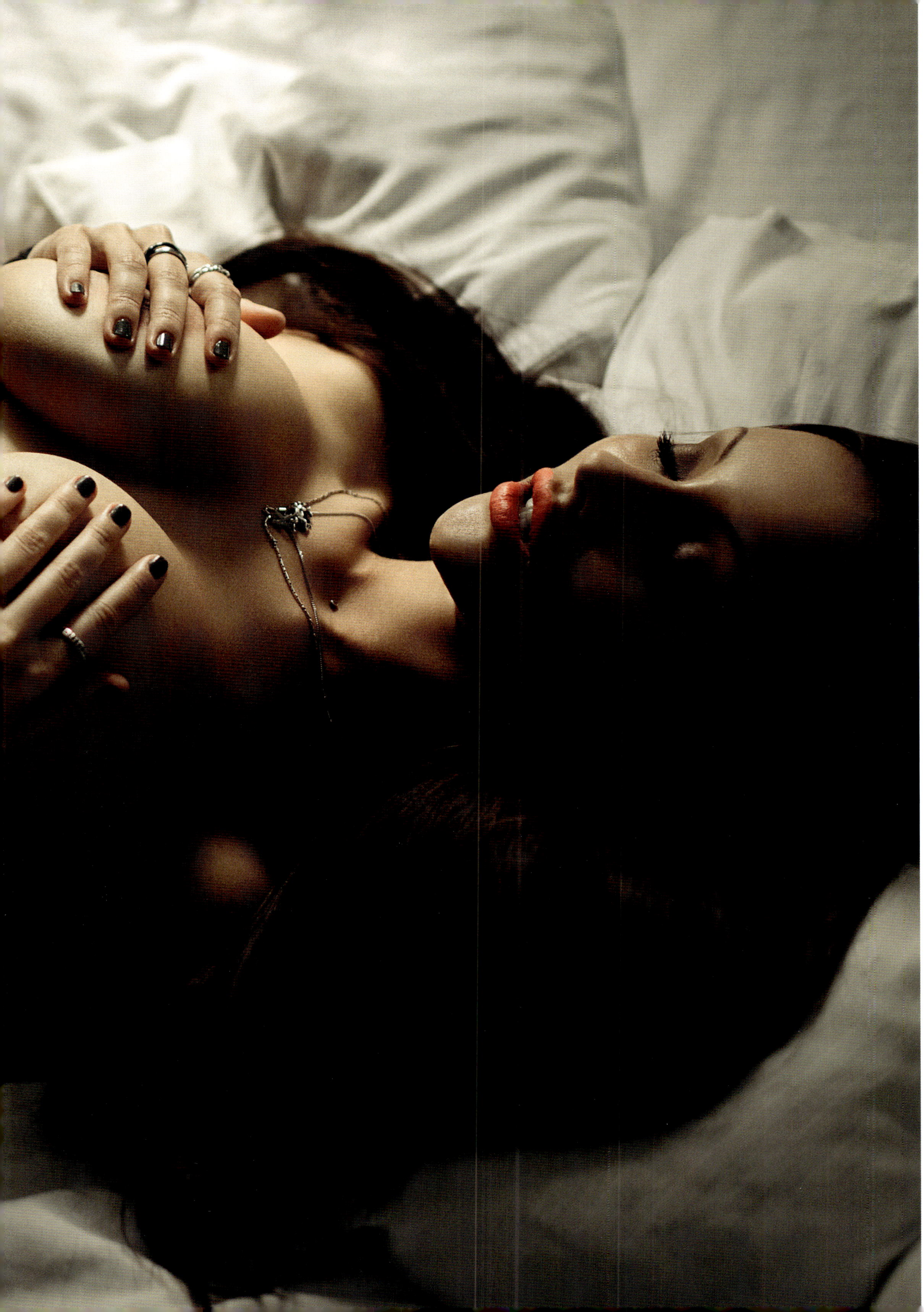

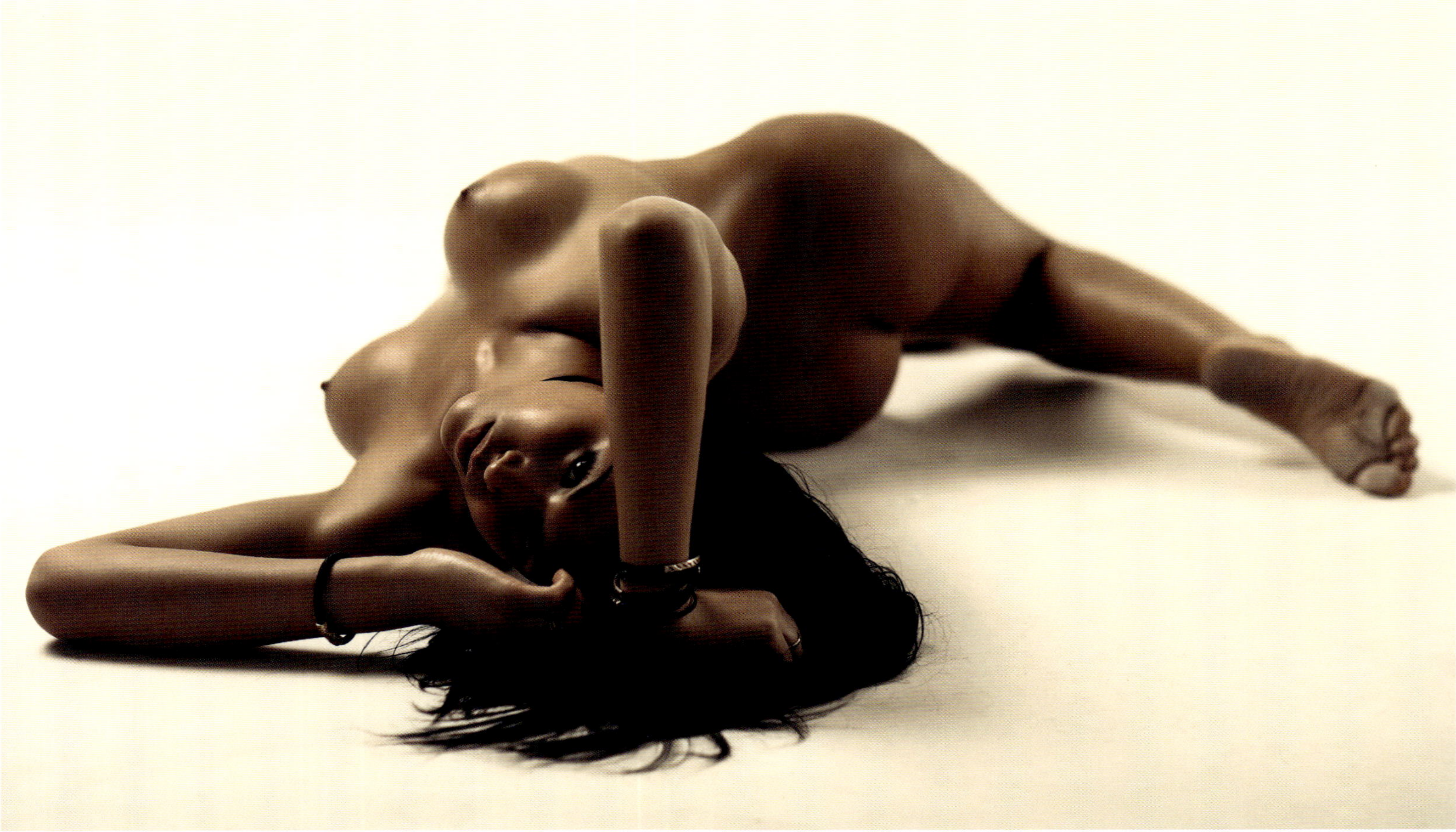

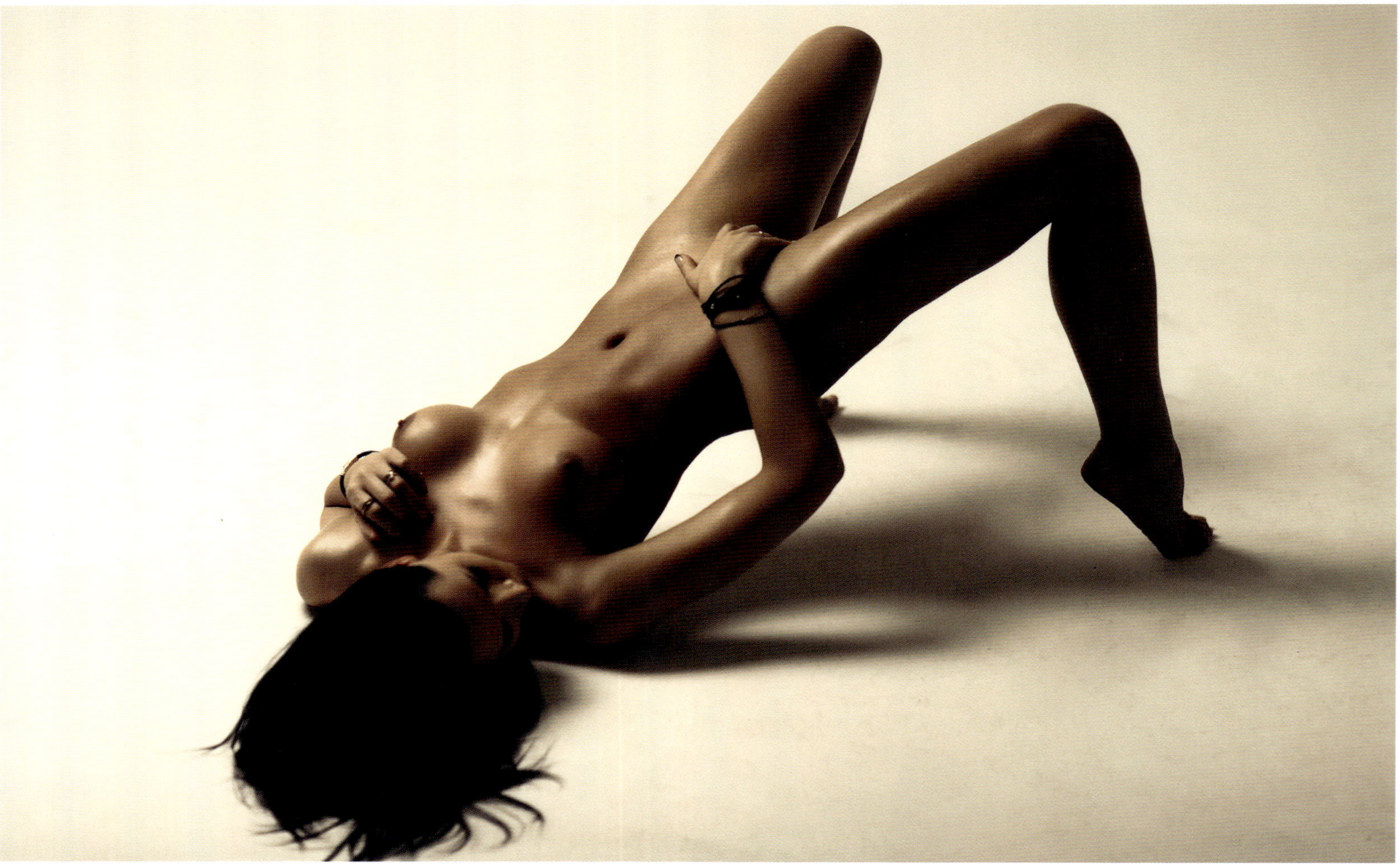

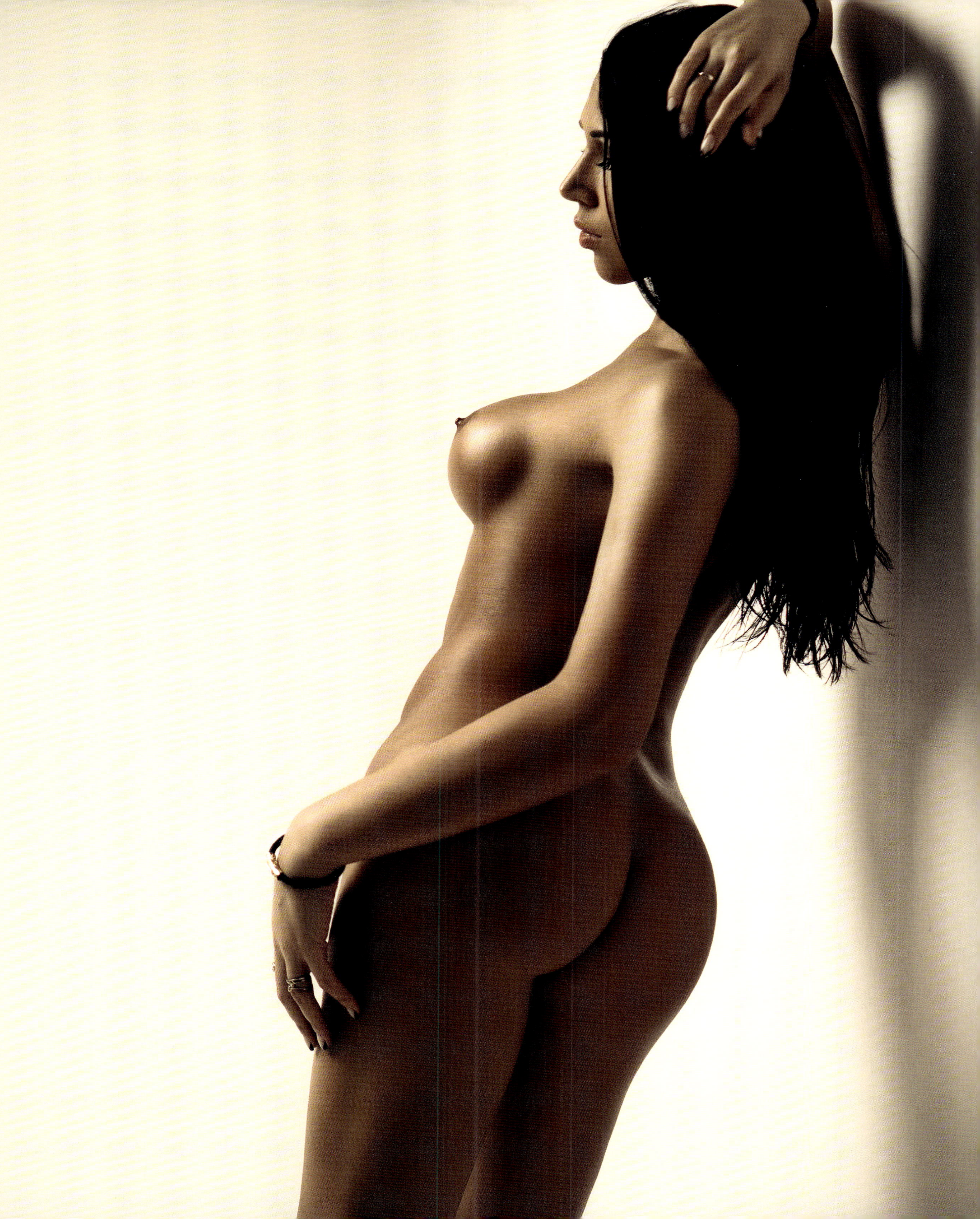

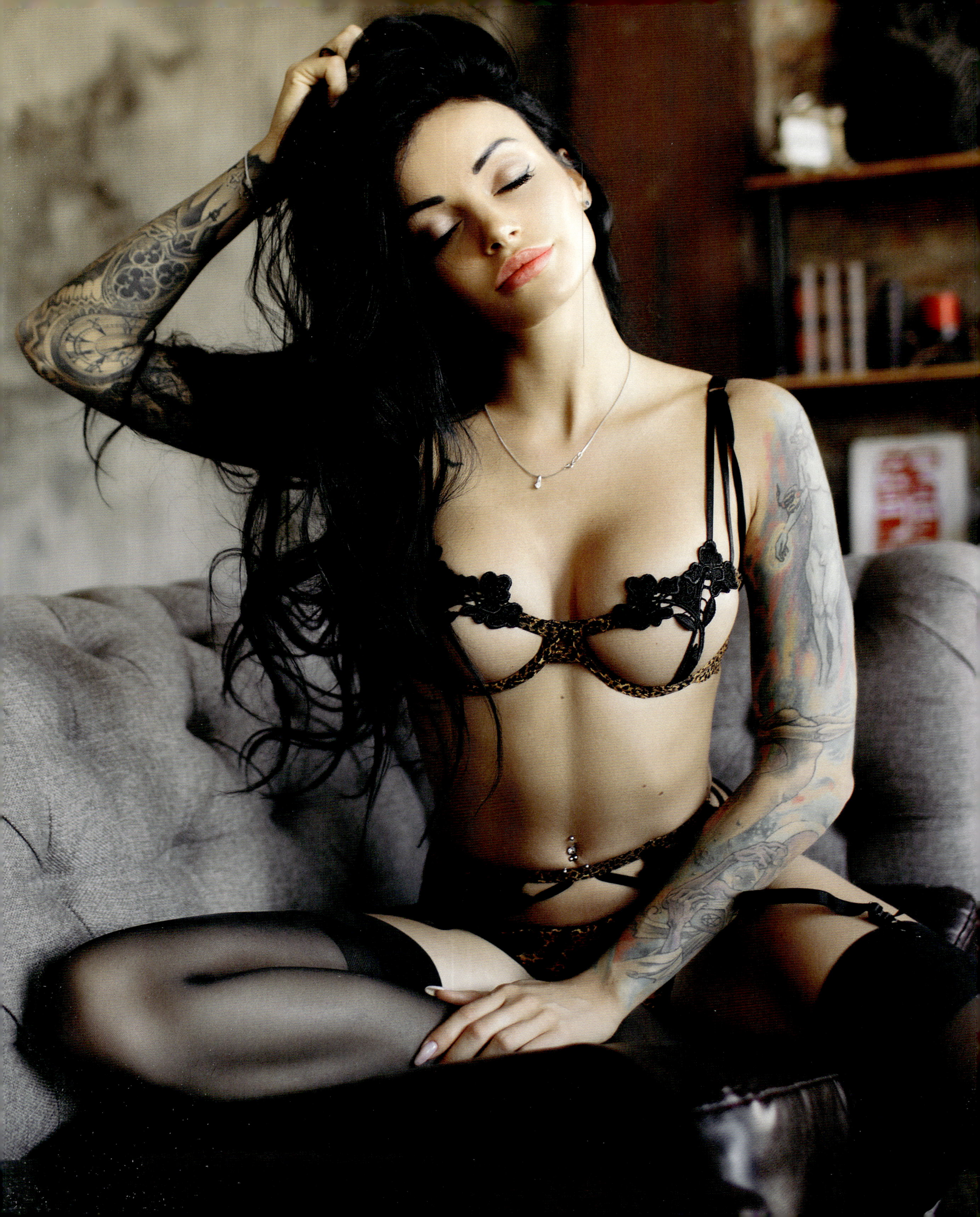

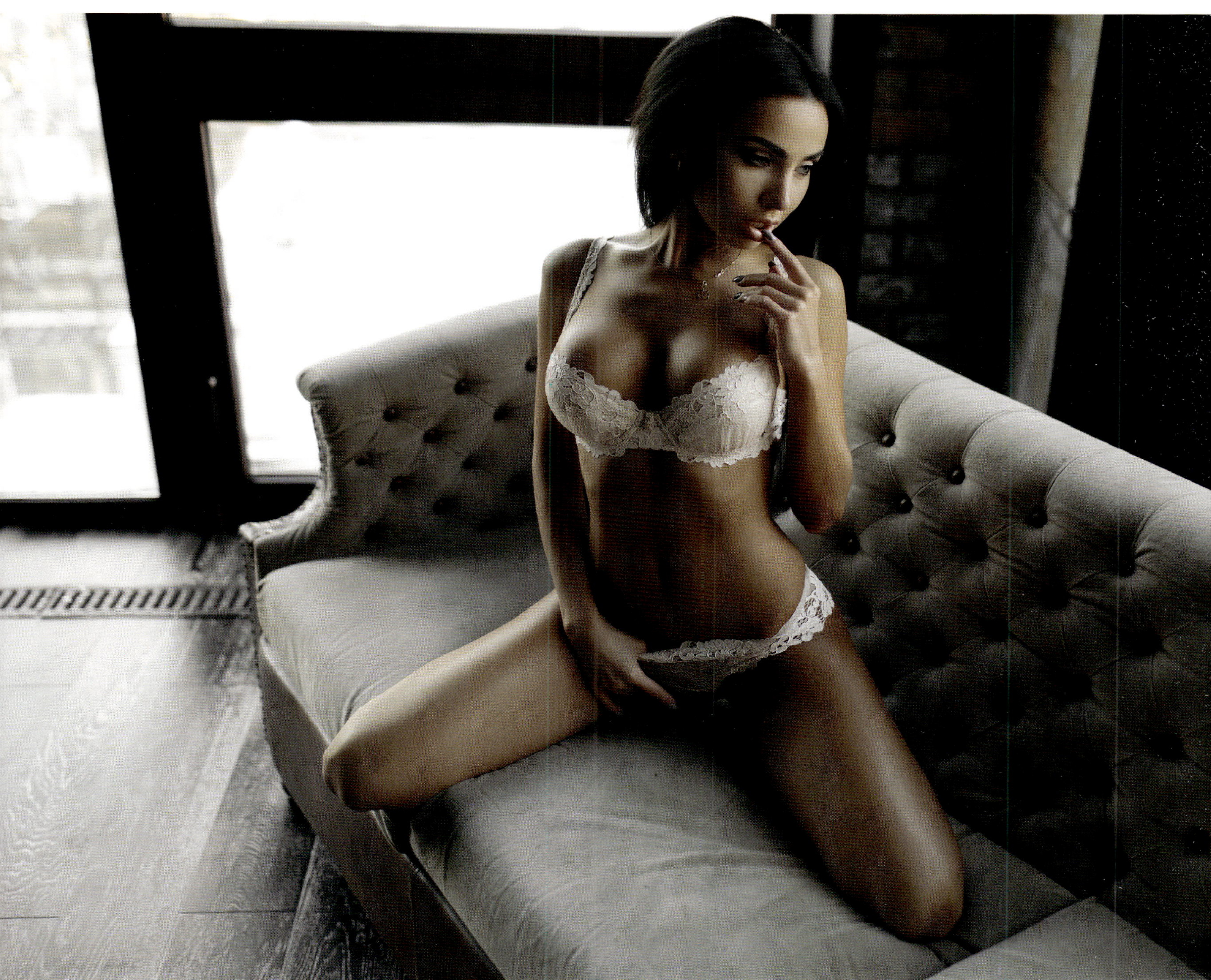

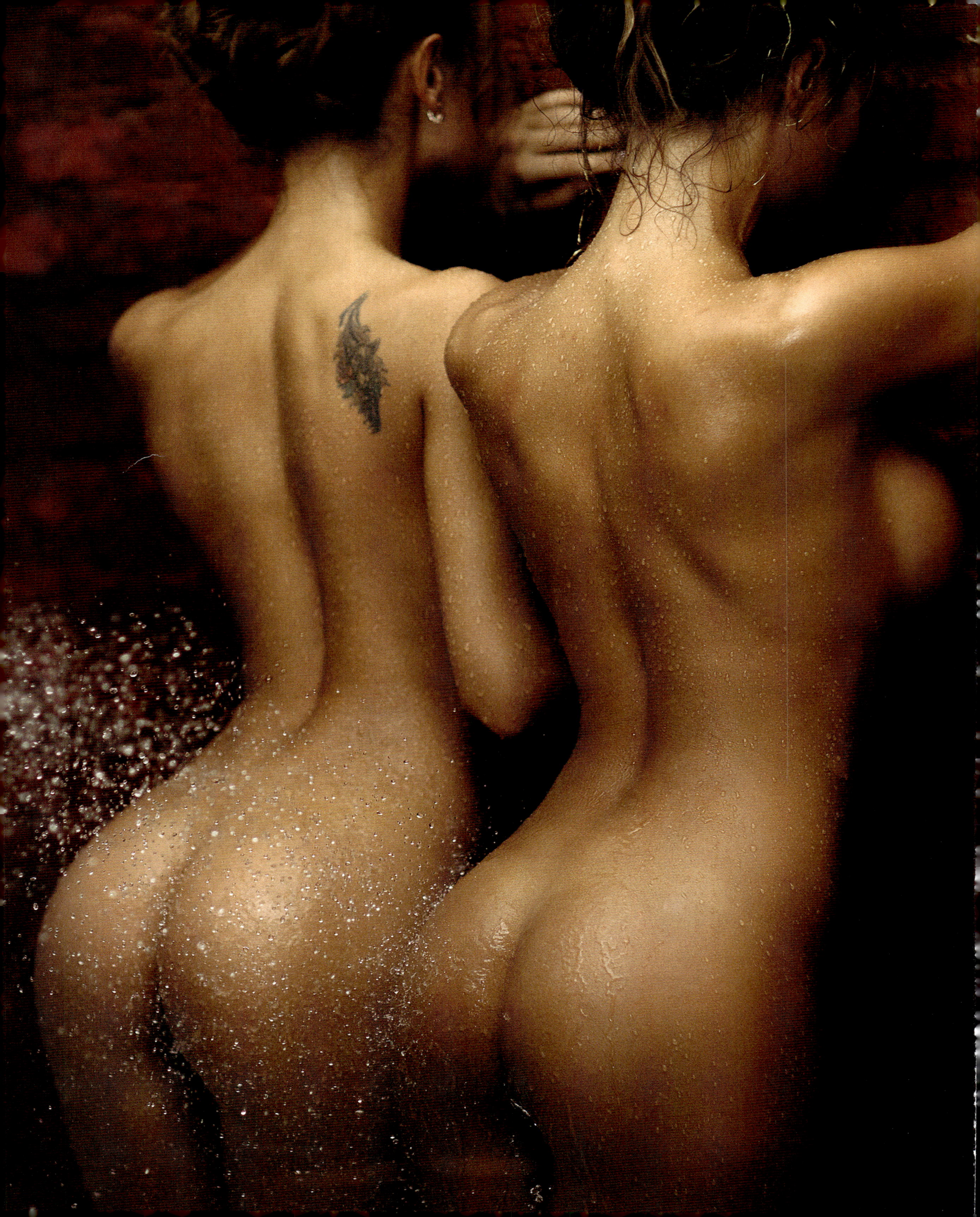